Praise for previous editions of
100 Best Resorts of the Caribbean

"There are too many resorts to count in the Caribbean:
This takes the guesswork out of picking the best."
—*The Bookwatch*

"A vital resource . . . from Aruba to the Virgins, the pages show
a great variety of resorts, not just the most expensive."
—*Associated Press* Broadcast Services

"A big help for travelers thinking about a Caribbean vacation . . . describes each
resort's accommodations, rates, ambience,
room amenities, dining, sports facilities, nightlife, activities for
children, and age range and nationality of most guests."
—*New York Post*

"Showker will help you find your particular version of paradise. . . ."
—*Sun-Sentinel,* Ft. Lauderdale

Help Us Keep This Guide Up to Date

Every effort has been made by the author and editors to make this guide as accurate and useful as possible. However, many things can change after a guide is published—establishments close, phone numbers change, facilities come under new management, and so on.

We would love to hear from you concerning your experiences with this guide and how you feel it could be made better and kept up to date. While we may not be able to respond to all comments and suggestions, we'll take them to heart and we'll also make certain to share them with the author. Please send your comments and suggestions to the following address:

The Globe Pequot Press
Reader Response/Editorial Department
P.O. Box 480
Guilford, CT 06437

Or you may e-mail us at:
editorial@globe-pequot.com

Thanks for your input, and happy travels!

100 *Best* Resorts *of the* Caribbean

Fifth Edition

KAY SHOWKER

The Globe Pequot Press

GUILFORD, CONNECTICUT

Text design by Nancy Freeborn
Map by Stefanie Ward
For photo credits, see page 254

ISBN 0-7627-2404-8
ISSN 1546-5799

Printed in Korea
Fifth Edition/Second Printing

CONTENTS

A WORD OF THANKS

When a book covers 100 resorts on thirty-nine islands, it goes almost without saying that the author needs the help of many people to complete the task. I am certainly no exception. This book has required an incredible amount of research, discussions with knowledgeable people, and follow-up. Dozens of people were tireless in their efforts to help me. I only wish I could name them all, but I would be remiss not to mention some.

First, I would like to express my everlasting gratitude to Marcella Martinez of Marcella Martinez Associates, New York, and her staff, who helped me every step of the way.

The questionnaire for the Green Leaf Awards was based on months of discussions with environmentalists, experienced hotel managers, architects, and others working in the conservation field. But none of it would have been possible without the help of Stan Selengut, the proprietor of Maho Bay Camp and a recognized authority and adviser to governments and tourism officials around the world on ecotourism, and Peggy Bendel of Development Counsellors International, whose work for the U.S. Virgin Islands formed the basis of my questionnaire.

Others who made generous efforts on my behalf are Katharine Dyson; Barbara Daley, Grand Cayman; Kim Greiner, Karen Weiner Escalera Associates, New York; Kim Duvall-Hutchinson, Premier World Marketing, Miami; Myron Clement and Joe Petrocik, Clement-Petrocik, New York; Alison Ross and Roland Alzoni, Peter Martin Associates, New York; Frances Borden, Frances Borden Public Relations, New York; Roberta Garzaroli, Jensen/Boga Inc., New York; Virginia Haynes, BCA Communications, New York; Marilyn Marx, Marilyn Marx Associates, New York; Martha Moreno, E&M Associates, New York; Candice Adams, Adams Unlimited, New York; Ginny Craven, Progressive Public Relations, Miami Beach, Florida; Laura Davidson and her staff, Laura Davidson Public Relations, New York; and Cheryl Andrews and her staff, Cheryl Andrews Marketing, Coral Gables, Florida.

Text Contributions

Because the time constraints of writing this book made it impossible for me to revisit every resort prior to my deadline, as I had wanted to do, I called on my writing colleagues for help. Some contributed specific material written for this book; others allowed me to use material from articles that had been published recently elsewhere. In every case they are writers who specialize in the Caribbean and are as qualified as I to write this book. Indeed, several have written books on the Caribbean.

Several entries are based on articles that first appeared in *Caribbean Travel and Life,* and I am particularly grateful to the authors for their generous cooperation. Specifically these are Hotel Carl Gustaf, Hotel Saint Barth Isle de France, and Eden Rock (St. Barts) and Grace Bay Club (Turks and Caicos) by Susan Pierres; and Stan Murray for his input on Casa de Campo (Dominican Republic) and Parrot Cay (Turks and Caicos).

There were also contributions from John Buchanan for Hotel Kura Hulanda (Curaçao) and The House (Barbados); Michael DeFreitas for The Inn at Old Bahama Bay (Grand Bahama); Stan Murray for Altamer (Anguilla); Gay Myers for Carenage Bay Beach & Golf Club (The Grenadines); and Eleanor Wilson for La Luna (Grenada).

Suzanne McManus advised and helped me with the research on all the resorts in Jamaica. Joan Ioancotti researched some of the resorts in the Grenadines. Christy Marshell updated Little Dix and Caneel Bay.

Katharine Gordon Dyson not only helped me edit much of the material in the book but also contributed *Sandcastle* (Jost Van Dyke, B.V.I.) and helped in the research to update this edition. I am deeply grateful to Susan Pierres, who has continually shared her extensive knowledge of the Caribbean resorts with me.

—Kay Showker

INTRODUCTION

Ask any ten Caribbean cognoscenti to name the best or even their favorite resort in the Caribbean and you will probably get ten different answers. You will certainly start an argument.

In the twenty-five years or so that I've been writing about the Caribbean, the questions I'm asked most often are, "What's your favorite place?" and, "What's the best place to stay?" It is not surprising, since the choice of a hotel is usually a traveler's first concern. But the best resort, like beauty, is in the eye of the beholder. And resorts, like people, differ. Not every resort suits everyone's needs and style.

Any of us can recognize high quality and good service. We all appreciate good architectural design and interior decor. But to be the best, a hotel or resort must have that "something special" that is almost impossible to define and strikes each of us differently.

Then, too, there was a time not long ago when the choices in the Caribbean were clearer, because good resorts were few. But now, after more than a decade of steady building throughout the region, the number has more than doubled. (The Caribbean Hotel Association's reference guide lists almost 1,500 entries.) The choice is more difficult, but, happily, the selection is more interesting.

Consider, too, that these hotels, inns, and resorts are spread over nearly forty separate islands, or island groups, and you will see that the task is daunting. *100 Best Resorts of the Caribbean* is meant to make the choice easier. Most people do not want or need the standard long list of options with brief descriptions that appear in many Caribbean guidebooks; they prefer some selectivity, and selectivity is precisely the aim of this book.

Since standards vary so much from island to island, it is difficult to set up arbitrary rules or criteria to apply across the board. What passes as the best in Guadeloupe may be only acceptable in Anguilla. What has some travelers turned on in St. Barts would be turned down in Jamaica. A great deal also has to do with an island's tradition—British, French, Dutch, Spanish—and the kind of tourists it attracts.

The Caribbean best are recognized by the same attention to detail and quality of service, food, care, comfort, and facilities that distinguish the best hotels and resorts around the world. But in judging the Caribbean, you have to be generous. There are many problems in trying to operate a top-quality resort in the Tropics. This, coupled with the region's high operating costs, means that the best tend to be equated with the most expensive.

Yet it would have been a mistake to include only the most expensive resorts. The selection would have been easy, but you don't need me to tell you which are the 100 most expensive hotels in the Caribbean. Any good travel agent can tell you that. What's more, being expensive is no guarantee of being the best—or even good—and there are some real dogs out there. Rather, consideration was given to ambience, historic setting, management style, uniqueness, and other elements that make some resorts the best for other than traditional reasons.

What impresses me, even after twenty-five years, is the enormous variety that the Caribbean offers. I wanted the 100 resorts in this book to reflect that variety and to represent a broad range of establishments: large and small, beachside and hillside, modest and deluxe, homey and elegant.

I made a conscious effort to provide diversity, choosing the resorts I considered the best in each category

across the broadest possible spectrum on as many islands as possible. The selections run the gamut from rustic retreats to private island hideaways to large, full-service layouts. They range in their degree of luxury from minimal to extravagant. That's why you will find such widely differing entries as back-to-nature Maho Bay Camp on St. John, U.S. Virgin Islands, at one end of the spectrum and posh Malliouhana on Anguilla at the other.

What Is a Resort?

But first, what is a resort? Because my selection covers such a broad range, you may wonder how I define resort, and you will certainly want to know the criteria I used.

Webster defines *resort* as a place providing recreation and entertainment, especially to vacationers. Roget's *Thesaurus* and Rodale's *The Synonym Finder* list as synonyms *hotel, inn, club, lodge, spa, watering place, camp*. This book includes places fitting all these appellations, along with *haven, hideaway,* and *retreat*.

But let me make it simple. I define resort as "a place to go for a vacation." It is a broad definition, but it reflects a reality—namely, that vacationers are an extremely diverse group whose ideas of a vacation differ as much as their interests, needs, and expectations. What is paradise for one person might be hell for another.

For some people the ideal resort is a pleasure palace by the sea—the more luxurious, the more pampering, the more exclusive, the better. For others it is the exact opposite. They willingly trade creature comforts to be close to nature with as few man-made intrusions as possible.

Then there are the honeymooners, golfers, divers, birders, hikers; those who want action; those who want serenity; those who care about cuisine; those who take family vacations; those who want to be directly on the beach; those who want a vacation in the mountains; those who select a resort by the variety of sports and recreation available; those who care little about activities. All of these people will find resorts in this guide to suit them. Yet the traveler's needs did not guide my initial selection—only the fine-tuning. My first concern was the quality of the resort itself.

Criteria

So what were my criteria? To be the best a resort needs a combination of factors: location, setting, layout, service, appearance, ambience, dining experience, sports facilities, management, and staff. But then it must have something beyond these—the intangibles, that *je ne sais quoi*.

Maybe it's warmth, maybe it's style. It is a certain quality, a feeling that is hard to define but that you know instinctively when you find it. When I described my dilemma to a fellow writer, he replied instantly, "Yes, I know what

you mean. Would you want to spend a week there?"

"That's it." I replied. "That's it." Would you want to spend a week there? And perhaps more important, at the end of the week, do you long to return? Every entry in this book was put to that test. There were other tests, too. Does the resort live up to the goals it designed for itself? Does it fulfill its role—whatever the style, price, category—better than any other?

Another important criterion: The resort had to have been in business for at least one year. Most of those included here have been around much longer than a year; they have stood the test of time. A few, which barely got in under the time requirement, were included because the owners have established track records for running outstanding hotels and because the inn or resort is of such quality and distinction that it merits early recognition.

Certainly some testing was influenced by my personal likes and dislikes. When I go to the Caribbean, I want to know I'm in the Caribbean. I want to feast on its beauty as well as its bounty, to feel the balmy air and hear the sea. My ideal resort takes advantage of its location; it lets the trade winds cool the air and blow away the sand flies. Its rooms and restaurants are open to the sea, with breezy balconies and splendid views. Architecture is to me as important as ambience—the two work together to make a place special. Good architectural design fits its environment and helps create the ambience. I also care a great deal about the Caribbean's heritage—natural, historic, cultural—and have more to say about this later in the Green Leaf Awards section.

I like places that make me feel good as soon as my taxi pulls up to the front door. I like places that look as though they are expecting you, from an alert doorman to a friendly check-in desk to a bellhop who tells me everything I need to know about my room and points out the features of the hotel that I am likely to need soon after my arrival. I appreciate one who takes the time to find the luggage rack and place my suitcase on it, and checks the ice bucket or water in the fridge to ensure that I can have a cool drink of water after my long trip.

Little things mean a lot: good reading lights, firm mattresses, efficient bathrooms with a place for toiletries, fresh flowers, lit footpaths or flashlights to light the way. I like omnipresent but unobtrusive managers, and I want to shake hands with the person minding the store.

Although I let my experience guide me, I sought the opinions and advice of many others—travel agents and other writers who specialize in the Caribbean, hoteliers with long Caribbean experience, friends who live in the Caribbean part or all of the year, and, most important, dozens of vacationers I met along the way. They gave me their overall impressions and were particularly helpful in highlighting the features that had made their visit to a particular resort memorable. But in the end the choices are mine. So, too, are the comments and criticism.

The Goal

My principal objective in the resort profiles was to define a resort's personality and stress the elements that make it different and distinctive from other resorts to enable you to identify with those best suited for you. But defining a resort's personality is not an exact science. Sometimes it is the history of the structure that helped shape the resort's character, sometimes the owner or manager whose imprint is indelible, sometimes the setting, the staff, the ambience, or a specific feature—or all of the above.

In the beginning I thought finding 100 different ways to describe 100 different resorts would be the hardest part about writing this book. I found instead that the resorts have such distinctive personalities, the descriptions almost wrote themselves. In a way the ease of writing about them further confirmed my choices.

Small Versus Large

Those who know the Caribbean well will not be surprised to learn that out of the total 100 resorts in this book, more than half have fewer than fifty rooms, and forty-one have fewer than thirty rooms. Less than a third are large resorts with a hundred or more rooms. This was not a deliberate decision. In fact, I had not even analyzed the numbers until after I had written all the entries.

There's no mystery about the results. Big resorts are better known because they have the muscle to market and promote themselves, but small ones of less than fifty rooms are more typical of the Caribbean and are its strength, providing a more authentic Caribbean experience.

Small hotels have a personality—that's what makes them worthy of attention—while large ones tend to be homogenized. Let me quickly add, however, that the large resorts included here run counter to the norm; they, too, have strong character.

The size of a hotel makes a difference in the type of Caribbean holiday you have. Large hotels have a greater array of activities and facilities, a busier atmosphere, and more round-the-clock staff and services than a small hotel, where the atmosphere is usually quiet and very relaxed.

At the smallest ones you get more personal care and attention from the manager, who is often the owner, and from the staff, who will call you by name and learn your preferences from the first day of your visit. Usually you feel as though you are a guest in a friend's home or at a weekend house party. The service may not be as polished as at large resorts, but it is warm and genuine.

Commitment

The Caribbean is full of wonderful stories about people with a dream. Owning a small hotel in the Caribbean is a fantasy that's right up there in popularity with buying a boat and sailing around the world. So irrepressible is the idea that many, many people have done it and continue to do it. Most give up after a few years when they learn how difficult it is to run a really good hotel in the Caribbean. The innkeepers in this book are people who made it; invariably, they reflect the high degree of personal commitment it takes to succeed.

Amenities

Many small hotels, including some of the most expensive, do not have air-conditioning, television, or phones in the rooms. Not having a phone is a blessing to some people, an inconvenience to others. The Calabash in Grenada has the ideal solution: All guest rooms have telephones—along with a printed note that says, "The phone will be removed if you find it a nuisance."

As for air-conditioning, you may be surprised (I was amazed) to discover how many resorts don't have it—and don't need it. Ceiling fans and natural breezes do a better job. Generally, the absence of air-conditioning in a good

hotel says the structure was built to be architecturally sensitive to its setting.

In the past Caribbean hoteliers believed they could not attract guests, particularly Americans, if they did not have air-conditioning. But during the oil crises of the 1970s, when skyrocketing fuel bills almost put them out of business, many returned to Mother Nature out of necessity. The response from guests was so positive that more and more have followed suit.

Architects with Caribbean experience have long since abandoned square concrete-block hotels in favor of styles that suit the natural environment, stressing open-air dining, louvered windows and doors, shaded terraces, and tile and terra-cotta floors. What a joy!

Paradise Isn't Perfect

Even the best resorts aren't perfect. Where I feel it's warranted, I point out weaknesses. And you may notice that I save my toughest judgment for the posh corners of paradise, where prices unhappily have risen to heights as heavenly as the pleasures. To me, expensive resorts have a greater responsibility to deliver what they promise than those that keep rates low and don't try to be fancy. Higher rates, however, are usually justified as the degree of luxury increases, since almost everything is imported, and catering to Americans—a demanding lot—is costly. Nonetheless, people who seek luxury still want their money's worth.

Maintenance in the Tropics, government taxes, and service charges also drive up costs. High labor costs and restrictive policies—often more politically than economically motivated, since hotels are usually the island's largest employers—are contributing factors, too. Which brings me to the matter of service.

Service

The Caribbean offers service at a stroll. Swift, at-the-snap-of-a-finger, professional service is unusual. If that's your yardstick for judging service, you'll be disappointed even in the best of the best places. If you require this kind of service to be happy, the Caribbean is the wrong place for you.

Caring, cheerful, and thoughtful service from a friendly staff, not speed or polish, are the criteria on which to make a judgment here. Turn off your motor, leave your watch at home, relax. This is not a cop-out or apology for service in the Caribbean. Rather, it is said to help you enjoy your vacation by knowing the parameters within which Caribbean resorts operate.

Careers in service industries are only now getting the respect they deserve from people who, having only recently passed from colonialism to independence, traditionally equated such work with servitude. Fortunately, this attitude is fading as islanders have come to recognize their need for tourism and as local ownership of hotels has broadened. Professionalism, too, is increasing as training and opportunities grow and the hospitality profession, as it matures, offers meaningful advancement to young people.

Cuisine

The time has come for travelers and travel writers to stop saying, "You can't get a good meal in the Caribbean." It simply isn't true. I've enjoyed wonderful meals from the Bahamas to Trinidad. It may be difficult, but it's not impossible; too many restaurants and hotels have demonstrated otherwise.

Instead, it's time to hold hotels to higher standards. In judging a resort I gave cuisine a great deal of attention. Some places have brought a quality and creativity to their cuisine not associated with the Caribbean in the past. Many have young, imaginative chefs who are turning out great dishes.

Trouble in Paradise

Idyllic places today must be more than pretty to get our attention and gain our loyalty. They must be reasonably efficient, if not always convenient, and secure. Trouble in paradise is troubling whenever it rears its ugly head, but with the exception of a few islands—ironically, those that have the most tourists—crime is less of a problem at hotels in the Caribbean than in any major city in the United States.

We who live by security systems and double-bolted doors have forgotten what it's like not to worry about security. But imagine! There are still Caribbean islands where people don't lock their doors. And there are still resorts where you aren't given a room key because they don't have them—or need them. When I visit some of my favorite places where there are no locks on the doors, I find it unsettling at first, until I realize I can shed those city fears. The freedom is exhilarating.

Crawling Critters

Welcome to the Tropics. If this is your first visit, I have some explaining to do. If you have been to Florida or the Mississippi Delta, you already know about bugs and other creatures that thrive in warm, humid climates. Ninety-nine percent are harmless. They may not be cheering to see, but they won't hurt you. "I saw a roach 2 inches long," I've heard visitors new to the Tropics say. And I reply, "Yes, I see them often."

This is true even at the best Caribbean resorts. Recently, at one of the very finest, most expensive resorts in this book, I opened a drawer, and there it was—a huge

water bug flat on its back, dead.

You'll also see geckos or chameleons and, after the first shock, you'll grow fond of them, like pets. They are wonderfully interesting to watch; some have great color, too.

At certain times of the year, mosquitoes can be fierce, particularly after a rain. I know; they love me. I never go anywhere without insect repellent. Most good hotels provide a can of repellent in their guest rooms and usually have a can on hand at the bar. People with allergies may have a problem using repellents and should consult their doctors. Needless to say, in air-conditioned places you are less likely to be bothered. It's the best reason I know for air-conditioning.

How the Book Is Organized

100 Best Resorts of the Caribbean covers thirty-nine separate islands in twenty-seven island groups arranged alphabetically by island and within its group. For example, under the U.S. Virgin Islands, you will find St. Croix, St. John, St. Thomas, in that order. Each island or island group starts with a profile intended as no more than a quick introduction. I have made the assumption that you have been to the Caribbean before or have other guidebooks by me or other writers with the nitty-gritty details for planning a vacation.

At the end of each entry, you will find an information block providing standard information on the resort that is not included in the text, such as where to make reservations or how much local tax or service charges are levied.

Other information, such as room amenities like television and air-conditioning or sports facilities such as tennis courts and water-sports equipment, is also listed for quick reference. If, however, a resort is known for a particular sport like golf or diving, more information on its special features is provided in the text.

Seasons and Symbols

There is absolutely no uniformity in designating the beginning and ending of high season and low season in the Caribbean. The dates differ from island to island and hotel to hotel. Unless specified to the contrary, the definitions throughout this book are those used generally in the region: High season is the winter months from mid-December to mid-April, low season is comprised of the balance of the year when hotel rates are reduced by 30 percent or more. More and more resorts are adding a third season, known as the shoulder season (mid-April to late May and/or September to October), when rates are also reduced substantially.

Rates peak during holiday periods, particularly during Christmas and New Year's and in February, when most resorts require a one-week or longer stay. When your priority is a winter vacation, paradise can be pricey, but you can often save a bundle by shifting slightly from March to mid-April or by going in November instead of December. And do not overlook packages. Even the fanciest resorts have them, particularly in the shoulder and low seasons. They usually represent meaningful savings and have additional bonus features.

Rates found at the end of each resort indicate the resort's price range rather than the rates for each different type of accommodation. All rates are subject to change, and if the past is prologue, they will change. Consult the resort's U.S. representative (listed at the end of each resort) or a travel agent who can get the most current information. Prices are quoted in U.S. dollars unless indicated otherwise.

The symbols used are as follows:

EP   (European Plan): Room only, no meals.

CP   (Continental Plan): Room with continental breakfast.

FAB   (Full American Breakfast): Room with full American breakfast.

MAP   (Modified American Plan): Room with breakfast and dinner.

A   (American Plan): Room with three meals daily.

FAP   (Full American Plan): Room with three meals; full American breakfast daily.

ALL-INCLUSIVE   The rate includes accommodations, all meals, on-premises sports and entertainment, drinks, tax, and service.

You should know that many resorts call themselves all-inclusive or say they have all-inclusive packages when in fact they do not. The hotel's brochure spells out what is and is not included. It is important to *read the fine print*.

Facilities

Almost any of the resorts in this book can arrange those sports not available at their property and island tours or boat trips to nearby islands. Most have tennis and beachside sports, but it is important when you compare prices to factor in these additional costs when the use of facilities is not included in room rates.

Dress Code

Specific guidelines are given under each resort, as the code does vary, but generally throughout the Caribbean, dress during the day and evening is casual and informal. This, however, does not mean sloppy, tacky, or tasteless. West Indians are often quite offended by the way some tourists dress. Hotel owners are also. They ask that beachwear be kept for the beach. Many resorts require a jacket for dinner in the winter season, but only a very few still require ties for men. Some of the smallest, least pretentious hotels have the strictest dress codes for evening.

Children

More and more couples are vacationing with their children. Most Caribbean resorts welcome children, but a few do not, or they limit the age or the time period. The policy is spelled out for every resort in this book. Those that welcome families often have special rates for children; some have special meals and supervised activities. All that take children can arrange baby-sitters, although some resorts request that you notify them in advance.

Meetings

Almost all resorts now take meetings, but some small ones are likely to take them only at certain times of the year. Alternatively, you can book the entire hotel—not a bad idea for small groups.

Stargazing

Since I have already selected 100 resorts out of the 1,500 hotels in the Caribbean, you may wonder why I added stars. I'm wondering, too, since it will probably cause me nothing but grief—from readers who will tell me I over-rated this or that resort, and from hoteliers who will think I've underrated them. I agonized over each one, but I don't claim that I always got it right.

The distinctions are as follows:

- **★★★★★** A league of their own. Not only do they stand out as the best on their island, but they stand up to each other as well.
- **★★★★** Close to the top but not quite in a league all their own.
- **★★★** All-around good but not quite in the top league.
- **★★** All-around good but on a modest scale.
- **★** Small, very modest.
- **N/S/T** A few resorts were not given stars because they are (N) too new to be judged, (S) too specialized to be classified in the usual manner, or (T) in transition under new owners or management.

Green Leaf Awards 🍃

Protecting the environment is not a fad but a concern that we must maintain day in and day out. In no place in the world is this more essential than the Caribbean. The natural environment is this area's number one asset and protecting it must be its number one priority. The need is as great, if not greater, for the people who live there as for visitors. Without it, they have nothing.

More and more people are becoming aware of their role as travelers, and many (myself included) want to support those who demonstrate an environmental awareness and are making an effort to protect this heritage through their daily actions.

In researching this book, I created an environmental profile that I asked every resort to complete; their participation was entirely voluntary. To my knowledge it is the first time a guidebook has made such an attempt in any part of the world. My purpose was not to serve as critic, since there are, as yet, no internationally recognized standards by which to judge and I do not consider myself an expert, only a concerned citizen. Rather, I wanted to survey this group in particular to learn if the 100 that are the best at operating their resorts treat their environment with the same care they give their guests. I awarded Green Leaves to those who demonstrate an ongoing concern through their conservation policies and practices.

I was surprised and pleased by the results. Of the 100 resorts, seventy-five responded. Environmental awareness and conservation among these hotels is at a much higher level than I had realized. This being the first time anyone has made such a selection, I limited the Green Leaf Award to seventeen resorts. I would be pleased to send you a copy of the questionnaire if you request it, and I welcome your suggestions for future editions.

Author's Postscript

I want to assure you that there was no charge for a hotel to be in this guide—a practice not uncommon for books of this kind, particularly in Europe. Nor did I incur any obligation whatsoever in the course of researching the resorts and making my selections.

The choices are entirely my own. I sought opinions often and listened to advice. I tried to cast myself into the mold of the people for whom a resort was designed. But in the end the process was subjective. I don't claim to be all-knowing; nor do I expect everyone to agree with all my selections. However, I can say without hesitation that there is no resort in this book I wouldn't be happy to return to many times. Indeed, I believe that sentiment is the most valuable criterion a writer can use.

From time to time the Caribbean region experiences hurricanes and tropical storms that can cause damage. If there has been a hurricane or storm recently in the area you plan to travel to, you should phone ahead to make sure that the resort you'd like to visit is open and that any storm damage has been repaired.

The prices and rates listed in this guidebook were confirmed at press time but under no circumstances are they guaranteed. We recommend that you call establishments before traveling to obtain current information.

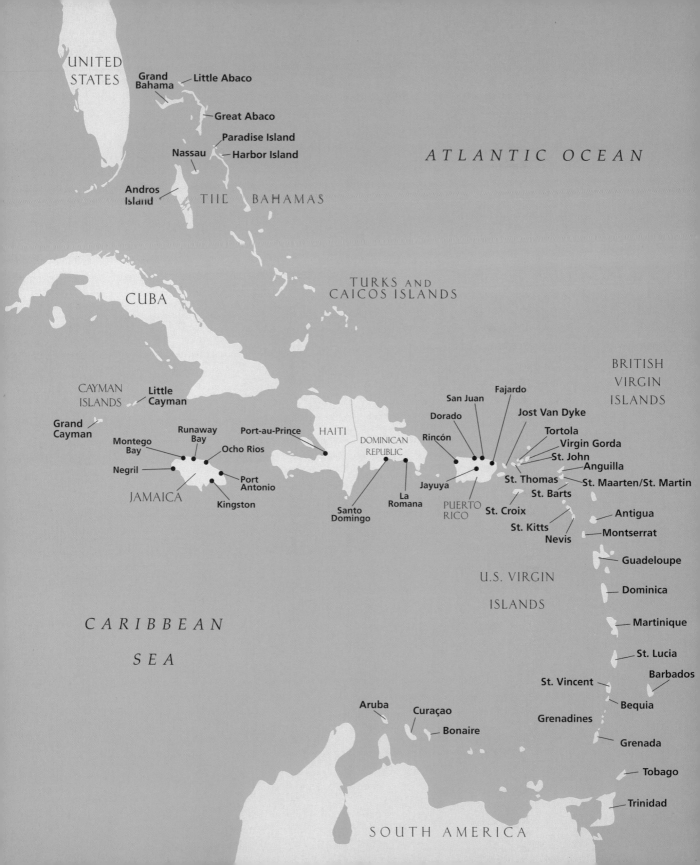

UNITED
STATES

Grand
Bahama   Little Abaco

Great Abaco

Paradise Island

Nassau   Harbor Island

Andros
Island   THE   BAHAMAS

ATLANTIC OCEAN

CUBA

TURKS AND
CAICOS ISLANDS

CAYMAN
ISLANDS   Little
Cayman

BRITISH
VIRGIN
ISLANDS

Grand
Cayman

Runaway
Bay   Port-au-Prince   HAITI   San Juan   Fajardo

Montego
Bay   Ocho Rios   DOMINICAN
REPUBLIC   Dorado   Jost Van Dyke

Negril   Rincón   Tortola

Port
Antonio   Virgin Gorda

JAMAICA   Kingston   St. John   Anguilla

Jayuya   St. Thomas   St. Maarten/St. Martin

Santo
Domingo   La
Romana   PUERTO
RICO   St. Barts

St. Croix   Antigua

St. Kitts   Montserrat

Nevis

Guadeloupe

U.S. VIRGIN

ISLANDS   Dominica

CARIBBEAN   Martinique

SEA   St. Lucia

Barbados

St. Vincent

Bequia

Grenadines

Aruba   Curaçao

Bonaire   Grenada

Tobago

Trinidad

SOUTH AMERICA

Anguilla

Sea, sand, and serenity—these are the assets of this tranquil hideaway in the northeastern corner of the Caribbean. Anguilla (pronounced Ann-GWEF-la), 5 miles north of St. Martin, is a dry, low-lying coral island that receives only 35 inches of rainfall per year.

What Anguilla lacks in mountains and tropical foliage, it makes up for in powdery white beaches, which you can have almost to yourself, and fantastically clear aqua and cobalt-blue waters that have attracted yachtsmen for decades and fishermen for centuries. More recently the spectacular waters have been luring snorkelers and scuba divers to the large reefs that lie off Anguilla's coast.

Yet until it burst on the scene in the 1980s with some superdeluxe resorts, Anguilla was the best-kept secret in the Caribbean. Since then trendsetters have been flocking to this little-known spot to learn what all the fuss is about. A beachcomber's island at heart, Anguilla even now is so laid-back that you might need to practice doing nothing to enjoy its tranquillity. Over the years the island has gained an array of good restaurants, shops, and tourist facilities—all low-key—and it even has a budding artist colony. Yet, the island still has no golf courses, casinos, or shopping arcades, and all but a few small cruise ships pass it by. If you want a change of pace, though, Anguilla is only a twenty-minute ferry ride from the casinos and duty-free shopping of St. Martin.

Traditionally among the region's most skilled boatmen and fishermen, the Anguillans supply the markets and restaurants of St. Martin with much of their fish. You can watch the fishing boats come in at Island Harbor on the eastern end. The Anguillans also make boats, including an unusual racing vessel that gets tested during Anguilla's annual Race Week in August. Sleek yachts and humble fishing boats are available to take you to nearby atolls for a picnic and a day of snorkeling.

For a destination whose total number of guest rooms is less than that of a large hotel, Anguilla has a surprising range of accommodations, from guest houses to posh hotels.

Information

Anguilla Tourist Information, (800) 553–4939; www.anguilla-vacation.com;
e-mail: atbtour@anguillanet.com

CAP JULUCA
Maunday's Bay, Anguilla, B.W.I.

Casablanca by the sugary shores of the Caribbean . . . I must be dreaming, you will say to yourself. But this Arabian Nights fantasy is no mirage, although there is enough deep sand around it to make you think you got lost in the Sahara.

Cap Juluca could win any contest for being the most beautiful resort in the Caribbean, if not the world. It is sensual, romantic, and glamorous. Situated on 179 acres at Maunday's Bay, on Anguilla's leeward shores, with St. Martin in the distance, Cap Juluca is a villa resort stretching for a mile along the curve of a magnificent beach.

The posh resort is comprised of superdeluxe villas in Moorish style, complete with arches, domes, turrets, and keyhole doorways in a fairyland of colors. The blue skies, azure sea, magenta bougainvillea, and green gardens seem all the more intense against the snow-white villas. Cap Juluca is fittingly named for the Arawak god of the rainbow.

Guest rooms, in two-story "hotel" villas and pool villas with up to five bedrooms, come in a bewildering variety: from a bedroom with only a kitchenette and shower to a large villa with a private pool. Bedrooms and suites are rented separately, as in a hotel, and the pool and sundeck are shared. Or you can take an entire villa and have a pool to yourself.

The sumptuous interiors vary, but they all have Italian tile floors and louvered doors of Brazilian walnut. Generally, those east of the main pool have built-in banquettes of white masonry with colorful cushions and pillows that give the interior a clean, sophisticated look. Moroccan artifacts and design elements inspired by colorful Moorish motifs are set against pure white walls, conveying the impression of a palace in Tangier. The newer villas are furnished rather grandly in European colonial style, which seems to my eye a bit heavy and pretentious for the airy, dreamy ambience that Cap Juluca is meant to convey.

The huge, luxurious bathrooms found in some suites are second to none. They are fabulous, if not downright decadent. They feature a king's ransom of Italian marble and mirrors along with an oversize bathtub, double sinks, a separate shower, and a bidet. Some even have a double bathtub with leather headrests and a private solarium.

You can sink into the mile of soft, deep white sand at your doorstep, or loll about the large freshwater pool of the Azzamour complex. A continental breakfast served in your room is part of the luxury at Cap Juluca. But if your room does not have a terrace from which to enjoy an early-morning sea view, you can have breakfast and lunch at the pool terrace and refreshments at the Beach Pavilion under its onion-shaped dome. Roving beach waiters offer chilled towels, complimentary mineral water, and drinks on request.

The eastern end of the beach is anchored by Pimm's, the main restaurant. Named for a refreshing drink popular with the British in the days of the raj, Pimm's has an enchanting setting directly by the sea, looking across the sweep of Cap Juluca by the bay. In the evening the candlelit tables and the sound of the water lapping at the rocks make it even more romantic.

Lunch and dinner menus feature seafood selections based on the island's supply of fresh fish, along with chicken, lamb, veal, and beef specialties, and too many yummy desserts—but all prepared with a light touch. Not surprisingly, they will lighten your wallet as well. A restaurant by the central pool pavilion, George's, named for award-winning Anguillan chef George Reid, serves Mediterranean cuisine tinged with Caribbean flavors. Two special nights—West Indian night and a beach bonfire barbecue—are held here weekly. For lunch George's serves light fare and grilled chicken, seafood, and burgers. The resort's newest restaurant, Kemia (meaning tapa or mezza), is located next to Pimm's. It is presided over by a former chef at New York's famous Gramercy Tavern and specializes in hors d'oeuvres or tapas.

Should you care to leave your villa or haven by the pool, Cap Juluca has three Omni-turf tennis courts (two lighted) and a pro shop. The use of Sunfish, snorkeling gear, windsurfers, and Hobie Cats is included in the rate. Excursions farther afield are available on Cap Juluca's 34-foot, twenty-passenger *Justice*, an Anguillan-crafted powerboat. You could also try working on your golf stroke at Cap Juluca's new aqua driving range. Located in front of the lagoon, which is marked for yardage, play is with golf balls that float and are then driven back to shore by the breeze. In addition, a sand bunker is in place so that difficult shots can be practiced, hitting to a target. A putting green with tee-areas of 50, 75, and 150 yards has also been added. There is a $10 charge for golf balls; clubs are complimentary.

The resort has an herb garden and self-guided walking trails that lead to a lagoon behind the resort—a popular bird-watching location. The garden supplies fresh herbs for the chef and is a novelty for guests. Cap Juluca is one of the few resorts in the Caribbean to have a full-time horticulturist on staff.

There is not much entertainment at Cap Juluca. A West Indian buffet is offered on the pool terrace on one evening, along with the manager's cocktail party, and several evenings feature dancing in the Beach Pavilion. Cable television is available in the media room in the main house, as are VCRs and cassettes on request. The main building near the entrance has a library and boutique.

Cap Juluca has a reception area in the main building, where you check in while you sip a welcome drink. There is also a fitness center where Cardy, an Anguillan and a cricket player who plays professionally in England during the season, puts you through your paces. The spa, which Cardy also operates with a staff of professionals, has been expanded to offer many more Asian and other trendy specialty treatments than were available in the past. There are two treatment rooms along with in-room availability, which most guests seem to prefer.

Cap Juluca has been designed as a secluded, stylish retreat for sophisticated travelers and is meant to have a mystique of exotic, erotic luxury about it. Reports continue to be good, although not every problem has been solved. It's better to go to Cap Juluca with lower expectations and give the genie of this Arabian Nights fantasy time to work his magic.

Cap Juluca ★★★★

P.O. Box 240, Maunday's Bay, Anguilla, B.W.I.
Phone: (264) 497–6666; Fax: (264) 497–6117;
e-mail: capjuluca@anguillanet.com; www.capjuluca.com

Owner: Cap Juluca Holdings, Ltd.
General Manager: Eustace Guishard
Open: Year-round
Credit Cards: American Express, MasterCard, Visa
U.S. Reservations: Cap Juluca, (888) 8–JULUCA (888–858–5822), 866–458–5822, 305–466–0916
Deposit: Three nights; twenty-one days cancellation
Minimum Stay: Seven nights during Christmas/New Year's
Arrival/Departure: Guests met at airport by hotel representative; complimentary transfer service in packages
Distance from Airport: *(Wallblake Airport)* 5 miles: taxi one-way, $20; via ferry from Marigot, St. Martin: 4 miles (fifteen minutes), $15
Distance from The Valley: 5 miles; taxi one-way, $20
Accommodations: 85 rooms and 13 suites in 12 hotel villas and six pool villas; most with terraces or interior patios; all have king-size beds; some suites have extra queen-size daybed
Amenities: Air-conditioning, ceiling fans; refrigerator with icemaker, stocked minibar; telephone; some baths with tub, some with solarium and double tub, some with shower only; hair dryer, deluxe toiletries, bathrobe; nightly turndown service, room service as requested; bottle of rum and fruit in room; kitchen in villas
Electricity: 110/220 volts
Fitness Facilities/Spa Services: Fitness center; in-room massages upon request
Sports: Freshwater swimming pool, six villa pools; tennis, Sunfish, Hobie Cats, snorkeling gear, waterskiing free; scuba, fishing, golf in St. Martin arranged for charge
Dress Code: Casual by day; casually elegant in evening; no jacket or tie required
Children: All ages, but advance inquiry requested for those under three; cribs; baby-sitters; supervised children's program
Meetings: Up to forty people
Day Visitors: No
Handicapped: No facilities
Packages: Honeymoon, Romantic Retreat; weddings
Rates: Per room, daily, CP. *High Season* (January 4–March 31): $735–$2,315. *Shoulder Season* (April 1–30 and November 15–mid-December): $420–$1,315. *Low Season:* $325–$935. Three- and five-bedroom villas priced separately; inquire.
Service Charge: 10 percent
Government Tax: 8 percent

CUISINART RESORT & SPA
Rendezvous Bay, Anguilla, B.W.I.

A resort for the twenty-first century, CuisinArt is a hideaway for baby boomers who want it all—large comfortable rooms with the latest electronic gadgets, huge marble bathrooms, a beautiful beach, a vanishing-edge swimming pool, gourmet cuisine by a celebrated chef, a hydroponic farm (no pollution, no pesticides), a full-service spa for pampering, with a fitness center and par course for just enough exercise not to feel guilty. What else could you ask for?

Set on the beautiful white sands of Rendezvous Bay on Anquilla's southern coast with views of St. Martin across the Caribbean Sea, the stylish resort's lavishness makes it clear that no costs were spared, no shortcuts taken.

The resort is approached by a drive along a flower-bordered boulevard that leads to the grand entrance of the blue-domed main building with the reception and concierge desks, a boutique, a reading and video library, a game room with a billiards table, a bar, a lounge, and two restaurants. Everywhere the whitewashed walls are ablaze with vivid, decorative paintings by Italian artists, establishing one of the resort's dual goals—art patronage. And you thought it was named for a kitchen appliance!

(I will let you in on a little secret. Many people seem puzzled by the name, CuisinArt. The quick explanation: The resort's owner, Lee Rizzuto, owns Le Cuisinart.)

The resort is set around tropical gardens centered by a large swimming pool from which a series of small pools and waterfalls drop to the beach. To each side are five large, three-story whitewashed villas of Mediterranean-inspired architecture. Flower-filled courtyards at each entrance are framed by an archway with a wooden door that adds an accent and stairs whose art deco brick glass is integrated into the white stucco walls.

All ten villas are directly on the beach; each has eight spacious units. The first and second floors have junior and one-bedroom suites with patios or terraces, while the top floor has two two-bedroom suites. The verandas are large enough for a table with two chairs and two chaise lounges. Most one-bedroom units have connecting doors to a neighboring unit and can be converted to a two-bedroom suite. All have cable television with forty-seven channels and a telephone with dataport; luxury suites have living room sound systems. Large bathrooms are set in soft-toned Italian marble and have double sinks, deep oval tubs, and a separate shower. Some suites have a private solarium for sunning.

The three-story main building has nine accommodations: seven luxury rooms and two spectacular penthouses. Of the latter, one is a 4,300-square-foot, three-bedroom suite, the other a 7,600-square-foot, two-bedroom suite. Each has a living room, a fully equipped kitchen (with Cuisinart appliances), and wraparound terraces with expansive views.

The spacious accommodations—double the size of most hotel rooms—are furnished in a comfortably elegant style with fine rattan and wood furniture imported from Asia and brightly colored Italian fabrics, predominantly in blue and yellow. Indeed, the resort is coordinated in these strong primary colors right down to the napkins on your breakfast tray, the chairs and cushions in the restaurants and around the pool, and even the blue soap in your bathroom. The result: a certain flashiness.

There are three venues for dining. CuisinArt's cuisine is directed by executive chef Denis Jaricot, who comes with more than twenty years of experience, most recently as executive chef of Four Seasons Toronto's highly rated Truffles Restaurant. Chef Jaricot hosts cooking demonstrations in the open kitchen of Santorini, the resort's gourmet restaurant offering a creative menu of Mediterranean cuisine infused with the flamboyant flavors and spices of the Caribbean. Cafe Mediterraneo, overlooking the pool,

serves seafood, grilled items, pizza, and salads of fresh home-grown vegetables. Bring money: Prices here are on a par with those of top eateries in New York.

The Hydroponics Cafe, set outdoors next to the "farm" (which looked like a greenhouse to me), offers lunch daily, featuring salads and other light fare of vegetables, edible flowers, and herbs grown hydroponically.

CuisinArt has three lighted tennis courts, a boccie court next to the swimming pool, a championship croquet field, and a 1-mile par course with exercise stations. There are facilities for water sports.

The resort's full-service spa and fitness center is situated in a three-story building with three indoor and two outdoor treatment rooms. The trained staff offers massages, seaweed wraps, reflexology, aromatherapy, hot stone therapy, sea salt scrubs, and an array of other treatments.

In addition to what you'll find on the walls throughout the resort, more of the art of CuisinArt is found on the top floor of the spa building, which is devoted to an art gallery featuring a changing collection of original art.

CuisinArt's gardens, created by landscape designer and horticulturalist Caryl Clement as an oasis within Anguilla's dry environment, showcase more than 150 species of trees, fragrant flowers, and exotic plants.

CuisinArt's prices might give you sticker shock, but money seems not to be a problem for the new millionaires, celebrities, and other people who come here—the highest-priced suites are the first to go.

CuisinArt Resort & Spa ★★★

P.O. Box 2000, Rendezvous Bay, Anguilla, B.W.I
Phone: (264) 498–2000; Fax: (264) 498–2010;
e-mail: reservations@cuisinart.ai; www.cuisinartresort.com

Management: Olympus Hospitality Group
General Manager: David W. Flack
Open: Year-round except early September–early October
Credit Cards: American Express, MasterCard, Visa
U.S. Reservations: (800) 943–3210, (800) 937–9356, (212) 972–0880
Deposit: Three nights; thirty days cancellation
Minimum Stay: Seven nights during Christmas/New Year's
Arrival/Departure: Guests met at airport by hotel representative
Distance from Airport: *(Wallblake Airport)* 4 miles (ten-minute drive): taxi one-way, $20; via ferry from Marigot, St. Martin, to Blowing Point Ferry terminal, 3 miles (twenty-five minutes), $15
Distance from The Valley: 4 miles; taxi one-way, $20
Accommodations: 93 rooms and suites, all with terraces
Amenities: Air-conditioning, ceiling fans; refrigerator; telephone and dataport; bath with tub and shower, hair dryer, deluxe toiletries, bathrobe; nightly turndown service, room service; art gallery, boutique
Electricity: 110/220 volts
Fitness Facilities/Spa Services: Full-service spa, fitness center, 1-mile parcourse, hair salon, Jacuzzi
Sports: Freshwater swimming pool; three lighted tennis courts; boccie court; championship croquet field; snorkeling, windsurfing, waterskiing, deep-sea fishing, sailing
Dress Code: Casual by day; casually elegant in evening; no jacket or tie required
Meetings: Up to fifty people
Children: All ages; no supervised children's program
Day Visitors: No
Handicapped: No facilities
Packages: Summer
Rates: Per room, daily, CP. *High Season* (mid-December–March 31): $490–$1,900. *Shoulder Season* (April 1–May 31 and November 1–mid-December): $340–$1,340. *Low Season:* $260–$1,030. Owner's suite priced separately; inquire.
Service Charge: 10 percent
Government Tax: 8 percent

LA SIRENA
Mead's Bay, Anguilla, B.W.I.

Soothing to your mind and gentle on your pocketbook, this small ridgetop resort refutes the ill-founded image that Anguilla is a hideaway only for the filthy rich.

Only a short slope—200 yards, maybe—from powdery sands, La Sirena gives you fabulous Mead's Bay Beach but at a third of the cost of Malliouhana, the pricey preserve of celebrities and moguls that anchors the beach's eastern end.

To be absolutely accurate and not to mislead, La Sirena has accommodations of two types in two locations. There are villas near the shore; the walk to the beach for villa guests takes about one minute. At the top of the rise is the main hotel, an attractive complex of two- and three-story buildings housing the restaurants, bar, lounge, a new boutique, small spa, Internet cafe, and most accommodations. Guests here take a three-minute walk along a path to the same fine beach—hardly an inconvenience.

Designed by a Swiss architect, La Sirena combines Mediterranean tradition with Caribbean touches: white stucco walls and arches, peaked ceilings, weathered red tile roofs, and generous balconies trimmed with white latticework.

The main building has guest rooms on three floors, each with a balcony overlooking the gardens and the large swimming pool. Rooms are modest and uncluttered. They have terra-cotta tile floors and tiled bathrooms, and are furnished with wicker, green plants, and fresh flowers. A wicker chest conceals a stocked mini bar. All rooms have safes, and most standard and superior rooms, plus the villas, have air-conditioning at no extra charge. Cable television is available for an extra charge of $50 per week. Room service is available for breakfast only.

I would have been happy had the rooms been just a wee bit larger with a tad more closet space (pack lightly). They are functional and immaculate. La Sirena even includes single rooms—an almost unheard-of commodity in Caribbean resorts. The singles are small with a queen-size bed and a tiny terrace. The most desirable double rooms are the top-floor ones, which have high ceilings and the best views. Rooms 301 and 302 have access to a roof terrace with expansive views. Even more desirable are the recently added junior suites, two on the top floor of the main building and two in a new building in the gardens.

Stone pathways through the gardens lead to the six comfortable, but rather modest, villas and the mile-long beach. Three villas have two bedrooms with two baths, and three have three bedrooms, each with a bath and a separate entrance. The villas have lounges, fully equipped kitchens, a private patio or rooftop sundeck, a telephone, barbecue equipment, daily maid service, and their own freshwater pool. Dishwashers and cable television are available at an extra charge. The villas are particularly well suited for families.

The hotel's restaurant, Top of the Palms, offers French cuisine with a Caribbean flavor. A Caribbean evening on Monday includes music by a steel band, and Thursday night features performances by local music groups.

The resort has a full-service PADI Dive Center on the property and offers a range of dive packages, from beginning to advanced diving. It also has added spa services

P.O. Box 200, Mead's Bay, Anguilla, B.W.I.
Phone: (264) 497–6827; Fax: (264) 497–6829;
e-mail: lasirena@anguillanet.com; www.la-sirena.com

Owner/General Manager: Rolf Masshardt

Open: Year-round

Credit Cards: All major

Reservations: Direct to hotel, (800) 331–9358; or International Travel and Resorts (ITR), (800) 223–9815, (212) 251–1800; Fax: (212) 545–8467

Deposit: Three nights; ten days confirmation; thirty days cancellation

Minimum Stay: Ten nights during Christmas/New Year's

Arrival/Departure: Transfer arranged upon request for fee

Distance from Airport: *(Wallblake Airport)* 9 miles; taxi one-way, $16

Distance from Main Town: 9 miles; taxi one-way, $16

Accommodations: 20 units with balcony or patio in three-story main building (16 doubles with queen, king, or two full-size beds; four singles with queen); four junior suites (with king and queen sleeper sofa); and six villas with 15 bedrooms, each with two queens or one king

Amenities: Ceiling fans; telephone; clock-radio; bath with shower only, hair dryer, basket of toiletries; minibar, room service for breakfast only; safe; air-conditioning in most standard and superior rooms, plus all suites and villas; cable television in villas and available in hotel rooms for charge; Jacuzzi tubs in junior suites; massage center

Electricity: 110 volts

Sports: Two freshwater swimming pools; free snorkeling gear; bicycles for fee; tennis, boating, fishing, horseback riding arranged; full-service PADI Dive Center on premises

Dress Code: Informal

Children: All ages; cribs; baby-sitters; children's activity program in summer; up to two children under twelve stay free in room with two adults

Meetings: No

Day Visitors: Welcome

Handicapped: No facilities

Packages: Summer, pre-Christmas, winter

Rates: Per person, daily, EP. *High Season* (mid-December–March 31): $200 (rooms); $400 (suites); $400-$500 (villas). *Low Season:* $110–$165 (rooms); $230 (suites); $230–$360 (villas). Return guests get 10 percent discount on room rate. Single rates available; inquire.

Service Charge: 10 percent

Government Tax: 10 percent

such as massage and reflexology at its Massage Center.

La Sirena's owners have children of their own and welcome families. In the summer months the resort offers a children's program that includes snorkeling trips, glass-bottom boat excursions, and other activities. Up to two children under twelve stay free in a room with two adults.

Opened in 1989, La Sirena is owned and operated by a young, personable Swiss couple who have blended Swiss efficiency with a Caribbean ambience. They often join their guests for drinks or dinner in the evening.

La Sirena may not have the panache of its ritzy neighbors, but many people would probably find its casual and comfortable digs far more suitable for a relaxed beachside vacation.

Generally, La Sirena receives more Europeans, particularly in the summer, than Americans. Its low-key, friendly atmosphere is well suited to singles who want a quiet vacation, young couples, and families with children who are happy building sand castles on the beach and can go without a daily fix of television or Nintendo.

MALLIOUHANA
Mead's Bay, Anguilla, B.W.I.

Located on Anguilla's northwestern coast on a twenty-five-acre bluff overlooking two spectacular beaches, Malliouhana (the Arawak Indian name for Anguilla) is a sybaritic fantasy in Mediterranean design set in a garden of Eden.

Almost from the day it opened in 1983, the resort won rave reviews for its extraordinary interiors, style, refinement, gourmet cuisine, and attention to detail. It raised deluxe to a lofty new level that few can equal.

Before creating Malliouhana, British industrialist and well-traveled bon vivant Leon Roydon and his late wife, Lyane, had dreamed of building a Caribbean resort with the standards to which they were accustomed in Europe. Like most people, the Roydons fell in love with Anguilla when they visited it for the first time, in 1980.

There are no signs pointing the way to Malliouhana. A driveway passes through landscaped gardens exploding with color and shaded by stately palms to a cluster of white stucco buildings with arched galleries and red tile roofs that look more like palatial Mediterranean hilltop mansions than a hotel.

From the elegant lobby you step through a series of tall, cool white arches that rise to cathedral ceilings of warm Brazilian walnut. They lead to terraced gardens and high-ceilinged, breeze-filled lounges with light terra-cotta tile floors and upholstered rattan furniture.

Malliouhana's accommodations all feature huge bedrooms with king size beds; they are located in wings of the main building and other buildings on the cliff and in villas with one- and two-bedroom suites directly on the beach. Junior suites have large bedrooms and dressing rooms; one-bedroom and two-bedroom suites have separate bedrooms, living-dining rooms, and covered patios. Guest rooms have marbled and mirrored bathrooms almost as large as the bedrooms, and terraces overlooking Anguilla's peacock-blue waters.

Exquisitely designed tropical furniture of the highest-quality rush and bamboo and rich Brazilian mahogany louvered doors and windows with solid-brass fittings contrast with the stark white bedcovers, tile floors, and walls adorned with subdued Asian prints and vibrant Haitian paintings.

The resort has a mile of powder-fine beach on one side and a small, intimate cove, accessible only from the hotel (or by boat), on the other. There are four Laykold tennis courts (lighted), which are managed by a Peter Burwash International pro. You'll also find a water-sports center and fitness center. The hotel's launch is available for trips to nearby islets and reefs for snorkeling and picnics and for excursions to St. Martin.

At cocktails guests enjoy light musical entertainment, but the evening's highlight is dining on haute cuisine in the casually elegant terrace restaurant overlooking the sea. Chef Alain Laurent has continued the tradition of his teacher, the late Jo Rostang of La Bonne Auberge—a two-star Michelin restaurant on the French Riviera—who developed Malliouhana's cuisine. In the winter season staff from La Bonne Auberge come to work with the Anguillan staff, some of whom have been given training in France. Malliouhana also has an outstanding wine cellar, stocked with 35,000 bottles of fine wine selected and shipped by connoisseur Leon Roydon, mostly from France.

For those who prefer a casual day, the resort has another pool and poolside cafe, Le Bistro, by the beach. The second floor of the cafe has a large room for meetings; it can be converted into a disco.

If you had any doubt that times are changing, Malliouhana's children's addition is proof positive. For the increasing number of guests traveling with their children and grandchildren, the posh hideaway has added the

Children's Place, a well-equipped beachfront playground with a paddling pool and two Playworld Systems areas: one for ages two through five, the other for ages five through twelve. The playground is supervised daily from 8:30 A.M. to 4:00 P.M. and is free for guests.

In another bow to new trends, the resort has built an elaborate 12,000-square-foot spa. The beachside facility offers massage, skin and hair care, and body treatments that use island herbs, spices, flowers, and fruits creatively. For example, the Malliouhana Massage uses blends of oils such as passionfruit, ginger, lemongrass, and hibiscus. Guests can take an exotic coconut milk or lemon basil bath in one of the spa suites or request "bath turndown service" in their room.

Roydon clearly understands the needs of his discerning guests. A staff-to-guest ratio of more than two to one and the high level of service by the resort's staff of 200 Anguillans, more than half of whom have been with the resort since it opened, ensure that those needs are met in a gracious atmosphere.

From the time it opened, Malliouhana has attracted celebrities, movie stars, and a loyal following of well-heeled, sophisticated travelers. Leon Roydon and his son Nigel manage the hotel with meticulous care. One of them is on hand to greet guests on arrival and to say farewell at the end of their stay. At other times, however, the managers keep their distance, believing that people come to Malliouhana for privacy. As a result, some people find Malliouhana cold. Malliouhana's ambience is not for everyone, especially if you prefer your beachside elegance to be barefoot.

Malliouhana ★★★★★

P.O. Box 173, Mead's Bay, Anguilla, B.W.I.
Phone: (800) 835–0796, (264) 497–6111; Fax: (264) 497–6011;
e-mail: malliouhana@anguillanet.com; www.malliouhana.com

Owner: Leon Roydon
General Manager: Nigel Roydon
Open: Year-round except September–October
Credit Cards: None
U.S. Reservations: Direct to hotel, (800) 835–0796
Deposit: Three nights; thirty days cancellation
Minimum Stay: Seven nights, December–March
Arrival/Departure: Transfers not available
Distance from Airport: 8 miles from *Wallblake Airport* and Blowing Point Ferry terminal; taxi one way, $16
Distance from Main Town: 9 miles; taxi one-way, $18
Accommodations: 55 rooms (including 34 double rooms, six junior suites, seven one-bedroom suites, three Jacuzzi suites, one pool suite, and two two-bedroom suites)
Amenities: Air-conditioning, ceiling fans (also in bathrooms); telephone; stocked mini bars; ample closet space; bathroom vanities with makeup lights, deep tub, shower stall, bidet, plush towels, bathrobes, hair dryer, toiletries; room service until 10:00 P.M.; beauty salon; designer boutique, sundries shop; cable television in television room and library; some televisions and VCRs for rent
Electricity: 110 volts
Fitness Facilities/Spa Services: Fitness center and full-service spa; personal trainer
Sports: Three freshwater pools and large heated Jacuzzi; snorkeling; four tennis courts (three lighted); fishing gear, waterskiing, windsurfing, Sunfish, Lasers, Prindle catamarans; deep-sea fishing, diving arranged for fee
Dress Code: Casual but chic sportswear by day; casually elegant in evening
Children: All ages; baby-sitters available; children's pool and playground
Meetings: Small groups on request
Day Visitors: No
Handicapped: No facilities
Packages: Honeymoon, anniversary; June 1–August 31, four or more nights; for couples, November 1–December 18, five nights or more
Rates: Single or double, daily, EP. *High Season* (mid-December–March 31): $555–$2,510. *Shoulder Season* (April 1–May 31 and November 1–mid-December): $365–$1,620. *Low Season* (June 1–August 31): $265–$1,175. Surcharge for Christmas holiday period.
Service Charge: 10 percent
Government Tax: 8 percent

Antigua

Shaped somewhat like a maple leaf, Antigua has protruding fingers that provide its coastline with sheltered bays, natural harbors, and extra miles of beautiful beaches—one for every day of the year, the Antiguans say—fringed by coral reefs. These assets have made Antigua one of the most popular beach and water-sports centers in the Caribbean. As a bonus, low humidity and year-round trade winds create the ideal climate for tennis, golf, horseback riding, and a variety of other sports and sightseeing.

Antigua (pronounced Ann-TEE-ga) is the largest of the Leeward Islands. Located east of Puerto Rico, between the U.S. Virgin Islands and the French and Dutch West Indies, Antigua is a transportation hub of the region and the home of LIAT (Leeward Islands Air Transport), the regional carrier of eleven Eastern Caribbean states.

After English settlers from St. Kitts established a colony near Old Town on the southern coast in 1632, Antigua remained a British possession until 1981, when full independence was achieved. Today the island's British heritage and historic character are most evident at English Harbour, once the headquarters of the British navy, where the buildings of the old wharf (now known as Nelson's Dockyard) have been restored to house shops, inns, restaurants, and museums.

St. John's, the capital and once a sleepy West Indian village, has become a popular tourist mecca. Charming historic buildings of West Indian architecture house attractive boutiques and restaurants.

This relaxed and quietly sophisticated island has a few large resorts and casinos, but most of Antigua's hotels are small and operated by their owners—a feature that helps give the island a less commercial atmosphere than some other Caribbean destinations.

Information

Antigua and Barbuda Department of Tourism, 610 Fifth Avenue, Suite 311, New York, NY 10020; (212) 541–4117, (800) 268–4227; Fax: (212) 757–1607; www.antigua-barbuda.org

CURTAIN BLUFF

St. John's, Antigua, W.I.

Ideally located on a secluded promontory on Antigua's southern coast, with Atlantic surf washing the beach on one side and the tranquil Caribbean lapping the shore on the other, Curtain Bluff is an exclusive enclave of tropical splendor spread across twenty beachfront acres against a backdrop of verdant hills.

The time-tested resort has been called Antigua's blue-chip address for conservative travelers by some and a tropical paradise with a country club ambience by others, but perhaps the best description was offered by the guest who said, "This is a place where you fall in love with your wife all over again." Not a bad vote of confidence for a resort that set a new standard for the Caribbean when it was opened in 1961, watched a host of competitors blossom— and wither like dandelions—and is still going strong.

Whatever Curtain Bluff is, for sure it is a reflection of its creator, Howard Hulford. A legend in his own time, he has been called by many the best hotelier in the Caribbean. Gruff, opinionated, love-me-if-you-dare Hulford is as famous for his silver mustache as he is for his manner. He and his fine staff have made sure his standard of excellence has been maintained at Curtain Bluff for almost four decades. As a result the resort is usually booked a year in advance, primarily by repeat visitors.

Curtain Bluff operates as an all-inclusive resort. Included in the price are all meals, afternoon tea, and table wine; most sports; deep-sea fishing; and even postage stamps. Room service is available for all meals, and bar service is provided at no extra charge—an unusual amenity for an all-inclusive resort.

Accommodations include seafront double rooms with sitting areas as well as one- and two-bedroom suites in two-story, low-rise buildings, all with terraces and dreamy views. The tastefully appointed rooms have tile floors and wicker furniture dressed in pastels. The two-bedroom, two-level suites offer a breeze-cooled patio with a hammock just waiting to be used; the second bedroom can be rented as a separate accommodation.

The most luxurious: deluxe suites perched in stair-step fashion near the top of the bluff. Each unit has a bedroom larger than most New York apartments, a spacious living room that opens directly onto a large terrace with spectacular views, five ceiling fans, and a well-equipped marbled bathroom. A new building with eighteen marvelous junior suites has replaced the twelve deluxe rooms that were in one of the buildings by the beach. Seven of the new suites

are connecting pairs accommodate families. During the summer of 2002, the resort was closed to construct twenty more junior suites to replace sixteen deluxe beachfront rooms. Each of the new suites has 750 square feet; eight pairs connect. Above the two floors of junior suites are two extravagant suites comprising the entire third floor; each is the equivalent in size of three junior suites. The Morris Bay and Grace Bay Suites have two oversized bedrooms, a marble-accented bathroom with double sinks, tub and walk-in shower, spacious living room, and sliding glass doors that open onto broad terraces with sweeping views of the Caribbean.

Your introduction to Curtain Bluff begins at the central building, surrounded by a riot of flowers with a pretty white filigree gazebo in the gardens. At the reception and concierge desk, you will be greeted by the amiable Wendy Eardley, the resort's very efficient concierge who seems to have the answer to your every need. Beyond is a small patio, shaded by a large tamarind tree, and the dining terrace. To one side is a boutique and the Sugar Mill Bar, the gathering spot for predinner drinks and hors d'oeuvres.

Daytime activities are centered on the calm, palm-fringed Caribbean beach, which offers the Beach Club, where informal lunches are served; the Wednesday bar-

becue buffet is a beach party with steel band music. You'll find umbrellas, changing rooms, showers, and water-sports equipment. Here, too, is the large swimming pool in a pretty grove overlooking the beach.

Tennis is one of Curtain Bluff's main attractions. It has four all-weather championship courts (lighted), a squash court, viewing stands, a resident pro, and a pro shop. Beyond the tennis courts is an air-conditioned fitness center with a full line of exercise equipment and an outdoor area where aerobic and other exercise sessions are held with a professional trainer four times weekly.

Meals are served in the main restaurant, tea on the Bar Terrace. The kitchen at Curtain Bluff is now directed by Christophe Blatz, the former sous-chef, following the retirement of chef Reudi Portmann who had been with Curtain Bluff for thirty-seven years. Blatz, like Portmann, keeps his menus limited, changing them daily to maximize the use of fresh products.

Lunches are light, but dinners are a real treat with your choice of hot and cold soups, appetizers, salads, six different entrees, and too many yummy desserts each night. The wine cellar, with approximately 25,000 bottles of the finest vintages, is Hulford's pride, second only to his fabulous gardens. You can take a guided tour of either.

Hulford and his charming wife, Chelle (who is responsible for the resort's fine decor), along with their able managing director, Rob Sherman, run the resort like a country club. The Hulfords live in a lovely villa on the bluff, where they often entertain hotel guests.

Curtain Bluff is not for everyone, but it does not try to be. The ambience may seem a little old-fashioned to some, but it appeals to Curtain Bluff's loyal patrons, who enjoy dressing for dinner and dancing under the stars to the sounds of the oldies, updated for the young and young-at-heart with jazz, rock, reggae, and calypso.

Curtain Bluff *****

P.O. Box 288, Old Road, St. John's, Antigua, W.I.
Phone: (268) 462–8400, –8403, (888) 289–9898, (212) 289–8888; Fax: (268) 462–8409; www.curtainbluff.com

Owner: Howard Hulford
Managing Director: Rob Sherman
General Manager: Calvert A. Roberts
Open: Mid-October–May 20
Credit Cards: American Express
U.S. Reservations. Direct to hotel or (212) 289–8888
Deposit: Three nights; thirty days cancellation except mid-December–January 1, for which payment must be received before November 1
Minimum Stay: Ten nights during Christmas
Arrival/Departure: Hotel transfers not available due to local taxi regulations
Distance from Airport: 16 miles (thirty-five minutes); taxi one-way, $22
Distance from St. John's: 13 miles; taxi one-way, $22
Accommodations: 71 rooms and suites, all with terraces. All accommodations have either two double beds or one king.
Amenities: Ceiling fans; telephones (suites have them in bath); wall safes; bath with tub and shower, bathrobes, hair dryers available; fresh flowers daily; full room service; suites have mini-bars; no television, radio, air-conditioning; television room; room service 10:00 a.m.–11:00 p.m.
Electricity: 110 volts
Fitness Facilities/Spa Services: See text
Sports: Tennis (see text); squash; croquet; putting green; Sunfish, snorkeling, waterskiing, windsurfing; diving for certified divers only; deep-sea fishing; 47-foot ketch for optional whole- and half-day sails; swimming pool; hiking trips in nearby hills; area offers some of the best birding locations in Antigua
Dress Code: Casual by day; cover-up required in dining room; jacket (tie optional) required after 7:00 p.m. in public areas five nights a week December 19–April 14
Children: All ages, except early January–March 10, when only those twelve years and older welcome; cribs; baby-sitters
Meetings: Up to twenty people
Handicapped: Limited facilities
Day Visitors: No
Packages: Tennis Week, wedding
Rates: Per room doubles, daily, All-inclusive. **High Season** (mid-December–mid-April): $725–$1,075. **Low Season** (mid-April–mid-May and mid-October–mid-December): $555–$850.
Service Charge: 10 percent
Government Tax: 8.5 percent

GALLEY BAY

St. John's, Antigua, W.I.

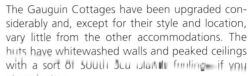

By the time you have made the long drive from the airport, through St. John's and down the narrow country road to Galley Bay, you may be having second thoughts. But press on. It's worth it!

Galley Bay (not to be confused with Galleon Beach on the eastern side of Antigua) has one of the prettiest away-from-it-all settings in the Caribbean. Tucked away on the western coast on forty tropical acres—some landscaped, some natural—the resort is bordered on one side by ½ mile of uninterrupted white-sand beach and, on the other, by a lagoon and bird sanctuary, banded by green hills.

After a hurricane all but leveled the resort in 1995, it was completely rebuilt by its new owner, Robert Barrett, who also owns St. James's Club on Antigua. The rebuilding modernized Galley Bay without changing its essential character, although it is no longer quite as rustic, nor does it have the makeshift look of the past. All the facilities were upgraded, the gardens tamed and greatly embellished, and a much-needed swimming pool added, as well as six two-story cottages with twenty-four deluxe guest rooms directly on the southern beach.

Galley Bay offers three types of accommodations: beachfront rooms, suites directly on the beach, and thatched-roof huts called Gauguin Cottages, resting under shade trees by the lagoon, a stone's throw from the sea. The original beachfront rooms, in two-unit cottages with patios, have terra-cotta floors, rush rugs, and a fresh look with rattan furniture covered with attractive prints and louvered windows that catch the breezes.

Rooms in the new cottages are about a third larger and have huge marble bathrooms with a long, wide counter over two sinks and a big shower. There is a walk-in closet and enough hangers for a year's stay. All have air-conditioning, ceiling fans, telephone, television, coffeemakers, and minifridges stocked with soft drinks. In 1998 another beachfront group of more luxurious one-bedroom suites was added on the southern side of the beach.

The Gauguin Cottages are much more comfortable than you might expect upon first sight. They are two rooms whose masonry walls are covered with white stucco and wooden strips and topped with thatched roofs made to look like huts; they are connected by a thatch-covered breezeway-patio. One "hut" is a spacious bedroom with a sitting area; the other has a bath/dressing room where you will find extra-plush towels and toiletries.

The Gauguin Cottages have been upgraded considerably and, except for their style and location, vary little from the other accommodations. The huts have whitewashed walls and peaked ceilings with a sort of South Sea island feeling—if you use your imagination.

The resort has a hard-surface tennis court, racquets, and balls; bicycles; a rough track around the lagoon for walking and jogging; a shaded Ping-Pong table in its own thatched hut; and a small exercise pavilion beside the lagoon. Galley Bay has a splendid beach, but be aware that in the winter months the sea is often rough with swells, which is why the new swimming pool was such a welcome addition. Equipment for snorkeling, windsurfing, and sailing is provided.

Another of Galley Bay's distinctive features is its open-air beachside bar, which sits under a high pyramid of weathered wood and plaited palms and adds to the rustic ambience. Next door, the open-air lounge, furnished with easy chairs, traditional planter's chairs, and comfortable sofas, is the gathering place for most activities—drinks, daytime chats, afternoon tea, and lots of doing nothing. By cocktail time in the evening, when folks have gotten dressed a bit fancier, there's something of a house-party atmosphere for after-dinner socializing and dancing.

The open-sided dining room bordered by an attractive boardwalk of weathered wood, is the venue for all meals and offers full menus and table service—in other words,

no buffets, a feature that distinguishes Galley Bay from most all-inclusive resorts. Menus change daily and offer an imaginative selection. Dine by candlelight with the sea lapping at the shore and the stars twinkling overhead—it's as romantic a setting as you will find in the Caribbean. The service is outstanding. There is piano music most nights; live entertainment, featured three or four evenings a week, might be a calypso singer, a combo, or a steel band.

The Gauguin, a second, rustic restaurant serving grilled food, is situated at the far end of the beach. Here some tables by the sea are under their own separate thatched roof, giving them an intimate, romantic feeling.

Galley Bay is a comfortable, laid-back, informal retreat. It was opened in 1962 by Pennsylvania native Edie Holbert, who gave it a funky, deserted-island atmosphere that attracted a loyal following. Some of her friends and fans are still coming, along with the next generation. Most guests in winter are British and European; in summer more are American.

Galley Bay has the advantage of seeming to be on a remote island when, in fact, it is only about fifteen or twenty minutes by car (which you will need) from town and nightlife at nearby hotels. That should be ideal for active urbanites who are attracted to a totally relaxed lifestyle but unaccustomed to vegging out and might get restless.

If you have hesitated about returning to Galley Bay, unsure of the upgrading or the new management, you need not delay. In my opinion Galley Bay is better, prettier, and more comfortable than ever. What's more, the staff is one of the best, most friendly, and most caring I have encountered anywhere in visiting the Caribbean.

Galley Bay ★★★★

Box 305, Five Islands, St. John's, Antigua, W.I.
Phone: (268) 462–0302; Fax: (268) 462–4551;
www.antigua-resorts.com

Owner: Rob Barrett
General Manager: Britton Foreman
Open: Year-round
Credit Cards: All major
U.S. Reservations: (800) 345–0271, (954) 481–8787
Deposit: Three nights; fourteen days cancellation; for arrivals during February, reservations and complete payment must be received no later than forty-five days prior to arrival. Cancellations within thirty days will result in a three-night penalty fee.
Minimum Stay: Five nights year-round, except seven nights mid-December– January 1
Arrival/Departure: Transfer service not provided
Distance from Airport: *(Bird Airport)* 8 miles; taxi one-way, $17
Distance from St. John's: 4 miles; taxi one-way, $12
Accommodations: 70 rooms with patios (including 39 superior and deluxe beachfront rooms; 16 beachfront suites; 14 thatched cottages) with twin or king-size beds
Amenities: Ceiling fans, air-conditioning; bath with shower; bathrobe, safe, hair dryer, deluxe basket of toiletries; mini-refrigerator, coffeemaker; no television, radio. Premium suites have large tubs, bidet, and his and hers showers.
Electricity: 110 volts
Fitness Facilities/Spa Services: Small pavilion with minimal exercise equipment
Sports: Tennis, sailing, snorkeling, windsurfing, kayaking, bicycling equipment included; diving, golf arranged; pool; Ping-Pong; jogging track; bird sanctuary
Dress Code: Casual by day; after 7:00 P.M. no shorts, jeans, or T-shirts in bar and restaurant areas
Children: None under sixteen years of age
Meetings: No
Day Visitors: No
Handicapped: No facilities
Packages: All-inclusive
Rates: Two people, per room, daily, All-inclusive. *High Season* (mid-December–mid-April): $670–$860. *Low Season:* $550–$730. For single, deduct $100 per day.
Service Charge: Included
Government Tax: Included

JUMBY BAY

Antigua, W.I.

Less than a mile off the northern coast of Antigua is the ultimate private-island resort, Jumby Bay. Situated on a 300-acre dot of land walloped with pearly beaches, the exclusive eighty-eight acre resort was created in 1983 by real estate investor Homer Williams. Within a year he had sold 80 percent of his holdings to the owners of New York–based Villa Banfi, vintners and wine importers who added several million dollars' worth of improvements and changed the name, Long Island, to Jumby Bay. After several years of uncertainty about its future, the resort was purchased by the Half Moon Golf, Tennis and Beach Club of Jamaica, whose managing director, Heinz Simonitsch, is one of the leading hoteliers in the Caribbean.

But in April 2002, Simonitsch sold the resort back to the island's fourteen homeowners from whom he had purchased it two years earlier. The homeowners have engaged Rosewood Hotels & Resorts of Dallas to manage the property. (Rosewood's other Caribbean properties are Caneel Bay and Little Dix Bay.) Jumby is scheduled to be given a $2.5 million-plus refurbishment, which follows the extensive renovations Simonitsch made that restored Jumby Bay to its five-star luster.

Jumby Bay offers quietly luxurious accommodations, facilities, and amenities, as fine as can be found in the Caribbean, for one all-inclusive price. That means all meals, cocktails and wine with meals, afternoon tea, rum and soft drinks in your room, all sports and recreational facilities on the property, transfers, and even postage stamps. At the airport in Antigua, you are met by a Jumby Bay representative and whisked off to the nearby Beachcomber dock, where the Jumby Bay high-speed catamaran is waiting.

Jumby Bay has three groups of accommodations, all near, but not directly on, the beach. Semi-rondavel villas, each with two suites, are set along paved paths leading from the main beach to a 200-year-old plantation house, the centerpiece. More junior suites are located in Pond Bay House, a graceful Spanish-mission-style structure on a finger of land overlooking a long beach. All accommodations have been newly renovated.

The beautifully appointed rooms, all with sitting areas, are furnished in custom-designed rattan with pillows and bedcovers in quality fabrics of bright prints. Another four superdeluxe villas inspired by traditional West Indian architecture are the most luxurious of the lot. Set alongside Pond Bay House, each villa has two spacious suites and a veranda facing the sea. The four attached villas share a swimming pool. On the south side of the island are the newest accommodations, Harbor Bay and Harbor Beach villas—one three-bedroom villa and ten huge two-bedroom suites with large living rooms and kitchens.

Each cluster of villas is different, but all of the resort's accommodations have walls of louvered doors and windows of Brazilian walnut, adding a rich accent to the decor and providing cross ventilation. High, beamed ceil-

ings create a sense of space and airiness. Bathrooms are unusually large. Bicycles are standing outside the doors.

The beautifully restored Estate House, with its red tile roof, whitewashed arches, and delightful garden courtyard, is reminiscent of a Mediterranean palazzo. The courtyard opens onto a pretty indoor-outdoor dining terrace used for dinner. Courtyard steps lead to a second-floor lounge with a cozy bar and library.

Daytime activity is centered in the large, flower-bedecked Verandah Bar, a beach pavilion near the entry dock and main beach. Breakfast, lunch, and afternoon tea are served on its open-air terraces—and shared with a host of bananaquits and hummingbirds. The resort does not have traditional room service, but continental breakfast can be delivered to your room upon request.

Next to the beach pavilion are three Laykold tennis courts (lighted); a full-time pro is available. The Beach Hut serves as the sports center. If you feel less ambitious, you can take up residence on a lounge chair beneath a thatched umbrella by the 1,800-foot white-sand beach.

A more romantic evening than alfresco dining at the Estate House would be hard to find. The candlelit terrace sits at the edge of the gardens under the spreading arms of an enormous mimosa. In the distance are the twinkling lights of Antigua.

Jumby Bay maintains an impressive greenhouse to grow an enormous variety of tropical plants. Except for the flower-festooned resort grounds, the island is covered with dry woods; nature trails and biking paths meander past sumptuous villas and lead to beaches. One path goes to Pasture Bay, where the endangered hawksbill turtle comes to lay her eggs from May to November. Under a watch directed by WIDECAST (Wide Caribbean Sea Turtle Conservation Network), Jumby Bay hosts marine biology students studying the endangered species during the nesting season.

Jumby Bay, with its gracious informality and aura of well-being, is made for honeymooners and romantics, but it appeals equally to those who simply want to get away from it all in spacious, sophisticated surroundings.

Jumby Bay ★★★★

Box 243, Jumby Bay Island, Antigua, W.I.
Phone: (268) 462–6000, –6002, –6003; Fax: (268) 462–6020;
e-mail: jumbygs@candw.ag; www.jumbybayresort.com

Management: Rosewood Hotel & Resorts
Managing Director: Peter Bowling
Open: Year-round
Credit Cards: Most major
U.S. Reservations: Direct to hotel, (800) 237-3237
Deposit: Three nights; forty-five days cancellation
Minimum Stay: Ten nights during Christmas/New Year's
Arrival/Departure: Transfer service included
Distance from Airport: Less than 1 mile (five-minute ride) to ferry dock; ten-minute boat ride to Jumby Bay dock; Jumby Bay operates its own scheduled water shuttle between resort and Beachcomber dock in Antigua
Distance from St. John's: 7 miles (fifteen minutes) from Beachcomber dock in Antigua; taxi one-way, $10
Accommodations: 39 suites (with king-size beds, doubles, or twins); 11 suites in Harbor Bay and Harbor Beach villas
Amenities: Air-conditioning, ceiling fans; hair dryers, deluxe toiletries, bathrobes, plush towels changed twice daily; wall safe; umbrellas, walking sticks; cable television in suites and villas, telephones, CD player; VCR on request; room service for breakfast on request, ice service daily; flowers and champagne in room on arrival; golf carts for guests in Harbor Bay and Harbor Beach villas
Electricity: 110 volts
Fitness Facilities/Spa Services: Spa and fitness center
Sports: Freshwater swimming pool, putting green, croquet court, three tennis courts, windsurfing, snorkeling, Sunfish, waterskiing, hiking trails, bicycles included; scuba diving, deep-sea fishing, golf in Antigua arranged for fee
Dress Code: Casual by day; slightly more formal for evening; no jacket or tie required
Children: All ages; playground; children under two years old free; two–twelve years old, $275 per stay in winter, $75 in summer
Meetings: Pond Bay House or entire island can be rented in summer
Day Visitors: Welcome with reservations
Handicapped: Most facilities accessible
Packages: Honeymoon, wedding
Rates: Two people, daily, All-inclusive. *High Season* (mid-December–mid-April): $950–$1,500. *Low Season:* $650–$1,000.
Service Charge: 10 percent
Government Tax: 10 percent

Aruba

Aruba was little more than a sleepy sandbar in the 1950s before the gracious Arubans began to develop their tourism industry. Now they have created one of the most popular, fun-loving playgrounds in the Tropics. And they never stop: This Dutch island is booming with new resorts, marinas, smart boutiques, and more.

Fifteen miles off the Venezuelan coast, this dry, low-lying island in the Netherlands Antilles has surprisingly diverse landscapes and natural attractions for an island only 20 miles long. Similar to the American Southwest, with rocky desert terrain and less than 20 inches of annual rainfall, the island has two totally different faces.

On the southern coast tranquil beaches, sophisticated resorts, and glittering casinos line Palm Beach, a beautiful 5-mile band of sand where most of the hotels are located. In sharp contrast, the rugged northern shore reveals moonscape terrain with pounding surf, shifting sand dunes, caves with prehistoric drawings, and strange gigantic rock formations sculpted by the strong winds. The countryside is dotted with tiny farm villages of Dutch colonial architecture. They're surrounded by cactus fields, which turn overnight from a lifeless gray to flowering green following a good rain, and the distinctive ever-present divi-divi tree. The outback can be fun to visit on horseback or by jeep safari with a naturalist guide.

Aruba is ringed by coral reefs, making snorkeling and diving popular; deep-sea fishing is good, too. But the most popular sport is windsurfing; the strong winds that shape the divi-divi trees and keep the island cool have made Aruba one of the leading windsurfing locations in the Caribbean. In June an annual international windsurfing competition is held at Eagle Beach, where winds can exceed 25 knots.

In the capital of Oranjestad, a redesigned town center and shopping plaza showcase Aruba's Dutch colonial past. The Aruba Historical Museum, housed in Fort Zoutman, and William III Towers, one of the island's oldest landmarks, reveal its ancient past. The museum and other examples of historic preservation reflect Aruba's increased emphasis on its cultural and historic heritage. Folkloric shows presented regularly at hotels, as well as restaurants serving authentic Aruban dishes, are other indications.

Information

Aruba Tourist Authority, 1000 Harbor Boulevard, Main Floor, Weehawken, NJ 07087;
(800) TO–ARUBA, (201) 330–0800; www.aruba.com

HYATT REGENCY ARUBA
Palm Beach, Aruba

Located on Palm Beach, along twelve beautiful beachfront acres on Aruba's southwestern coast, the Aruba Hyatt proves that you can have your cake and eat it, too. In other words, with good design it is possible to have a large, full-service resort and still retain the warmth and grace of a small hotel.

Opened in 1990 and totally renovated in 1996, the hotel's handsome design is inspired by Spanish mission architecture. It consists of a nine-story tower flanked by two wings of four and five stories, respectively, that overlook the hotel's centerpiece: a landscaped, multilevel pool and lagoon. It starts as a waterfall by the open-air lobby, flows into a series of interconnected pools in flower-filled gardens, and leads to a wide, white-sand beach. You can slip quietly into the pool at one end and splash down a two-story winding water slide at the other, or swim up to the bar on yet another side.

In the public areas the decor plays on Aruba's gold mining days at the turn of the century. Mock ruins, special carvings, textured and tinted concrete, and weather-beaten rocks in the gardens and around the pool create the look of the old mines still found in several locations on the island. By the Ruinas del Mar restaurant, a rock wall, which seems to float in the lagoon near the center of the gardens, is built of a native limestone called Aruba rock, quarried on the island's northern coast.

All guest rooms have water or garden views, and most have balconies. They are furnished in lively tropical prints with brightly colored accessories and original art by local artists, commissioned for the hotel. The furniture in guest rooms and throughout the hotel blends bleached ash, wicker, and rattan, often with leather trim. Electronic locks on doors and voice mail on the phones are other features.

The Regency Club, Hyatt's executive rooms enhanced with more luxurious amenities, is located on the ninth floor. It has a private concierge and a lounge where complimentary continental breakfast and evening cocktails and tasty hors d'oeuvres are served daily.

There are several suites with one to four bedrooms, large living rooms with cathedral ceilings, stocked wet bars and guest baths, as well as rooftop terraces with wraparound views of Palm Beach and the Caribbean. One of the master bedrooms, furnished with a king-size bed, has a spacious bathroom with a whirlpool tub.

Low-key compared to other large Aruban resorts, the Hyatt has as many services and facilities as its flashier neighbors, if not more. The Ruinas del Mar, an indoor-outdoor restaurant, offers a breakfast buffet and nightly dinner. Next to it is Cafe Piccolo, a small Italian cafe specializing in regional cuisine, particularly northern Italian dishes and pizza hot from a large brick oven, and Cafe Japengo, a Japanese restaurant, the newest addition. The more casual Palms is also a beachfront indoor and outdoor restaurant where lunch and dinner are available daily; it offers local seafood, salads, sandwiches, and Hyatt's Cuisine Naturelle. Wednesday is steak night; Friday is an all-you-can-eat fajita and margarita night with Mexican music. The poolside Balashi Bar and Grill features grilled meat and seafood, sandwiches, and salads during the day. A TCBY store has been added next to the lobby. In the evening you can take in a sunset cruise, a comedy show, or the disco. The Casino Copacabana has a nightly live musical show and offers introductory clinics on casino games. The alfresco Lobby Bar overlooking the pools offers live entertainment nightly.

Tierra del Sol, Aruba's first eighteen-hole golf course (6,800 yards, par seventy-one), is 2 miles from the hotel on the northwestern end of the island. The course was designed by Robert Trent Jones II and is part of a golf community. The course, landscaped with Aruba's indigenous flora, has its own irrigation system and water supply separate from the island's desalinization plant—a major

consideration on this arid island. During construction, environmentalists were consulted to protect local wildlife, including birds at a nearby sanctuary. The hotel has golf packages that include tee times for guests.

The resort offers a full range of water sports operated by Red Sail Sports, including free daily windsurfing clinics, dive programs for the disabled with instructors certified by the Handicapped Scuba Association, and special-interest dives such as a PADI underwater naturalist course. It has cruiser and mountain bicycles for rent and arranges escorted biking tours of the island.

The Stillwater Spa is the resort's newly expanded spa and fitness facility, offering a wide range of body and beauty treatments and state-of-the-art exercise equipment, a sauna and steam room, massage rooms, men's and women's locker rooms, and showers. Pool and beach aerobics, volleyball, pool basketball, and other activities are offered daily. In conjunction with the health club, the Hyatt maintains an arrival/departure lounge with lockers and showers, allowing early-arriving or late-departing guests full access to hotel facilities.

While you are checking out the gym, you can check the kids into Camp Hyatt, a program of supervised day and evening activities for children ages three to twelve, available daily year-round. Camp Hyatt facilities include a children's outdoor playground, arts and crafts, a Nintendo play station, and more than a hundred different types of games and toys. Activities, led by professional counselors, include nature walks, Papiamento lessons, pool and beach games, swimming and windsurfing lessons, and movies. Prices range from $18 for a half day to $68 for a full day with meals. Children get special menus, special room rates, and special check-in packets.

Casual and friendly, the Aruba Hyatt has a certain glamour and attracts a wide range of guests, mostly from the United States and Latin America. It appeals to couples, families with children, and water-sports enthusiasts.

Hyatt Regency Aruba ✱✱✱✱

J. E. Irausquin Boulevard #85, Palm Beach, Aruba
Phone: (297) 8–61234; Fax: (297) 8–61682; www.hyatt.com

Owner: Aruba Beachfront Resorts
General Manager: Barry Kaplan
Open: Year-round
Credit Cards: All major
U.S. Reservations: Hyatt Worldwide, (800) 233–1234
Deposit: Varies, depending on season; fourteen days cancellation, except sixty days for Christmas
Minimum Stay: Ten nights during Christmas
Arrival/Departure: No transfer service
Distance from Airport: 7 miles; taxi one-way, $14
Distance from Oranjestad: 4½ miles, taxi one way, $7
Accommodations: 360 guest rooms and suites with twin or king-size beds, most with terrace; Regency Club floor (29 rooms)
Amenities: Air-conditioning, ceiling fans; bath with tub and shower, basket of toiletries, hair dryer; telephones; stocked minibar; coffeemaker; iron and ironing board; personal safe; television with CNN and other cable services, clock, radio; nightly turndown service, twenty-four-hour room service; floor of non-smoking rooms; concierge; business services; quality boutiques; hair salon. Regency Club: Club lounge; continental breakfast, evening cocktails and hors d'oeuvres; concierge; upgraded amenities and linens.
Electricity: 110 volts
Fitness Facilities/Spa Services: Full-service health club and spa (see text)
Sports: Three-level pool with waterfalls and slide; wide white-sand beach; two free tennis courts (lighted); biking; water sports; dive resort and specialty courses; PADI certification for fee; dive boat departs from beach on trips daily; luxury glass-bottom catamaran with private-yacht amenities; deep-sea fishing arranged; eighteen-hole golf course 2 miles from resort
Children: All ages; cribs, high chairs; baby-sitters; Camp Hyatt for ages three to twelve. Children under eighteen may stay free in parent's room or purchase second room at 50 percent discount, depending on availability.
Meetings: Up to 600 people
Day Visitors: Yes
Handicapped: Facilities fully accessible; dive program for disabled
Packages: Honeymoon, dive, golf
Rates: Per person, daily, EP. **High Season** (mid-December–mid-April): $365–$650. **Shoulder Season** (April 15–May 31 and October 1–December 19): $260–$395. **Low Season** (June 1–September 30): $220–$496.
Service Charge: 12 percent on room
Government Tax: 6 percent

The Bahamas

An archipelago of more than 700 tropical islands stretches south from the eastern coast of Florida over 100,000 square miles of peacock-green and cobalt-blue seas. The Bahamas are so close to the U.S. mainland that many people hop to them in their own boats or private planes for the weekend.

Proximity, together with the foreign but familiar cultural influence of Great Britain (which ruled the Bahamas for more than two centuries), helps make this island nation the tropical destination most visited by Americans—more than three million a year. The variety and range of activities are further attractions.

Most people's introduction to the Bahamas includes Nassau, the capital and commercial center, and Paradise Island, across the harbor. Both bustle with activity day and night, but when you want to exchange the razzle-dazzle for tranquillity, you need only escape to the "other Bahamas," where life is so laid-back and serene that ten people make a crowd. The Out Islands, as they are called, offer lazy, sunny days of sailing, snorkeling, scuba diving, fishing, windsurfing, or doing nothing at all, and evenings of dining on fresh fish and homemade island specialties.

But visiting the Out Islands can present a case of you-can't-get-there-from-here. Fewer than three dozen islands and cays (pronounced keys) have hotels, and even fewer have regular air service. Unless you use a private plane or boat, you must usually double back to Nassau or Florida for connections.

The Abacos: At the northern end of the archipelago, a group of islands is strung in boomerang fashion for 130 miles around the Sea of Abaco, whose sheltered waters offer some of the Bahamas' best sailing. Marsh Harbour is the hub, and New Plymouth is a Cape Cod–like village with palm trees.

Andros: Directly west of Nassau, Andros is the largest of the Bahamas but one of the least developed islands. The interior is covered with forests and mangroves. The Barrier Reef, third largest in the world, and, just beyond, the Tongue of the Ocean, 1,000 fathoms deep, lie off the eastern coast and attract divers and sport fishermen from afar. The towns, hotels, and airstrips are also on the eastern coast.

Eleuthera: First-timers in search of the other Bahamas will delight in the quiet and beauty of this island paradise with its 300 years of history, comfortable hotels, and good dining and sports facilities. Eleuthera, 60 miles east of Nassau, is a 110-mile-long slice of land never more than 2 miles wide (except for splays at both ends). Historic villages and unpretentious beach resorts dot the entire length of the island and nearby cays.

Governor's Harbour, near the center of the island, is the main town and commercial hub. Harbour Island, almost touching the northeastern tip, is one of the Bahamas' most beautiful spots and the site of Dunmore Town, its original capital.

Information

Bahamas Tourist Center, 19495 Biscayne Boulevard, Suite 804, Aventura, FL 33180;
(800) 4–BAHAMAS, (305) 932–0051; Fax: (305) 682–8758.
Offices also in Chicago, Dallas, Los Angeles, New York, and Toronto; www.bahamas.com

GREEN TURTLE CLUB AND MARINA
Abaco, Bahamas

Set on a point overlooking White Sound on the south and Coco Bay on the north, and surrounded by green forested hills, the Green Turtle Club has been a favorite of yachtsmen since it started as a boathouse bar in the 1960s.

The Charlesworth family, who own the resort, came to the Bahamas from Britain in search of a family vacation house. When you see Green Turtle Cay, you will understand immediately why they decided to stay. It has one of the most idyllic settings in the Abacos, if not the entire Bahamas.

The wooden cottages are painted a fresh yellow with white trim; inside, the spacious rooms and villas are furnished with attractive colonial-style mahogany furniture, Meissen prints, and Oriental rugs.

There is a variety of accommodations. Some rooms and suites, as well as cottages with kitchens for up to four people, are located on a small rise by the swimming pool. Other villas directly on the water have private docks and can accommodate up to ten people.

The pine-paneled dining rooms with high-pitched ceilings and colonial-style furnishings accommodate the many day visitors, mainly boaters, along with guests of the hotel. Dinner menus are changed daily, and you are asked to make your selection by 5:00 P.M. each day. The fare is good quality and very traditional—even a bit dated (and heavy on the sauce). Dinner is served promptly at an uncompromising 7:30 P.M., which might bother some free-spirited souls.

Following a hurricane in 1999 when the resort was severely damaged, it undertook an extensive eighteen-month, two-million-dollar renovation that resulted in a new marina, an outdoor patio restaurant, a new restaurant kitchen, swimming pool and deck, and a new road to the Turtle Point Villas. All rooms have been refurbished and extensive landscaping completed. The resort now has its own nursery and every month approximately sixty plants on the property are added or replaced.

Green Turtle has the ambience of a club, and indeed, it has a private membership club, Green Turtle Yacht Club, to which all hotel guests pay $1.00 per day temporary membership. It is also associated with the Birdham Yacht Club in England, the Palm Beach Yacht Club, and some other boating clubs in Florida.

The bar, with its dark wood and beamed ceiling, is in the original boathouse and decorated with flags from yacht clubs around the world. Its walls are papered with one-pound British sterling notes, U.S. dollars, and other currency, maintaining a tradition begun in World War II when RAF pilots, about to depart on a mission, left money for a round of drinks in their memory in case they did not return. Just outside the bar is a new patio restaurant.

The bar is the social center in winter, but in summer the crowd moves out to the pretty terrace by the marina. At sunset and after dinner, this is probably the liveliest place in the Abacos, particularly on the nights when there is live music for listening and dancing. A lounge by the bar has cable television.

Green Turtle Club and Marina **

Green Turtle Cay, Abaco, Bahamas Out Islands
Phone: (242) 365–4271; Fax: (242) 365–4272;
e-mail: info@greenturtleclub.com; www.greenturtle.com

Owners: The Charlesworth family

General Manager: Lynn Johnson

Open: Year-round

Credit Cards: All major

U.S. Reservations: Direct to hotel

Deposit: Five nights for Christmas, three nights balance of year; twenty-one days cancellation for holidays, fourteen days balance of year

Minimum Stay: Five nights during holidays, three nights balance of year

Arrival/Departure: No transfer service

Distance from Airport: (Treasure Cay Airport) 31/2 miles; taxi one-way, $5.00 for one, $6.00 for two; ferry one-way, $8.00

Distance from New Plymouth: 2 miles; free water taxi daily

Accommodations: 34 rooms with deck or terrace in cottages and villas (seven with twin beds; 21 with king); some with kitchens

Amenities: Air-conditioning, ceiling fans; six rooms have bath with tub, twenty-two have shower only; small refrigerator; no telephones, television, room service

Electricity: 110 volts

Sports: Freshwater swimming pool (heated); boating, snorkeling, diving, windsurfing, deep-sea fishing available for fee; golf nearby

Dress Code: Casual

Children: All ages; cribs; baby-sitters

Meetings: Up to fifty people

Day visitors: Welcome; reservations required for meals

Handicapped: No facilities

Packages: Dive

Rates: One or two people, daily, EP. *High Season* (late December–mid-April and Race Week, late June–early July): $184–$235 (rooms); $320–$470 (villas). *Low Season:* $140–$185 (rooms); $245–$365 (villas).

Service Charge: 15 percent, including government tax

Government Tax: Included in service charge

Tucked in the corner to one side of the terrace is a quiet cove with a small beach where lounge chairs and thatched umbrellas draw sun worshipers during the day. Up a small hill where the rooms are located, there is a pretty, newly rebuilt, tiled lap swimming pool, which is solar-heated in winter. The deluxe villas overlooking the water on Turtle Point are a medley of colors found in a West Indian village. Each villa is named for the fruit or flower of its color, such as key lime; and inside, the decor reflects a West Indian theme.

For those who are more energetic, a path behind the cottages leads to secluded Coco Bay, a beautiful white-sand beach where there is good snorkeling. A narrow dirt road leads to New Plymouth, the main settlement on Green Turtle Cay, about an hour's walk from the resort. Water sports, boats for fishing (including a Bertram for deep-sea fishing), and dive excursions are available daily. The club's dive operation offers a wide range of services and top-of-the-line equipment. Golf can be arranged at Treasure Cay, a twenty-minute boat ride away.

Getting here is definitely not half the fun, unless you arrive in your own yacht. The nearest airport is on Treasure Cay; from there you take a taxi to the ferry dock, a ferry to New Plymouth, and a water taxi to the club. But after a couple of the resort's famous Tipsy Turtle Rum Punches, you'll forget about the long trip and be happy that you discovered the club.

SMALL HOPE BAY LODGE
Andros, Nassau, Bahamas

The very antithesis of the glitz and glitter of Nassau and Paradise Island is Small Hope Bay Lodge, a rustic retreat in an idyllic setting on the eastern coast of Andros. Here, friendly conversation replaces casinos and floor shows, and natural means not only an almost undisturbed landscape but also genuine people and an ambience where guests blend into the "family" and love it—or quickly find they are in the wrong place.

When the late Dick Birch decided to give up cold Canadian winters and the fast track to create a resort on an undeveloped island, he found the ideal spot: a white-sand beach on Andros, facing the third longest barrier reef in the world, only an hour's flight from Florida. When he began building in the 1960s, Andros had no roads, electricity, or running water, and only one telephone.

Hidden under pine and palm trees on the shallow bay from which it takes its name, Small Hope Bay Lodge has twenty bungalows for forty guests at the edge of a crescent beach. Birch, an engineer by profession, built the bungalows and lodge himself out of local pine and coral stone. The bungalows have large rooms with newly tiled floors and are decorated with colorful handmade batiks created at Androsia, the factory begun by Birch's former wife, Rosie, and now a mainstay of the island's economy. Hammocks wide enough for two are placed about the property. Romantic? You bet.

The lodge, the focal point of the resort, has a large living room rather than a hotel lobby. (Check-in means having your name hung up at the bar.) The homey lounge has a large stone fireplace and walls lined with well-read books: everything from scientific treatises to science fiction. An old fishing boat, the Panacea, serves as the bar (drinks are included in the all-inclusive price).

Meals are informal, in keeping with the resort's laid-back ambience. Breakfast and lunch are served buffet-style. By early evening guests have gathered in the lodge to sample a Bahamas Mama or another cocktail at the bar, along with conch fritters and a veggie platter served every evening before dinner.

Dinner is a communal affair at which guests dine family-style with family members, dive masters, and staff. It is slightly—but only slightly—more formal than other meals, with table service. The chef specializes in Bahamian-style home cooking and favors fresh seafood supplied by local fishermen, with fresh vegetables from the island's farms.

Entertainment after dinner might be an impromptu party or slide show in the lounge. On cool winter evenings guests settle on huge cushions by a warm fire to continue their conversations. Others play chess, backgammon, or Ping-Pong. Someone strumming a guitar might bring on a song; a CD might inspire dancing.

Children are easily included in the informal atmosphere. There is plenty for them to do, but they must be ten years old to dive. Children eleven and under have a separate dinner hour. Some Birch grandchildren are likely to be around. Son Jeff manages the lodge and son-in-law Alex operates the resort's aircraft, which will ferry you from Florida.

The star attraction is the 142-mile-long barrier reef, less than fifteen minutes from the lodge. A conservationist and record-setting diver, Birch (and his family) worked hard to have the Bahamian government declare the Andros reef a national reserve. The reef has a tremendous variety of

coral and fish, and virgin dive sites are frequently found.

The dive center offers excursions several times daily, ranging from 10 feet on one side of the reef to "over the wall," a dive to 185 feet that looks down a sheer vertical 6,000-foot drop into the Tongue of the Ocean. You can have a personalized video of your dive made by the lodge's resident diver-photographer. Nondivers snorkel in shallow water either from shore or on the second morning dive, or they can learn scuba at no cost. Equipment is provided. A special program provides one-on-one diving with two dive masters to some of the Blue Holes, part of the intricate cave system beneath Andros. The center also offers shark diving under controlled, environmentally conscious conditions. It offers Nitrox and Nitrox certification and is capable of offering tech dive training.

Bonefishing is as popular as diving, and you can't find better waters for the sport than those of Andros. Small Hope can arrange everything you need, along with some of the best bonefishing guides in the Bahamas.

The resort has a variety of weekend and special week packages: yoga groups, a birding and ecology week with experts, a safari into the interior of Fresh Creek with the opportunity to snorkel with dolphins, or overnight camping in the wilderness on western Andros.

Small Hope operates as an all-inclusive resort; rates include accommodations, meals and hors d'oeuvres, open bar, hotel taxes and service charges, and use of windsurfers, bikes, sailboats, kayaks, nature trails, beachfront hot tub, and introductory dive lessons for nondivers.

Following Dick's sudden death in 1996, his son, Jeff, and other members of the family have carried on the spirit of this unspoiled paradise, which is not just a business but a way of life. It's like spending the weekend at a beach cottage with friends from all over the world. While diving continues to be the main attraction, nondivers in search of tropical bliss and beauty, good food, and good company will be happy here, too. "Rest, relax, and rediscovery" is the resort's motto, and it delivers.

Small Hope Bay Lodge ★★

Fresh Creek, Andros Island; P.O. Box N1131, Nassau, Bahamas
Phone: (800) 223–6961, (242) 368–2014; Fax: (242) 368–2015;
e-mail: SHBinfo@SmallHope.com; www.smallhope.com

Owners: The Birch family
General Manager: Jeff Birch
Open: Year-round
Credit Cards: All major
U.S. Reservations: Direct to lodge, (800) 223–6961
Deposit: One night per person within ten days of reservation
Minimum Stay: Five nights during Christmas/New Year's and Easter
Arrival/Departure: Free taxi transfer
Distance from Airport: 5 miles; Bahamasair or Western Air, about $110, from Nassau or Small Hope's flight service from Fort Lauderdale, $230 per person, round-trip, two-passenger minimum; children under twelve, $180. Book directly with hotel. Be sure to bring passport or birth certificate with photo identification.
Accommodations: 20 cottages with twin beds or king (good mattresses), all with patios; four two-bedroom cottages for families with children
Amenities: Ceiling fans; bath with shower; oceanfront hot tub; tile floors; nightly turndown service, room service on request; no telephones, television, locks on doors
Electricity: 110 volts/60 cycles
Fitness Facilities/Spa Services: Masseuse on premises; hot tub on beach
Sports: Diving (see text); windsurfing (equipment free), Laser sailboat, kayaks; nature walks; birding; biking; no swimming pool; great bonefishing, $200 half day for two people, boat, guide, equipment; reef fishing, deep-sea fishing available
Dress Code: Informal resort wear, day and evening. Small Hope has only one rule: No ties.
Children: All ages; cribs; playroom and supervised activities; baby-sitters available; children's rates; special rates for single parents; family discounts on scuba certification
Packages: Scuba, wedding, fishing, family, honeymoon, snorkeling
Meetings: Up to forty people when renting entire resort
Day Visitors: Welcome
Handicapped: Limited facilities
Rates: All-inclusive. *Year-round:* $175 per adult per night, $100 per teen, and $75 for children two to eleven.
Service Charge: Included
Government Tax: Included

DUNMORE BEACH CLUB
Harbour Island, Eleuthera, Bahamas

This small cottage colony has won the hearts of its many loyal fans and the coveted Hideaway Small Inn of the Year Award for good reason. Still, to understand what it is and is not, let's step back briefly in time.

Three decades ago Long Islander Basil Albury converted a house on the crest of the ridge overlooking Harbour Island's famous pink-sand beach into a small inn and added some cottages. For twenty-five years he ran it like a private club, preferring guests who were in the social registry and not accepting anyone who was not recommended. Albury did not like tourists, did not allow Bahamians, and was outspoken to a fault.

Still, the resort garnered praise, loyal fans, and legions of repeaters—more than 90 percent. Most say it was the outstanding food. So concerned was Albury that Dunmore remain as it was that when he decided to sell, he looked for and found buyers from among his previous guests.

Today some of the "our club" atmosphere remains, but the new owners have introduced a more open attitude and fresh spirit—not to mention some fresh paint and professionalism. The Club now takes anyone, with or without recommendations, who fits. Fitting in has more to do with understanding what the club is than with who you are.

Dunmore Beach is a small, quiet—very quiet—resort set high above the beach on eight well-kept acres shaded by tropical trees and colorful flowers. The half-dozen guest cottages, each with two units, are spaced far enough apart from one another to provide a great deal of privacy.

The structures are squares, more or less, painted in pretty pastels, each a different color. What they lack in architectural merit on the outside, they make up for in their comfortable interiors—all with pitched roofs, air-conditioning, new furniture and furnishings, and completely new bathrooms.

The guest rooms are large suites with pickled-wood-beamed ceilings. Each is individually furnished in attractive and cheerful English country style, with tropical touches and island paintings. All units were recently upgraded and expanded and now have a separate sitting room and an enlarged bathroom with a 6-foot-long Jacuzzi tub, oversized shower stall, vanity with double sinks, and lighted mirror. A refrigerator and stocked wet bar have also been added. Each one has a breezy porch with fabulous views, where it is easy to spend hours reading, sipping a cool drink, snoozing, watching the changing colors of the beautiful sea, and feeling completely removed from the cares of the world.

The main house serves as clubhouse and social center. It has a large, comfortable living room with a library. A lounge with a bar is invitingly furnished with white rattan and pretty prints. The lounge extends to an indoor dining room with an oceanfront terrace. The clubhouse is being enlarged and a business center added to provide computers with Internet and e-mail access. A lacy gazebo by the dining terrace is another good perch for viewing the gorgeous beach and deep blue sea. The bar is open on a self-service honor basis all day, but is attended during prelunch and predinner cocktail hours, which quickly take on a house-party ambience.

The resort's reputation for having the best cuisine on the island is well deserved. Guests enjoy creative and imaginative interpretations of Bahamian dishes and international classics by chef/general manager Richard Hamilton, whose prior stints included such prestigious places as Daniel in New York and Mansion on Turtle Creek in Dallas. He's aided by his wife, Shannon. The staff members who serve meals are also wonderful: attentive, caring, and delightful.

Breakfast and lunch are served on the outdoor terrace, in full view of the pretty pink-sand beach and the sea, or in the rather spartan dining room with walls reaching to a high-pitched hip roof with a pickled-wood-beamed ceiling. Snow-white wooden tables, with white captain's chairs, are brightened with bouquets of fresh pink hibiscus.

At dinner the room gets much dressier and more formal, as do the guests. Dunmore Beach is one of the few places in the Tropics that still requires a jacket for dinner during the winter. Most of the guests would not have it

Dunmore Beach Club **

Box 122, Harbour Island, Eleuthera, Bahamas
Phone: (242) 333–2200, toll free (877) 891–3100; Fax: (242) 333–2429; e-mail: DBC@batelnet.bs; www.dunmorebeach.com

Owner: Dunmore Beach Club, Ltd.
General Manager: Richard Hamilton
Open: Year-round except September–October
Credit Cards: Visa, MasterCard
U.S. Reservations: Direct to hotel, toll free (877) 891–3100
Deposit: Two nights; thirty days cancellation
Minimum Stay: None
Arrival/Departure: No transfer service
Distance from Airport: *(North Eleuthera International Airport)* 3 miles; from airport to ferry, 1 mile, $3.00; from dock to Harbour Island, 2 miles, $4.00; from Harbour Island to hotel: taxi one-way, $4.00
Distance from Dunmore Town: 1/2 mile; taxi one-way, $3.00
Accommodations: 14 units in seven cottages, all with terraces; with twins or kings; one four-bedroom villa
Amenities: Air-conditioning, ceiling fans; bath with Jacuzzi tub and separate shower, hair dryer, robes, basket of toiletries; refrigerator, wet bar, ice service; nightly turndown service; no telephone, television, radio, clock; room service during breakfast and dinner hours
Electricity: 110 volts
Sports: Tennis court, racquets, balls, and snorkeling gear free; diving, fishing, waterskiing, windsurfing, sailing, glass-bottom boat rides arranged; bikes, $10 per day; no swimming pool
Dress Code: In winter jackets and collared shirts required for dinner; May– August, jackets requested
Children: All ages; children under twelve years old dine separately; cribs, high chairs; baby-sitters
Meetings: Up to twenty-eight people
Day Visitors: No
Handicapped: Facilities, but beach access difficult
Packages: No
Rates: Per room, two people, daily, FAP. *High Season* (mid-December–April 30): $395–$425. *Shoulder Season* (May and November 1–mid-December): $370–$400. *Low Season:* $345–$375.
Service Charge: 22 percent for gratuities and government tax
Government Tax: Included in service charge

any other way. The dining room tables are dressed in white linen and candlelight, and meals are served on fine china with crystal stemware and silver flatware. Dinner is served at one sitting, at 8:00 P.M. When space is available, nonresident guests are accepted if they have reservations. Occasionally there is musical entertainment in the evening. There is a special early dinner for children under twelve years of age.

From the dining room terrace, steps lead down to the beach—as nice a spot for walking or jogging as it is for sunning and swimming. There are beach chairs and umbrellas for lounging. The resort offers tennis and snorkeling and other water sports; bonefishing and deep-sea fishing can be arranged.

Recently, Dunmore acquired another nine acres, and plans are underway to add more cottages there. Next door, too, the resort acquired a four-bedroom villa that is available for rent.

Dunmore Beach has an informal, clubby atmosphere, and if you feel you belong, you'll love it. Although the owners are from Locust Valley, New York, southern accents predominate. Guests are affluent, mostly professionals and CEOs. Families with children come frequently.

PINK SANDS
Harbour Island, Eleuthera, Bahamas

Long one of Harbour Island's best hotels, Pink Sands was all but blown away during Hurricane Andrew in 1992. The hotel was acquired the following year by Chris Blackwell of Island Records fame (see Compass Point) and extensively rebuilt as the second Bahamian member of his Island Outpost group. Opened in 1996, the luxury resort of simple elegance can lay claim to being one of the most stylish hideaways in the Bahamas.

Located on sixteen tranquil oceanfront acres near the northern tip of Harbour Island, the resort anchors a prime location on the island's famous 3-mile stretch of gorgeous pink sands. Conventional on the outside, in keeping with Harbour Island's very low-key ambience, the hotel's interiors are anything but traditional.

Designed by Barbara Hulanicki, who created Compass Point's exteriors and is well known for her unorthodox interiors of the art deco hotels along Miami's South Beach, the Pink Sands decor is soft and muted by comparison. It makes elaborate use of wood, copper, marble, and other natural materials and a palette of pastels.

All guest rooms are large, very comfortable one- and two-bedroom suites in cottages with ocean or garden views. Each has a sundeck with lounge chairs and breakfast table. The pitched-roof cottages of pink and white stone with rough-cut Italian marble floors are cooled with both air conditioners and ceiling fans and amply furnished with king-size bed, desk, area rugs, and local artwork. But the most distinctive features are the oversize chairs, which are something of a planter's and an Adirondack chair combined. The rooms have mini kitchenettes and tiled baths. All guest rooms have phones, a satellite television with VCR, a stocked wet bar, and CD players with a selection of CDs—a standard feature of Island Outpost hotels.

Pink Sands ✴✴✴

Harbour Island (Eleuthera), Bahamas
Phone: (242) 333–2030; Fax: (242) 333–2060;
e-mail: reservations@islandoutpost.com; www.islandoutpost.com

Owner: Island Outpost

General Managers: Nancy and Clemens Von Merveldt

Open: Year-round except for several weeks in October

Credit Cards: Most major

U.S. Reservations: (800) OUT–POST

Deposit: Three nights

Minimum Stay: Three nights

Arrival/Departure: No transfer service

Distance from Airport: *(North Eleuthera International Airport)* 3 miles; taxi to Harbor Island ferry one-way, $3.00; boat to Harbor Island one-way, $4.00; taxi to hotel one-way, $4.00

Distance from Dunmore Town: ½ mile; taxi one-way, $3.00

Accommodations: 23 one-bedroom and three two-bedroom cottages, with twin or king-size beds; each with sundeck

Amenities: Air-conditioning, ceiling fans; minibar; phones, VCR, television, CD player with CDs; tiled bath with tub and shower, hair dryer, toiletries, and sundries; towels changed twice daily, nightly turndown service, fresh flowers, robes; breakfast-only room service with $15 charge; video library

Electricity: 110 volts

Fitness Facilities/Spa Services: Exercise room; massage, pedicure, manicure arranged

Sports: Three tennis courts (one lighted), walking paths, kayaks, bikes, water sports, snorkeling; deep-sea fishing, diving arranged; freshwater pool

Children: All ages; baby-sitters arranged

Dress Code: Casual but always chic

Meetings: Small executive groups

Day Visitors: No

Handicapped: Limited facilities

Packages: Honeymoon

Rates: Per room, two people, daily, MAP. *High Season* (mid-December–mid-April): $655–$2,100. *Low Season:* $525–$1,400. Rates for two-bedroom cottages, single, triple, and quads available; inquire.

Service Charge: 10 percent

Government Tax: 8 percent

Facilities include a freshwater pool set in a jungle of tropical foliage, three tennis courts (one lit for night play), an exercise studio, a gift shop, and a 125-video library for in-room viewing. Golf carts and bikes are available for rent.

Pink Sands has two restaurants, both with a casual but sophisticated atmosphere where you can enjoy Caribbean fusion cuisine. The main dining room, with indoor and outdoor garden settings, serves breakfast and dinner; the Blue Bar, with a super setting overlooking magnificent Pink Beach, gathers guests for lunch and a weekly Bahamian buffet evening.

Most of the resort's tony guests are from the United States, particularly the Northeast; some are European. They come to Pink Sands to get away from it all in the atmosphere of a luxury resort—without leaving it all behind.

RUNAWAY HILL CLUB

Harbour Island, Bahamas

Getting there is not half the fun—nor any fun at all—and if what awaits at the other end weren't so utterly delightful, it might not even be worth the trip. Getting to Runaway Hill requires at least one plane ride (usually two), a taxi ride followed by a short boat ride, and another taxi ride before you see the resort. Still, lots of people think it's worth the effort—myself included.

A long driveway through the resort's eight wooded acres leads to a pretty, pink stone manor, reminiscent of a gracious old Bermuda house. When you walk through the front door, you will feel as though you are walking into a friend's home. The reception is something like that, too.

Depending on the time or the day, you might be greeted by Roger or Carol Becht, the managers and part owners, or a staff member from the front office who will fix you a welcome drink and show you to your room. When no one is around to make you a drink, the honor bar system is in operation.

A New England–style inn with palm trees, the Runaway Hill Club is a small, intimate hotel overlooking the pink sands of Harbour Island. Built in the early 1940s as a private home, it was converted into a small inn in the early 1960s, when a second floor and a terrace (now the dining room) were added. A group of Brilanders headed by the Bechts took over the property in 1980, after it had been closed for two years. They renovated it and opened it as a hotel again the following year.

The house nestles in a grove of casuarina trees on a bluff overlooking the Atlantic. It sits at road level on the town side but high above the beach on the ocean side, thus capturing both balmy breezes and spectacular views. There are guest rooms in three buildings: the main house, which has three on the ground floor in the original building and two on the second floor—all with patios or balconies and views of the sea; in the garden wing by the main entrance; and in one of the two new villas.

Each guest room is different and individually decorated, but all are furnished comfortably, like a private home rather than a hotel. Room 1, for example, is the size of a large suite. White bamboo and wicker furniture sits on ceramic tile floors patterned like a Spanish rug. The pink tile bath has a tub and double sinks. There are lots of good lamps, and the rose curtains, bedcovers, and watercolors on the wall give the room a homey informality.

The cozy lounge with a fireplace for chilly winter evenings has walls of books, while the bar and dining room are in one large space, divided by furniture and flowers rather than walls, and opening onto a breezy veranda looking out over the beach.

Runaway Hill Club ✱✱

Box 31, Harbour Island, Bahamas
Phone: (242) 333–2150; Fax: (242) 333–2420;
www.runawayhill.com

Owner: Dunmore Development Group
General Managers: Roger and Carol Becht
Open: Year-round except September–October
Credit Cards: All major
U.S. Reservations: Direct to hotel, (800) 728–9803
Deposit: Four nights with thirty days cancellation in winter; three nights with twenty-one days cancellation in summer
Minimum Stay. Seven nights mid-December–Easter
Arrival/Departure: No transfer service
Distance from Airport: 3 miles; taxi to ferry one-way, $3.00; ferry to island one-way, $4.00; taxi to hotel one-way, $3.00
Distance from Dunmore Town: ½ mile; taxi one-way, $3.00
Accommodations: Ten rooms in three buildings (five rooms in main house, three with kings, two with twins; three in garden wing, two with twins, one king; two in villa with kings); all with terrace, patio, or balcony
Amenities: Air-conditioning, ceiling fans; safe; seven baths with tub and shower, three with shower only; hair dryer, dressing gown; ice service; room service on request; no telephone, radio, television
Electricity: 110 volts
Sports: Freshwater swimming pool; hammocks overlooking beach; snorkeling gear available; water sports and fishing arranged; bike, golf cart
Dress Code: Casual; jacket requested in evening; shoes required in bar and lounge
Children: Sixteen years and older
Meetings: No
Day Visitors: With reservations
Handicapped: No facilities
Packages: No
Rates: Two people, per room, daily, EP. *High Season* (mid-December–mid-April): $260–$275. *Low Season:* $230–$245. Single rates available; inquire.
Service Charge: 10 percent
Government Tax: 10 percent

Breakfast and lunch are served on the ocean-view veranda, weather permitting, while dinner by candlelight is set in the indoor dining room. Outsiders with reservations are accepted for dinner when space is available.

The bar becomes the social center at cocktails and after dinner for guests who do not retire early. On Tuesday evening during the winter, Danny and the Dana-Lites are on hand in the lounge. On most nights one of the other nearby resorts has entertainment featuring island musicians, who play a range of music from calypso to easy-listening tunes.

From the veranda, steps lead down the terraced bluff through tropical greenery to a freshwater swimming pool, set about midway between the main building and the beach. Lazy days are spent in shaded hammocks catching up on reading, with an occasional swim in the reef-protected waters or a walk along the magnificent 3-mile beach. Diving and other water sports can be arranged, as can fishing trips, particularly for bonefish.

A surprising variety of people run away to this hideaway. Although most are from the States, they also come from Canada, Europe, Latin America, and now Japan. The ages and backgrounds vary greatly, too, from honeymooners to retirees, from a police captain to captains of industry. Many are repeat guests who first saw Runaway Hill while sailing by in their yachts. The friendly, family atmosphere appeals to people who travel alone, and its setting and tranquillity make romantics of us all.

BRITISH COLONIAL HILTON NASSAU

Nassau, Bahamas

In October 1999 Hilton International opened its first Bahamian property, the British Colonial Hilton Nassau, after its now owners, RHK Capital of Toronto, completed an eighteen-month, $68 million restoration that converted the historic property into a deluxe business and leisure hotel with downtown Nassau's only private beach.

Located in the heart of Nassau's business center, the British Colonial is the city's oldest continuously operating hotel, first opened in 1922. It is part of a development project that houses the first stock exchange in the Bahamas, along with offices. An apartment complex and a marina are to be added.

Formerly known as the British Colonial Hotel and built on the historic site of old Fort Nassau, the new seven-story Hilton preserves the Caribbean colonial charm of the old landmark while adding the amenities that today's travelers want and expect.

The restoration encompassed a total makeover of the guest rooms, meeting rooms, restaurants, landscaping, and more. A special business floor was installed on the fifth floor; it has forty-six rooms with over-size desks, modems, fax machines on request, and nightly turndown service. The sixth and seventh floors have fifty-eight executive rooms offering the same amenities as the business-floor rooms along with an Executive Club Lounge, where guests enjoy private check-in and check-out as well as complimentary breakfast, evening hors d'oeuvres, and drinks on the lounge's outdoor terrace. The seventh floor also holds the Prime Minister's Suite and two junior suites.

In addition to the private beach, the landmark property has a large freshwater swimming pool set in pretty tropical gardens, a fitness center, and a full-service diving and snorkeling facility. Recently, the hotel added a spa with seven treatment rooms, most with views of the gardens, and a beauty salon. They are open daily from 8:00 A.M. to 8:00 P.M. The spa offers a full roster of treatments—massage, body wraps, scrubs, aromatherapy, and more, plus spa packages.

Portofino, an Italian cafe, is open for breakfast, lunch, and dinner. The Wedgwood features grilled meats and fish, while the outdoor Patio Grille offers Bahamian and American-style snacks. For cocktails there's Blackbeard's Cove Bar and the Palm Court Lounge.

The British Colonial Hilton has a fully equipped business center. Its meeting facilities include the spacious Governor's Ballroom, the Victoria Room with garden and ocean views, the Sir Harry Oakes Boardroom, and five meeting rooms. Situated at the head of Bay Street, the hotel is within easy walking distance of Nassau's famous Straw Market, duty-free shops, historic sites, and the port. Golf and nightlife are only a few minutes away by car.

The British Colonial was the setting for two James Bond films with Sean Connery: *Thunderball* (1965) and *Never Say Never Again* (1983). (Connery has a home on the island.) To promote its James Bond connection, the hotel has a series of 007 packages, the first being Live and Let Dive. The hotel can arrange for Stuart Cove (who trained the Bond movie doubles) to take divers down to see the 120-foot freighter that was sunk for the movie *Never Say Never Again* as well as the *Valkin Bomber* airplane from *Thunderball*. Both wrecks are the actual sets from the movies and lie 40 feet beneath the surface.

In another promotion the hotel is offering a free night's stay to anyone who can provide memorabilia of the old British Colonial Hotel, such as photos, postcards, matchbooks, hotel bills, and the like.

British Colonial Hilton Nassau (N)

One Bay Street, Nassau, Bahamas
Phone: (242) 322–3301; Fax: (242) 322–2286; www.hilton.com

Owners: RHK Capital of Toronto
Management: Hilton International
General Manager: Michael Hooper
Credit Cards: All major
U.S. Reservations: Hilton Reservations Worldwide, (800) HILTONS
Deposit: One night
Minimum Stay: None, except Christmas/New Year's
Arrival/Departure: Guests referred to local company for transfer service
Distance from Airport: *(Nassau International Airport)* 10 miles; taxi one-way $20
Accommodations: 291 rooms (46 business-floor rooms; 58 executive rooms with Executive Lounge; one penthouse; two junior suites; one Double-O James Bond suite)
Amenities: Air-conditioning; telephones; television; hair dryer; toiletries; room service, nightly turndown service. Business-floor rooms: oversized desks; modems, fax machines on request.
Electricity: 120 volts
Fitness Facilities/Spa Services: See text
Sports: Beach, swimming pool; water sports and dive operation on premise
Children: All ages
Dress Code: Business casual
Meetings: Facilities for up to 400 people. Five meeting rooms; boardroom; business center
Day Visitors: Yes
Handicapped: Yes
Packages: Yes
Rates: Per room, single or double, daily: January 3–February 4 and June 1–December 25: $250-$315, $355–$1,200 (suites); February 5–May 31: $295–$355, $400–$1,275 (suites); December 26–31: $335–$400, $420–$1,360 (suites)
Service Charge: $3.50 per day
Government Tax: 12 percent
Energy Surcharge: $3.50 per person per day

COMPASS POINT
Nassau, Bahamas

After three centuries of orderly British colonial architecture in pink with white trim, Compass Point came to the Bahamas as a breath of fresh air—particularly since it is so well done and so much fun.

Bold in concept and design, Compass Point is a collection of highly original, wildly outrageous, colorful cottages that interpret indigenous designs in a modern, sophisticated way. Upon seeing the resort for the first time, you might wonder if you have arrived in a village designed by the people who make the costumes for Junkanoo, the Bahamas' annual Carnival. In a way, you have.

Opened in 1995, Compass Point is the first of two hotels in the Bahamas belonging to Island Outpost, a group created by Chris Blackwell, founder of Island Records (responsible for discovering reggae superstar Bob Marley and other pop music greats). Both of Blackwell's hotels bring fresh, new ideas to preserving the Caribbean's heritage.

Located at the western end of Nassau on two secluded acres next to Love Beach, one of the island's best, Compass Point is about a six-minute ride from the international airport. The resort's entrance faces Compass Point Recording Studios, where many Island Records favorites have been produced.

Accommodations are found in five cabanas, four low-rise "huts," and nine elevated cottages on stilts with studio, one-bedroom, and two-bedroom units, all with louvered windows and private decks facing the ocean to catch the breeze.

The exteriors of the octagonal huts and cottages, painted in a rainbow of bright colors, were designed by Barbara Hulanicki, who also created Pink Sands's decor. The interiors, with handcrafted natural woods and batik accents by the Island Trading Company, are equally interesting.

Rooms are furnished with king- or queen-size beds, coffeemakers, mini-bars, satellite televisions, CD players, and

Compass Point ★★

P.O. Box CB 13842, West Bay Street, Nassau, Bahamas
Phone: (242) 327–4500, (800) OUT–POST; Fax: (242) 327–3299;
e-mail: reservations@islandoutpost.com; www.islandoutpost.com

Owner: Island Outpost
General Manager: Kelly Roberts
Open: Year-round
Credit Cards: Most major
U.S. Reservations: (800) OUT–POST
Deposit: First night
Minimum Stay: None
Arrival/Departure: No transfer service
Distance from Airport: *(Nassau International Airport)* Six minutes; taxi one-way, $5.00
Distance from Nassau: 10 miles; taxi one-way, $15
Accommodations: 20 rooms (five cabanas with air-conditioned studios; four huts with one bedroom, two two-bedroom cottages, seven one-bedroom cottages, all with ceiling fans but no air-conditioning)
Amenities: Ceiling fans; telephones; television; hair dryer, toiletries; room service, CD stereo with CDs, nightly turndown service. Cabanas have air-conditioning
Electricity: 120 volts
Sports: Beach, swimming pool, water sports
Children: All ages; baby-sitters on request
Dress Code: Casual
Meetings: By advance arrangement
Day Visitors: Only on request, except for restaurant
Handicapped: Limited facilities
Packages: Honeymoon
Rates: Per room, daily, CP. *High Season* (mid-December–mid-April): $245–$2,100. *Low Season:* $235–$1,600.
Service Charge: 7 percent plus a daily maid-gratuity charge
Government Tax: 8 percent on room only

VCRs. Nine rooms have open-air kitchenettes and dining terraces on the ground level; the others have refrigerators.

Compass Point's oceanfront restaurant, open daily for three meals, offers a creative menu of original dishes blending American and European cuisine with Caribbean flavors. It quickly became Nassau's hottest new dining spot after it opened, and it continued to be so popular that it was enlarged after the first year. The resort has an oceanfront, freshwater swimming pool, a beach, water sports including a dive shop, and tennis with lighted courts. There is also an activities desk, a CD and video library, and a boutique.

OCEAN CLUB
Paradise Island, Nassau, Bahamas

Paradise on Paradise. In the ups and downs of the Bahamas' development, the posh Ocean Club has been the one resort that's kept its panache. Located on thirty-five acres along a white-sand beach across the bridge from Nassau, this tony resort is one of the most beautiful in the Tropics. It has style.

In 2000–2001, the Ocean Club underwent an extensive renovation and expansion that added fifty new beachfront rooms, a new beachfront restaurant headed by a noted chef, an elaborate spa, and a redesigned golf course. All the resort's rooms, public areas, and grounds were renovated. There is a newly-designed reception area with views of the ocean from its terrace and a new open-air bar and grill by the swimming pool. The project was part of a $100-million development, which has included the construction of Ocean Club Estates—luxurious homes available for sale—and a marina.

Long a hideaway for the rich and famous, the Club was originally the private winter home of a wealthy Swedish industrialist, who named it Shangri-La. In the 1960s A&P heir Huntington Hartford built the Ocean Club adjacent to Shangri-La, got government permission to rename the island Paradise Island (originally called Hog Island), and turned it into a premier resort for his wealthy friends. In 1968, Resorts International acquired the majority interest in Hartford's holdings and expanded Paradise Island into a major resort. In 1988, in a highly publicized deal with Donald Trump, showman/producer Merv Griffin bought Resorts International, which included the Ocean Club; and in 1994, Sun International bought out Merv Griffin and built the nearby mammoth resort complex, Atlantis. The Ocean Club was left in its secluded splendor.

But now with its latest makeover, the new Ocean Club—to borrow a phrase—is not your father's Oldsmobile. Kerzner International (formerly Sun International) has reinvented the resort, preserving its timeless elegance while updating it with new facilities and fresh amenities for a new generation of travelers in the twenty-first century.

Located on the eastern end of Paradise Island, a forty-minute drive from Nassau International Airport, hotel services of the reborn Ocean Club begin upon your arrival at the airport with town car transfer to the resort.

As soon as you turn into the long drive through gardens and manicured lawns to the main entrance, you know you have arrived at a special place. The Ocean Club's style begins with check-in. If you have been a guest before, the staff will remember your name and probably your preferences for breakfast, newspapers, sports, and any special services you require.

The main building is a graceful two-story mansion, with rooms set around a tropical garden courtyard with an ornamental pool and fountain at the center. The rooms overlook turquoise waters edged by 2 miles of beach along lawns where hammocks swing in the breeze under palms and giant eucalyptus trees. Rooms have verandas and are furnished in colonial-style mahogany with bedspreads and draperies in colorful prints.

The new addition, The Crescent, made up of five, two-story buildings by the beach, has forty oceanfront rooms (each measuring a spacious 550 square feet) and ten suites (each with a huge 1,100 square feet)—all with private balcony or terrace with unobstructed views of the club's long white-sand beach. Dressed in subdued colors and British colonial decor but still Caribbean in feeling, the accommodations have large marble bathrooms, separate showers, double-sink vanities, and the latest technology—Internet access, portable telephone, DVD and CD players, and DMX music. Crescent suites also have steam shower, Jacuzzi bathtub, a bathroom television, and a Bose entertainment system.

All accommodations enjoy butler service, which includes packing and unpacking, dinner and activity reservations, personal wake-up calls, daily fruit bowl delivery, shoeshine service, afternoon tea, champagne, and strawberries delivered to guest rooms. There is thrice-daily maid service, including nightly turndown, and guests can borrow from the CD and DVD library. Laptops are available for guest in-room use. Guests in suites and garden cottages have in-room check-in.

To the south is the freshwater swimming pool, which you can have to yourself in the early morning. The pool has a wonderful setting overlooking the terraced Versailles Gardens, which flow for 1/4 mile in seven tiers to an authentic twelfth-century French cloister on the highest rise at the far southern end. The cloister, with its graceful arches and columns, was originally part of an Augustinian monastery brought, piece by piece, from France to the United States by William Randolph Hearst. Hartford purchased the stone structure, shipped it from Florida, and had it reassembled here. Beyond the cloister, at the end of the garden by the water's edge, you'll find a pretty gazebo and a lovely view across Nassau harbor. The romantic setting is enormously popular for weddings.

The new beachfront restaurant, Dune, created by

renowned chef and restaurateur Jean-Georges Von-gerichten and designed by famed French interior designer Christian Liaigre, is stunning. Set in the dunes at the edge of the beach, the decor interprets the British Colonial heritage of the Bahamas in a modern context, rendering it casual and elegant at the same time. Liaigre, who is known as the most environmentally sensitive of designers, blends natural woods and fibers with a sophisticated patina of color that ranges from the ash of weathered wood around the bar to the slate of chairs and the charcoal of highly polished Ivory Coast hardwood table tops in the dining room. Running full length across the back of the restaurant is the display kitchen, designed by California-based Mark Stech-Novak of Restaurant Consultation & Design, himself a chef of fifteen years. The kitchen is encased in glass partitions that reflect the ocean into the room. During the day, the sun filters through bamboo

blinds and louvered screens creating geometrical patterns around the room.

Daily at breakfast, lunch, and dinner, diners may sit inside under a high-pitched, beamed ceiling and look in one direction to the turquoise sea and in the other direction to the activity in the kitchen. Or, they can dine under white umbrella tables on the outdoor patio overlooking the beach. At one end of the building is an outdoor white marble bar, which has become a popular rendezvous almost any time of day.

Dune is Jean-Georges's first island restaurant. The menu offers signature dishes from his top-rated New York restaurants—Jean Georges, Mercer Kitchen, Vong, and JoJo—with Bahamian ingredients whenever possible. To underscore his commitment to using local products, Jean-Georges engaged Bahamian Teresa Kemp to create a garden of local herbs in front of the restaurant. Jean-Georges was also responsible for training the Bahamian staff, bringing chefs and staff from his stateside enterprises, as well as sending Bahamians to further their training at his U.S. restaurants.

The Ocean Club's other restaurants include the elegant Courtyard Terrace, in a romantic setting around a fountain in the courtyard of the hotel's original building and open daily for dinner; and the Pool Terrace, adjacent to the pool and tennis courts, and open throughout the day for light fare and drinks.

The Ocean Club Golf Course was totally revamped into an eighteen-hole championship course by pro golfer and course designer Tom Weiskopf. The brand-new course (7123 yard/par 72), designed for every caliber of player, takes advantage of the Bahamian landscape and crosswinds, challenging golfers' precision and accuracy. It offers seaside greens and tees, alternating fairways, lakes, and a new clubhouse—all enjoying panoramic views of the lush course against the waters of the Atlantic Ocean and Nassau Harbour. Particularly outstanding is the seventeenth hole, which plays entirely along scenic Snorkelers Cove.

The Ocean Club's new spa, operated by Mandara, has an open air pavilion; there are eight private spa suites, each with a garden Jacuzzi and outdoor waterfall shower. The spa suites use natural materials—Javanese teak massage tables, Thai-silk pillows, and coconut bowls filled with fresh flowers and floating candles. In the serene atmosphere for which it is known, Mandara offers a full range of body and beauty treatments and the ultimate indulgence—the Mandara Massage—two spa therapists simultaneously massaging the guest for a full hour.

On the beach—one of the most beautiful in the world—you are served afternoon sorbet and cooled off with Evian misting. Beach attendants and food and beverage service are available. Water sports include sailing, kayaking, and snorkeling; diving can be arranged. A fitness room with Nautilus equipment has men's and women's lockers and changing facilities. Bicycles are available without charge.

The Tennis Club has nine Har-Tru courts (four lighted for night play); a staff pro available for private lessons; and a pro shop with racquet rentals and full line of apparel.

Ocean Club guests have the best of both worlds: peace and tranquillity in a romantic setting and a glittering nightlife at the nearby Atlantis. Guests have access to Atlantis's other facilities and restaurants as well. Free shuttles run every half hour to Atlantis, the golf course, and the casino.

In addition to its romance, this fashionable resort appeals to people who like a quietly elegant and slightly European ambience. It attracts golf enthusiasts at any time of year and honeymooners in spring and summer when prices are reduced.

Ocean Club ★★★★

Box N-4777, Paradise Island, Nassau, Bahamas
Phone: (242) 363–2501, (800) 321–3000; Fax: (242) 363–2424; www.oceanclub.com

Owner: Kerzner International Bahamas

General Manager: Russell Miller

Open: Year-round

Credit Cards: Most major

U.S. Reservations: Kerzner International, (800) 321–3000

Deposit: Two nights

Minimum Stay: None, except at Christmas/New Year's; inquire.

Arrival/Departure: Transfer service via town car, $60 one-way

Distance from Airport: *(Nassau International Airport)* Forty minutes; taxi one-way, $22; five minutes from *Paradise Island Airport*

Distance from Nassau: 3 miles; taxi one-way, $6.00 plus $2.50 bridge toll; water taxi between Paradise Island and Nassau one-way, $2.50

Accommodations: 106 rooms and suites and five two-bedroom/two-bath garden cottages; all with terraces and king-size beds

Amenities: Air-conditioning, ceiling fans; television (including one in bathroom); marbled bath with tub and shower, hair dryer, toiletries; telephones (including one in bathroom); stocked minibar; room service, terry robes, thrice-daily maid service including nightly turndown; butler service; daily fruit bowl, afternoon champagne and strawberries; laptop for use in suites and villas, shoeshine service. Crescent: VCR, Jacuzzi baths, steam shower, Bose entertainment system, in-room check-in; Internet access, DVD and CD player, and DMX music.

Electricity: 110 volts

Fitness Facilities/Spa Services: Fitness room with Nautilus equipment, men's and women's lockers and changing facilities; full-service Mandara spa

Sports: Beach, freshwater pool; tennis, golf, walking paths, bikes, water sports

Children: Baby-sitters; Discovery Channel Camp offers daily supervised activities operated by Atlantis.

Dress Code: Casual but always chic; jackets requested in evening

Meetings: Small executive groups

Day Visitors: Not encouraged

Handicapped: Limited facilities

Packages: Golf, tennis, honeymoon, wedding

Rates: Per room or suite, daily, EP. **High Season** (mid-December–early May): $695–$1,750. **Low Season:** $400–$910.

Service Charge: $3.50 per person daily housekeeping-gratuity

Government Tax: 12 percent resort tax based on room rate

Barbados

Barbados is an elegant place in a quiet sort of way. Whether it is the 300 years of British rule, the Bajans' pride and natural grace, or the blue-stocking vacationers who return annually like homing birds to their roost, this Caribbean island feels something like *Masterpiece Theatre* in the Tropics.

Independent since 1966, Barbados still seems as British as the queen. Bridgetown, the capital, has a Trafalgar Square, now renamed National Heroes Square. Bewigged judges preside over the country's law courts, hotels stop for afternoon tea, and a police band gives outdoor concerts.

The 166-square-mile island of green rolling hills even resembles the English countryside and is a pleasure to explore. On an island only 21 miles long, you can visit stately homes and gardens, more than fifty important historic sites, and the outstanding Barbados Museum.

A coral island 100 miles east of the Lesser Antilles, Barbados is the easternmost land in the Caribbean. Its western coast, fringed with attractive beaches, is bathed by calm Caribbean waters; the eastern shores are washed by the whitecapped rollers of the Atlantic. It is one of the main locations for windsurfing in the Caribbean and often a venue for international competitions. The island is surrounded by coral reefs good for snorkeling and learning to scuba dive. Sailing, fishing, golf, tennis, horseback riding, and polo are also available.

Barbados has one of the widest selections of accommodations of any island in the Caribbean, ranging from modest guest houses to ultraposh resorts with great style. Each is different and distinctive. Their ambience is often more European than that found in hotels on Caribbean islands closer to the United States, because the majority of Barbados's visitors come from Britain and other European countries.

Information

Barbados Tourism Authority, 800 Second Avenue, New York, NY 10017;
(800) 221–9831, (212) 986–6516; Fax: (212) 573–9850;
and 3440 Wilshire Boulevard, #1215, Los Angeles, CA 90010;
(800) 221–9831, (213) 380–2198; Fax: (213) 384–2763; www.barbados.org

COBBLERS COVE
St. Peter, Barbados

This cozy complex of two-story cottages in gardens overlooking a gorgeous beach can induce love at first sight in those who want a casual, romantic resort with just enough history to lend it charm—but with attractive, modern, spacious accommodations to boot.

The centerpiece of this quiet resort is a pale pink villa built in the early part of the twentieth century by a Bajan sugar baron as a summer home. The former living room, similar to an English country drawing room, now serves as a reading lounge with daily U.S. and European newspapers.

The villa's open-air, seaside terrace doubles as the dining pavilion and bar, a favorite meeting place for hotel guests and local friends. During the winter season you'll hear a strong British upstairs accent, but in summer the voices are likely to have a more familiar American ring.

In the evening the pavilion and another terrace next to the lounge become romantic settings for candlelight dining on some of the best hotel cuisine in Barbados. Blending traditional European dishes with fresh local products, the chef has developed an innovative, sophisticated cuisine. Because all dishes are cooked to order, guests give their selections to the headwaiter while they enjoy a drink at the bar adjacent to the dining terrace. Cobblers Cove has a dinner exchange with a number of other deluxe island hotels.

The cottages, each with four suites, sit snugly in a V in three acres of tropical gardens alongside the main house and around a small pool overlooking the Caribbean. The pool area can be crowded when the hotel is full, but you'll get plenty of solitude on the picture-perfect beach, one of Barbados's finest and most secluded, only 10 yards away.

All accommodations are suites with large bedrooms, ample closets, and special drying racks for wet bathing suits and towels. Each suite overlooks the garden or sea and has a wet bar and separate sitting room with louvered doors that, when folded back, open onto a furnished patio or balcony to create one large, airy space.

The most sensational accommodations are the bilevel Camelot and Colleton Suites on the top floor of the main villa by architect Ian Morrison, known for his handsome

design of nearby Glitter Bay and Royal Pavilion hotels. These posh love nests offer the ultimate in privacy, along with marble floors; a king-size, canopied four-poster bed; and a lounge area with a settee, writing desk, and chaise lounge—all in fresh blue and white decor. The huge bathrooms have whirlpool tubs, twin sinks, bidets, and his and hers showers with twin showerheads. Each suite has a small plunge pool and wet bar that overlooks a wonderful view of the sea. These suites may well be the most heavenly honeymoon hideaways in the Tropics. The price is up there, too.

The resort's sports facilities include complimentary water sports and day and night tennis. You can go snorkeling directly off the beach. Cobblers has a gift shop and an exercise facility, both housed in a pair of colorful chattel houses. Exercise equipment is top of the line. There is a treatment room for massages—which can be arranged in your room as well. Also, through an arrangement with the nearby Royal Westmoreland Club, Cobblers guests have access to that club's excellent golf, tennis, and health club facilities. The latter offers massages, beauty treatments, exercise, yoga, and other services.

Life at Cobblers Cove is very low-key. There's the manager's weekly cocktail party and occasional live musical entertainment, but essentially the resort is a friendly, easy-living sort of place where guests meet and mingle or go their own way. It all happens under the watchful eye of Hamish Watson, a hands-on, wonderfully friendly manager.

The resort's informality is suited to families, while its cozy, romantic ambience attracts couples of all ages. Cobblers Cove is a member of the prestigious Relais et Châteaux.

Cobblers Cove ★ ★ ★

Road View, St. Peter, Barbados
Phone: (246) 422–2291; Fax: (246) 422–1460; e-mail: cobblers@caribsurf.com; www.barbados.org/hotels/cobblers.htm

Owner: Hayton, Ltd.
General Manager: Hamish Watson
Open: Year-round except September–mid-October
Credit Cards: All major
U.S. Reservations: Karen Bull Associates, (800) 890–6060; Fax: (404) 237–1841
Deposit: Three nights in winter, except seven nights during Christmas, one night in summer; twenty-eight days cancellation in winter, fourteen days in summer
Minimum Stay: Ten nights during Christmas/New Year's
Arrival/Departure: Transfer service arranged for fee
Distance from Airport: 18 miles (forty-five minutes); taxi one-way, $21
Distance from Bridgetown: 12 miles (twenty-five minutes); taxi one-way, $18
Accommodations: 38 suites in two-story cottages (22 garden view, 16 deluxe and oceanfront) with twin beds in ten, all with terraces and patios; two superdeluxe suites with plunge pool
Amenities: Air-conditioning, ceiling fans; direct-dial telephones; individual safes; television arranged on request; radio at front desk; bath with tub and shower, hair dryer, terry robes, basket of toiletries; stocked minibar, ice service, room service 8:00 A.M.–9:00 P.M.
Electricity: 110 volts/50 cycles
Fitness Facilities/Spa Services: Fitness facility with exercise equipment and some spa services
Sports: Freshwater swimming pool; free waterskiing, windsurfing, Sunfish, snorkeling, tennis; special fees for golf at Sandy Lane and Royal Westmoreland courses; diving/water sports can be arranged
Dress Code: Informal by day; elegantly casual in evening; men wear slacks and open-neck shirts. Jeans, shorts, and swimwear are not allowed in bar area after 7:00 P.M.
Children: All ages except mid-January–mid-March, when none under twelve years old; cribs; baby-sitters with advance notice
Meetings: No
Day Visitors: With reservations
Handicapped: Facilities available
Packages: Honeymooners, gourmet, golf, summer
Rates: Per room, two people, daily, MAP. *High Season* (early January–mid-April): $728–$1,080; Camelot and Colleton Suites, $1,833 and $2,068. EP *Low Season* (mid-April–September 30): $300–$447; suites, $870 and $1,010. EP *Shoulder Season* (October 1–mid-December): $365–$494; suites, $940–$1,081. Single, two-bedroom, Christmas, MAP low and shoulder rates available; inquire.
Service Charge: Included
Government Tax: Included

CORAL REEF CLUB
St. James, Barbados

This is a family affair. The O'Hara family—mother, two sons, a daughter, two daughters-in-law, and a son-in-law—own and operate this resort and give it a special cachet.

The Coral Reef Club, together with the Sandpiper, its sister hotel next door, enjoys a coveted location on Barbados' Caribbean coast, amid a string of fashionable resorts and trendy restaurants. Spread over twelve acres of flowering trees and gardens and fronting a mile of casuarina-shaded powdery sands, the resort blends an upscale British style with a comfortable, relaxing, friendly atmosphere.

Coral Reef Club was born almost by accident in the 1950s when Ted Powell, an Englishman and owner of Coral Reef's original coral-stone house, began taking in guests to help defray expenses. Over the next three decades, the beachfront property grew from a four-bedroom beach house to a sixty-nine-room resort. The late Budge O'Hara, the patriarch of the family who arrived as manager with his bride, Cynthia, in 1956, eventually acquired both hotels after Powell's death in 1976.

Meanwhile, the O'Hara children were being schooled in England and gaining hotel and business experience. Patrick and Mark had stints at such prestigious hotels as Inn on the Park and Capital Hotel in London and the George V in Paris, while Karen studied interior decorating.

After their father passed away in 1995, the younger O'Haras and their spouses assumed day-to-day management of Coral Reef and Sandpiper, putting their training to use, refurbishing, redecorating, updating, and expanding the properties, while their mother became chairman.

Now, Mark and Patrick jointly manage Coral Reef, helped by Mark's wife Maria, an artist, in refurbishing, housekeeping, and gardening. Patrick's wife, Sharon, who owns an antiques business, takes care of the resort's flower arrangements in the public areas. Sister Karen, a director of Coral Reef, is involved in management, sales, and marketing, and her husband, Wayne Capaldi, manages the Sandpiper. As we said, it's a family affair.

A tree-lined drive leads to the original coral-stone villa overlooking the beach, passing the cottages and the newer, two-story buildings nesting in the gardens. The main building houses the island- and antique-dressed lobby, lounge, restaurant, and bar, which open onto a balustrade terrace overlooking the beach and gardens.

Accommodations are in garden rooms and cottages providing the most privacy; rooms in the main house; and the newer two-story colonial-style buildings with gingerbread trim. Some, built around a large swimming pool, house luxury junior suites and the newest category of luxury plantation suites. Some cottages have a separate dressing room that is suitable as a bedroom for a third adult or for children; and there are two four-bedroom villas with kitchens. A few single rooms with double bed are also available.

All accommodations have tile floors with straw mats from Dominica; patios or balconies; king-size or twin beds; air-conditioning, ceiling fans; small refrigerators, direct-dial telephones, safes, hair dryers, and homey touches, such as toasters, a shelf of paperback books, and fresh flowers.

Coral Reef closed for almost six months during the summer and fall of 2002 to rebuild and upgrade the four rooms in the main building and all the cottages on the north side of the main drive, bringing all accommodations up to one high standard throughout the hotel.

The resort's most posh accommodations are four superdeluxe Plantation Suites with private pools. Situated on the second floor of two separate buildings and fronting the sea, the beautifully furnished, luxury suites have four-poster canopied beds, spacious living rooms, a dressing area, bathrooms with separate tub and large shower, a complimentary starter bar, and—a first for Coral Reef—television/VCR, fax machine, CD player with a selection of CDs, and a covered terrace and sundeck with a private plunge pool.

The breeze-cooled restaurant serves all three meals plus afternoon tea and a Sunday brunch buffet; during the winter season, it also serves a buffet lunch daily. Dinner offers an à la carte menu nightly except Monday, when a buffet of Bajan dishes, plus English standards of roast beef and Yorkshire pudding, are featured. For a change of scenery, Coral Reef has a dining exchange with neighboring Sandpiper, as well as with Treasure Beach and Cobblers Cove up the road. Room service for meals is available during restaurant hours.

The main bar is open twenty-four hours, and there is musical entertainment and dancing nightly in the winter, less frequently in other months. There is a weekly folklore show and beach barbecue, television room, and billiards room.

Coral Reef has two freshwater swimming pools and two lighted tennis courts, as well as a ten-station, air-conditioned exercise room. Guests enjoy free use of small sailboats, windsurfers, kayaks, and equipment for water skiing and for snorkeling on the resort's reef, only a few yards from the beach. They have access to a 32-foot catamaran and scuba diving can be arranged for a fee, as can golf at the Royal Westmoreland and Sandy Lane courses. A new boutique in the style of a Barbados chattel house is found in the gardens. A complimentary shuttle to Bridgetown goes daily for shopping.

Neighboring Sandpiper has spacious one- and two-bedroom suites well suited to families; guests have unlimited access to Coral Reef. The accommodations are air-conditioned, have ceiling fans and refrigerators, are furnished with rattan or pickled pine, and have Bajan art on the walls; suites come with full kitchens.

Coral Reef has many loyal fans who, like the owners, are into the second and third generations. Most are Brits but many are affluent Americans who appreciate the resort's certain Old World character blended into a New World setting and its friendly family ambience. The O'Haras usually greet guests on arrival, invite them to their home for the manager's cocktail parties, and give gifts to those staying at Christmas. Many of the staff have been with the hotel for years.

Television and fax machines may be this west coast veteran's bow to the twenty-first century, but it draws the line at cell phones. No cell phones are allowed in the bar or restaurant and are acceptable elsewhere if used "with discretion." We approve.

Coral Reef Club ★★★★

St. James, Barbados
Phone: (246) 422–2372; Fax: (246) 422–1776;
e-mail: coral@caribsurf.com; www.coralreefbarbados.com

Owner: O'Hara Family

Managing Directors: Patrick and Mark O'Hara

Open: Year-round except late May–mid-July; in 2002, closed until December 15

Credit Cards: All major

U.S. Reservations: Ralph Locke, (800) 223–1108; Fax: (310) 440–4220

Deposit: Three nights, seven at Christmas; twenty-eight days cancellation winter, fourteen in summer

Minimum Stay: Fourteen days at Christmas

Arrival/Departure: No transfer service due to government regulations

Distance from Airport: 18 miles (forty-five minutes); taxi $22 one-way

Distance from Bridgetown: 8 miles (twenty minutes)

Accommodations: 85 units, all with terraces, patios, or balconies (24 king or twin double; four singles; 14 superior junior suites; 37 luxury junior suites; four Plantation suites with sundeck and plunge pool; two four-bedroom villas)

Amenities: Air-conditioning, ceiling fans; direct-dial phones; safe; refrigerator, toaster; hair dryer, bath with tub and shower, bathrobes, basket of toiletries; daily newspaper; nightly turndown service; television on request ($50 per week); hair salon; boutique; twenty-four-hour room service; e-mail and Internet access

Electricity: 110 volts/50 cycles

Fitness Facilities/Spa Services: Fitness center, massage

Sports: Two freshwater swimming pools; two tennis courts, lighted; snorkeling, Sunfish, kayaking, waterskiing, and windsurfing included; golf, diving, deep-sea fishing arranged for fee

Dress Code: Smart casual by day; elegantly casual in evening; jacket and tie or black tie Christmas and New Year's

Children: Children welcome year-round except in February when those under twelve years old cannot be accommodated; children under five not allowed in restaurant or lounge after 7:00 P.M.

Meetings: Up to twenty-four people

Handicapped: Certain accommodations suitable

Packages: Honeymoon, wedding

Rates: Per room, for two, MAP, including service charge and taxes. **High Season** (December 14, 2002–January 5, 2003, and January 20-February 28, 2003): $750-$1,280, single $485. **Shoulder Season** (January 6-19 and March 1-April 23): $670-$1,190, single $450. **Low Season** (April 24-October 31): $440-$645, single $260; (November 1-December 14): $480-$720, single $290. For EP rates and 2-bedroom suites for four people, inquire.

Service Charge: Included

Government Tax: Included

GLITTER BAY

St. James, Barbados

The minute you enter the front gate that opens onto twelve beachfront acres of landscaped gardens and stately trees, you get the impression that someone important once lived here. He did.

Glitter Bay, overlooking Barbados's Caribbean coast, was once the seaside retreat of Sir Edward Cunard of British steamship fame. In its heyday, when his passengers came to winter in the Tropics, his guests were a glittering gathering of lords and ladies. In more recent times the retreat has attracted a sparkling array of Hollywood stars, Wall Street lights, and Washington luminaries.

If you want to make a dazzling arrival yourself, you can be transported from the airport by the hotel's stretch Mercedes (for $100 plus 15 percent tax). A glass of champagne awaits you on arrival, and on departure the concierge will arrange airport executive check-in for a fee of $48 per person. For $60, you can have precheck-in and access to The Club Caribbean Lounge; for $75 you get precheck-in, transportation, and access to Lounge.

Glitter Bay is a baronial spread of quiet grandeur, with stately royal palms leading the way to flower-trimmed walkways, a split-level swimming pool with a waterfall and wooden footbridge, and a ½-mile-long white-sand beach with a water sports center that it shares with its sister hotel, Royal Pavilion.

Cunard's gracious coral-stone mansion serves as the centerpiece of the resort. In the 1990s, a new marble-floor wing was added to provide space for a fitness center, a concierge desk, and a small courtyard of quality boutiques and a residents' lounge.

On both sides of the extensive gardens are clusters of three-story, white stucco buildings with red clay roofs and a cascade of terraces reflecting the Mediterranean design that is architect Ian Morrison's signature. All units have private verandas overlooking the gardens and the pool. The suites and penthouses are furnished like living rooms, making the accommodations very spacious. Most of the standard rooms are interconnected to provide a second room for a one-bedroom suite.

The units are decorated in fresh blue and white, and the bathrooms have tubs, showers, and bidets. Rooms have minibars, and suites have kitchens. All accommodations are furnished with king-size beds; twin beds, rollaways, and cribs are available on request.

Off to one side, beyond the main complex, is the Beach House—a replica of Cunard's Venetian mansion—with five superposh rooms, the most desirable of the lot. They offer the best of both worlds: the intimacy and privacy of a small resort with the facilities of a large one.

Beside the pool is a breeze-cooled restaurant, Piperade, serving international and local cuisine. Friday night features a buffet with a local show. Afternoon tea is served by the pool.

Glitter Bay offers complimentary water sports, along with two tennis courts (lighted) and a fitness center with Lifecycle equipment, a treadmill, a stair climber, weights, daily aerobics classes, massage, and personalized training. Guests at Glitter Bay also enjoy the use of all facilities at Royal Pavilion. Through an arrangement with the nearby Royal Westmoreland Club, Glitter Bay and Royal Pavilion guests have access to that club's excellent golf course, designed by Robert Trent Jones II; complimentary transfers are provided.

Shared facilities do not mean, however, that the two resorts are similar. Glitter Bay defines itself as a more informal and family oriented resort than Royal Pavilion. Its large apartment-type accommodations, space, and facilities are well suited to families. The mix of patrons, too, is different, with more coming from Britain than the United States.

Glitter Bay ★ ★ ★ ★

Porters, St. James, Barbados
Phone: (246) 422–5555; Fax: (246) 422–1367;
www.fairmont.com

Owner: Fairmont Hotels
General Manager: Jan Schöningh
Open: Year-round
Credit Cards: All major
U.S. Reservations: Fairmont Hotels, (800) 866–5577, Fax: (246) 422–3940
Deposit: Three nights, thirty days cancellation in winter; one night, fourteen days cancellation in summer
Minimum Stay: Twelve nights during Christmas/New Year's
Arrival/Departure: Limousine transfer service arranged
Distance from Airport: 12 miles; taxi one-way, $35
Distance from Bridgetown: 8 miles; taxi one-way, $20
Accommodations: 27 double rooms, 32 suites with kitchens, five penthouses; all have balconies; most have garden views; some have sea view or partial sea view
Amenities: Air-conditioning, ceiling fan; direct-dial telephone, radio, cable television; safe; bath with tub, shower, bidet, hair dryer, bathrobes, basket of toiletries; stocked minibar; ice service, nightly turndown service, twenty-four-hour room service, concierge
Electricity: 110 volts/60 cycles
Fitness Facilities/Spa Services: Air-conditioned fitness center; massage (see text)
Sports: Freshwater swimming pool, children's pool; free tennis, waterskiing, Hobie Cats, Sunfish, snorkeling, windsurfing; diving for fee; golf, fishing, horseback riding arranged
Dress Code: Informal by day, casually elegant in evening, coverups requested in dining room for all meals; at dinner men are asked to wear trousers; no shorts, T-shirts, or jeans allowed in public rooms in evening; no swimwear at lunch or afternoon tea
Children: All ages year-round; children's pool and menus; cribs; baby-sitters; Cubs Club, an activities program for ages four to twelve available summer and major holidays, $60
Meetings: Up to fifty people
Day Visitors: Welcome with reservations
Handicapped: Limited facilities
Packages: Four, seven, and fourteen nights; honeymoon, wedding, family
Rates: Two people, daily, EP. *High Season* (mid-December–mid-April): $475–$825. *Low Season* (mid-April–early November): $255–$440. *Shoulder Season* (early November–mid-December): $330–$470. Inquire for suite and two- and three-bedroom rates.
Service Charge: 10 percent
Government Tax: 7.5 percent on room; 15 percent on food and beverages

ROYAL PAVILION

St. James, Barbados

Adjacent to Glitter Bay—its sister hotel and designed by the same architect, Ian Morrison—the Royal Pavilion is aimed directly at today's affluent travelers. Although grand luxe in the European tradition, it has made a point of being more contemporary in style and attitude than the grandes dames of Barbados's hotels.

Set amid thirty acres of immaculate tropical gardens directly on a white-sand beach in the quiet cove it shares with its sister resort, the pastel pink Royal Pavilion combines Spanish mission and Mediterranean elements in its design. An imposing avenue of royal palms leads to the flower-encircled portico of the main entrance. There you step into a marbled reception hall with a concierge desk and a colonnaded Andalusian courtyard cooled by a fountain. As at Glitter Bay, if you wish to have your arrival match the hotel's grand entrance, you can be met at the airport in one of the resort's stretch Mercedes limousines.

The resort's accommodations, all facing the sea, are in two wings of three-story buildings. All are large, deluxe rooms with terraces designed and furnished as part of the room—making the rooms all the more spacious. One of the best features of each terrace is a built-in settee of white sculpted masonry set off with colorful cushions that pick up the hues of the flowers in the gardens and of the Caribbean Sea, directly in view. All guest rooms are attractively decorated in fashionable prints against pickled-wood furniture. Completing the roster is a villa with three additional accommodations.

Royal Pavilion's triumph is the Palm Terrace, an elegant, pink marble dining room by the sea. Here the romantic palm-court effect is enhanced by a skylight pavilion roof shaded by living palm trees that are part of the decor. Adjacent to the restaurant is a spacious lounge

Royal Pavilion ★★★★

Porters, St. James, Barbados
Phone: (246) 422–5555; Fax: (246) 422–0118;
www.fairmont.com

Owner: Fairmont Hotels
General Manager: Jan Schöningh
Open: Year-round
Credit Cards: All major
U.S. Reservations: Fairmont Hotels, (800) 223–1818, Fax.
(212) 832–1564
Deposit: Three nights, thirty days cancellation in winter; one
night, fourteen days cancellation in summer
Minimum Stay: Twelve nights during Christmas
Arrival/Departure: Limousine transfer service arranged for fee
Distance from Airport: 12 miles; taxi one-way, $35
Distance from Bridgetown: 8 miles; taxi one-way, $20
Accommodations: 72 oceanfront deluxe rooms with king-size
beds and private balconies in two three-story buildings; one
three-bedroom villa
Amenities: Air-conditioning; bath with tub and shower, hair
dryer, basket of toiletries, bathrobe; direct-dial telephone, radio,
cable television; safe; stocked minibar; twice-daily maid service,
twenty-four-hour room service; concierge
Electricity: 110 volts/60 cycles
Fitness Facilities/Spa Services: Air-conditioned fitness center;
massage (see text for Glitter Bay)
Sports: Freshwater swimming pool; complimentary tennis and
equipment (lessons extra), Hobie Cats, Sunfish, snorkeling,
waterskiing, windsurfing; diving additional; horseback riding,
golf, fishing arranged
Dress Code: Informal by day, casually elegant in evening; for
dining, jeans, T-shirts, rubber shoes, sneakers not accepted; no
shorts in bar after 6:00 P.M., no swimwear at lunch or after-
noon tea
Children: No children under thirteen years old year-round
except in July–August; cribs; baby-sitters
Meetings: Up to fifty people; equipment available
Day Visitors: With reservations
Handicapped: Limited facilities
Packages: Honeymoon, wedding
Rates: Per room, daily, EP. **High Season** (mid-December–mid-
April): $575– $675. **Low Season** (mid-April–early November):
$280. **Shoulder Season** (early November–mid-December):
$380. Inquire for two bedrooms and villa rates.
Service Charge: 10 percent
Government Tax: 7.5 percent on room; 15 percent on food
and beverages

with graceful arched doorways and windows opening onto views of the gardens and sea. Here guests enjoy afternoon tea, cocktails, and after-dinner drinks. The Palm Terrace has an elegant cigar lounge offering fine cognacs and after-dinner drinks as well as a selection of cigars.

On the northern side of the resort, Cafe Tabora is a casual, open-air restaurant where breakfast and lunch are served. It is named for Fernando Tabora, a well-known Latin American landscape architect who designed the exquisite gardens for Royal Pavilion and Glitter Bay. Cafe Tabora is terraced by the sea on one side, with the swimming pool and a large sunning deck on the other.

The hotel has two hard-surface tennis courts (lighted) and shares the water-sports, fitness, and restaurant facilities of Glitter Bay next door. One of the courtyards has a cluster of fashionable boutiques and a hair salon. Through an arrangement with the nearby Royal Westmoreland Club, Royal Pavilion guests have access to that club's excellent golf course, designed by Robert Trent Jones II; complimentary transfers are arranged.

Royal Pavilion is tony but not snobbish and enjoys a high number of repeat guests, mostly from Britain, Italy, and the United States. It is well suited for those who want a relaxing vacation in a stylish yet casual ambience, where the emphasis is on pretty surroundings, comfort, and sophisticated cuisine.

Bonaire

The second largest island in the Netherlands Antilles, Bonaire is located 50 miles north of Venezuela and 86 miles east of Aruba. For three decades it has been a haven for divers, who come to enjoy the island's remarkable marine life. The entire coastline, from the high-tide mark to a depth of 200 feet, is a marine park with more than eighty dive sites.

Most island hotels cater to divers and have excellent operations on their premises. In some places the reefs are so near you can wade to them; others are only a swim or short boat ride away. Thus, divers can enjoy unlimited diving from the beach at any time of day or night—the kind of ease and convenience few places in the world can duplicate. Indeed, there's no better place in the Caribbean to learn scuba.

Even for travelers with no higher aspiration than snorkeling, this 24-mile crescent-shaped island offers plenty. Two of its attractions are certainly unusual, if not unique, and easily accessible. The hilly northern end is covered by the Washington/Slagbaai National Park, a 13,500-acre wildlife sanctuary that includes the island's highest point, 784-foot-high Brandaris Hill. The park is a showcase of island flora and fauna with a variety of unusual formations and 130 species of birds.

The flat, dry southern part of the island has an equally interesting attraction. Salt pans, more than 150 years old and covered with white sparkling mountains of salt, are worked commercially, but amid the pans is a 135-acre flamingo sanctuary and breeding ground for about 10,000 birds. You can tour the perimeter of the pans to watch and photograph the birds.

A quiet island of 10,400 inhabitants, Bonaire's peaceful ambience belies its turbulent past. Discovered in 1499 by Amerigo Vespucci—for whom the Americas were named—it was colonized by the Spaniards, who carted off the entire Arawak population to Hispaniola. Later the island was captured by the Dutch, fought over by the French and British, and leased to a New York merchant. Finally, in 1816, the Dutch took it over and kept it.

Kralendijk, the capital, is a colorful miniature city with distinctive Dutch colonial architecture. Among the oldest structures is historic Fort Oranje and the original administration building, which dates to 1837. It has been restored as the Government Office. The island has a surprising variety of good restaurants and a neat little shopping area in the heart of town.

Information

Tourism Corporation of Bonaire, 10 Rockefeller Plaza, #900, New York, NY 10020;
(212) 956–5911, (800) BONAIRE; www.infobonaire.com

CAPTAIN DON'S HABITAT

Kralendijk, Bonaire, N.A.

A resort for divers, Captain Don's Habitat was founded by a diver who has become a legend in his own time.

I met Don Stewart, a salty California expatriate, on my first trip to Bonaire in the early 1970s, long before Habitat was born. He had wandered into Bonaire in 1962 from a 70-foot schooner called the *Valerie Queen* because, as he said in his wry way, "I was thirsty and heard they had water." The good ship *Valerie* sank; Stewart stayed. He started Bonaire's first hotel and later opened his own very rustic inn for divers, one of the first of its kind.

Stewart, known to all as Captain Don, bent my ear most of the day and evening on the wonders of scuba diving, the unique qualities of Bonaire, the need to protect the marine environment, and just about anything else that came to his mind. He was not a man at a loss for words.

Since then not much has changed, except that this interesting character has managed to get enough of the right people to listen. Today, after almost four decades of adhering to careful management of its reefs and sea life, Bonaire has one of the most magnificent marine parks in the world; diving is its number one industry. On the thirtieth anniversary of his arrival on the island and in appreciation for his contributions, the Bonaire government honored Stewart by proclaiming "Capt. Don Week" with all the associated fanfare, a memorial plaque sponsored by the Council of Underwater Resort Operators was placed on a reef bearing his name.

Along the way Stewart's once dinky little inn grew into quite a nice resort. Perched on a coral bluff north of town, overlooking a 1/2-mile shore line of great diving, Captain Don's Habitat is a very casual, relaxed resort. It is designed as clusters of white stucco town houses, some in attractive Dutch colonial architecture with high-pitched red roofs, others more modern with Spanish features such as courtyards and dark wood doors and windows.

In the past few years, the hotel has been substantially updated, upgraded, and expanded, now offering enough variety and flexibility to meet almost any need. There are two-bedroom garden-view cottages with kitchenettes set back from the water; deluxe junior suites with two queen-size beds, a refrigerator, and a furnished balcony overlooking a large freshwater swimming pool; and two- and three-bedroom villas.

The interiors are spacious, particularly in the newest units, with wood-beamed ceilings and French doors leading to a patio overlooking the sea. Separated from their neighbors by greenery and walkways, the units convey a feeling of privacy and offer an unexpected level of luxury for their moderate rates. All the guest rooms are tastefully furnished, mostly with rattan.

Happy hour at the Decompression Stop Bar, the oceanfront watering hole, attracts divers from far and wide. Rum Runners, the open-air seaside restaurant, offers an eclectic menu of Italian, Cajun, and local dishes, along with freshly made pizza. A Texas barbecue one night and a Tex-Mex dinner another night are merry evenings that are usually well attended. Captain Don usually appears for these special nights dressed in cowboy boots, Stetson, and fringe. You can't miss him.

The dive operation is one of the main PADI five-star training facilities in the Caribbean. You can dive at Captain Don's twenty-four hours a day, any day of the year. The resort has eight boats and a photo shop and offers every level of instruction, including underwater photography courses. Most guests come on packages that include tank, weights, belt, unlimited free air, and at least one boat dive daily. Nitrox rebreathers are available for rent with instruction. A sister resort, Habitat Curaçao, which opened in 1997 on the western coast of Curaçao, offers similar programs.

Although Habitat caters mainly to divers and would-be divers, it offers other diversions such as Sunfish sailing and windsurfing. You can swim in the main pool, set into a wooden deck by the sea, or soak up the sun on the resort's tiny strand of sand, appropriately named Seven Body Beach.

Captain Don, as loquacious as ever, is still a man with a mission. Although retired from the daily operation of Habitat, he is very active with a weekly slide show called "The Family Album." Most of the show consists of black-and-white slides made from original photographs during the early days of diving on Bonaire; it provides a fascinating look back at how the diving industry started here, with a few of the captain's sea stories thrown in for good measure.

Couples between the ages of thirty and fifty and families with kids old enough to dive make up the majority of guests. Most come on packages, which represent good value. You should, too.

Captain Don's Habitat ** 🌿

P.O. Box 88, Kralendijk, Bonaire, N.A.
Phone: (599) 717–8290; Fax: (599) 717–8240;
e-mail: info@maduro.com; www.habitatdiveresorts.com

Owner: Hambo/Maduro Holdings
Managing Director: Albert Romijn
Resident Manager: Nick Davies
Open: Year-round
Credit Cards: Most major
U.S. Reservations: Captain Don's Habitat, Maduro Travel, (800) 327–6709, (305) 438–4277; Fax: (305) 438–4220
Deposit: $100 per person; full payment thirty days prior to arrival
Minimum Stay: None
Arrival/Departure: Transfer normally included in packages
Distance from Airport: 6 miles; taxi one-way, $10
Distance from Kralendijk: 1 mile; taxi one-way, $3.00
Accommodations: 82 rooms and suites in cottages and villas (21 two-bedroom cottages, garden view; 24 deluxe junior suites with mini-refrigerators, furnished balcony; ten two- to three-bedroom villas with living room, kitchen on ground floor, two superior bedrooms, private entrance on second floor, one bedroom with king-size bed and balcony, second with twin; three-bedroom villas similar with third bedroom on ground floor)
Amenities: Air-conditioning, ceiling fans; some baths with tub, most with shower, basket of toiletries; no room service; photo shop; car rental and tour company on premises
Electricity: 120 volts
Sports: Freshwater swimming pool; full scuba program (see text); mountain bikes for rent; boating, snorkeling, windsurfing, deep-sea fishing, hiking arranged
Dress Code: Bathing suits and shorts appropriate at all times
Children: All ages, but must be twelve or older to scuba dive
Meetings: Up to one hundred people; seminar and conference facilities
Day Visitors: Yes
Handicapped: Facilities
Packages: Dive, nondivers, family
Rates: Per person, weekly, with six boat dives and unlimited twenty-four-hour per day shore diving, CP. *High Season* (mid-December–mid-April): $1,081–$1,440. *Low Season:* $747–$981. Inquire for nondiver rates.
Service Charge: Included
Government Tax: Included

British Virgin Islands

This archipelago of about fifty green, mountainous islands and cays scalloped with idyllic coves of white-sand beaches is spread over 59 square miles along Drake's Channel and the Anegada Passage between the Caribbean Sea and the Atlantic Ocean. Mostly volcanic in origin and uninhabited, the British Virgin Islands are almost as virgin as the day Christopher Columbus first saw them. Popular hiding places of pirates in olden days, these gems are today favorite hideaways of yachtsmen (for their good anchorage) and of vacationers fleeing the crowd.

The largest and most populated islands of this British Crown Colony are Tortola, the capital, and Virgin Gorda, to the east of Tortola. Several islands, such as Guana Island off Tortola's northeastern coast and Peter Island to the southeast, have been developed as private resorts.

Tortola is best known as a yacht-chartering center. Its main town and port, Road Town, is the British Virgin Islands' commercial and residential hub. Other entry points are West End, where ferries from St. Thomas stop, and the airport on Beef Island, connected to Tortola's eastern end by a small bridge.

Virgin Gorda's largest settlement, Spanish Town, is located about midisland. Little more than a hamlet a decade ago, the town has grown by leaps and bounds as the island has prospered from sheltering several of the Caribbean's most celebrated hideaways.

The B.V.I., as aficionados call them, do not appeal to everyone. They have no golf courses or casinos, and nighttime activity is very low-key. But they more than make up for the lack of razzle-dazzle with fabulous scenery and facilities, particularly for water sports.

Information

British Virgin Islands Tourist Board, 370 Lexington Avenue, Suite 313, New York, NY 10017; (212) 696–0400, (800) 835–8530; Fax: (212) 949–8254; www.bviwelcome.com

SANDCASTLE

Jost Van Dyke, B.V.I.

Feel like dropping out? Want to hide out for a few days? Try Sandcastle. It's on tiny Jost Van Dyke, a remote island northeast of Tortola that's home to only 135 people.

That number is just fine for those who find their way to this heavenly haven. There are no casinos, no native floor shows, no discos here. And until recently, there was no electricity either.

Sandcastle sits on White Bay, a gorgeous 1/2-mile stretch of powdery white sand with a lot of palm trees and tropical flowers, which seem to grow where they will. You stay in one of the four cottages, two of which have two rooms, or in one of two new spacious rooms. They are modestly but adequately furnished with almost everything you'd need on a castaway island: king-size beds and a twin-size daybed, comfy chairs, a coffee table, books, and an efficient toilet.

All rooms have electricity for lights and fans; the newest two rooms, in a storm-resistant building, even have air-conditioning. Romantics will be pleased to know that oil lamps are available for guests who want mood lighting in their cottages. The water comes from heaven. Outdoor shower stalls are attached to each cottage. The newest rooms have full baths with indoor hot-water showers. All accommodations now have hot-water showers.

The Soggy Dollar, the beachfront restaurant and bar, is the hotel's focal point and the food one of its highlights. Dinner finds many other guests from yachts anchored offshore sitting down to savor dishes such as fresh grilled fish and Key lime pie.

Sandcastle's reputation for superb food is well known in yachting circles; sailors simply pull their boats into the bay and transfer to shore via their dinghies. There is no dock; you must usually take a step or two in the water before hitting dry land. Tables are lit by candlelight and adorned with soft pastel cloths and fresh flowers. It's all very romantic. Conversation can be lively or quiet, depending on the mix of guests.

You won't be at Sandcastle long before you'll be tempted to try the hotel's specialty drink, the Painkiller. This yummy concoction (rum, coconut cream, fruit juice,

and nutmeg) may have originated here. Two at midday and it's hammock time.

There's wonderful snorkeling on a reef within swimming distance of the beach. The first reef is in only 12 feet of water; the sea bottom then slopes to about 40 feet for a second reef, and about 400 yards farther out is a wall with an 80-foot drop. It's great diving, too, if you come with dive gear.

For excitement it's a half-hour walk or a quick taxi ride to Foxy's Tamarind Bar, the most famous watering hole in this part of the Caribbean. Foxy, the consummate Caribbean character, has a well-deserved reputation for his quick wit and talent on the guitar.

You could take an excursion or two to neighboring islands, but for most people the combination of sand, sea, and sun, along with the great cooking and friendly owners and staff, is enough.

Getting to Sandcastle requires a bit of scheduling and a lot of determination. You can fly to Tortola or St. Thomas. From Beef Island Airport on Tortola, it's a forty-five-minute taxi ride to the West End Ferry dock. From St. Thomas there's a ferry to West End several times daily, which takes one hour.

At West End Sandcastle's boat will meet you, and a half hour or so later, you'll kick off your shoes and wade ashore while your boatman brings your luggage. Alternatively, from Red Hook on St. Thomas, the *Mona Queen* runs via St. John twice on Friday, Saturday, and Sunday directly to Jost Van Dyke in forty-five minutes.

Pack light. You won't need much—just bathing suits and shorts. This is barefoot living at its best. Obviously, Sandcastle is not for everyone, but for some it's as near paradise as they need to be.

Sandcastle *

For the speediest mail: 6501 Red Hook Plaza, Suite 201, St. Thomas, U.S.V.I. 00802
Phone: (284) 495–9888; Fax: (284) 495–9999;
e-mail: relax@sandcastle-bvi.com; www.sandcastle-bvi.com

Owners/Managers: Debby Pearse and Bruce Donath
Managing Director: Ross Justice
Open: Year-round
Credit Cards: Visa, MasterCard
U.S. Reservations: Direct to hotel
Deposit: $500 to confirm reservations; thirty days cancellation
Minimum Stay: Three nights during winter season
Arrival/Departure: See text
Distance from West End: (Tortola) Thirty minutes by boat; from Red Hook, St. Thomas: forty-five minutes
Accommodations: Four cottages (two directly on beach with sitting rooms, king-size beds, and daybed); two garden rooms with kings and air-conditioning
Amenities: Electricity for lights and fans; outside shower stalls connected to each cottage; gift and sportswear shop
Electricity: 110 volts/60 Hz (same as in U.S.)
Sports: Kayaking and snorkeling equipment included; hammocks on beach
Dress Code: Very casual: bathing suits and bare feet
Children: None under ten years of age
Meetings: No
Day Visitors: Welcome at restaurant and bar
Handicapped: No facilities
Packages: Seven-night MAP, including transportation from Tortola
Rates: Two people, daily, EP. *High Season* (mid-December–mid-May): $200– $250. *Low Season:* $125–$175. Singles rate available; inquire.
Service Charge: 10 percent on room, 15 percent on food and beverages
Government Tax: 7 percent on room

GUANA ISLAND
Guana Island, B.V.I.

A secluded resort tucked into a far-from-it-all setting, Guana Island is one of the Caribbean's true hideaways. Low-key to a whisper, it is the sort of place that makes you happy to be alive to enjoy the simple beauty of nature.

Located off the northeastern coast of Tortola, 850-acre Guana Island began as a private club in the 1930s. After purchasing it in 1974, its new owner modernized the facilities while retaining its rustic style and made it into a private nature sanctuary, leaving all but the small resort area crowning the topmost ridge undeveloped.

The resort, encased in gardens of hibiscus and oleander and shaded by flowering trees, accommodates a total of thirty guests in the main building and two clusters of whitewashed cottages. The cottages vary in size and layout, but each has its own special appeal. My favorite is Eleuthera, where you wake up to a fabulous view across the island and sea and in the evening take in 200 degrees of magnificent scenery bathed in sunset orange and red. Only the sounds of birds and crickets disturb the peace.

The guest rooms are actually junior suites with large verandas. The rooms are earthy, airy, comfortable, and cozy, furnished in rattan and local art against whitewashed stucco walls, set off by wood-beamed ceilings. All accommodations have been upgraded and made very comfortable, particularly the bathrooms. Gone are the pull chains that used to be in the showers. Two new generators and a desalinization plant, greatly increased the island's power and water supplies, and the electricity is no longer turned off at midnight as in the past.

Grenada House, with the resort's only pool, was added to the original six cottages. It rents as a two-bedroom unit with the pool or as two separate guest rooms without it. Another addition is North Beach Cottage, a very private, one-bedroom house with a living room, kitchen, and bath on its own 1/3 mile of beach with a private sea pool. North Beach Cottage is surrounded by open and covered decks for lounging or sunbathing and dining. Meals are offered there, or you can eat at the resort's main dining terrace. The trail to the cottage from the main resort winds along an old Quaker stone wall. North Beach Cottage guests are provided with a golf cart to drive across the flat to White Bay Beach activities and tennis courts. Transportation up the hill to the club is provided by the club's Land Rover, if you want it.

The main house, Dominica, is the social center. It includes a homey lounge with an honor bar, a library where a rare winter evening chill could be warmed by a fireplace, and dining terraces where all meals and afternoon tea are served.

The lively atmosphere at cocktails in the lounge before dinner is more like a weekend house party than a hotel. Dinner seating is arranged by the manager nightly. You may choose to dine with other guests or on your own. You dine by candlelight on a menu that includes fresh seafood, home-baked breads, locally grown fruits and vegetables, and good wine. There is a weekly beach barbecue.

After dinner you can join other guests in the lounge to listen to music over coffee, dance to recorded music, enjoy more conversation, or plan the next day's activities.

Guana Island boasts six untrampled porcelain beaches. Reef-protected White Bay, the "arrival" beach below the main house, is a powdery ½-mile crescent bathed by gin-clear waters ideal for swimming and snorkeling. A Land Rover will shuttle you to and fro, or you can walk on one of the island's two paved roads. The more isolated beaches can be reached on hiking trails; two are accessible only by boat. A new trail of about 150 steps down a cliff on the northern end of Guana will take you to Chicken Rock—so named because it looks like a sitting hen—where at the end of a long hike you can cool off in pristine sea pools before hiking back or being picked up by boat.

The owners' interest in conservation led them to make Guana a nature and wildlife preserve. They underwrite an autumn program that, due to the island's unusual nature—an ecosystem almost undisturbed for a century—brings a small army of scientists from Harvard University, The Conservation Agency, and other institutions from afar to study and document its rich flora and fauna. They are also helping to restore the natural environment and reintroduce native species.

About fifty bird species and thirty-one butterfly species can be seen regularly, and another fifty bird species come at different times of year. The pristine reefs near shore have 125 species of fish and dozens of species of coral. Maps of the island's two dozen trails are available. Be sure to bring comfortable walking shoes or sneakers with tread and binoculars.

While the personable managers are attentive and the friendly staff—most of whom have been at Guana for years—are helpful, no one pampers you. You set your own pace, doing as little or as much as you want. There's lots of walking—*hiking* would be more accurate—to get to meals and the beach. (Transportation is available, too.) But then, nature is what Guana is all about. If you need entertainment or waiters at your beck and call, this is not the place for you.

Guana Island is limited to its guests; yachters, cruise passengers, and day trippers are not welcome, and there are no facilities for them. Although they have a legal right to come ashore, few do. The policy helps preserve Guana Island's ecology and the resort's exclusivity.

Guana is designed for travelers who seek tranquillity and can operate on their own juices. Your company will be mostly Americans, with a few British and other Europeans in the thirty-to-sixty age group. Younger guests and honeymooners come in spring and summer. If it's privacy you want, you can rent the entire island—as CEOs, wedding parties, and families on reunion sometimes do.

Guana Island ★★★ 🏖

Guana Island, B.V.I.
Phone: (284) 494–2354; Fax: (284) 495–2900;
e-mail: guana@guana.com; www.guana.com

Owners: Henry and Gloria Jarecki
Resident Managers: Roger Miller and Bridget MacArthur
Open: Year-round except September–October
Credit Cards: Visa and MasterCard; personal and travelers checks preferred
U.S. Reservations: Guana Island, (800) 54–GUANA, (914) 967–6050; Fax: (914) 967–8048
Deposit: Three nights per booking; thirty days cancellation unless resort is able to rebook accommodation. Policy differs for Christmas/New Year's; inquire.
Minimum Stay: Four nights—less at some times of year; inquire.
Arrival/Departure: Guests met at Beef Island Airport by Guana Island representative and taken to nearby dock to board resort's launch for ten-minute ride to island; $35 per person is added to bill for round-trip boat and taxi transfer.
Distance from Airport: Ten minutes by boat
Distance from Road Town: Thirty minutes by boat and road; from launch dock to town one-way, $15
Accommodations: 15 rooms in seven hillside cottages, all with twin or king-size beds and verandas; one bedroom in North Beach Cottage
Amenities: Ceiling fan; umbrella; rack for wet bathing suits; bath with shower only; no air-conditioning, telephone, radio, television
Electricity: 110 volts
Sports: Two tennis courts (clay and all weather Omni-turf); self-service beach bar with water-sports equipment, dressing and rest rooms, lounging chairs, hammocks; use of courts, racquets, fishing rods, snorkeling gear, sailboats, kayaks, water skis, windsurfers free; deep-sea fishing charters and diving arranged; tennis balls and fishing tackle sold at tiny boutique
Dress Code: Casual; cover-up and shoes at breakfast and lunch; dinner smart casual
Children: Inquire in advance.
Meetings: Up to thirty people can rent whole island
Day Visitors: No
Handicapped: Very limited facilities; inquire.
Packages: No
Rates: Two people, daily, AP. **High Season** (December 15–mid-March): $850. **Low Season:** $650. **Shoulder Season** (November–mid-December): $650. North Beach Cottage (daily, two people): **High Season:** $1,500. **Shoulder and Low Season:** $1,250. Entire island (daily, up to thirty people): High Season: $15,000. **Shoulder and Low Season:** $11,500. Single occupancy, $75 less; triple $150 more.
Service Charge: 17 percent, including government tax
Government Tax: Included in service charge

PETER ISLAND RESORT & YACHT HARBOUR
Road Town, Tortola, B.V.I.

Set on some of the most beautiful beaches in the Caribbean and surrounded by forested hills with pretty vistas at every turn, posh Peter Island has evolved from a small, exclusive yacht haven created in 1971 into a full-scale resort.

Covering 1,050 of the private island's 1,800 green, hilly acres, Peter Island is perennially named as one of the Caribbean's top resorts. It was all but blown away by Hurricane Hugo in 1989. Rebuilding took fifteen months, only to be damaged again in 1995. This prompted Amway Hotel Corporation, who owned it at the time, to close the resort for six months in 1997 to undertake a major, multi-million-dollar renovation of the entire property that added a welcome gazebo, an expanded lobby with an atrium, redesigned guest rooms and restaurants, new fitness facilities in a new location, and new landscaping.

Ownership of Peter Island Resort passed to a family member of the Amway owners in 2000 and is now privately owned. The new owner closed the hotel again in late summer 2001 for yet another renovation. This time the twenty beachfront rooms were almost completely redesigned and upgraded and most of the resort and grounds were refurbished. Peter Island has never looked better in my thirty years of going there.

The resort is laid out in two areas: the original A-frame cottages overlooking the yacht basin, and the more deluxe villas hidden beneath a forest of palm trees on Deadman's Bay, the main beach. The latter have the spacious beachfront junior suites that were improved with an open floor plan with large windows and doors that look out at the lush surroundings and ocean views. The rooms have lavish new bathrooms with imported Spanish tile and original hand-laid stonework, walk-in Euro showers, Jacuzzi tubs, and walls of glass that open on to ocean or garden views; a new air-conditioning system; new furniture, decor, and lighting; and redesigned closets by Designs for Living, Inc. A certain formal look in period furnishings is blended with Caribbean decor to create a sophisticated yet comfortable ambience. Although the resort has not abandoned its long-standing policy of no-television-in-guest-rooms, Peter Island is looking to the future—fiber-optic cable lines and dataports in room telephones were part of the upgrading. Some signature items such as Peter Island beach sandals and a compact disk of Caribbean music await you upon check-in.

The upgraded A-frames are less expensive than the beachfront rooms. Each cottage has four large bedrooms: two on the ground floor with patios and two above with high, beamed ceilings and decks overlooking the harbor on the south and Drake's Channel on the north. They are slated for more upgrading next year.

The Crow's Nest, a fabulous villa with decor by designer Carlton Varney, has four bedrooms, each with a private balcony and bath, game room, entertainment system, library, wine cellar, and saltwater pool surrounded by flagstone terraces. The villa is staffed with two maids, a gardener, and a cook; a jeep for your exclusive use is provided. Situated on the highest point of the resort, with spectacular views, its price is spectacular, too.

The two hillside villas at Hawk's Nest, which are suitable for families, have two bedrooms, two baths, living room, television, kitchenette, sundeck, and air-conditioning.

The open-air lobby, next to the infinity pool, is convenient to the dock and A-frame cottages. The adjacent library has television that carries CNN and other cable programs. The air-conditioned Tradewinds restaurant has large waterfront windows with views of Drake's Channel and Tortola. Tradewinds offers weekly vintner's wine-pairing dinners, focusing on a particular region to showcase wines from that area. Each course is prepared to complement the wines being served. The cost is $55 per person for hotel guests and $65 nonguests to participate. Peter Island also revamped its cuisine, making it more contemporary, and launched an ambitious staff training program, which shows.

The Beach Bar and Grill on Deadman's Bay Beach, which has a new kitchen and wood-fired oven, is the casual setting for lunch. It offers an interesting menu as varied as pizza, roti, and fresh fish, along with a salad bar and dessert table. Tea is served daily in the bar area near the pool. Dinner by candlelight is set in both the main dining room and alfresco by the pool, weather permitting. Menus are changed daily, with light fare and a classic repertoire.

Peter Island operates as an all-inclusive resort. In addition to meals and tea, water sports, tennis, mountain biking, and use of the fitness center are included. Hotel guests must reserve for dinner, because the dining terrace is a popular stop for yachts sailing in the Virgin Islands. Drake's Channel, the main lounge, has a romantic terrace setting with music by a different combo nightly for dancing under the stars.

Each of Peter Island's five beaches is memorable. On Deadman's Bay Beach you will find thatched umbrellas and lounge chairs near the bar and the water-sports center; hammocks are hidden among the trees. The resort's fitness center, with an array of exercise equipment, and the Solé Spa are located at the eastern end of Deadman's Bay Beach, near the water-sports center.

Farther east, Little Deadman's Bay is a mini mirror image of the main beach, and farther on, secluded Honeymoon Beach has one thatched umbrella and two chairs. It's for all romantics, not just honeymooners, but only one couple at a time, please.

The grounds in the immediate vicinity of the resort are landscaped and well tended, but the remainder of the island has been left to nature. The resort offers a free tour of the island with guide, "Bonji" Benjamin, a mason by trade who laid most of the stonework in Tradewinds. He came to Peter Island as a teenager in 1973, and eventually authored a book on the spot. If you want to explore on your own, Peter Island has 10 miles of dirt roads and hiking paths to be taken on foot or by bike, conventional or mountain. "Nature Stops" are posted around the island to identify neighboring islands in the panorama and local flora.

Peter Island Resort & Yacht Harbour ✳✳✳✳

P.O. Box 211, Road Town, Tortola, B.V.I.; or P.O. Box 9409, St. Thomas, U.S.V.I. 00801
Phone: (284) 495–2000, (800) 346–4451; Fax: (284) 495–2500; e-mail: reservations@peterisland.com; www.peterisland.com

Owner: Barb Van Andel-Gaby
Managing Director: Wayne Kafcsak
Resort Manager: Jeff Humes
Open: Year-round
Credit Cards: All major
U.S. Reservations: Peter Island Resort Worldwide; Phone: (800) 346–4451, (770) 476–4488; Fax: (770) 476–4979
Deposit: Three nights within 5 days of reservation
Minimum Stay: Ten nights during Christmas/New Year's
Arrival/Departure: Guests arriving at Beef Island Airport transfer directly to resort's motor launch for 6-mile trip across Drake's Channel to Peter Island. Resort also operates up to eight round-trips of free ferry service to its dock at Baughers Bay in Tortola. Transfer by helicopter directly to resort's lighted helipad arranged from St. Thomas, San Juan, or neighboring islands.
Distance from Airport: (Beef Island) Approximately 6 miles
Accommodations: 52 rooms (22 in A-frames with kings; 20 junior suites in beachfront buildings with kings); one two-bedroom and one four-bedroom villa, all with verandas
Amenities: Air-conditioning, ceiling fans; minibar, coffeemaker; telephone; bath with double sinks, tub, shower, hair dryers, bathrobes, toiletries; room service for continental breakfast; no television
Electricity: 110 volts
Fitness Facilities/Spa Services: New fitness center with exercise machines; massage and beauty treatments
Sports: Four tennis courts (two lighted), tennis pro, equipment; small boats, windsurfers, and free introductory lessons; fishing charters and motor launch sightseeing; snorkeling gear free; Dive BVI, on-site operator
Dress Code: Men requested to wear sport coats (tie not necessary) in winter season
Children: Inquire.
Meetings: Entire island can be rented for up to fifty people
Day Visitors: Welcome
Handicapped: Limited facilities
Packages: Honeymoon, wedding, dive, sailing, four and seven nights off-season
Rates: All-inclusive, per person, double, per day. *High Season* (mid-December– March): $600–$930. *Shoulder Season* (April and November–mid-December): $575–$660. *Low Season:* $490–$595. Villa rates: Inquire.
Service Charge: 10 percent
Government Tax: 7 percent

SUGAR MILL HOTEL
Apple Bay, Tortola, B.V.I.

Set on a hillside overlooking Apple Bay on Tortola's quiet northern coast, Sugar Mill is a cozy country inn as well known for its restaurant as for its hotel. It is owned and operated by veteran travel and food writers Jinx and Jeff Morgan.

Sugar Mill is divided into two sections by the small road that skirts the northern coast of Tortola. Instead of the usual lobby, at the hotel entrance you will find an outdoor gazebo lounge all but concealed in a riot of flowers and tropical greenery. It is adjacent to the bar, which doubles as the reception area, library, and boutique, and leads to an open-air terrace where breakfast is served. Behind it is the restored remnant of a 350-year-old sugar mill for which the inn is named and that houses the main dining room.

Hugging the steep hillside above the mill are clusters of two-story buildings containing the hotel's rooms and suites—all with balconies overlooking the lovely gardens and a small terraced swimming pool. The rooms, furnished mainly in wicker, are comfortable but not fancy. The rooms contain small kitchen units that families with children particularly appreciate. A new cottage with a suite of rooms was added recently near the hotel entrance gazebo. It has two deluxe bedrooms, each with a patio, that can be rented individually or as a two-bedroom cottage.

The lower section of the hotel sits at the edge of the sea alongside a small beach with lounging chairs; here, too, is Islands, an informal, open-to-the-breezes restaurant where, as the name suggests, the specialties are Caribbean fare. It is open for lunch daily and serves dinner Tuesday through Saturday during high season.

The old stone sugar mill, under a high, cedar-lined

Sugar Mill Hotel ★★

Box 425, Road Town, Apple Bay, Tortola, B.V.I.
Phone: (284) 495–4355, (800) 462–8834; Fax: (284) 495–4696;
e-mail: sugmill@surfbvi.com; www.sugarmillhotel.com

Owners: Jinx and Jeff Morgan
General Manager: Patrick Conway
Open: Year-round except August–September
Credit Cards: Most major
U.S. Reservations: (800) 462–8834, (284) 495–4355
Deposit: Three nights; thirty days cancellation in order to issue full refund
Minimum Stay: Seven nights during Christmas/New Year's; three nights rest of high season
Arrival/Departure: Transfer arranged on request for reduced fee
Distance from Airport: (Beef Island Airport) 18 miles (forty-five minutes); taxi one-way, $30
Distance from Road Town: 10 miles, taxi one-way, $20.00; from West End ferry dock, 3 miles, taxi one-way, $5.00
Accommodations: 24 units (including two standard rooms; 17 double rooms with terrace and kitchen including four family suites; one two-bedroom villa; two Plantation House suites); twin and king-size beds
Amenities: Ceiling fans, air-conditioning; bath with shower only, hair dryers; telephone; iron and ironing boards; refrigerator and coffeemaker; microwave in deluxe rooms
Electricity: 110 volts/60 cycles
Sports: Freshwater swimming pool, small beach, beautiful long strands nearby; free snorkeling gear; scuba, deep-sea fishing, hiking, other sports arranged
Dress Code: Casual
Children: Over eleven years old in winter; baby-sitters
Meetings: No
Day Visitors: Welcome in small numbers
Handicapped: Inquire.
Packages: Honeymoon, adventure
Rates: Two people, daily, EP. *High Season* (mid-December–mid-April): $215–$310. *Shoulder Season* (mid-April–May 31 and November 1–mid-December): $190–$245. *Low Season* (June 1–July 31 and October 1–31): $180–$225.
Service Charge: 10.7 percent
Government Tax: 7 percent

roof with ceiling fans, the warm glow of candlelight, fresh flowers, colorful Haitian paintings, and classical music playing in the background—all this makes up the inviting setting in which you will enjoy the inn's celebrated cuisine. The Sugar Mill is usually filled with patrons from other hotels and residents of Tortola.

Menus are a la carte and feature such specialties as chilled mango or curried banana soup, poached scallops with roasted red pepper sauce, fresh fish with coral sunset sauce, grilled quail with mango-papaya sauce, and chicken breast with chutney cream sauce. Many of the recipes are included in the *Sugar Mill Hotel Cookbook*.

Given Jeff's expertise in California wines (he has written three books on the subject), it's no surprise that the extensive wine list highlights California vintages. Jeff has provided brief descriptions of each wine to help guests make their selections.

Sugar Mill gets a great variety of guests—celebrity friends, movie stars, artists, writers, and just plain folks. Many are repeaters—Americans, Canadians, and British—who appreciate the food and enjoy the inn's homey, informal atmosphere. Some come for the workshops conducted by established artists and sponsored by the Morgans from time to time.

Sugar Mill is a bit remote—for many that's part of its charm. Car rental can be arranged through the hotel; you'll need it if you want to explore the island.

BIRAS CREEK
Virgin Gorda, B.V.I.

A masterpiece of British understatement far off the beaten path, Biras Creek is a hideaway in every sense. Small and secluded, the quietly posh resort is designed for relaxing and luxuriating in privacy in a casual, unpretentious, yet sophisticated ambience.

Much of the resort's privacy is all but guaranteed by its location: It's accessible only by boat and reached by the resort's private launch—or by your own yacht. Set in 140 acres of nature preserve on an isthmus of green hills that brackets the northern end of Virgin Gorda, the resort overlooks North Sound, a huge deep-water bay that has long been a yachtsman's mecca. On the north and east is the Atlantic, and to the west—the side on which you arrive—the Caribbean.

When you approach from the water, all you see is a fortresslike stone structure with a steep carousel roof atop a small rise at the center of the property. Built in terraces and approached by several sets of interconnected stone steps, the "castle" serves as the reception, dining, and social center with an indoor-outdoor terraced restaurant and bar commanding a lovely panoramic view.

The resort's size and layout also help ensure privacy.

Hidden under enormous almond and sea grape trees that provide shade and maximize privacy are sixteen cottages, each with two suites. They skirt the crest of Bercher's Bay, where the Atlantic roars in—too rough for swimming but great for cooling breezes to lull you to sleep. Cottage 11A is so close to the sea, it's like being on a ship—in a storm.

Each suite has a large bedroom and sitting room with a comfortable chair, writing desk, and sofa with mountains of pillows. Sliding glass doors open onto an ocean-view terrace with lounging chairs—the perfect nook for afternoon reading or dozing. The bathroom features a delightful open-air shower with a tropical garden, enclosed by an 8-foot patio wall but open overhead to trees and blue skies.

Terra-cotta tile floors and the ocean breezes sailing through the screen doors and louvered windows keep the tree-shaded rooms cool. A bottle of wine and soft drinks will be awaiting your arrival. Near your cottage door you'll find two bicycles for your exclusive use.

In 1995, after being bought from its Norwegian owners by Dutchman Bert Houwer, a loyal guest at Biras Creek for fourteen years, the resort was closed for four months to complete a multimillion-dollar renovation that improved the resort without changing its character. All the guest rooms were refurbished with light interiors by the talented artist-designer Marti Schmidt, who brightened the decor with color and unusual objets d'art. They complement the cheerful designs on the fabrics and the handcrafted furniture from Bali that accent the bedrooms and sitting rooms. Telephones, air conditioners, more powerful ceiling fans, safes, and reading lights that you can actually read by were all added in the bedrooms, along with hair dryers, robes, and coffeemakers with a selection of coffees and herbal teas.

Among other nice touches, the oceanfront room patios have low wooden railings and terra-cotta tiles line the patios and entrances; bathroom vanities and mirrors are bordered with pottery tiles from St. John; and outdoor walkways are illuminated with ground-level lighting.

The two grand suites—17A and 17B—are superdeluxe with luxuriously spacious sitting rooms, bedrooms, and baths and some of the most handsome, unusual decor of any hotel room in the Caribbean. A premier suite, ideal for a family, has two bedrooms with three terraces, two baths, a spacious living area.

Running from the castle to the hillsides are twenty-five landscaped acres watched over by Biras Creek's gar-

dener, Alvin Harrigan, who has tended the gardens since the resort opened in 1974. Harrigan guides a weekly garden tour. The remaining 115 acres of the estate have been left to nature and include hiking trails and walking paths.

Biras Creek's freshwater pool, at the foot of the castle, has lounge chairs and thatched-roof sun shelters. A secluded beach at tranquil Deep Bay is a ten-minute walk or a five-minute bike ride from your cottage. En route you pass the tennis courts and a small estuary, a favorite spot for bird-watchers. Next to the beach a large thatched-roof pavilion has a bar (open daily) and picnic tables where lunch barbecues are served several days per week.

Biras Creek's open-air dining room in the hilltop castle is cheerful by day, with sunlight flooding the open terraces, and romantic by night, with candlelit tables and soft background music. The restaurant serves three meals daily, as well as afternoon tea.

From its inception Biras Creek established a reputation for fine cuisine and an impressive wine list. The bar adjoining the main dining room is a delightful open-air lounge and a popular gathering spot before dinner. The weekly manager's party here features a local combo. On Tuesdays there's calypso, on Thursday a ballad singer entertains at dinner, and on Saturday a steel band plays for dancing under the stars.

Biras offers several packages in the off season that are good value. Among the most popular is the Sailaway package, which gives you the best of both worlds—a stay at the resort plus overnight sailing through the British Virgin Islands on the resort's own crewed yacht. Summer specials provide seven days for the price of six and fourteen days for the price of eleven.

The service at Biras is as noteworthy in the restaurant (where a caring staff works quietly and efficiently) as in the rooms (where the housekeeping ladies keep your suite in top shape). They also change your towels twice daily, bring ice, take laundry, and turn down your bed at night.

Biras Creek ★★★★

Box 54, Virgin Gorda, B.V.I.
Phone: (284) 494–3555; Fax: (284) 494–3557;
e-mail: biras@biras.com; www.biras.com

Owner: Bert Houwer
General Managers: Michael and Luciana Nijdam
Open: November to August
Credit Cards: All major
U.S. Reservations: Ralph Locke Islands, (800) 223–1108;
Fax: (310) 440–4220; or Relais et Châteaux, (800) 735–2478
Deposit: Three nights
Minimum Stay: Ten nights during Christmas
Arrival/Departure: Free transfer with five-night stay. From Virgin Gorda Airport take twenty-five-minute jitney bus ride to dock at Gun Creek on northern end (almost length of island). There, resort's water taxi picks you up for ten-minute ride to Biras Creek. From Tortola the resort's water taxi zips you from dock near Beef Island Airport directly to Biras Creek. Ferries from Road Town go to Bitter End's dock, where Biras's boat picks you up.
Distance from Airport: (Spanish Town) 8 miles; taxi one-way, $20; ferry from Beef Island one-way, $20
Accommodations: 33 suites in 17 cottages with twin or king-size beds; one two-bedroom ocean-view suite; three suites interconnect
Amenities: Ceiling fans, air-conditioning in bedrooms; coffeemakers, small refrigerator; phones; iron and ironing board; e-mail and Internet access; in-room dataport; safes; hair dryers, showers; robes; no locks on doors or room service
Electricity: 110 volts/60 cycles
Fitness Facilities/Spa Services: Massage upon request
Sports: Freshwater pool; two lighted tennis courts, free use of courts, equipment; sailing, snorkeling, windsurfing equipment and instruction; hiking trails; motorized Boston Whalers; snorkeling trips three times a week and frequent trips to nearby secluded sands; waterskiing, fishing charters, day and sunset cruises; dive courses with certification arranged for fee. Dive BVI dive masters conduct free introductory scuba lessons.
Dress Code: Casual by day; cover-up and footwear required in dining room and bar; informally elegant for evening; tie and jacket not required
Children: Over eight years old
Meetings: None
Day Visitors: None
Handicapped: No facilities
Packages: Off season, honeymoon, Sailaway, family, wedding
Rates: Per person, double, daily, FAP. *High Season* (mid-December–early April): $750–$1,050. *Low Season:* $525–$825. Rates include use of tennis courts and water-sports equipment and round-trip airport transfers. Weekly and single rates available.
Service Charge: 10 percent
Government Tax: 7 percent

THE BITTER END YACHT CLUB AND RESORT

Virgin Gorda, B.V.I.

Although The Bitter End Yacht Club and Resort shares the waters of North Sound with Biras Creek, the two resorts are as different as you could imagine. Bitter End, stretching almost a mile along the northern shore of the sound, is as big and busy as Biras Creek is small and serene.

The twenty-five-acre Bitter End began in the 1960s as a watering hole for yachtsmen. When a Chicago businessman, Myron Hokin, sailed by on a fishing trip in 1972, he recognized the value of Bitter End's superb anchorage—the last outpost before the open waters of the Atlantic—and bought the property.

In 1988 Bitter End merged with neighboring Tradewinds, a more upscale resort, and overnight doubled in size. In addition to more facilities and rooms, Bitter End gained a wider range of style, broadening its appeal and transforming it from a boating haven to a full-scale resort.

Only steps from the beach, the original thatched cottages (upgraded in 1999) and Beachfront Villas continue to be the most popular accommodations. They are nicely but simply furnished, most with twin or king beds.

Climbing the wooded hillsides above the Clubhouse restaurant to the east are the deluxe Commodore Suites in jungle gardens; they're connected to one another by wooden walkways and catwalks, much like tree houses. Each of the Commodore Suites has two units—one studio and one suite—and balconies with fabulous views of the sound. The two units can be combined into a two-bedroom cottage. The rooms have peaked, wooden ceilings and are tastefully decorated in wicker with rich fabrics and grass-cloth wall coverings. They are air-conditioned and have telephones, refrigerators, coffeemakers, VCRs, and king- or queen-size beds. The Estate House is a posh, secluded two-bedroom villa above the Clubhouse with a large living room, separate dining area, screened porch, and wraparound veranda.

This eastern section of the resort is called The Commodore Club and offers more luxuries than the original area. On the beach below the Commodore Suites is a freshwater pool, with bar and lunch service poolside. A new communications system has streamlined hotel operations and improved the check-in and check-out processes. It includes a phone system that enables guests to have twenty-four-hour phone service from their rooms.

If you can't decide between a land or sea vacation, or simply want to sample life aboard a sailboat, you have an alternative. In combination with a hotel stay, you can rent a Freedom 30 complete with provisions and sail through the Virgin Islands. Guests often take short day sails, returning to Bitter End each evening. The live-aboard package includes meals at the resort's restaurants and unlimited free use of the resort's watercraft and other amenities.

Bitter End's facilities are in a medley of buildings by the water. Dining is set in two beachside pavilions, both with a comfortable ambience. The cuisine, created by European-trained chefs, is popular with the sailing community, which often ties up at the marina to enjoy the cocktail and dinner hour and entertainment.

The Clubhouse, an indoor restaurant with a tree-

shaded terrace, serves three meals daily. Light lunches are available poolside; the English Pub at The Emporium offers a variety of choices for snacks. The more sedate English Carvery has a traditional carving board and fresh fish prepared to order. Candlelight dinners end with soft music and dancing. The Yachtsman Bathhouse and lounge accommodate visiting boaters. Almond Walk, a gazebo at the center of the resort by the beach, is one of several locations for weddings and special events.

The resort has good entertainment, attracting guests from neighboring hotels as well as boaters. You can enjoy music in the lobby; the mellow calypso melodies of guitarist Eldon John; beach barbecues with calypso; and sunset, dinner, and moonlight cruises. Movies, major sporting events, and CNN's daily news program are shown at the Sand Palace, an open-air video and television theater. There's dancing under the stars at Almond Walk, with music by The Latitude Stars, a local band, or The Reflections, Bitter End's own steel band combo made up of eight employees who entertain several nights weekly.

Even with its expansion, Bitter End remains above all a yacht club. Nautical themes are everywhere, and the flags of yacht clubs from around the world hang in the Clubhouse. The resort's fleet of more than one hundred craft is available to guests for their unlimited use. It includes Freedom 30s, Boston Whalers, Rhodes 19s, Lasers, Mistral Sailboards, and Sunfish, among others. The resort offers day charters, deep-sea fishing boats, snorkeling, and sightseeing boats.

And if you don't know the difference between a jib and a spinnaker, Bitter End provides free sailing lessons, along with windsurfing and snorkeling instruction. Nick Trotter's Sailing School, based here, holds classes for boaters of all skill levels. Fast Tack each November is a monthlong, action-packed promotion of Bitter End's sailing facilities and includes Women's Sailing Week and Family Thanksgiving Week. During the Annual Pro-Am Regatta, guests get to sail with America's Cup–winning skippers and Olympic medalists. It's said to be the only event of its kind in the world. Daily dive classes for beginners and trips for certified divers are also available. A Junior Sailing Program is offered year-round for kids six years old and over. The resort also has a children's program with supervised water sports, crafts, and hikes.

Bitter End's easygoing atmosphere attracts sports enthusiasts of all ages—singles, couples, honeymooners, and families. Most are affluent, active, and somewhat preppie Americans, but there is a sprinkling of Europeans. Life here is so water oriented that those who have no interest in sailing or water sports should look elsewhere. But if you love the sea, this little corner of the Caribbean is paradise.

The Bitter End Yacht Club and Resort ✱✱✱

North Sound, Virgin Gorda, B.V.I.
Phone: (284) 494–2746; Fax: (284) 494–4756;
e-mail: binfo@beyc.com; www.beyc.com

Owner: Dana Hokin

Open: Year-round

Credit Cards: All major

U.S. Reservations: Bitter End Yacht Club and Resort, (312) 944–5855, (800) 872–2392; Fax: (312) 944–2860

Deposit: Three nights

Minimum Stay: None

Arrival/Departure: Transfers included in five-night packages; otherwise cost is $40 round-trip

Distance from Airport: (Virgin Gorda Airport) Thirty-minute bus ride (one-way, $12), plus ten-minute boat ride; or from Beef Island Airport via Bitter End's own North Sound Express high-speed ferry, a thirty-minute scenic trip from the airport directly to the resort, $20 per person ($40 round-trip), included in five-day package

Accommodations: 85 rooms and suites with verandas (45 in rustic cottages; 38 in deluxe chalets with twin, queen-size, or king-size beds; two-bedroom villa); four live-aboard boats

Amenities: Air-conditioning in deluxe units, ceiling fans; bath with shower only, hair dryers on request; coffeemaker, refrigerator; VCRs in suites; towels changed twice daily, nightly turndown service; phones; shops and mini-market; no television or room service

Electricity: 110 volts/60 cycles

Sports: Sailing, water sports (see text); one swimming pool, three beaches; jogging and exercise trail; aerobics; marina with thirty slips

Dress Code: Informal

Children: Six years and older; supervised activities; sailing lessons; baby-sitters

Meetings: Up to one hundred people; conference center; audiovisual equipment

Day Visitors: Welcome

Handicapped: Limited facilities

Packages: Honeymoon, family, live-aboard, weddings, dive, sailing school, wind-surfing; Island Cruise, Fast Tack

Rates: Two people, daily, FAP. **High Season** (mid-December–April 30): $500–$700. **Low Season** (May 1–October 31): $375–$525. **Sailing Season** (November 1–December 22): $400–$550.

Service Charge: 8 percent

Government Tax: 7 percent

LITTLE DIX BAY
Virgin Gorda, B.V.I.

Opened in 1964, Rockresorts—exclusive enclaves renowned for their spectacular natural settings, begun by conservationist pioneer Laurance Rockefeller (hence the name)—became the standard against which all other Caribbean resorts were measured.

Understated and environmentally sensitive long before conservation became fashionable, they were a new kind of resort, where less is more. The accommodations were almost spartan in their simplicity: no phones, air-conditioning, radios, television, or room keys. Peace, privacy, and natural beauty—not man-made trappings—were their special appeal.

The people who patronized them were not unlike Mr. Rockefeller—eastern establishment. They were Wall Street bankers, old money, Ivy Leaguers, Junior Leaguers, and their preppie offspring.

Despite changes in ownership over the years, the Rockresorts formula has remained more or less intact, enabling Little Dix—one of the Caribbean's most expensive resorts—to boast a year-round occupancy, a repeat business of 70 percent, and a place on the coveted ten best list of *The Hideaway Report* year after year.

But times have changed, even at Little Dix, and since 1992 (when the Rosewood group of Dallas took over), Little Dix has been undergoing a much needed renewal that has made it better than ever. Now, it has launched another phase of development that will add even more amenities and facilities, including new luxury accommodations, a spa, and some unusual dining and sports facilities.

Little Dix is set in a 500-acre garden paradise along a ½-mile white-sand beach on the southwestern side of Virgin Gorda, with the green slopes of Gorda Peak as a backdrop. Still exclusive but not quite as snooty as in its formative years, Little Dix's service and country club atmosphere begin as soon as you step off the plane at the tiny Virgin Gorda Airport (which Little Dix Bay owns). There you are met, registered, and driven directly to your beachside room, where you will find fresh flowers, a bottle of rum, and soft drinks.

Camouflaged under dense tropical foliage, Little Dix's spacious guest rooms, each with its own terrace overlooking the sea, are in clusters of cottages—some hexagonal and cone topped, some conventionally shaped—with two to eight rooms. Those rooms behind the beachfront cottages are perched on stilts like tree houses to catch the trade winds; they have ground-level patios and hammocks.

The rooms make use of native stone and island hardwoods in their decor created by a team from Vision Design of Dallas, and the results are fabulous. Without changing the spirit or character of Little Dix, the designers have put together an eclectic mix of traditional and contemporary decor in the wonderful manner of understatement that is Little Dix. The rooms are light and elegant yet comfortable and inviting as never before. They use earthy tones, accented with bleached wicker and cane furniture and made more plush; there are good reading lamps.

Bowing to today's needs, phones (which can be removed) and air-conditioning have been added in all the units. Walk-in closets contain umbrellas, walking sticks, a safe, and flashlights to help you find your way along the paths at night. Outside each cottage is a footbath to rinse the sand from your feet.

Perhaps even more telling about changing times, Little Dix is adding two luxurious villa suites, each with three bedrooms and a private pool. They are located at the west side of the resort on a small beach. In 2003, the resort will add an exotic spa where treatment rooms will be in simple, thatched huts.

Daytime activities—most included in the room rate—can be as strenuous as lazing on a bright blue float on smooth azure water (a protective reef keeps it that way) or more demanding: tennis, Sunfish sailing, waterskiing, and scuba lessons. A water taxi will take you to one of seven pristine beaches to snorkel, sunbathe, and picnic. Most fun of all may be a tennis challenge, with six or more people kept in constant motion by the Peter Burwash–trained pro who makes getting a workout lots of fun. And soon guests will be able to play croquet and boccie on courts in the green field near the tennis courts.

The center of life at Little Dix Bay is The Pavilion, a terrace with four interconnected dining and lounge areas topped with a soaring, four-point shingled roof where lavish breakfasts and lunch buffets, afternoon tea, and candlelight dinners are served. For Thursday lunch guests are taken by Boston Whalers to Spring Bay for a beach party. By the beach, the new Beach Grill specializes in Pacific Rim or fusion cuisine offering sushi, dim sum, and other pan-Asian specialties. The resort can also arrange private dinners on the beach with full service, tiki lights, and steel pan music, at an extra cost of $75.

Another new addition is a special private dining room for twelve with its own china and decor and personalized menus. The room, situated off to the side of The Pavilion, is equipped for meetings.

Cuisine in Rockresorts has traditionally been American and dependably good, but under Rosewood's executive chef, the cuisine has been upgraded and greatly improved with lighter, more imaginative and sophisticated fare.

The informal Sugar Mill Restaurant and Bar, adjacent to the main terrace, is a dinner alternative where wonderful seafood cuisine is the specialty and the service is first class all the way.

Indeed, service is one of Little Dix Bay's strengths. Most employees are Virgin Gorda natives who have been at Little Dix for more than two decades, giving the resort a sense of family.

As with so many other exclusive resorts, the need to attract a younger market and cater to the ever-increasing family market led Little Dix in 1995 to add a children's facility, The Children's Grove, which operates year-round. Children are divided into three age groups. All activities are supervised by a full-time, professional staff. The Children's Grove is open from 9:00 A.M. to 4:30 p.m. and 6:00 to 9:30 P.M., Monday to Saturday; closed on Sunday. Cost is $40 per child, per day, and $35 evenings.

Little Dix Bay ★★★★★

P.O. Box 70, Virgin Gorda, B.V.I.
Phone: (284) 495–5555, (800) 223–7637; Fax: (284) 495–5661; e-mail: www.rosewood-hotels.com

Owner/Management: Rosewood Hotels and Resorts
Regional Vice President Caribbean/Managing Director: Peter Shaindlin
Hotel Manager: John Macon
Open: Year round
Credit Cards: All major
U.S. Reservations: Rosewood Hotels and Resorts, (800) 928–3000, (214) 871–5454; Fax: (214) 871–5444; e-mail: guest-services@surfbvi.com
Deposit: Three nights; twenty-eight days cancellation in peak season; seven days cancellation in low season
Minimum Stay: Applies in high season; inquire in advance.
Arrival/Departure: Local transfer service included. For those arriving via St. Thomas, Little Dix has a new shuttle service that reduces transfer time and complicated plane connections. Guests are met and escorted to Crown Bay Marina to board a Sunseeker for the one-hour trip to Little Dix, complete with champagne and check-in. Round-trip: $250 per person.
Distance from Airport: *(Virgin Gorda Airport)* About 1 mile
Distance from Spanish Town: 2 miles; taxi one-way, $5.00
Accommodations: 97 double rooms
Amenities: Ceiling fans, air-conditioning; bath with double sinks, tub and shower, bathrobes, slippers, toiletries, hair dryers; telephones; minibars; safes; nightly turndown service, towels changed and ice service three times daily; room service
Electricity: 110 volts/60 cycles
Fitness Facilities/Spa Services: Fitness center with cardiovascular equipment; massage available
Sports: No swimming pool or windsurfing. Seven tennis courts (two lighted), clinics, resident pro; hiking trails; dive trips for fee
Dress Code: Gracious informality; trousers, collared shirts, and closed-toe shoes (no beach attire) required after 6:30 P.M.; jackets and ties not required
Children: All ages; Year-round program (see text); nanny service
Meetings: Up to twenty people
Day Visitors: Individuals welcome with reservations
Handicapped: Four rooms with facilities
Packages: Honeymoon, family, wedding
Rates: Two people, daily, EP. **High Season** (mid-December–March 31): $550–$1,400. **Shoulder Season** (April 1–31 and mid-November–mid-December): $325–$575. **Low Season:** $250–$400.
Service Charge: 5 percent of room; 15 percent of meals
Government Tax: 7 percent
Daily Surcharge: 5 percent

NECKER ISLAND
Virgin Gorda, Tortola, B.V.I.

For the ultimate escape to the ultimate private-island getaway, there is no better choice: the island haven created by Richard Branson, Britain's boy-wonder entrepreneur (founder of Virgin Records and Virgin Airways), as a holiday retreat for his family and friends.

As laid-back as his resort, Branson is so low-key that it's hard to link the man with the success story—until you see how it all comes together in his Caribbean paradise. Located at the northeastern end of the British Virgin Islands, Necker is a small, dry, rocky island encircled by coral reefs and lapped by the waters that run from cobalt and peacock blue to aquamarine. The island has dramatic scenery at every turn: jutting headlands interspersed with pristine beaches, panoramic hills, and cactus-studded ridges—and, always, that spectacular water.

By his telling, in the 1970s Branson (then still in his twenties) was in New York on business when he heard that some of the B.V.I. were up for sale. He went to have a look, but it took two years before the price was right. An environmental-impact study to help maintain the seventy-four-acre island's ecological balance was carried out, and construction atop Devil's Hill began in 1982. Wherever possible, natural materials—including the stone removed from the hilltop—were used in construction.

"I wanted the house designed in an airy Balinese style . . . where the architecture blends so well with the country and culture," Branson says. "I also wanted the house to become the apex of Devil's Hill, as if it grew out of the rock."

He got his wish. As you approach Necker you must look hard to see the Balinese-style villa, it harmonizes so well with the landscape.

The palatial mansion divides into two sections: an enormous living room and dining area in the front, and ten bedrooms on two levels to the back. The huge, open living room with exposed beams of Brazilian hardwood overhead and Yorkshire granite floors underfoot is created around a tropical garden. Large sections of the roof left as natural skylights and a retractable roof allow sunlight to shower the garden, creating a magical effect during the day and a canopy of stars at night.

The enormous room is a combination living-dining-bar area furnished with elephant bamboo chairs and over-size cushions on natural stone banquettes. A giant oak refectory table seating twenty-six people occupies one corner, a snooker table sits in another, and a piano and television and video cabinet with a library of movie cassettes a third. Steps in the center of the room lead up to a gallery lined with books, tapes, and games.

Surrounding the house on all sides are spacious terraces festooned with brilliant bougainvillea, allamanda, and other tropical flowers. The terraces overlook the sea and drop down to a lower level, where there is a swimming pool and

Jacuzzi. There's a telescope for serious stargazers and hammocks for guests who simply want to dream.

A breezeway with tropical greenery leading to the bedroom wing ends in front of a ceiling-to-floor waterfall that catches the light as it tumbles through a chain sculpture. The bedrooms, all with terraces, have views that embrace the sea, sky, sun, moon, and neighboring islands, too.

Named for Indonesian islands, the bedrooms combine vibrant Balinese fabrics—each with a different color scheme—and elephant bamboo furniture, accented by Haitian paintings. The master suite on the upper level is Branson's Bali—and it was Princess Diana's during her stay. It has a huge terrace and a large wooden deck with its own Jacuzzi. The villa has ten comfortable bathrooms with stone-grotto showers that cleverly conceal the drainpipes.

Menus feature sophisticated fare as fresh as the chef can make it. You are summoned to dinner by a gong and will feel as royal as a princess when you sit at the regal dining table. There are outside dining areas as well.

Both sides of the island are etched with dreamy white-sand beaches. Turtle Beach, on the west, has a fine coral reef only a short snorkel away. Well Bay, a long curve of sand on the southeast, has a raised Balinese pavilion with giant bamboo chairs and ottomans. It overlooks the tennis courts and the new swimming pool. Alongside the pool is a bar in the shape of a 30-foot crocodile, seating thirty.

Off in the distance on the northwestern tip of Necker is a smaller version of the main house—Bali Hi, as it is called, and to the right is Bali Lo. They are fully furnished in the same manner as the main house. Bali Hi has a plunge pool; Bali Lo, a full-size pool. Bali Cliff, attached to Bali Hi, has a rather bizarre layout with a living room on one level, a bedroom on a higher level that virtually hangs over a cliff, and an open-air bath downstairs—all with expansive views.

Walks around the island are wonderful. A nature trail runs downhill to mangroves and ponds; other paths lead to lookouts. Part of Necker has been designated a bird sanctuary, and whales are often sighted offshore in February and March. The island has a full array of watersports equipment for guests to use at will.

Necker is not rented in the conventional way of a hotel, and the price is prohibitive for most people unless they can round up twenty-three friends—even twelve affluent ones will do. The price includes the entire island and all its facilities; managers and a staff of twenty-eight; all meals for up to twenty-four people; an open bar, wine, and champagne. A local calypso band for a party evening is also included. Four times a year, during Celebration Weeks, the resort takes bookings on an individual basis.

Necker is very romantic and very glamorous, and it would probably appeal to anyone who can afford it. But it helps if you relish unforgettable natural beauty and exquisite man-made comfort.

Necker Island ★★★★★

Box 1091, Virgin Gorda, Tortola, B.V.I.
Phone: (284) 494–2757; Fax: (284) 494–4396;
www.virgin.com/necker

Owner: Richard Branson

General Managers: Rebecca Leigh and Martayn Brouwer

Open: Year-round

Credit Cards: None

U.S. Reservations: Resorts Management, Inc., (800) 557–4255, (212) 696–4566, Fax: (212) 689–1598

Deposit: 20 percent at booking, 40 percent six months prior to arrival, balance three months prior. Inquire regarding refund policy.

Minimum Stay: None

Arrival/Departure: Transfers included by boat from Virgin Gorda (fifteen minutes) or Beef Island (forty minutes)

Distance from Other Islands: Virgin Gorda, 1 mile; Tortola, 8 miles

Accommodations: One master and nine double bedrooms (four convertible to two suites, all with terraces and twin beds or king), ten bathrooms; one cottage for two people; one cottage for four people

Amenities: Ceiling fans; satellite television, VCR; bath with shower only, hair dryer, toiletry amenities, bathrobe; business facilities; helicopter landing pad; video, book, and music libraries

Electricity: 110 volts

Sports: Two freshwater swimming pools, two Jacuzzis; snorkeling, waterskiing, sailing, sea kayaking, windsurfing; two lighted tennis courts and equipment; gym with exercise equipment; Lasers, Sunfish, catamaran, light tackle, fishing equipment; snooker table, children's books and games

Children: All ages

Dress Code: None

Meetings: Up to twenty-six people

Day Visitors: No

Handicapped: No facilities

Packages: All-inclusive

Rates: Daily, All-inclusive. One–seven people, $15,000; eight–fourteen people, $22,500; fifteen–nineteen people, $28,500, twenty–twenty-four people, $36,000. Two additional people can be accommodated; inquire. Celebration Weeks: Twice a year, bookings on an individual basis; inquire.

Service Charge: 2.5 percent

Government Tax: Included

Cayman Islands

Known as the Mount Everest of diving, the Cayman Islands are a British Crown Colony tucked under the western end of Cuba. The group is comprised of three low-lying islands almost completely surrounded by reefs: Grand Cayman, the resort and commercial center; Cayman Brac, a string bean of untamed wilderness, 89 miles to the northeast; and Little Cayman, the smallest, 5 miles west of Cayman Brac.

One of the most prosperous places in the Caribbean, the islands have excellent communications, their own airline and currency—and a population of only 25,000. Early in their history they were a favorite hiding place for pirates, and Pirates' Week, held in October, is a frolicking annual commemoration of the islands' history.

Grand Cayman, with the capital at George Town, is the largest of the trio. Seven Mile Beach, where the majority of the hotels are located, is a magnificent crest of powdery white sand just north of George Town. The 22-mile-long island rises only 60 feet above sea level and is made up largely of lagoons and mangroves rich in bird life.

Across one of these areas, North Sound, lies a barrier reef, and just inside the mouth is one of the Caribbean's most unusual sites. Dubbed Stingray City, it offers divers and snorkelers a thrilling opportunity to touch, feed, and photograph a dozen or more friendly stingrays in only 12 feet of water.

Grand Cayman also has the world's only sea turtle farm, where you can see turtles at various stages of development in their breeding pans. For a nominal fee you can sponsor a turtle for release to the ocean.

Under the sea the Caymans are surrounded by extensive cliffs, slopes, and valleys of submerged mountains, collectively known as the Cayman Wall, and densely encrusted with forests of corals, giant sponges, and other marine life. Nondivers can see the Caymans' underwater splendors thanks to recreational submarines.

Cayman Brac is 12 square miles of untamed tropics yet to be discovered by nature buffs for its hiking, fishing, birding, and caving. Little Cayman is even less developed. The 10-mile-long island has large expanses of mangroves and lagoons and is surrounded by long stretches of white-sand beaches, extensive reefs, and spectacular walls that some experts consider to make up the finest diving in the Western Hemisphere.

Information

Cayman Islands Department of Tourism, 6100 Blue Lagoon Drive, Miami, FL 33126;
(305) 266–2300; www.caymanislands.ky. Offices are in Chicago, Houston, New York, and Toronto.

HYATT REGENCY GRAND CAYMAN
Grand Cayman, B.W.I.

Whether you are lounging around the elegant pool with its colonnaded gazebo and swim-up bar, sipping a cool drink on your private veranda by the golf course, or trying your hand at croquet, at the Hyatt a glance in any direction pleases the eye.

The overall impression is of harmony and beauty. Buildings, landscaping, lounges, guest rooms, and courtyards all point to the fact that the architects and interior designers really got this one right. Another element that pleases is the pristine quality of the property.

Located only a few miles outside George Town, the Hyatt Regency Grand Cayman is the centerpiece of the ninety-acre Britannia resort complex, which includes a golf course, a private marina, and a residential community of attractive villas. Its design is British colonial inspired, but don't look for any faded chintz-covered chairs or sofas here. At the Hyatt all furnishings have a spit-and-polish look that speaks to travelers who seek a luxurious yet low-key ambience. The architecture actually incorporates a variety of classic elements—French doors, colonnaded gazebos, Spanish courtyards, and high, beamed ceilings—that create a wonderful airy, sumptuous, tropical ambience on one of the Caribbean's driest islands.

The plush appointments use custom-designed bleached ash, rattan, wicker, teak, and Honduran mahogany furniture throughout, some accented with leather trim. Designer fabrics awash with Caribbean colors—aqua, coral, pink, lilac, and earth tones—complement the flowers in the magnificently landscaped grounds.

Hyatt's sports facilities are a big attraction. Leading the list is the unusual golf course, designed by Jack Nicklaus. It's an eighteen-hole course built within the acreage normally required for a regulation nine-hole course. Nicklaus had only forty acres, so he designed a special ball, known as the short ball, which goes only half the distance of a normal

one. The resulting game is now known as Cayman Golf.

The undulating greens are reminiscent of some famous Scottish layouts; to create a course in this dry environment that has the morning-dew look of the Highlands is an amazing achievement. The course can be played three ways: as a nine-hole championship course, an eighteen-hole executive course, or an eighteen-hole Cayman Ball course. There are clinics and a pro shop. Hyatt guests may book tee times up to forty-eight hours in advance.

Guest rooms and suites, housed in clusters of low-rise buildings, are outstanding, with luxurious appointments in casual island style. All rooms have step-out French balconies—except terrace rooms, which have large furnished patios. The suites are bilevel and have king-size beds and stocked minibars. Some guest rooms look out at the tennis courts or croquet lawn, others at the golf course or the manicured gardens of the courtyard with waterfalls and a reflecting pond. Two buildings house the Regency Club's one- and two-bedroom villas. The club has a concierge and lounge where continental breakfast and cocktails are served.

Along the edge of the golf course and by the marina are beautiful one- and two-bedroom villas, ideal for families. They have private patios or balconies that open onto the golf course through elegant French doors and come equipped with kitchens with a microwave, dishwasher, washer, and dryer. Each has large walk-in closets and two bathrooms. Villa guests enjoy all the amenities and facilities offered at the Hyatt.

In 1998 the Hyatt added a brand-new complex directly on the beach. This $15 million annex is a hotel-within-a-hotel with its own concierge, forty-four one-bedroom junior suites, and nine two-bedroom suites. All suites have full kitchens with microwave ovens and stoves, as well as upgraded in-room amenities including a fax machine, terry robes, and keyed elevator access. The complex is built around a landscaped garden with waterfalls and three interconnected freshwater pools embellished with bronze sea turtle sculptures and mosaic tile designs of stingrays and other marine life. There is a coffee bar and ice cream cafe, a rooftop sundeck, a health club, a Red Sail Sports facility with a scuba training center, retail shops, a TCBY, and Bamboo, a new sushi restaurant. The health club, open daily from 6:30 a.m. to 8:30 p.m., is equipped with Nautilus weight stations, free weights, Lifecycles, treadmills, and Stairmasters. There is a second health club on the first floor of the Britannia Beauty Spa.

The Hyatt's main buildings are not on the beach but directly across the road from Grand Cayman's famous Seven Mile Beach, where the resort has a private beach club with a swimming pool, restaurant, and bar. The resort's main free-form pool with a swim-up bar and

Jacuzzi covers one-third of an acre. There are tennis courts and an English Tea Garden with a croquet lawn.

The main restaurant, the Garden Loggia, has a lovely indoor-outdoor setting in the interior courtyard gardens. Casual for breakfast, it is more elegant with candlelight when dinner is served here during the winter season. Sunday brunch is an elaborate affair. Light lunches and sunset dining can be enjoyed at Hemingway's at the beach club. The Britannia Golf Club Bar and Grill also serves lunch and dinner, and there are grills by the pool and beach. Live entertainment can usually be enjoyed in the restaurants or bars daily, except Sunday.

Red Sail Sports, Hyatt's water-sports operator, offers a full range of water sports, a dive program, and deep-sea fishing for an extra charge. The hotel's own 65-foot catamaran offers daily snorkeling and sunset and evening cruises. From the marina, boats have direct access to North Sound, the main area for diving, fishing, and snorkeling, and Rum Point, where Hyatt operates a beach facility that includes a restaurant in a pretty outdoor setting with picnic-style tables and another restaurant open for dinner. Red Sail Sports has a full-scale water-sports center here, too. Rum Point overlooks Grand Cayman's famous Stingray City, where you can swim with a dozen friendly rays in gin-clear water only 12 feet deep. The Rum Pointer Ferry, which Hyatt operates, makes several trips daily to Rum Point.

The Britannia Beauty Spa at the Hyatt Regency is a full-service spa offering hydrotherapy, seaweed wraps, reflexology, massage, aromatherapy, body exfoliating, and more. The two-story facility, staffed with eight European-trained therapists, has two wet and four multipurpose dry treatment rooms—each with its own stereo system, shower and changing facilities, and relaxation room. The resort's second health club is on the ground floor, and an outdoor pool is adjacent to a juice bar. The spa, open from 8:00 a.m. to 8:00 p.m., serves health-conscious Cuisine Naturelle and natural juice drinks. Treatments are available a la carte as well as in four- and eight-day spa packages.

For families with children, Camp Hyatt is a year-round program of supervised activities for children three to twelve years old. Housed in an 1,800-square-foot facility for the exclusive use of Camp Hyatt, it offers arts and crafts, sand castle building, movies, excursions, and more. There are special children's menus, a frequent-stay program, and a chance for families to book a second room at half the price of the parents' room, subject to availability.

The Hyatt Regency Grand Cayman is geared to an upscale audience. It works very well for couples, singles, and families, as well as for business meeting participants and anyone who wants to play golf on one of the Caribbean's most unusual courses. And it would certainly make a fabulous prize for any incentive-award winner.

Hyatt Regency Grand Cayman ★★★★

Seven Mile Beach, Grand Cayman, B.W.I.
Phone: (345) 949–1234; Fax: (345) 949–8528; www.hyatt.com

Owner: Britannia/Ellesmere Development Ltd.

General Manager: Mark Bastis

Open: Year-round

Credit Cards: All major

U.S. Reservations: Hyatt Worldwide, (800) 233–1234

Deposit: Varies with season

Minimum Stay: Applies in holiday seasons; inquire.

Arrival/Departure: Transfer service arranged for fee

Distance from Airport: (Owen Roberts International Airport) 2½ miles; taxi one-way, $15.50 per person

Distance from George Town: 2 miles; taxi one-way, $8.00

Accommodations: 289 guest rooms and suites in two- to four-story buildings, including 44 Regency Club rooms, 53 one- and two-bedroom suites in beachfront annex, and 50 one- to four-bedroom villas; guest rooms have two doubles or king; one-bedroom villas have king; two-bedroom have king, two doubles, and Roman tub in master bath

Amenities: Air-conditioning, ceiling fans; bath with tub and shower, hair dryer, toiletries basket; international direct-dial telephone, clock-radio, television; stocked minibar; coffeemakers; iron and ironing board; safe; washer and dryer in villas; room service twenty-four hours daily; shops, concierge, beauty salon; Regency Club: Club lounge; continental breakfast, evening cocktails and hors d'oeuvres; concierge; upgraded amenities and linens

Electricity: 110 volts

Fitness Facilities/Spa Services: Two health clubs/fitness centers; full-service spa (see text)

Sports: Freshwater swimming pool, Jacuzzi; free use of four lighted tennis courts; croquet, dive shop, water sports extra; golf (see text)

Dress Code: Casual

Children: All ages; cribs; baby-sitters; Camp Hyatt; children's menus; frequent-stay program; second room at half price of parents' room, subject to availability

Meetings: Up to 300 people

Day Visitors: Day room available

Handicapped: Facilities

Packages: Honeymoon, golf, dive, spa

Rates: Per room, single or double, daily, EP. **High Season** (mid-December–mid-April): $375–$675. **Shoulder Season** (mid-April–May 31 and October 1–mid-December): $260–$525. **Low Season** (June 1–September 30): $210–$480. For special suites and villa rates, inquire.

Service Charge: 10 percent on room; 15 percent on food and beverages

Government Tax: 10 percent on room only

PIRATES POINT RESORT
Little Cayman, Cayman Islands, B.W.I.

Unusual if not unique. Pirates Point is a diver's resort owned and operated by Gladys Howard from Tyler, Texas.

What's unusual about that?

Gladys also happens to be an award-winning cookbook author and a Cordon Bleu chef who has studied with Julia Child, James Beard, and Lucy Lo. And she operated an international cooking school and gourmet catering service in East Texas for twenty years.

When you arrive at the Edward Bodden International Airport, Gladys meets you in her van or truck for the 1/2-mile ride to the resort. Don't let the airport name fool you. It's a grass strip with a wooden shack; Little Cayman has a total population of one hundred people.

Pirates Point consists of a central pavilion that includes the front desk, lounge and bar, dining room and outdoor barbecue, and four cottages constructed of cut stone and wood. They're only twenty steps from the beach. Three of the cottages have two units each, and one has five units. Two cottages have large verandas.

The little inn is immaculate. Rooms are spacious and surprisingly pleasant and comfortable, given their rustic setting. They have white stucco and wood-paneled walls and high wood-beamed ceilings. Furnished in wicker, they have either two twin beds or one king. In the bathroom you'll find fluffy towels, terry robes, and a shower with hot and cold water. Pirates Point has its own reverse-osmosis plant, which helps ensure a freshwater supply. The resort has one telephone and a VCR and videocassettes in the lounge.

Each year Gladys repaints all guest rooms and buildings as well as overhauls and refits the *Yellow Rose III,* the resort's 42-foot custom dive boat. For her tenth anniversary in 1996, she built a new kitchen and added an Olympic-size freshwater pool and a ten-person Jacuzzi surrounded by an 8-foot deck. She also added a second 1,200-gallon reverse-osmosis plant and 24,000-gallon cistern. Now, she has enlarged the bar.

The complex is shaded by large almond, sea grape, and coconut palm trees. Along the path by the cactus garden leading to the reception area, you will notice some sculptures made from coconuts, driftwood, and other natural material. What started as a pastime has developed into a wacky tradition, and now these "works of art" by guests decorate the bar and add character to the inn. Since 1988 Gladys has run an annual contest for the most original creation; the prize is a week's vacation at the resort.

You can count on the food to be good. Gladys uses whatever she can get and works miracles in her new kitchen. It is difficult to get products locally, except fish. Her supplies come by boat from Grand Cayman, and she flies in fresh fruits and vegetables.

For this caterer and gourmet chef, dining is serious business. There's no roughing it here: You'll dine with crystal stemware and linen napkins even at picnics. Lunch, an outdoor buffet under the sea grape trees, is in your swimsuit, and dinner offers a buffet and table service in the dining room. There is a barbecue on Thursday and Saturday, weather permitting, and sunset wine and cheese.

A coral atoll 10 miles long and 1 mile wide, Little Cayman is one of diving's last frontiers. Its Bloody Bay Wall is one of life's great diving experiences. Rising to within 20 feet of the surface and plunging in sheer cliffs more than a mile deep, these pristine formations offer marine life found nowhere else. There are giant sponges, trees of black coral, elaborate sea fans, and eagle rays, to name a few. The late Philippe Cousteau called it one of the three finest dive areas in the world.

Pirates Point is located only 2 miles or a five-minute fast boat ride from the wall. The resort has a full scuba operation with six instructors on staff who handle everything from a short resort course to full certification and advanced training. The resort offers two dives daily and night dives by request.

Good snorkeling (gear costs extra) can be enjoyed directly in front of the resort about 10 feet from shore. There is diving nearby, and the resort has a fast boat to reach the more dramatic dive sites on the wall. You can have an underwater video of your dives shot for an additional charge.

The resort has a sandy beach, but the entrance into the water from shore is rocky and better made from its small pier, which puts you into about 3 feet of water. Pirates Point often takes all the guests for a picnic lunch on nearby cays and can arrange fishing and group-dive programs on request.

Gladys chairs the Little Cayman National Trust, which has created trails for hiking and bird-watching. The Caymans are a flyover for North American birds, and Little Cayman is a sanctuary for the red-footed booby and frigate bird. It also has its own island lake for tarpon fishing, with an endemic subspecies.

Pirates Point is operated as an all-inclusive resort. The package includes accommodations with private bath, three meals daily with wine, an open bar with unlimited drinks, two boat dives daily, tanks, weights, belt, guide, transfer to and from the airport, and the use of bicycles, beach towels, and terry robes. Add the experience of diving at Little Cayman and Gladys's food, and Pirates Point tallies up as one of the best buys in the Caribbean.

Pirates Point Resort * 🌿

Box 43LC, Little Cayman, Cayman Islands, B.W.I.
Phone: (345) 948–1010; Fax: (345) 948–1011;
www.piratespointresort.com

Owner/Manager: Gladys B. Howard

Open: Year-round except mid-September–early October

Credit Cards: Visa, MasterCard, Discover

U.S. Reservations: Direct to hotel

Deposit: Half total reservation within ten days of booking; thirty days cancellation, refund half of deposit; fewer than thirty days, deposit forfeited

Minimum Stay: Three nights

Arrival/Departure: Complimentary transfer service

Distance from Airport: *(Boden Airport)* ½ mile; no taxi service (Little Cayman is 90 miles northeast of Grand Cayman; Island Air provides daily flights from George Town.)

Distance from South Town: ¾ mile

Accommodations: 11 rooms in bungalows (five air-conditioned; six oceanfront); doubles have twins or king; maximum of twenty divers

Amenities: Ceiling fans, floor fans; five rooms with air-conditioning; baths with shower only; custom 42-foot Newton dive boat; no room service

Electricity: 110 volts

Sports: See text

Dress Code: Very casual

Children: Over five years of age, but must be over twelve to dive

Meetings: Up to twenty people

Day Visitors: Welcome, with reservations

Handicapped: No facilities

Packages: All-inclusive, dive

Rates: Per person, double, daily, AP. *High Season* (mid-December–mid-April): $250 diver; $195 nondiver. *Low Season:* $220 diver; $170 nondiver. Single supplement, $80 per day.

Service Charge: 15 percent

Government Tax: $8.00 per room daily

Curaçao

Only 30 miles off the coast of Venezuela, the cosmopolitan capital of the Netherlands Antilles is noted for its commerce, diversity of restaurants, and fashionable shops with goods from around the world. These features are found side by side with the colorful colonial harbor of Willemstad, making it easy and fun to explore on foot.

At the heart of the compact historic old city are Fort Amsterdam, the Governor's Palace, the eighteenth-century Dutch Reform Church, and, nearby, Mikve Israel-Emanuel Synagogue, the oldest synagogue in the Americas (founded in 1654).

Juxtaposed against the sophisticated city center is the little-known landscape of windswept shores, chalky mountains, and rugged terrain, as well as two of the best nature parks in the Caribbean. In the 3,500-acre Christoffel National Park, the cactus grow as tall as trees. Dominated by the rocky peak of 1,238-foot Mount Christoffel, the park has 20 miles of roads with color-coded routes for self-guided tours and hiking trails.

Curaçao is completely surrounded by reefs with an extraordinary variety of coral and fish that are only now being discovered by divers. The 1,500-acre Curaçao Underwater Park, stretching for 121/2 miles from the Princess Beach Hotel to the eastern tip of the island, protects some of Curaçao's finest reefs. Many areas can be enjoyed by snorkelers as well as divers. East of the marine park is the Curaçao Aquarium, a private facility where 400 species of marine life native to Curaçao waters are displayed.

Quiet seas wash Curaçao's western shores, but wild surf crashes against the windward north. The coast has many small coves with beaches and large bays or lagoons with very narrow entrances and wide basins. These waterways are among Curaçao's most distinctive features. Some lagoons are used for commerce, others for sport.

On the east, Spanish Water is one of the island's largest, prettiest lagoons with a long, narrow opening to the sea. It has hilly green fingers and coves, islands and beaches, and is the boating and fishing center with marinas and water-sports facilities. Santa Barbara, on its eastern side, is a popular public beach with changing facilities.

The constant northeastern trade winds that cool the island have made windsurfing one of Curaçao's most popular sports, with international recognition and an Olympic champion. Annually in June the Curaçao Open International Pro-Am Windsurf Championship attracts world masters. The most popular windsurfing area is on the southern coast between Willemstad and Spanish Water, also the site of the island's main hotels and water-sports centers.

Information

Curaçao Tourism Development Bureau, 475 Park Avenue South, Suite 2000, New York, NY 10016; (212) 683–7660, (800) 270–3350; www.curacao.tourism.com

CURAÇAO MARRIOTT BEACH RESORT & EMERALD CASINO

Curaçao, N.A.

Curaçao's first large, deluxe beach resort in more than twenty years when it opened in 1992, the Curaçao Marriott Beach Resort & Emerald Casino is something of a monument to the island's architecture and rich history. From the magnificent facade of the hotel in deep ochre stucco and white gabled trim to the traditional red tile roof and colonnaded promenades, you can pick up echoes of the island's past.

More so than other former colonies, Curaçao's Dutch heritage is evident throughout the island in its architec

ture. The colorful stucco buildings that line the harbor and streets of Willemstad, the capital; the historic landhuis, or manor houses, that dot the countryside; the homes in the Scharloo area, during the nineteenth century a lively neighborhood of wealthy merchants—all are relics of the colonial era. In addition to the Dutch touch, the architecture was shaped by the spirited colors and exuberant flair of Spanish, Latin American, and African influences.

All served as the inspiration for original designers Mary Jane Rosa and John Olson, who spent days combing neighborhoods, noting details, getting ideas, and even collecting paint chips to re-create authentic colors. The results are subtle and sophisticated—a modern interpretation of historical tradition without the use of excessive curlicues and other decorative touches solely for effect.

Set on Piscadera Bay, the tropically elegant three-story resort stretches along a white-sand beach on the southern end of the island, ten minutes from the airport and from downtown Willemstad and next door to the World Trade Center Curaçao.

A circular driveway fronted by a massive gabled roof, a fountain, a garden driveway, and pith-helmeted bellhops makes for a grand entrance. As you walk up a set of steps into the hotel, you can look through the open-air lobby to a fabulous view of the white sandy beach and the turquoise Caribbean waters.

On the periphery of the hotel, a shaded promenade of bellied columns, symmetrically bowed in the typical fashion of Curaçao, frames the marvelous ocean views and blurs the line between indoor and outdoor living. The lobby, with its rich wooden ceiling and weathered brass fixtures, is meant to recall the Curaçao of the eighteenth and nineteenth centuries, when it was a major hub for trade ships cruising between Europe and South America. The result was the Curaçao style, an eclectic blend of decorative themes and products from all over the world.

The lobby's front desk is made entirely of wood panels crisscrossed with carved, rope-style moldings. Sturdy unfinished wooden furniture with carved detailing and textured upholstery in deep colors lends a Dutch flavor to the sitting areas.

A modern accent is added by a large metal abstract wall sculpture by local Curaçaoan artist Yubi Kirindongo,

and Grille reflects this pleasing melting pot of styles. The mahogany bar, chairs, and couches are of differing styles, though the dark woods and rich tapestry fabrics help unite the room and make an inviting setting for evening relaxing.

Recalling the elegant Scharloo court-yards, tiled pathways—lined with more white columns and flaming bougainvillea—lead to the turquoise doors of the plush guest rooms. The large, air-conditioned rooms, with furnished balconies or terraces and full or partial ocean views, are appointed in pale wood with gentle pastel florals and original art.

The immense pool and beach area, graced with fountains and lush tropical greenery, is the center of the hotel—and the action. Comfy chaise lounges ring the free-form pool, which has a swim-up bar, a wading pool, and two large whirlpools. A shack dispenses beach towels, and an outdoor grill serves up burgers and barbecued chicken. A beach hut for resort activities is also available for special events and groups of up to a hundred.

The man-made beach—the largest of any Curaçao resort—is wide, long, and studded with thatched shelters under which you can escape the hot sun. Caribbean Sea Sports, which operates directly on the beach, offers snorkeling, waterskiing, windsurfing, sailing, and scuba diving lessons and equipment rentals. It also has a new lobby shop.

The Palm Cafe on the terrace overlooking the pool and beach is open from early morning to 11:00 A.M. and noon to 9:30 P.M. to provide convenient dining all day. The casual restaurant, reminiscent of a Spanish colonial courtyard, has a semi-enclosed garden setting with white-lattice-trimmed coral walls and verdigris iron terrace chairs and tables. The restaurant is not inexpensive, but servings are generous.

which hangs near the concierge desk. Two fiber wall hangings by Alexander Calder and a commissioned floral painting by Lucio Pozzi are just across the way.

Matching pieces of furniture or one singular design style were rare in Curaçaoan households. The Emerald Bar

For dinner, Portofino is a glass-enclosed restaurant with high ceilings, palm-frond fans, hand-painted tiles, and Renaissance-style murals around the walls. It provides an elegant setting for enjoying outstanding northern Italian cuisine as well as pizza and pasta. Recently it has been expanded to offer alfresco dining on the patio adjacent to the restaurant. The Emerald Bar and Grille is a classic American steakhouse featuring premium cuts of beef and grilled fish and poultry in a setting reminiscent of an English men's club. The restaurant and bar feature light jazz piano background music nightly.

Across from the restaurant, the Emerald Casino—fashioned after the patios or courtyards at the center of Scharloo homes—glitters with elegance and sophistication. An opulent French crystal chandelier 8 feet in diameter sparkles overhead against a white-clouds-on-blue-sky mural. The custom-woven carpet has a tile pattern of tulips and circles found on the exterior of a nineteenth-century Scharloo home. The casino offers blackjack, roulette, craps, mini-baccarat, and slot machines.

In addition to water sports, the resort's sports and fitness facilities include two lighted tennis courts, a health club with a gym, two saunas, two steam rooms, and a massage room. There are aerobics classes, Universal machines, exercise bikes, stair climbers, and free weights. The Fitness Center provides exercise and strength-training equipment. The resort has a beauty salon, shopping arcade, and business center offering fax, copying, computer and Internet access, and business services. The hotel offers shuttle service to town.

The hotel welcomes children through its program for ages five to twelve. The center has supplies, toys, and a nearby playground. There is a fee of $5.00 to $10.00 per day, depending on the activities scheduled. It is open from 10:00 a.m. to noon and 1:30 to 4:30 p.m. Wednesday through Sunday and from 6:30 to 9:30 p.m. on Saturdays. Up to two children under twelve may stay in their parents' room and eat for free.

Meeting facilities are centered on the Queen's Ballroom, which has a distinctly Spanish flavor and Old World, formal atmosphere. It takes its cue from the Scharloo *salas*, rooms saved for special celebrations filled with music and dancing.

The Marriott was a welcome addition to Curaçao; it has rejuvenated the island's lackluster hotel scene and helped raise the standard of service and luxury on the island. The resort has received the coveted Four Diamond rating from the AAA.

On a clear night—and every night in Curaçao is clear—there's a touch of Caribbean magic when you sink your body into the bubbling waters of an outdoor Jacuzzi and watch moon shadows dance upon the yellow gables, white columns, and crimson tiles of this most modern yet delightfully traditional resort.

Curaçao Marriott Beach Resort & Emerald Casino ★★★★

Piscadera Bay, P.O. Box 6003, Curaçao, N.A.
Phone: (599) 9–736–8800; Fax: (599) 9–462–7502;
wwwmarriotthotels.com/curmc or www.offshoreresorts.com

Owner: Reef Resorts
General Manager: George Landa
Open: Year-round
Credit Cards: Most major
U.S. Reservations: (800) 223 6388
Deposit: One night with credit card; three days cancellation in high season
Minimum Stay: Five nights Christmas/New Year's; none in low season
Arrival/Departure: Transfers not available
Distance from Airport: 10 miles; taxi one-way, $15
Distance from Town: 5 miles; taxi one-way, $7.00
Accommodations: 247 rooms and ten suites, with balconies or patios (eight terrace suites and two Presidential Suites with ocean view; 124 with king, 123 with queens)
Amenities: Air-conditioning; bath with tub, shower, toiletries, hair dryer; remote control television with cable; radio; stocked minibar; telephone; safe; iron and ironing board; casino; turn-down service on request, room service 6:00 A.M.–midnight
Electricity: 110 volts
Fitness Facilities/Spa Services: Fitness center with aerobics classes, Universal equipment, steam rooms, massages, saunas; beauty salon
Sports: Freshwater swimming pool, two outdoor whirlpools; two free, lighted tennis courts; water-sports center for snorkeling, waterskiing, windsurfing, sailing, and diving lessons and equipment rentals
Dress Code: Casual by day; casually elegant in evening; jackets and ties not required
Children: Up to two children under twelve years old free in parents' room, including meals; children's program (see text); cribs, high chairs; baby-sitters
Meetings: Up to 400 people; hotel adjacent to the World Trade Center Curaçao
Day Visitors: May use pool, beach, fitness center, tennis courts, and other facilities for $20 per person; limited if hotel is busy
Handicapped: Available on request
Packages: Family, diving, honeymoon; Ultimate Indulgence
Rates: Per room, EP. *High Season* (early January–March): $259–$299. *Low Season* (June–mid-December): $139–$169. Meal plans available.
Service Charge: 12 percent
Government Tax: 7 percent

Dominican Republic

The Dominican Republic is a land of superlatives: the oldest country of the Caribbean, with the tallest mountains and the lowest lake. Historic Santo Domingo was the first Spanish settlement in the New World. Here the Spaniards built their first cathedral, first hospital, first university, and first fortress.

The Old City has been beautifully restored and is alive with restaurants, shops, art galleries, and museums. Columbus Square boasts the oldest cathedral in the Americas.

Modern Santo Domingo, the fun-loving, sophisticated capital with Old-World charm, has more than one million people and about the lowest prices in the Caribbean. The modern Plaza de la Cultura is the heart of the capital's cultural life. It includes the National Theatre, where plays, concerts by the National Symphony Orchestra and jazz ensembles, and performances by visiting artists are held.

But Santo Domingo is far more than history and culture. Dominicans are warm and friendly and love to have a good time, and their city bounces with every sort of entertainment, from piano bars and smart supper clubs to brassy cabarets.

Shopping is best at the central market, Mercado Modelo. You'll know you're in the right place when you smell freshly roasted Dominican coffee. It's for sale at the entrance. The Mercado is stacked with fruits and vegetables and so many great buys that you could stock up on a year's worth of presents and pay for your trip with the savings!

One of the city's most unusual attractions, Los Tres Ojos (the three eyes) Park, is a subterranean cave with three lagoons, each with different water: sweet, salt, and sulfur.

From the rolling terrain of the east and south, the land rises toward the island's center in two tree-covered spines where two national parks contain the country's highest peaks—three that are more than 10,000 feet high and several rising to almost 9,000 feet—with trails.

In the northeastern corner Samana Peninsula and Bay is one of the most beautiful and least developed areas. From December to March whales play at the mouth of the bay. On the Rio Limon, in the center of the peninsula, a footpath leads to a magnificent waterfall, all but hidden amid the savage beauty of the thickly forested mountains. On the southern side of the bay, Los Haitises National Park is a 100-mile karst region with dense mangroves, estuaries, and tiny cays that are rookeries for seabirds.

Information

Dominican Republic Tourist Office, 1501 Broadway, Suite 410, New York, NY 10036;
(888) 374–6361 or (212) 575–4966; Fax: (212) 575–5448; www.dominicana.com.do

CASA DE CAMPO
La Romana, Dominican Republic

Think big. Three golf courses, fourteen swimming pools, thirteen tennis courts, fifteen restaurants, three polo fields and 150 polo ponies, a hundred-station sporting clays center, a fitness center, a water-sports center, a fleet of sport-fishing boats, a 5,000-seat amphitheater, a museum, an art school, a replica of a sixteenth-century Mediterranean village, an international airport, 300 guest rooms, and 150 villas on 7,000 acres.

Yes, it's big. But Casa de Campo is never overwhelming or noisy or crowded, as megaresorts often are. On the contrary, it's tranquil and very private. *Casa de campo* means "a house in the country" in Spanish and despite its size, Casa actually has that feeling to it.

Set in pretty rolling countryside in the southeastern corner of the Dominican Republic near the sugar-producing town of La Romana, Casa de Campo began in the early 1970s as a private retreat for local sugar barons, who played polo and golf on a preserve owned by Gulf & Western whose founder, the late Charles Bluhdorn, developed the property into a sprawling resort. Later Gulf & Western sold it to the present owners, brothers Jose "Pepe" and Alphonso Fanjul, who developed it further. Today it is something of a sophisticated amusement park and a posh country club with Caribbean attractions and Spanish charm, appealing to families, honeymooners, sportsmen, incentive winners, and just about anyone who wants a vacation with lots of choices at affordable prices.

In 1999, after being hit broadside by storms, Casa de Campo closed for three months to complete a $24 million renovation. It retained its casually elegant style, but returning guests see a new entrance and palm-thatched porte cochere leading to the new lobby of the main building. This building holds the guest services area, Excel Club VIP lounge, transportation center, La Cana Bar, and Business Center—all sporting a new look created by Dominican designer Patricia Reid, who combined the textures and colors of fine fabrics and plantation-style furniture with island craftsmanship, local coral rock, rich woods, and woven palms to integrate Dominican cultural elements into the decor throughout the resort.

All 300 guest rooms and many facilities were completely redecorated and upgraded. Rooms come in three categories: standard, superior, and luxury. All are spacious and furnished with two double beds or a king and have a private balcony or terrace with views of the golf courses or gardens. Each room is equipped with a minibar, a coffeemaker, cable television, air-conditioning, a Bose Wave radio with thirty-one channels of commercial-free music, a refrigerator bar, direct-dial telephones with voice mail and dataport, a separate vanity and dressing area, a hair dryer, a walk-in closet with a safe, an iron and ironing board, and a terrace. All have retiled bathrooms with new features installed. Luxury rooms have extra amenities such as Serta pillow-top mattresses, a cozy seating area, bathrobes, a dressing area with a marble-topped vanity, a lighted makeup mirror, three phones, and a writing desk.

The resort's private villas, located near the tennis club, around the golf courses, and in the countryside, have two to four bedrooms, each with air-conditioning and private

bath. Each villa has a comfortable living room, a dining room, a fully equipped kitchen, and a screened terrace; it comes with a maid, baby-sitting services, and other amenities. The villas are particularly popular with families and friends traveling together.

Of the group, some thirty sumptuous, commodious Excel Club villas have three and four bedrooms, some with swimming pools, others whirlpools. They come with an array of amenities, including a maid and butler, two golf carts, and concierge and transportation service. The cognoscenti say that a villa is the place to stay.

Perched on a cliff overlooking the Chavon River, several miles from the main hotel area, Altos de Chavon is a replica of a sixteenth-century Mediterranean village conceived by Bluhdorn and created by Italian cinematographer Roberto Copa to foster the culture of the Dominican Republic. Begun in 1976, with local artisans building the village of stone, wood, and iron by hand, it was completed and officially inaugurated with a concert by Frank Sinatra in its 5,000-plus-seat amphitheater in 1982.

At the heart of the village in a cobblestone square stands the Church of St. Stanislaus. Nearby, the Regional Museum of Archaeology houses a comprehensive collection of artifacts of the Taino Indians (the island's inhabitants at the time of Christopher Columbus's arrival). Three art galleries showcase the works of Dominican, European, and American artists. Altos de Chavon School of Design, in affiliation with New York's prestigious Parsons School of Design, offers degrees in various design fields and the arts. The amphitheater is home to the school's performing arts department and has hosted Julio Iglesias and Gloria Estefan, among others. Along the narrow streets, local shops sell handmade jewelry, pottery, and Dominican crafts.

The variety and quality of sports are among Casa de Campo's prime attractions. Its three (soon to be four) eighteen-hole championship Pete Dye–designed courses (one for private membership only) attract players from around the world and regularly host international tournaments. The Teeth of the Dog course, with seven holes skirting the Caribbean, is one of the most beautiful in the world and was recently named the top course in the Caribbean by *Golf* magazine. (Dye's thatched-roof villa compound is along the seventh fairway.) The Links is an inland, rolling course with water coming into play on five holes. Both are dedicated resort courses, with no public access. Carts are de rigueur, although caddies are used by most players, even when using carts.

Casa de Campo's fourth golf course (third resort course), also by Pete Dye, is scheduled to open in late 2002. Laid out around Altos de Chavon with fabulous views of the Chavon River, the surrounding countryside, and the Caribbean, it has a distinctive feature that is bound to make history.

The new course is being planted with two new strains of grass, or paspalum, that thrive on salt water—Sea Isle One (for tees and fairways) and Sea Isle 2000 (for greens)—and can be watered directly from the ocean. Some predict it will change the face of golf in the Caribbean or any place where fresh water is in short supply.

La Terraza Tennis Center offers thirteen Har-Tru tennis courts, ten lighted for night play. Ballboys are available, and games are guaranteed at all times for all levels of expertise. Clinics and private lessons are offered.

Casa de Campo's equestrian and polo facilities are without rival. The Equestrian Center offers guided rides along trails and the beach, along with jumping and riding lessons for beginners and experienced riders; it is the venue for authentic rodeos. The facility has more than 150 trained polo ponies and equipment for players of any level. From November to May polo is played at least three times a week on three playing fields.

For skeet or trapshooting, the 245-acre Sporting Clays Center is outstanding. Michael Rose, long associated with Purdy's of London and director of the center, is acknowledged to be the world's leading gun fitter and a sought-after instructor.

Casa de Campo has plenty of water toys—fourteen swimming pools, including a children's pool, dot the resort. Water sports are featured at the resort's private Minitas Beach, and there are trips to the offshore islands of Saona and Catalina for snorkeling and beach picnics.

The resort's newest addition is Casa de Campo Marina and Yacht Club, a boating and residential community at the mouth of the Chavon River where it empties into the Caribbean Sea. Designed by Italian architect Gianfranco Fini to resemble an Italian seaside village, the first phase of the development consists of a private yacht club and marina; the residential communities will follow.

The heart of the complex is the Italian Plaza, an oceanfront two-story structure with restaurants, a bakery, delicatessen, pizzeria, ice cream shop, and piano bar on the first floor and two- and three-bedroom apartments on the upper floor. Behind the plaza on a single level are a drugstore, bank, travel agency, art gallery, beauty parlor, gift shops, and boutiques—all open to Casa de Campo resort guests.

The other residential areas are Ensenada with two- and three-bedroom apartments with boat slips in front; and the even more luxurious Darsena with fourteen villas in three-, four-, and five-bedroom configurations and forty-one boat slips (30 feet to 50 feet). Each villa has its own pool; boat slips are an option sold separately.

The marina has a fleet of 31-foot Bertram sport-fishing boats for deep-sea fishing, and others for river fishing and sailing. Marlin is the main catch on the ocean, while you can fish for snook in the Chavon River with a local guide.

Casa de Campo's children's program, Kidz 'n Casa, is a day camp offered daily year-round from 9:00 A.M. to 4:00 P.M. for children ages three to twelve. The $15 daily fee includes lunch and snacks. During a week's stay children visit a ranch, see artisans working at Altos de Chavon, take a riverboat cruise, and receive tennis and arts and crafts instruction. Swimming lessons are given daily. There is a separate program for older children. The resort's fifteen restaurants offer children's menus and high chairs, and even the most elegant eateries welcome kids.

Casa de Campo offers many dining choices. In the main hotel area, Tropicana is a steak house specializing in imported Angus beef and seafood for dinner. El Patio, a tropical cafe, serves authentic Dominican fare, pasta dishes, and seafood for lunch and dinner. It features a different gastronomic adventure monthly, from Asian and Cajun to an all-chocolate festival. The Upper Deck, above the main pool, serves sandwiches and snacks. La Cana Bar, a thatched-roof lounge, features merengue bands, a folkloric ballet, and different international artists nightly.

The newest addition, the Safari Club at the shooting center, is dressed in African decor with carved wood furnishings and African artifacts and hand-painted ceilings under a 30-foot thatched roof. The club and bar are open for lunch and dinner during high season.

Some of the resort's best restaurants are located at Altos de Chavon, where nighttime offers floodlit views over the ravine several hundred feet below. Casa del Rio, the resort's gourmet restaurant, serves fresh local fish, nouvelle Caribbean cuisine, and continental specialties. La Piazzetta is an Italian restaurant with strolling musicians, and Cafe del Sol, an open-air pizza parlor, has daily specialties, ice cream, and desserts.

To explore the resort you need one of its fleet of red touring carts, which can be rented by the day or for your entire stay. Shuttle buses are available to carry guests back and forth to Altos de Chavon, the beach, the tennis courts, and the riding center.

Casa de Campo is the Good Life—a fun-filled destination, especially for families, providing options, privacy, security, and the kind of friendly service usually associated with smaller resorts.

Casa de Campo ★★★★

P.O. Box 140, La Romana, Dominican Republic
Phone: (809) 523– 3333; Fax: (809) 523–8548;
e-mail: res@pwmonline.com; www.casadecampo.cc

Management: Premier Resorts and Hotels, Claudio A. Silvestri, President

Managing Director: Ana Lisa Brache

Open: Year-round

Credit Cards: All major

U.S. Reservations: Premier World Marketing, 2600 Southwest Third Avenue, Miami, FL 33129; (800) 877–3643, (305) 856–7083, (305) 856–5405; Fax (305) 858–4677

Deposit: Two nights within seven days of booking; balance fourteen days prior to arrival

Minimum Stay: None

Arrival/Departure: Direct flights daily from Miami and New York to Casa de Campo's international airport of La Romana (LRM) via American Airlines (time: one hour, fifty minutes); American Eagle daily from San Juan (fifty minutes)

Distance from Airport: From La Romana: ten minutes; from Santo Domingo: one and a half hours

Distance from Santo Domingo: One and a half hours

Accommodations: 300 standard, superior, and luxury hotel rooms in two-story buildings with balcony or terrace; 150 two- to four-bedroom villas, including 30 Excel Club villas, some with pool or whirlpool

Amenities: Air-conditioning, ceiling fan; minibar, coffeemaker; cable television, Bose Wave radio with thirty-one channels, direct-dial telephones with voice mail and dataport; hair dryer, separate vanity and dressing area; baths; walk-in closet, safe, iron and ironing board. Excel Club: Private maid and butler, baths, bathrobes, golf carts, twenty-four-hour concierge.

Electricity: 110 volts

Fitness Facilities/Spa Services: Fitness center, free weights, exercise equipment

Sports: Three championship eighteen-hole golf courses; thirteen Har-Tru tennis courts (ten lighted); shooting center; fourteen pools; equestrian center, polo; marina, water sports, river fishing, boating

Dress Code: Smartly casual

Children: All ages

Meetings: Up to 500 people

Day Visitors: Yes

Handicapped: No facilities

Packages: Golf, villa, honeymoon

Rates: Per person, double, per night, EP. *High Season* (January–April): $225–$670. *Low Season:* $155–$439.

Service Charge: 10 percent

Government Tax: 13 percent on room; 8 percent on food

RENAISSANCE JARAGUA HOTEL & CASINO
Santo Domingo, Dominican Republic

Robert Redford once spent weeks here while filming Havana. So what else do you need to know? Yes, it's big, brassy, and painted in colors that will make you reach for your sunglasses. But it's also wonderfully Dominican.

Located on the Malecon, Santo Domingo's popular seashore boulevard overlooking the Caribbean, the Jaragua (pronounced Ha-RAG-wa) offers the best of two worlds: a resort set in fourteen acres of tropical gardens in the heart of the capital and a city full of history, culture, and fun.

The Jaragua doesn't have a beach (there are no beaches in Santo Domingo), but it has lagoons spilling into a huge swimming pool, a health club and spa, a tennis complex, four restaurants, four bars, a nightclub, a disco, a casino, shops, and beautiful rooms. And it's all within easy reach of any of Santo Domingo's many attractions.

Opened in 1987 on the site of the first Jaragua, a pop-ular Havana-in-the-old-days hotel with outdoor gardens and a splashy nightclub, the new Jaragua is *today*. A modern high-rise of ten floors combined with garden low-rise buildings, its design is sleek and the decor sophisticated, with stylish art deco details throughout. You will be impressed by the quality and high standards. Marble floors and satiny, hard-finished fixtures are kept polished to such a shine, you'll think they're mirrors. And the luster on the floor isn't one bit more impressive than the polish of the service. The Jaragua puts the country's other hotels to shame and demonstrates what Dominicans can do with a resort when they set their mind to it.

You arrive at the hotel by way of a grand driveway graced with fountains and gardens and step from a large portico directly into the lobby. Prepare yourself for the experience. On your left is the huge, wide-open casino, brimming with action and bouncing with merengue music most of the time. To your right is the quiet, elegant reception area with soft indirect lighting that highlights the lobby's art deco features. The contrast of the two sides is amazing. But it works.

The guest rooms are in two areas: the majority in the main ten-story tower, with the others in two-story garden buildings on the western side of the main building. All are large, luxurious, and attractive, and the penthouse suites with their own Jacuzzis are small palazzos. The stylish appointments use wicker of contemporary design with plush upholstery, draperies, and bedspreads.

The rooms, designed as much with business travelers in mind as tourists, each have a desk and three phones, including one in the marbled bathroom, where there is also a mini-television. The tower rooms, most with views of the sea, are for those who want to be at the center of the action. Being more removed, the garden rooms provide greater privacy and quiet and are particularly popular with guests enrolled in the spa program.

Directly in front of the guest-room tower is the spa, which offers saunas, massage, herbal wraps, facials, aerobics classes, Nautilus equipment, and more. This facility is one of the Caribbean's best. The hotel has packages for a full spa program.

Beyond the lagoon and gardens is the swimming pool, which is likely to be crowded, particularly on weekends, because it has a local membership. It can also be noisy with kids and music. To the rear is the tennis complex with four lighted clay courts, a viewing stand, and a pro shop.

The Jaragua has four dining outlets; each is a specialty restaurant with different chefs and menus. Quisqueya Restaurant, open twenty-four hours a day, is located in a quiet corner on the main floor. It is the main venue for breakfast and lunch and offers American entrees along with their Spanish counterparts. Las Cascadas, overlooking the waterfalls and lagoon, serves snacks during the day. Champions Sports Bar offers good food, good sports, and good times, day into night. The grill and bar by the pool serves lunch and snacks.

The Jaragua jumps in the evening, and there's plenty of opportunity to be part of the action. In addition to the casino and the casino bar, the 1,600-seat La Fiesta Room often has headline entertainers. You'll also find Las Cascadas, where happy hour features guitars and different types of musical entertainment five times weekly; the Merengue Lounge for cocktails, live music, and dancing; and the disco.

The Jaragua indeed has glamour and style—not so much Caribbean as Latin—and is as popular with Latin Americans as it is with gringos. This hotel is not for the traveler who wants a laid-back Caribbean retreat on a beach. If you prefer having the facilities and services of a large luxury hotel, thrive on a glittering, lively nightlife, and like to be in the center of the action, though, you'll love the Jaragua.

Renaissance Jaragua Hotel & Casino ★★★★
367 George Washington Avenue, Apartado Postal 769-2, Santo Domingo, Dominican Republic
Phone: (809) 221–2222; Fax: (809) 686–0528;
www.renaissancehotels.com/sdqgw

Owner/Management Company: Marriott International
General Manager: Jorge Berrio
Open: Year-round
Credit Cards: Most major
U.S. Reservations: Renaissance Worldwide, (800) 468–3571; or direct to hotel, (800) 331–3542; Fax: (809) 221–8271
Deposit: One night
Minimum Stay: None
Arrival/Departure: Transfer service arranged for charge
Distance from Airport: *(Santo Domingo Las Americas International Airport)* 20 miles (forty minutes); taxi one-way, $25
Distance from Old City: 1 mile; taxi one-way, $6.00
Accommodations: 300 rooms and suites with double or king-size beds (200 deluxe rooms, including nine suites, in ten-story tower; 100 in two-story garden buildings)
Amenities: Air-conditioning, ceiling fans; bath with tub and shower, hair dryer, makeup mirror, mini-TV, basket of toiletries, bathrobe; cable television, radio, direct-dial telephone, high-speed Internet access; minibar and refrigerator, ice service; nightly turndown service; concierge; twenty-four-hour room service; Jacuzzis in penthouse suites
Electricity: 110 volts
Fitness Facilities/Spa Services: See text
Sports: Freshwater swimming pool; free use of tennis courts; tennis rental equipment and lessons for fee; golf, horseback riding, water sports, fishing arranged through concierge
Dress Code: Casual
Children: All ages; cribs, high chairs; baby-sitters; up to two children under eighteen stay free in garden room with parents
Meetings: Up to 1,000 people
Day Visitors: Yes, for casino and restaurants
Handicapped: Limited facilities
Packages: Spa, honeymoon, merengue, other Renaissance standards
Rates: Per room, double, daily, EP. *Year-round:* $145-$305.
Service Charge: 10 percent
Government Tax: 12 percent

Grenada

Known as the Spice Island, Grenada is a tapestry of tropical splendor where banana trees by the side of the road grow as tall as the palm trees fringing the powdery beaches, and trade winds nourish the lush mountainous interior.

St. George's, the capital and one of the Caribbean's prettiest ports, is set on a deep horseshoe-shaped bay. Clinging to green hillsides behind it are yellow, blue, and pink houses topped with red roofs and historic buildings climbing to a series of colonial forts built to protect the strategic harbor.

Grand Anse Beach, south of St. George's, is a lovely 2-mile crescent of white sand bathed by calm Caribbean waters. It is the island's main resort and water-sports center, with snorkeling, sailing, diving, and windsurfing. Bay Gardens, a hillside botanic oasis, has trails covered with nutmeg shells that wind through woods of an estimated 3,000 species of tropical flora.

The main cross-island highway from the capital winds up the mountains to the Grand Etang Forest Reserve, crossing it at 1,910 feet within a few hundred yards of Grand Etang, an extinct volcano whose crater is filled with a lake.

The Grand Etang National Park, part of Grenada's national park system protecting most of the interior mountains, has hiking trails around the lake, through surrounding rain forests, and up to mountain peaks that showcase the island's exotic vegetation, birds, and wildlife.

North of St. George's, the road hugs the leeward coast, passing fishing villages and winding along the edge of magnificent tropical scenery on mountains that drop almost straight into the sea and hide little coves with black-sand beaches.

Grenada is one of the world's largest producers of nutmeg and just about every fruit known in the Tropics. In Gouyave you can visit the country's major nutmeg processing station. The staff at nearby Dougaldston Estates, a nutmeg plantation, have a wealth of information on the cultivation of spices and tropical fruits.

In the same vicinity Concord Falls, a triple-stage cascade set deep in the central mountains, is about an hour's hike; it requires some rock hopping, but your reward is a lovely waterfall that drops through jungle-thick vegetation to a pool where you can enjoy a refreshing swim.

Information

Grenada Tourist Board, 800 Second Avenue, 400-K, New York, NY 10017; (212) 687–9554, (800) 927–9554; Fax: (212) 573–9731; www.grenada.org

THE CALABASH HOTEL
St. George's, Grenada, W.I.

Having a private maid prepare your breakfast isn't a bad way to start a vacation—and she'll serve it to you in bed, if you like.

Since it opened in 1961, The Calabash has been the last word in British gentility, attracting lords and ladies and an occasional prince or princess, who fly in on their private planes. Once they've checked in, though, no one (except the staff, of course) will know who they are or see them being treated differently from you or me. This is true even though the times and owners have changed.

In 1989 when the new, young British owner, Leo Garbutt, took over, he updated, upgraded, and expanded the rather staid resort, making it much better (would you believe exciting?), but without diluting any of its grace. Among the improvements were more units with private pools and the addition of a keyhole-shaped swimming pool in a quiet area near the main building, which has men's and women's rest rooms and showers. The tennis court was lighted, and the beach bar moved to a more convenient location at the center of the beach.

Now there is regular live entertainment and a full range of water sports, which are included in the room rates. Telephones have been installed in all rooms but—as the management is quick to tell you—you may have yours removed if you consider it a nuisance. Now that's gentility.

The Calabash is spread over eight landscaped acres overlooking a quiet bay. Accommodations, each named for a tropical flower that grows in the gardens, are in one- and two-story cottages arranged in a horseshoe around a broad, open green with the main building at the center. Each of the spacious, airy units has a bedroom and a bathroom, sitting area, and patio or balcony. Some of the rooms are furnished with four-poster beds. In the older, cozier units, where the decor has a

warm, Caribbean feeling, the bedrooms and sitting rooms are separate. In the newer units they are combined in one spacious room and sport a contemporary look.

Adjacent to or, in some cases, within each unit is a small pantry where the maid appointed to your room prepares your breakfast each morning, unless you prefer to take breakfast in the restaurant.

In the newer two-story units, six on the ground floor have private plunge pools; those on the second floor have whirlpools. They also have pitched roofs, which make them seem all the larger and airier. Two units with pools were specially designed to accommodate handicapped or wheelchair bound guests.

Each unit has a garden view leading down to the sandy beach, where you will find lounge chairs and lots of shade trees as well as a beach bar and a casual restaurant where lunch is available.

In 1999 the resort added a new, unusually spacious accommodation—the Thorneycroft Suite, named for Lord Peter and Lady Carla Thorneycroft, who have spent many holidays at The Calabash. The suite, which has more than 2,000 square feet, has a large master bedroom leading out to a balcony, a huge marble-tiled bathroom with double shower and large double whirlpool bath, a walk-in closet, and a dressing area. A large and well-appointed lounge leads to a sundeck beside the private pool. The suite's luxurious interiors were created by Penny Barnard, a well-known designer from St. Lucia. For families that need more than one bedroom, the Thorneycroft Suite has a spiral staircase that can connect with the Calabash Suite below; the two suites can be booked as one family unit.

The Calabash has just embarked on its largest venture yet, Amber Belair, a luxurious villa community next to the resort on a peninsula that marks Grenada's most southerly

point. Several of the initial homes, which have set the style for the new development, were designed by the late Arne Hasselqvist, who created most of the famous posh homes on the island of Mustique. The complex includes a clubhouse, tennis court, fitness center, and meeting place. Owners will have access to all of the facilities of The Calabash. The first two of fourteen villas are being completed. Some of the villas will be available for rent through The Calabash.

The informal, breezy dining room, with natural stone walls and terra-cotta tile floors, sits under a trellis of thunbergia, a romantically decorative feature for which the hotel is known. Here you will find Cicely's, the main restaurant, open for dinner only, and one of the island's best restaurants. It serves continental cuisine with a Caribbean touch and excellent service in a lovely alfresco setting.

The hotel manager invites all the guests to cocktails at the beach bar on Monday, and there is live entertainment on different nights. Despite the assorted royalty that drops in, do not get the idea that The Calabash is a posh pleasure palace. Heaven forbid. It's anything but.

The Calabash is unpretentious and understated. It appeals to a wide range of visitors: couples, honeymooners, families with children, and nature lovers from ages twenty-five to seventy-five. Most come from the United States and Britain, but you'll find a sprinkling of Germans and other Europeans. All appreciate the quality that has long made The Calabash one of the best in the Caribbean.

The Calabash Hotel ✳ ✳ ✳

P.O. Box 382, L'Anse Aux Epines Beach, St. George's, Grenada, W.I.
Phone: (473) 444–4334, (800) 528–5835; Fax: (473) 444–5050;
e-mail: calabash@ caribsurf.com

Owner: Leo Garbutt
General Manager: Clive Barnes
Open: Year-round
Credit Cards: All major
U.S. Reservations: Direct to hotel
Deposit: Three nights; twenty-one days cancellation
Minimum Stay: Seven nights during Christmas and February
Arrival/Departure: Taxi Association rules do not permit hotels to send transportation to airport to pick up guests
Distance from Airport: *(Point Salines Airport)* 3 miles; taxi one-way, $10 day, $14 after 6:00 P.M.
Distance from St. George's: 5 miles; taxi one-way, $18
Accommodations: 30 units in one- and two-story cottages with terrace or patio (eight with pools, king-size beds; 22 with whirlpools and king-size, queen-size, or double beds; all units can be made into twins)
Amenities: Air-conditioning, ceiling fans; most baths with tub and shower (six with shower only), hair dryer, basket of toiletries; telephone; safe; minibar, CD player; tea and coffeemaker; iron and ironing board; nightly turndown service, room service 11:00 A.M.–8:30 P.M.; concierge; boutique; repeat guests greeted with fruit basket and bottle of wine
Electricity: 220 volts
Fitness Facilities/Spa Services: Fitness center with exercise equipment; aromatherapy and other spa treatments available for fee
Sports: Freshwater swimming pool; free use of lighted tennis court, racquets, balls; snooker and billiards room; shuffleboard and beach boules; snorkeling equipment, Sunfish, kayaks, windsurfing, and other water sports from beach concessionaire for charge; fishing, diving, yacht charters, and hiking with guide in national park arranged; golf with free green fees at Grenada Golf Club
Dress Code: Casual
Children: Over twelve years old in winter, all ages other times; cribs, high chairs; baby-sitters
Meetings: No
Day Visitors: With reservations
Handicapped: Facilities
Packages: Honeymoon, wedding, romantic escapes, gourmet getaways
Rates: Per person, daily, MAP. *High Season* (mid December–early April): $415– $625. *Low Season:* $250–$335.
Service Charge: 10 percent
Government Tax: 8 percent

LASOURCE

Grenada, W.I.

Those who know the health and fitness haven LeSport in St. Lucia will be pleased with its sibling.

Located on the southwestern corner of the island on forty hillside acres overlooking Pink Gin Beach, LaSource combines the facilities for an active beach vacation with pampering of the body and mind. The resort has two restaurants, a variety of land and water sports, two beaches, and the Oasis, a full-service spa.

Designed by Lane Pettigrew, a Miami-based architect and interior designer, the resort reflects Grenada's British and French heritage with West Indian- and Victorian-inspired architecture and colonial-style interior decor. The layout, set around a central courtyard with fountains and sculpture, is meant to suggest a West Indian colonial village; the main building would have been the governor's residence, complete with a clock tower permanently set at 5:10 P.M., the traditional time of the governor's cocktail hour in colonial days.

Guest rooms are housed in three- and four-story pastel buildings with terra-cotta tile roofs that fill a sloping hill facing the beach. The buildings are trimmed with hand-crafted wooden trellises, railings, doors, and shutters of such tropical woods as saman, mahogany, and teak from Venezuela, Trinidad, and Jamaica.

All guest rooms are finished with cream-colored Italian marble floors and furnished with hand-carved, four-poster beds from Jamaica covered with white chenille bedspreads in a woven pineapple pattern, embroidered lace bed cushions, Oriental rugs, and cream-colored stucco walls. Rooms on the top floor have 18-foot-high wood-beamed ceilings. The resort's nine suites enjoy views from bay windows with an overstuffed pullout sofa and armchair and tapestry-design floral cushions.

All rooms have walk-in closets, air-conditioning, ceiling fans, clock-radios, and mini-refrigerators. The large marble bathrooms were apparently measured for Amazons: The vanities are too high for most women, and the tubs have lips so wide that they are difficult to enter and exit. But there are hair dryers and bathrobes.

Upon arrival, guests are welcomed by the ocean breezes that cool the public areas, virtually all of which are open to the air. The reception opens onto a courtyard centered on a star-shaped fountain carved from stone from Grenada's sister island, Carriacou.

The French connection is in the name, inspired by La Source, a painting by the nineteenth-century neoclassic French artist Jean Ingres, known for his portraits and nudes. The resort's signature image—a female figure similar to that of a woman bathing in Ingres's painting—is incorporated into the design of the outdoor tiles and elsewhere throughout the resort.

The central pavilion, with cathedral wood-beamed ceilings and open on three sides, houses the Terrace, a casual restaurant where lunch and afternoon tea are served. It faces the beach and a large free-form swimming pool whose two levels are linked by a small waterfall. Adjacent is a large whirlpool, accommodating up to fifteen people. The pool and beach area look out at a spectacular view of Grenada's coast—all the way to St. George's, the capital.

The Great House, which suggests a West Indian plantation house of the olden days, has a double staircase

leading to a second level with an air-conditioned piano bar on one side and the main restaurant on the other. The room offers a choice of four areas to dine—a breezy open-air veranda overlooking the ocean and St. George's in the distance; a garden terrace; and two interior rooms for more formal dining.

A generous breakfast buffet of hot and cold cereals, fruits, fresh-baked breads and croissants, yogurt, and a selection of hot items is served here. Continental breakfast is also available in your room upon request. Dinners feature an a la carte menu of the chef's creations.

Cocktails are served in the piano bar and at the Terrace Bar, both of which also have nightly entertainment. In addition a variety of theme nights are held during the week, including a barbecue and beach party with steel band music and a Caribbean buffet.

The Oasis, the health and beauty facility, offers a program of restorative body and beauty treatments ranging from facials and massages to meditation and stress management. Like LeSport, but unlike traditional spa programs, LaSource is not regimented; participants set their own schedules. The main difference from LeSport is that LaSource emphasizes relaxation therapy rather than water-based therapies. Among the treatments available here are foot massage, aromatherapy, wraps, reflexology, Swedish massage, and salt loofah rubs.

A full roster of activities is posted daily at the Terrace Bar and includes day and night tennis, fencing, archery, volleyball, weight training, hiking, calypso dance classes, scuba diving, snorkeling, waterskiing, windsurfing, and sailing. Daily stress management, tai chi, and yoga classes are also available.

A nine-hole, par-three golf course at the entrance to the property features shorter lengths between holes and a lighter ball. Instruction and use of equipment for golf and all on-property activities are included in the price. Other resort facilities include a beauty salon and laundry service, at an additional cost, and a boutique.

LaSource rates include three meals plus afternoon tea, red and white wines at lunch and dinner, and all beverages (except for champagne and wines ordered from the wine list), as well as taxes and gratuities. Tipping is not allowed. Rooms for singles are now available at LaSource year-round in a new room category, Garden Single.

The resort is almost within walking distance of Point Salines International Airport; guests are met on arrival.

LaSource ✱✱✱✱

Pink Gin Beach, P.O. Box 852, St. George's, Grenada, W.I.
Phone: (473) 444–2556, (800) 544–2883; Fax: (473) 444–2561;
e-mail: lasource@caribsurf.com; www.lasource.com.gd

Owner/Management: Liberty Club Limited/Sunswept Resorts
General Manager: Adolf Fratton
Open: Year-round
Credit Cards: All major
U.S. Reservations: Tropical Holidays, (800) 544–2883
Deposit: $300 per person with booking; twenty-one days cancellation
Minimum Stay: None
Arrival/Departure: Transfer included
Distance from Airport: *(Point Salines International Airport)* Five minutes; taxi one-way, $8.00
Distance from St. George's: 7 miles; taxi one-way, $15
Accommodations: 100 rooms and suites (91 rooms and nine suites, most with ocean views) in three buildings of three and four stories; all with terrace; furnished with double or king-size beds
Amenities: Air-conditioning, ceiling fan; telephone, clock-radio; Internet access; mini-refrigerator; walk-in closets; marble bath with tub and shower, hair dryer, makeup mirror, bathrobe, basket of toiletries; room service for continental breakfast, nightly turndown service; boutique, hair salon; no television
Electricity: 220 volts; rooms have one 110-volt outlet
Fitness Facilities/Spa Services: Weight training, jogging, hikes, aerobics, stretch and dance classes, yoga, tai chi, stress management—all with instruction; personal trainer. Oasis: Loofah rubs, body and foot massage, seaweed wraps, facials, reflexology, aromatherapy. Beauty salon at extra charge.
Sports: Free-form pool, large whirlpool; two lighted tennis courts; fencing; croquet; Ping-Pong; archery; volleyball; golf (nine-hole, nonregulation, par three); snorkeling, waterskiing, windsurfing, sailing—all with instruction; complimentary dive resort course, PADI certification offered for fee
Dress Code: Sports- and beachwear by day; casually elegant in evening
Children: None under sixteen years of age
Meetings: No
Day Visitors: Day pass available for $60 with breakfast, lunch, tea, snacks, and activities, Monday–Friday, 10:00 A.M.–6:30 P.M.; evening pass for $60 includes dinner, drinks, and entertainment; $80 weekends; spa treatments subject to availability and priced separately
Packages: Honeymoon, wedding, others
Rates: All-inclusive, per person, daily. *High Season* (late December–late March): $275–$460. *Shoulder Season* (late March–mid-May): $255–$340. *Low Season* (mid-March–mid-December): $230–$315. Single, $330–$430; $280; $255, respectively.
Service Charge: Included
Government/Hotel Tax: Included

SPICE ISLAND BEACH RESORT
St. George's, Grenada, W.I.

A major expansion and refurbishment with new and upgraded accommodations, new facilities, and new services were completed in 2000 and Spice Island has never looked better. At the same time, it has become an all-inclusive resort with rates covering accommodations, three meals and afternoon tea, bar service, a dive lesson, and more. A landscaped swimming pool and large Jacuzzi were added near the beach, as were a fitness center, a full-service spa, two boutiques, and a new business center. The central building housing the dining room, bar, open-air terrace, reception area, lounge, and kitchen was completely redesigned and rebuilt and is now open from the entrance to the sea.

Giant almond trees shade the entrance to your cottage, where there's a pan with water to rinse your feet of sand from the beach. This is one of the special touches you'll find at the Spice Island Beach Resort.

Spice opened in 1961 as a rustic laid-back inn that defined the very notion of a Caribbean escape. In 1988 it was bought by some local businessmen headed by managing director Royston Hopkin, C.M.G., who was the 1991 Caribbean Hotelier of the Year and honored by Queen Elizabeth II in 1995. He has gradually updated, upgraded, and expanded Spice, now a Hopkin family enterprise, into a new hotel more than triple its original size.

The Spice welcome begins at the front door, where you are greeted upon arrival with a cooling tropical fruit drink or a Grenada-style rum punch. It comes with a generous sprinkling of nutmeg— Spice's friendly reminder that Grenada, the Spice Island, is the world's second largest producer of nutmeg.

Spice has several types of guest rooms. Stretching along the beach on both sides of the main building and the new pool are one-story cottages, each with two units. Behind them to the right are the honeymooners' favorites: suites with private pools a step away from a bedroom with a king-size bed. To the left of the main building and also set back from the beach are newer, two-story bunga-lows whose ground-level suites have plunge pools. The latest expansion includes twelve suites (six ocean-front), each with a sitting room, mini-bar, double whirlpool and twin vanity units in the bathroom, and covered or open patios. Sixteen of the original whirlpool beach suites and six private pool suites were upgraded with new furnishings and decor. Further enhancing the luxury, guests in the top category rooms sleep on fine Frette linens. By the way, there are Frette linens on the tables in Oliver's Restaurant, too.

The rooms, spacious and airy with tile floors and screened glass doors, are furnished in light rattan. All rooms have whirlpools big enough for two, found either in a tiny garden atrium open to the sky or in a corner of a large bathroom with a skylight. Four are ultraposh royal suites with pools, which are surrounded by high walls and large enough for laps—albeit short laps—and secluded enough for skinny-dipping.

The four royal suites, thought to be the only ones with a large, red-wood cedar in-room sauna at a Caribbean resort, have another unusual feature—a canopied fitness area, set in the gardens, with an exercise bike. Each has a sundeck with chaise lounges and patio table, along with a flower garden. Each suite, measuring 1,473 square feet, is decorated in bright Caribbean fabrics, custom-designed rattan furniture, and local art. There is a separate living room, a bedroom with a king-size bed, and a marble tile bathroom with double sinks and double whirlpools.

You enter your private paradise through a whitewashed, wooden door with the fitness area on one side, the gardens on the other. Inside, the amenities in the royal private-pool suites include a stocked minibar, a television, and a music center with stereo, cassette, and CD player. Each unit has a coffeemaker, radio, direct-dial telephone, hair dryer, air-conditioning, ceiling fan, and safe. These suites have special rates that include full breakfast and dinner daily, room service from 7:45 A.M. to 10:00 P.M., nonmotorized water sports, tennis,

bicycles, and green fees at the nearby Grenada Golf Club.

Breakfast and lunch are served a la carte in the dining room or delivered to your patio. Dinner is a set five-course menu with two or three choices of continental and local dishes. On Wednesday evening a West Indian buffet highlights the most popular native dishes, and a barbecue with steel band music livens up Friday night. During the winter season there is music for dancing five nights of the week.

Guests at Spice spend lazy days on the 1,200 feet of beach, occasionally cooling off in the languid waters or reading and dozing under leafy sea grape trees. Or, they can luxuriate in the new Janissa's Spa where they will find a full range of face, hair, and body treatments. If they are a bit more ambitious, they can try the Cybex equipment in the fitness center or check out the designer fashions in the new boutiques—one for men and one for women.

To maintain the setting's serenity, motorized water sports are not available in this section of Grand Anse.

Of all the resorts in this book, Spice seems to have fans the most ardent—and critics the most stern. The fans say the service is wonderful, caring, and attentive; critics tell me it is either indifferent or oversolicitous.

So I will tell you my experience. I have always enjoyed my stays at Spice and found the service and food good, though not brilliant. I preferred the halcyon days of its unpretentious past to its more posh present, but some people can spend hours neck-deep in the hot, gurgling water of their hot tub looking up at the puffy white clouds rolling by and reveling in such bliss.

Spice Island Beach Resort ✶✶✶✶

Grand Anse, P.O. Box 6, St. George's, Grenada, W.I.
Phone: (473) 444–4258; Fax: (473) 444–4807;
e-mail: spiceisl@caribsurf.com; www.spicebeachresort.com

Owner/Managing Director: Royston O. Hopkin, C.M.G.
Resort Manager: Brian Hardy
Open: Year-round
Credit Cards: All major
U.S. Reservations: International Travel and Resorts (ITR), (800) 223 9815, (212) 476 9444, (800) 742 4276; Fax: (212) 545–8467
Deposit: Three nights in winter; one night in summer; thirty days cancellation prior to arrival, mid-December–mid-April except during Christmas holidays and February when it is forty-five days
Minimum Stay: Seven nights in winter; none in summer (mid-April–mid-December)
Arrival/Departure: Transfer service not available due to local Taxi Association regulations
Distance from Airport: *(Pointe Salines Airport)* 4 miles; taxi one-way, $10 day; $14 after 6:00 p.m.
Distance from St. George's: 6 miles; taxi one-way, $10
Accommodations: 66 rooms and suites in two-unit bungalows with patio, most beachfront and ocean view, all with whirlpools; 17 suites with private swimming pools (six luxury pool suites, seven private-pool suites, four royal private-pool suites), each with king-size beds
Amenities: Air-conditioning, ceiling fans; whirlpool tub, shower, hair dryer, basket of toiletries; television, telephone with Internet access; clock-radio; stocked minibar, coffeemaker; iron and ironing board; safe; nightly turndown service; room service for meals and beverages; boutique; see text for royal suite amenities
Electricity: 220 volts
Sports: Tennis court, balls, racquets; snorkeling gear, Hobie Cats, windsurfers provided; boating, diving, fishing, hiking arranged
Fitness Facilities/Spa Services: See text
Dress Code: Casual by day; elegantly casual in evening
Children: None under five years old in high season; cribs; baby-sitters
Meetings: Up to seventy-five people; business center with Internet access and business equipment
Day Visitors: Yes
Handicapped: Limited facilities
Packages: Honeymoon
Rates: Two people, daily, All-inclusive. ***High Season*** (mid-December–mid-April): $570–$990. ***Low Season:*** $470–$780. Single rates are available.
Service Charge: 10 percent
Government Tax: 8 percent

TWELVE DEGREES NORTH

St. George's, Grenada, W.I.

Joe Gaylord, who has lived in Grenada since 1967, gave up the real estate business in New York for his patch of paradise. He created Twelve Degrees North—which takes its name from Grenada's latitude—out of the frustration of not finding the resort he wanted for his vacation. His nest is the most unhotel hotel you are ever likely to find. Joe believes it is unique in the Caribbean, and perhaps it is. It's also one of the Caribbean's best bargains.

The small complex has only eight units of one and two bedrooms. They are situated in four two-story buildings that are interconnected by steps. The rooms have terra-cotta floors and are decorated with rattan furniture and colorful fabrics and local art on the walls.

The bedrooms have a king or two twin beds joined by a king-size headboard. The two-bedroom suites have two baths and large living rooms. The suites on the second floor have pitched ceilings, which make them seem more spacious. All the units have kitchens and terraces with picture-postcard views of the Caribbean and the lush Grenada coast, and all face west, making your terrace the ideal perch at sunset for enjoying the full bottle of rum punch you will find in your refrigerator upon arrival. And that's not all you'll find in it.

Your refrigerator and pantry will be fully stocked with beverages and food—chicken, fish, fruit, vegetables, bread, and other staples—for your stay. The reason for this horn of plenty is one of the features that make Twelve Degrees so unusual: Namely, for your entire stay you will have a personal attendant (a combination maid, cook, and housekeeper) assigned exclusively to your suite.

Joe and his wife, Pat, have devised a system that seems to work like magic for them, the women attendants, and their guests. Each attendant's sole job is to care for the occupants of her unit and her unit only, year in and year out. She is available from 8:00 A.M. to 3:00 P.M. daily and will keep your room immaculate, change the linens, do your personal laundry, and cook and serve your breakfast and lunch.

If you don't want her to come as early as 8:00 A.M., it's no problem; just say so. If you don't need her to hang around to serve you lunch, just tell her. She can make your lunch and leave. For the evening you are on your own, but if you would like her to prepare your dinner in advance, she will do that too. If you don't care to bother with making dinner, there are restaurants nearby and some fine ones around the island.

You pay for the provisions that are stocked for you in advance of your arrival. If you do not intend to use certain items, you can tell Joe or your attendant, and they will be deducted from your bill.

You will find that these women are good cooks and are pleased to introduce you to Grenadian cuisine, but if you prefer your own style of cooking, they will prepare meals as you request.

Joe's care in selecting his location and staff extends to getting the right kind of guests—namely, ones who are suited to the quiet, intimate ambience of this resort. He does not welcome children, for example, simply because his guests do not want them around. Most people come for the tranquillity; anyone who needs activity or entertainment would definitely be in the wrong place.

Twelve Degrees North is about as low-key and laid-back as the Caribbean gets. It is set in a little cove on a hillside of tropical woods and gardens that slope to a small beach. A stone path leads from the cottages downhill to the beach. There you find an ample-size L-shaped freshwater pool, three hammocks, lounging chairs, a built-in gas barbecue, and a thatched hut with a self-service bar and library of well-read books. Pick a spot and spend the day.

You might converse with some of the other guests around the pool or by the beach. Most will be from the States—professionals, a university professor, a stockbroker, a television producer—and most are good company.

They usually are experienced travelers who have tried many of the better-known, ritzier places in the Caribbean. They probably heard about Joe's place from a friend or their own research. They are not likely to learn about it from their travel agent, unless they have a very knowledgeable one.

To the right of the beach is a 100-foot pier with a gazebo and benches. It juts out into the sea where the water is deep enough to swim (by the beach the water is very shallow), and there's a reef for snorkeling. The use of snorkeling gear, Sunfish, and kayaks, as well as the tennis court, is included in the rate. Scuba diving and waterskiing can be arranged for a fee.

There's a 720-square-foot over-the-water sundeck. When you look up from the beach or pier, you will see the Gaylords' home. If you think you have a wonderful view, wait until you see theirs. And you are likely to do so: The Gaylords often invite their guests to join them for cocktails. Most consider it the highlight of their visit. The house sits out on a point; the entire front is open to the view.

Oh, I forgot to mention: Twelve Degrees North has no office; it's in Joe's house. But if the Gaylords know you are coming, one of them will be standing by the driveway to greet you when you arrive. You can count on it.

Twelve Degrees North ✳✳

P.O. Box 241, St. George's, Grenada, W.I.
(473) 444–4580; Fax: Same as phone;
e-mail: 12degrsn@caribsurf.com; www.twelvedegreesnorth.com

Owners/Managers: Joe and Pat Gaylord

Open: Year-round

Credit Cards: None

U.S. Reservations: Direct to hotel

Deposit: Three nights

Minimum Stay: Seven–ten nights during Christmas and February

Arrival/Departure: No transfer service

Distance from Airport: (Pointe Salines International Airport) 5 miles; taxi one-way, $10

Distance from St. George's: 7 miles, taxi one-way, $12.00; from Grand Anse, 4 miles, taxi one-way, $8.00

Accommodations: Six one-bedroom suites; two two-bedroom suites, all with terrace, kitchen, and twin beds or king

Amenities: Ceiling fan; kitchen; bath with shower, basket of toiletries, hair dryer, shampoo and conditioner dispenser; complimentary rum punch; personal maid-cook-laundress

Electricity: 220 volts

Sports: Freshwater swimming pool; use of tennis court, snorkeling gear, kayaks, Sunfish included; scuba, fishing, waterskiing for fee; trail hiking, birding arranged

Dress Code: Casual

Children: None under fifteen years old, year-round

Meetings: No

Day Visitors: Not suitable

Handicapped: No facilities

Packages: No

Rates: Two people, daily, FAP. **High Season** (mid-December–mid-April): $225. **Low Season:** $150. Four people in two-bedroom unit, $350 and $265, respectively.

Service Charge: 10 percent

Government Tax: 8 percent

Jamaica

From the 7,400-foot peaks of the Blue Mountains, where the famous coffee is grown, Jamaica's terrain drops to foothills of banana groves and sugarcane fields and orchards of mangos and limes. Brilliant flowers, vivid birds, exotic fruit, gentle people whose voices lilt as though they are singing—these are the charms with which this Caribbean beauty seduces her admirers.

Jamaica, the land of reggae, is the quintessence of the Caribbean and offers diversity—in landscape and lifestyle, culture and cuisine, sports and attractions—that few islands can match. There are waterfalls to climb, mountains to hike, trails to ride, golf, tennis, polo, diving, fishing, plus attractions that are unique to Jamaica, such as rafting on the Rio Grande and trips into the mountainous Cockpit country that once sheltered the Maroons, runaway slaves who defied British rule.

Jamaica, 144 miles long and 49 miles wide, is located 90 miles south of Cuba. The third largest Caribbean island, Jamaica was called Xaymaca, meaning "land of wood and water," by the Arawaks who populated the island when Columbus arrived in 1494.

The British took Jamaica in 1655 and stayed for the next 300 years. Although the colonial trappings disappeared on the road to nationhood since independence in 1962, vestiges of the British, such as cricket and croquet, tea parties and polo, are still very much a part of the Jamaican fabric, incongruous as they may seem.

If its British past was the stock for the Jamaican bouillabaisse, the traders, slaves, and settlers who came to the island were the ingredients that created a culture as diverse as its scenery. Jamaica's influence in art, dance, and music extends far beyond the Caribbean.

Jamaica's diversity enables every visitor to find a niche. From the laid-back beaches of Negril on the west to the quiet coves and busy resorts along the 100-mile northern coast to Port Antonio on the east, there are resorts to suit most travelers, regardless of interest and budget.

Information

Jamaica Tourist Board, 1320 South Dixie Highway, Coral Gables, FL 33146;
(800) 327–9857, (305) 665–0557; www.jamaicatravel.com

STRAWBERRY HILL
Kingston, Jamaica, W.I.

What debuted as one of the most enchanting Caribbean havens of the 1990s is not on a beach but perched high in the Blue Mountains of eastern Jamaica, where eco-green must have been invented.

Strawberry Hill is the dream-come-true of Island Records mogul Chris Blackwell, who launched Bob Marley, U2, and others to superstardom and helped create the hip image of Miami's South Beach with his art deco hotels. Set amid gardens and wooded hills at an elevation of 3,000 feet near Irish Town, Strawberry Hill is a former coffee plantation whose manor house commands one of the island's most enviable views, with the mountains over 7,000 feet as the background and the sea at your feet.

The great house has been renovated as the centerpiece of the hotel, with a lounge and restaurant. Its decor is designed around Island Records memorabilia dating from the company's beginning in 1962 and including its many gold records and awards as well as items from its stable of recording stars. There's a library and a small conference room for up to thirty people.

Most accommodations are found in twelve veranda-encircled one- and two-story cottages. Designed by Jamaican architects Ann Hodges and Victor Haye in a modified gingerbread-trimmed West Indian style and painted in neutral colors, they have one-, two-, and three-bedroom suites with beautifully finished, local wood interiors.

Rooms are furnished in country-casual fashion by Tanya Melich, a British-by-way-of-the-Bahamas designer. They feature four-poster beds and antiqued, handmade island furniture.

The cottages are positioned to take maximum advantage of their heartstopping views. Each has a terra-cotta bathroom with recessed lights and a small kitchen nook—intended as a convenience for an early-morning or late-evening repast rather than serious cooking. The hammock on your veranda will be hard to resist for an afternoon nap or a cocktail-hour perch to watch the sun drop into the sea and Kingston light up for the evening show.

Each accommodation can be equipped with a state-of-the-art entertainment center for enjoying videos and recordings from a stocked library. Electronic gear enables you to stay plugged into the outside world, should you need to disrupt the serenity of this very private escape. You can request a television, VCR, or fax machine in your room. You will also find a cordless phone with answering machine, a CD player with a selection of CDs, a coffeemaker, a minibar, a large writing desk (that's to lay a guilt number on writers who goof off), and heated mattress pads (can you believe it actually gets cold at night in Jamaica!) on the huge four-poster beds. These pads are set on low to prevent mildew as well as to warm guests. Huge white pillows, down-filled comforters, and sheer mosquito netting—not necessary but aesthetically pleasing—make the beds very inviting.

Wooden walkways connecting the cottages wind their way up to the manor house and its crowning glory—a 60 foot swimming pool set in gardens on the highest point of the forty-five-acre property with vistas to infinity.

An Aveda Spa—the first in Jamaica—provides a wide range of treatments and services that encourage wellness. Designed by the same Jamaican architect (Ann Hodges) as the resort, the facility is the perfect complement to the resort's idyllic setting. It utilizes natural ingredients in a vari-

ety of services, including massage, hydrotherapy, facials, body care, as well as Aveda signature treatments such as the Himalayan Rejuvenation. The first step is to determine your unique "aroma identity" and formulate a personal aroma blend, which is used in all of your treatments. In addition to massage, yoga, and skin- and stress-relieving treatments, the spa has a full-service hair salon that offers manicure, pedicure, makeup consultation, facials, and body waxing. It also organizes hiking, mountain biking, and other outdoor activities in the Blue Mountains.

Chef Aris Latham creates truly unique and outstanding dishes that combine nouvelle cuisine techniques with traditional spicy Jamaican cooking; many praise it as the best food in Jamaica. A flan combining ackee (a local vegetable) with seafood and spices is superb. Gnocchi made with local vegetables, agnolotti (similar to ravioli) stuffed with goat and lamb, and soups of seafood and pumpkin are other selections on the ever-evolving menu. A variety of salads, pastas, grilled dishes, and spa cuisine are also available.

Meals can be enjoyed in the sun-dappled, high-ceilinged main dining room, which manages to be formal yet casual and relaxing all at the same time. Continental breakfasts (huge plates of fresh fruit, toast, and Blue Mountain coffee) are served, weather permitting, on the covered veranda that's just a few steps away. The restaurant, open from 7:00 A.M. until 10:00 P.M., serves all three meals, as well as high tea and Jamaican Sunday brunch. Room service is available from 7:00 A.M. to midnight.

Although Strawberry Hill is 5 miles from Kingston, the drive can take thirty minutes or more because of the narrow mountain roads. From the Kingston Airport on the far side of the city, you need to allow for at least a fifty-minute drive, depending on the traffic. Guests are met at the airport and escorted to the hotel in a customized van. Those who do not care to make the drive can arrive by helicopter (a seven-minute ride)—but it will cost a bundle.

If you fall in love with Strawberry Hill and can't bear to leave, ask about monthly rates—particularly if you're a writer.

Strawberry Hill ★ ★ ★ 🍃

Irish Town, Jamaica, W.I.
Phone: (876) 944–8400; Fax: (876) 944–8408;
e-mail: reservations@islandoutpost.com; www.islandoutpost.com

Owner: Island Outpost
General Manager: Jenny Wood
Open: Year-round
Credit Cards: All major
U.S. Reservations: (800) OUTPOST
Deposit: One night
Minimum Stay: None
Arrival/Departure: Shuttle from Kingston Airport (fifty minutes), $40; helicopter service available (seven-minute flight) for fee (very costly)
Distance from Airport: *(Kingston Airport)* 15 miles (fifty-minute drive on mountain roads)
Distance from Kingston: 5 miles (thirty or more minutes on mountain roads)
Accommodations: 12 villas with 14 rooms (four studio suites; four one-, two-, and three-bedroom villas); five kings, nine queens, four twins; all with balcony or veranda; some with kitchen
Amenities: Air-conditioning, ceiling fans; bath with tub and multihead shower; coffeemaker, minibar; large writing desk; heated mattress pads and heated closet rods (to prevent mildew); nightly turndown service, room service; massage and aromatherapy services; telephone, hair dryer, television, VCR, CD player, fax machine available on request
Electricity: 110 volts
Fitness Facilities/Spa Services: See text
Sports: Hiking; mountain biking in Blue Mountains; sightseeing excursions, coffee plantation tours; swimming pool
Dress Code: Casual
Children: Allowed but no facilities
Meetings: Small conference room for up to thirty people; state-of-the-art audiovisual equipment
Day Visitors: Welcome for lunch and dinner with reservations. Visitors may tour property; see manager at front desk upon arrival.
Handicapped: Not recommended
Packages: Honeymoon, wedding, spa
Rates: Per room, single or double, per night, CP. *High Season* (mid-December–March 31): $325–$775. *Low Season:* $315–$715. Monthly rates available; inquire.
Service Charge: 10 percent
Government Tax: Included

HALF MOON GOLF, TENNIS & BEACH CLUB
Montego Bay, Jamaica, W.I.

The entrance leading to the porte cochere is a long, flower-festooned driveway, a wedding cake of arches and filigree wrapped in bouquets of exuberant tropical flowers. It's so pretty that you barely notice you've passed security gates. Walls are camouflaged with flowered hedges to protect this fairyland of snow-white villas and gazebos.

From the porte cochere you are greeted by a large marble-paved lobby open all the way to the sea. This elegant lobby, furnished with Queen Anne–style mahogany chairs and other pieces, has a front desk with state-of-the-art computerized check-in facilities and a private check-in lounge for VIP guests. Beyond is a lobby bar and open-air lounge next to the Seagrape Terrace, the main indoor-outdoor restaurant by the sea.

Set in carefully tended lawns and gardens at the edge of a 2-mile stretch of white-sand beach, Half Moon is one of the most complete resorts in the Caribbean. Since it opened in 1954, it has grown from a cluster of cottages around Half Moon Bay—truly a perfect crescent—to a vast resort spread over 400 acres. It boasts a wide range of accommodations and extensive sports facilities, including a championship golf course, a tennis and squash complex, and fitness center, along with an array of activities and services.

Its plantation-style buildings house spacious guest rooms, most with sitting areas, large suites, and baronial one- and two-story villas with patios and balconies. The villas have kitchens, large tiled bathrooms, and separate dressing areas; some have private or semiprivate pools. Each of the thirty-two Royal Villas, the most luxurious of the accommodations, has a private pool. They offer privacy, but they are quite a distance from the main restaurant and bar. There is a grocery shop in the hotel's shopping arcade, and the resort can supply private cooks.

Throughout, from the lobby to the guest rooms and air-conditioned meeting rooms, British colonial architecture harmonizes with English country house interiors, using furniture made in Jamaica. Some rooms have four-poster beds.

The large, tree-shaded Seagrape Terrace restaurant and its breezy bar directly by the beach are the center of activity throughout the day. In the evening the setting, especially pretty for candlelight dining under the stars, offers a wide selection of continental and Caribbean-Jamaican cuisine. Next to the Terrace is Il Giardino, serving Italian cuisine. On the second floor is a piano bar with nightly entertainment and a meeting room. The bar opens onto a large balcony overlooking the beach, where tea is served in the afternoon and cocktails in the evening.

The Sugar Mill, on the hillside above Half Moon, has an enchanting garden setting next to a 200-year-old waterwheel. This gourmet restaurant offers its own original Caribbean haute cuisine.

Half Moon's beach is not deep, but it is long. Swimmers also have a choice of three large freshwater pools. Guests in some villas enjoy one of the seventeen private or semiprivate pools. Snorkeling, scuba diving, sailing, windsurfing, and deep-sea fishing (all at additional charge) are available from the water-sports center.

Half Moon's beautiful eighteen-hole championship golf course, designed by Robert Trent Jones, is one of Jamaica's best. Built on undulating terrain in the foothills and by the sea, the 7,115-yard, par-seventy-two course is made difficult by the tricky breezes that blow in off the ocean. A David Leadbetter Golf Academy helps golfers at all levels improve their swings—but the advice does not come cheap.

Half Moon's Fitness Center has been upgraded and expanded with the latest exercise equipment and beauty treatments. A personal trainer is available to help guests

develop a fitness program. The center has men's and women's sauna and steam rooms, Vichy and Swiss showers, and four massage rooms. Yoga and aerobics classes are offered daily. A championship tennis pavilion adjoins the tennis complex, which has squash and tennis courts. There are jogging and biking paths and horseback-riding trails.

The Children's Center, attended by a staff of trained counselors, is open daily and offers arts and crafts, nature walks, and other activities. It has a swimming pool, swings, tennis courts, playhouses, sandboxes, and a duck pond.

Live music—combo, calypso, or steel band—is available for dancing most evenings in the bar or Seagrape Terrace, and there is a folklore show at least one night a week. Half Moon has a group of shops next to the main lobby and a large, attractive upscale shopping center with high-quality boutiques located a mile or so east of the hotel in a separate complex that also houses restaurants, an ATM, a grocery, a pharmacy, and a conference center. The complex is part of Half Moon "village," with deluxe five-bedroom villas.

Half Moon has a new, unusual service—plastic surgery. Dr. Z. Paul Lorenc, a leading New York aesthetic plastic surgeon, brings his medical expertise with cosmetic procedures for face and body to the resort twice yearly. Dr. Lorenc performs at MoBay Hope Medical Centre, a fully accredited hospital located in Half Moon's Shopping Village and is assisted by a trained staff. Once surgery is completed, patient/guests may stay overnight at MoBay Hope or recuperate at one of the resort's private villas five minutes away where they have a butler, housekeeper, and cook to look after them. For those who want instant gratification, Dr. Lorenc treats wrinkles, crow's feet, and furrows with Restylane and Botox. Such treatments can be done in less than an hour and do not require an overnight hospital stay.

Half Moon is the very definition of barefoot elegance, combining a certain glamour and style with a laid-back Caribbean ambience. Guests are the most international you'll find at any of Jamaica's resorts: British and European princes and princesses—not to mention Hollywood ones—captains of industry, and sportsmen as well as business-meeting participants and Japanese honeymooners . Somehow it all seems to fit together.

Half Moon Golf, Tennis & Beach Club ✳✳✳✳
P.O. Box 80, Montego Bay, Jamaica, W.I.
Phone: (876) 953–2211; Fax: (876) 953–2731;
e-mail: reservations@halfmoonclub.com;
www.halfmoon.com.jm; www.eri-resorts.com

Owner/Managing Director: Half Moon Bay Ltd.
General Manager: Peter Komposch
Open: Year-round
Credit Cards: All major
U.S. Reservations: Direct to hotel (twenty four-hour service), (800) 626–0592; or Elegant Resorts International, (800) 237–3237
Deposit: Three nights
Minimum Stay: Fourteen nights during Christmas/New Year's
Arrival/Departure: Transfer service arranged for fee
Distance from Airport: (Montego Bay Airport) 5 miles; taxi one-way, $20
Distance from Montego Bay: 7 miles; taxi one-way, $30
Accommodations: 418 units (34 superior rooms; 119 deluxe, junior, and imperial suites; 60 royal suites with private pools; 32 five- to seven-bedroom villas), all with private pool and terrace; all doubles with twin beds or kings
Amenities: Air-conditioning, ceiling fans; direct-dial telephone, television; safe; bath with tub and shower (some with bidet, too), hair dryer, basket of toiletries; bathrobe in royal suites; mini-bar or refrigerator, kitchen in villas; nightly turndown service; room service 7:00 A.M.–midnight
Electricity: 110/220 volts
Fitness Facilities/Spa Services: Fitness center and spa (see text)
Sports: Three large freshwater swimming pools, forty-nine private or semiprivate pools, children's pool; bikes, four squash courts (lighted), thirteen Laykold tennis courts (seven lighted), free use; lessons, equipment for fee. Windsurfing, Sunfish, diving, snorkeling, guided horseback riding for fee; 50 percent discount on golf for hotel guests; pro, pro shop, equipment, caddies, carts for fee
Dress Code: Casual by day, but long-sleeved shirts after 6:00 P.M. in winter; informal in summer, but shorts, T-shirts, jeans not allowed at dinner
Children: All ages; cribs, high chairs; Children's Center with playground and supervised activities; baby-sitters
Meetings: Up to 1,000 people
Day Visitors: Welcome
Handicapped: Facilities
Packages: Golf, honeymoon, wedding; Platinum (all-inclusive)
Rates: Per person, daily, EP. *High Season* (mid-December–mid-April): $195–$595. *Low Season:* $120–$395.
Service Charge: Included
Government Tax: Included

THE RITZ-CARLTON ROSE HALL, JAMAICA
Montego Bay, Jamaica, W.I.

Located east of Montego Bay in the Rose Hall plantation area on Jamaica's north coast, the Ritz-Carlton Rose Hall, Jamaica opened in late 2000. The beachfront resort, owned by an affiliate of the Rollins Group of Wilmington, Delaware, is fifteen minutes from Montego Bay International Airport and within easy reach of the Half Moon Bay shopping center.

The layout, which fronts 1,500 feet of prime beach, includes the main building with a spacious lobby, looking out to the gardens and sea, and four separate wings with guest rooms overlooking the gardens or sea. The off-white stucco buildings with rust-colored roofs frame the swimming pool and the resort's tropical gardens and fountains. Arched doorways, vaulted ceilings, tall columns, and open-air spaces are architectural features throughout the hotel, which together with the British-colonial interior decor reflect the style of Jamaica's historic plantation homes. Vibrant hues of fuschia, gold, and turquoise are inspired by the island's blue waters, sunny skies, and colorful flora.

All guest rooms and suites have private, covered balconies with balustrade fronts. Tropical floral prints, mahogany bedposts, and rattan furniture are elements in the casually elegant decor. All rooms are equipped with Internet access and have television and a minibar. Bathrooms with white marble floors and walls have double sinks in a long white marble counter with the usual array

of Ritz-Carlton toiletries, hair dryer, and separate shower stall, tub, and toilet.

The Ritz-Carlton Club, accessed by elevator key only, has a dedicated concierge and private lounge where complimentary food and beverages are offered five times daily. It has thirty-three rooms, including two for handicapped, three suites, and the Presidential Suite.

The resort's eighteen-hole, 6,800-yard championship golf course, White Witch, is named after the famed storybook, *The White Witch of Rosehall,* by Herbert G. de Lesser. Designed by Robert Von Hagge and Associates, the course is situated across more than 200 acres of lush green mountainsides and rolling country with sixteen holes embracing dramatic views of the Caribbean Sea and several holes with water hazards. The clubhouse has an open-air restaurant with a 1,700 square-foot veranda and takes in views of the golf course, the ocean, and the mountains. White Witch has a resident pro, pro shop, and separate men's and ladies' locker rooms.

The Ritz-Carlton's outdoor swimming pool area, located between the central gardens and the beach, is crowded with lounge chairs. (An additional pool is planned near the meeting hall for use primarily by groups.) There is a small Jacuzzi hidden in the foliage near the pool. A walkway from the pool area leads to the beach where a variety of water sports is available. In

another area of the grounds, you find two tennis courts and a tennis pavilion with a juice bar and a tennis pro available for group or individual lessons.

The Spa and Fitness Center, one of the resort's most popular amenities, has ten treatment rooms and offers the full array of body treatments including deep-tissue massage, reflexology, shiatsu, and facials, including Ritz-Carlton's signature facial and facials for men.

The Spa's wet rooms offer a rain forest bath as well as scrub, seaweed, and mud therapies and wraps. Massages, facials, and wet treatments are also given in rooms designed specifically for two—couples, mothers and daughters, and siblings. Therapists are on hand to train spa guests to perform massage techniques on each other at home. The salon offers hair and nail services for men and women.

The Fitness Center has state-of-the-art cardiovascular and weight-training equipment. Ladies' and men's locker rooms have steam and sauna, shower facilities, and full-sized lockers. Island discovery hikes and nature tours are available through the center.

The Ritz-Carlton's dining options include Horizons for all-day dining indoors in air-conditioning or on an outdoor patio, located on the lower level of the lobby overlooking the gardens. Adjacent to it is Jasmine's, serving outstanding (but expensive), creative Asian-Jamaican fusion cuisine, an innovative concept, new to Jamaica; and Mango's, the casual poolside bar and restaurant with a wide selection of local and international choices. Afternoon tea with classical piano music, cocktails and evening cordials, and desserts are served in Cohoba's, the lobby lounge and outdoor terrace. Off the lobby are the main bar, a boutique, and the signature shop.

The hotel's extensive meeting and banquet facilities cover 16,745 square feet and include a 10,800 square-foot ballroom and four meeting rooms. The area for outdoor functions can accommodate up to 600 people.

The hotel has taken over management of the famous Rose Hall Great House, one of Jamaica's prime attractions, which recently won the Phoenix Award, the highly coveted recognition for historic preservation and conservation given annually by the Society of American Travel Writers. The lower level of the house has a bar and the manor house is available for weddings and special events. The Ritz-Carlton also manages the Rose Hall Beach Club where motorized sports are available (nonmotorized sports are at the hotel). The club is open to nonhotel guests during the day.

The Ritz-Carlton has brought to Jamaica a high level of service, associated heretofore in Jamaica with such top small hotels as Jamaica Inn and Round Hill, and which is apparent throughout the resort.

The Ritz-Carlton Rose Hall, Jamaica ★★★★

One Ritz Carlton Drive, Rose Hall, St. James, Jamaica, W.I.
Phone: (876) 953–2800; www.ritzcarlton.com

Management: The Ritz-Carlton Hotel Company, Atlanta, Georgia

General Manager: Martin Nicholson

U.S. Reservations: Ritz-Carlton, (800) 241–3333

Deposit: Three nights; seven days cancellation

Credit Cards: Most major

Minimum Stay: Seven nights Christmas/New Year's with forty-five days full, nonrefundable prepayment

Arrival/Departure: Transfer service by hotel's bus or by town car for $35 round-trip

Distance from Airport: (Montego Bay) 7 miles

Accommodations: 430 guest rooms and suites with private balconies (260 king; 118 double-doubles; 51 executive suites; one Ritz-Carlton suite) with garden, pool, mountains, and partial or full ocean views; 33 Ritz-Carlton Club rooms and three suites and private lounge

Amenities: Air-conditioning; safe; stocked bar; marble bathrooms with separate shower and tub and dual sinks; cable television, digital clock/alarm radio, three telephones with dual lines and dataports, computer and fax hook-ups; terry bathrobes and slippers, goosedown pillows; twenty-four-hour room service. Ritz-Carlton Suite: living room/dining area, pantry, foyer with powder room, master bathroom, dressing area, walk-in closet; twice-daily maid service.

Electricity: 120 volts

Fitness Facilities/Spa Services: See text

Sports: Swimming pool, water sports, tennis; golf, see text

Dress Code: Casually elegant

Day Visitors: Yes

Handicapped: Special rooms

Children: All ages; Ritz Kids program; baby-sitting

Meetings: Up to 800 people

Packages: Golf, wedding, spa, honeymoon, weekend

Rates: Per person, double, per day, EP: Through December 20: $150–$170. **High Season** (December 21–January 2): $475–$520. (January 3–April 30): $345–$395. **Low season:** To be determined. Ritz Carlton-Club rooms, inquire.

Service Charge: 10 percent

Government Tax: 8.25 percent

ROUND HILL HOTEL AND VILLAS

Montego Bay, Jamaica, W.I.

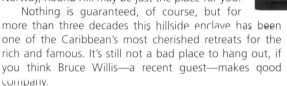

If you like the idea of sunset cocktails around the same piano Cole Porter once played, or dining on the terrace next to Ralph Lauren or the queen of Norway, Round Hill may be just the place for you.

Nothing is guaranteed, of course, but for more than three decades this hillside enclave has been one of the Caribbean's most cherished retreats for the rich and famous. It's still not a bad place to hang out, if you think Bruce Willis—a recent guest—makes good company.

You can't mistake the roadside entrance to Round Hill: white pillars with round (what else?) tops. The road along the ninety-eight-acre peninsula rounds the hill at the crest before descending quickly to the main building by the sea.

Round Hill was opened in 1953 by John Pringle, a prominent Jamaican who purchased the property. After selling land to some titled Europeans and affluent Jamaicans, he created a deluxe resort by getting his celebrity friends to become shareholders and build houses there. Noël Coward, Adele Astaire, the William Paleys, and the Oscar Hammersteins were among those who flocked here in the 1950s and came to regard Round Hill as their club.

Set amid acres of marvelous gardens, the villas cascade from the hilltop to the beach. Today they are more or less as they were originally built: light, airy, and unforgettably beautiful, combining easy Caribbean living with indulgent luxury.

Practical as well as pretty, villas are made up of two to four separate suites. Each has a private entrance, but they share the kitchen. You can rent the entire villa or a suite and still have your privacy, along with the services of the villa staff: a cook, maid, and gardener. Twenty-two of the twenty-seven villas have private swimming pools.

The exteriors are similar in design: All are one-story stone and white clapboard structures with shingled roofs and louvered shutters and doors opening onto terraces and seaward views. Inside, no two villas are alike, but most merit a spread in *House Beautiful*. Your housekeeper prepares and serves breakfast on your private terrace, from which you can feast on Jamaica's beauty framed by the flowering gardens that surround you.

Pringle's original hotel is now the beachfront Pineapple House, a white two-story building at the water's edge. All rooms have wide picture windows with louvered shutters. Rooms are furnished comfortably in traditional colonial style, some with four-poster mahogany beds with carved pineapple bedposts. All eighteen of the second-floor rooms blend light colors—cream and aqua, off white and blue—with dark wood in a sort of *Out of Africa* meets Jamaica way.

Pineapple House takes its name from Round Hill's logo, a Caribbean sign of welcome and a reminder that this was once a pineapple plantation. The emblem is everywhere: carved into headboards, shaped into lamps, and printed on all stationery. Pineapple House guests can breakfast in their rooms; on the upper level of the Georgian Pavilion, an open-air dining terrace; or at the seaside terrace.

Lunch for all is served alfresco on the hotel's tree-shaded dining terrace overlooking the bay. After a concerted effort to improve the fare, Round Hill can now boast some of the best cuisine of any hotel in Jamaica.

You will not have to wait for the manager's cocktail party on Tuesday to meet Josef Forstmayr. He is a hands-on, ever-present manager and gracious host. Either he or his assistant manager will greet you on arrival or the first time you dine on the terrace.

Evenings at the resort begin with cocktails in the piano bar, which was decorated by Round Hill home-owner Ralph Lauren. Dinner settings change from Monday night's barefoot picnic on the beach to Saturday

night's dinner dance in the Georgian Pavilion. Four nights a week, dinner in the dining terrace is followed by entertainment from the resident band and local artists, with dancing under the stars. Friday is Jamaica Night, featuring a folklore group and reggae band, while a steel band livens up the Monday scene.

The freshwater pool by Pineapple House compensates somewhat for Round Hill's small beach. A coral reef lies within swimming distance of shore, and use of snorkel gear is included in the rates (as are use of the tennis courts and transfers to nearby golf at Tryall). Whatever you do, don't overlook the art gallery. It specializes in the fabulous whimsical animal sculptures from Liz DeLisser's Gallery of West Indian Art in Montego Bay.

Recently Round Hill added Bunty's Cottage, a wellness center offering a comprehensive program of face and body treatments. Named for a beloved member of the Round Hill staff, the spa is the first in the Caribbean to use France-based Decleor Aromatherapy products, formulated entirely from natural ingredients. The center, in a tropical setting, has five indoor treatment rooms and one outdoor area. Guests may also receive treatments in their villas. The cottage's creamy beige decor, candlelight, and soft music are intended to create a soothing atmosphere. Among the services are stress-reduction aromatherapy massage; Reiki; reflexology; a holistic consultation; and a treatment to help regain skin firmness after weight loss. Also offered are facials, aromatherapy scalp and hand treatments, manicures, pedicures, and hairstyling. Treatments cost from $60 to $100. Wellness packages combining several treatments are available for men and women, from $165 to $350.

Times have changed and so have the owners of the villas, but Round Hill is still glamorous in a way that's hard to find these days. Hollywood must think so: Terry McMillan's *How Stella Got Her Groove Back* was filmed here. If you want to book Stella's villa, ask for Number 11.

Round Hill Hotel and Villas ✱✱✱✱

P.O. Box 64, Montego Bay, Jamaica, W.I.
Phone: (800) 972–2159, (876) 956–7050; Fax: (876) 956–7505; e-mail: roundhill@cwjamaica.com; www.roundhilljamaica.com

Owner: Round Hill Developments Ltd.
General Manager: Josef F. Forstmayr
Open: Year-round
Credit Cards: All major
U.S. Reservations: Direct to hotel, (800) 972–2159, Elegant Resorts of Jamaica, (800) 237–3237; Fax: (305) 666–8505; or Robert Reid Associates, (800) 223–6510
Deposit: Three nights
Minimum Stay: Ten nights, December 22–January 2
Arrival/Departure: Transfer service arranged for fee
Distance from Airport: *(Montego Bay Airport)* 10 miles; taxi one-way, $30; free daily shuttle to town
Accommodations: 110 rooms (36 in Pineapple House, 16 with twin beds, 20 king; 74 rooms and suites in 27 private villas with twins and kings; all villas staffed; 22 with private pools)
Amenities: Air-conditioning, ceiling fans; bath with tub and shower, bathrobes, basket of toiletries; telephone; kitchen in villas; ice service; nightly turndown service, room service 7:30 A.M.–9:30 P.M.; beauty salon; television, radio, VCR for rent, boutiques, afternoon tea in cocktail bar; free Internet access service
Electricity: 110 volts
Fitness Facilities/Spa Services: Fitness room with exercise equipment; aerobic, exercise, yoga classes; jogging trail, weekly nature walk; beauty salon with full-service spa
Sports: Hotel swimming pool, twenty-two private pools for villas; five Laykold tennis courts (two lighted), equipment free, proper tennis attire required; snorkeling gear; golf arranged at four Montego Bay courses; free transfers to Tryall for golf; water sports for fee; deep-sea fishing, horseback riding arranged
Dress Code: Casual, but shoes, shirts, cover-up required in dining areas; no T-shirts, shorts, sneakers after 7:00 P.M., except Monday
Children: All ages; cribs, high chairs; baby-sitters; children's dinner served from 6:00 P.M. May 1–October 31; family package lets children up to sixteen years old stay in separate adjoining superior or deluxe room in Pineapple House at no charge; half price meal plans for children under twelve; and more
Meetings: Up to 180 people
Day Visitors: Welcome
Handicapped: No facilities
Packages: Honeymoon, wedding; Platinum (all-inclusive)
Rates: Two people, daily, EP. *High Season* (mid-December–mid-April): $420–$850. *Low Season:* $260–$550. Two- to four-bedroom villas, weekly including full American breakfast daily, $7,000–$12,000 and $3,500–$6,000, respectively
Service Charge: Included
Government Tax: Included

THE TRYALL CLUB
Montego Bay, Jamaica, W.I.

To take afternoon tea on the terrace of the Great House at tradition-rich Tryall is to glimpse the grand style of colonial life in bygone days. (No wonder the British didn't want to give up the Empire!)

To spend a week in a villa at Tryall is to peek at the lifestyle of the rich, more than the famous—and today more American than British.

To play golf on Tryall's famous eighteen-hole championship course, one of the best in Jamaica, is to experience the island's beauty while being humbled by the difficulty of these benign-looking greens. And to travel the 2,200 acres of this former sugar and coconut plantation is to understand why its aficionados say, "There will never be another Tryall."

In recent years, Tryall seemed to be suffering an identity crisis—a parade of managers and name changes. However, since the owners brought in veteran hotelier Ted Ruddock and food and beverage consultant Herbert Baur, and undertook a major upgrade of facilities including the golf course, the enterprise has taken on new life.

Located on the northern shores of Jamaica, Tryall is an exclusive luxury suite and villa resort of great distinction. Its vast acres flow from forested mountainsides through manicured gardens to the sea. At the center, the restored early nineteenth-century manor house sits high on the hillside with gardens sloping down to the beach. The site catches a constant breeze and commands breathtaking,

wide-angle views. The waterwheel, installed in 1834 when the Great House was built, is the backdrop of the golf course's sixth hole.

The gracious Great House, with its antiques-filled parlors, dining room, and broad terraces, is the hub of the resort's social life. A long one- and two-story wing perpendicular to the Great House houses the hotel's spacious, elegant one- and two-bedroom guest suites, which are among the finest in the Caribbean. Some of the region's most palatial vacation homes, belonging to Tryall's owners, are in the hills framing the Great House and by the sea.

There are two categories of rooms, based on their view. All overlook the gardens and the fairways, with magnificent, expansive views stretching to Montego Bay. Some are duplex suites, others are on one level; all have living and dining areas and fully equipped kitchens. The upper floors of the duplexes have small balconies; those below have terraces.

The guest rooms are individually furnished in British-colonial style, accented with a museum collection of antiques and art belonging to individual owners. Recently all the rooms and suites were refurbished with handsome new fabrics and posh marble bathrooms, several with Jacuzzi baths.

You can take breakfast in your room (your housekeeper will cook breakfast and lunch for you at no additional charge; an excellent new food shop is on the

property) or in the Great House. A casual lunch can be taken in the delightful setting of the Beach Cafe or by the pretty pool with a swim-up bar.

The villas are Tryall's crown jewels. All in harmonious, traditional design, the privately owned mansions, with names like Linger Longer, Tranquillity, and No Problem, are exquisitely furnished and fully staffed. They are set in spacious lawns and gardens, providing greater privacy than the Great House suites. Each villa has its own pool and staff: cook, chambermaid, laundress, and gardener. The four- to seven-bedroom villas have a larger staff. You may choose to dine in your villa or at the Great House. (A shuttle service for all guests circles the property throughout the day and evening until 11:00 P.M.)

On Thursdays down by the beach, an early-evening barbecue features Jamaican dishes, entertainment by a

Jamaican folklore group, and a crafts fair. The setting for dinner—weather permitting, on the lamp-lit Great House terrace—may be more spectacular than the food, although new menus, changed daily and now relying more on fresh ingredients, have improved the fare noticeably. The service is exemplary. Dinner might be followed by light entertainment. Guests usually adjourn to the popular, newly enlarged bar.

A spacious and well-equipped center houses Tryall's recently added Kids Club, where the nature walks, craft lessons, and sessions on Jamaican folklore have scored high with young families.

Tryall's tennis center, recently rated among top resort facilities worldwide in an Internet poll, has a resident pro who organizes weekly tournaments and helps put together foursomes.

The golf course, familiar to television audiences as the host of the Johnnie Walker Championships, tops the list of Tryall's sports facilities. The attractive course runs along Tryall's 1½ miles of seafront and through palm groves and rolling terrain, with fairways bordered by fruit and flowering trees, and rises to forested hills before returning to the sea. There is a jogging track near the Great House and a range of water sports by the beach.

Tryall is tony, gracious living at its best with the facilities of a modern resort. Honeymooners and romantics of all ages will not find a more beautiful place, and families are among the most dedicated fans. But Tryall is a resort with a clubby ambience. If you are a part of the club, you will love it. If not, come with friends.

The Tryall Club ★★★

P.O. Box 1206, Montego Bay, Jamaica, W.I.
Phone: (876) 956–5660; Fax: (876) 956–5673;
www.tryallclub.com

Owner: Privately owned units

Managing Director: Edward H. "Ted" Ruddock

Open: Year-round

Credit Cards: All major

U.S. Reservations: Karen Bull Associates, (800) 238–5290; Fax: (404) 237–1841; karenbull@mindspring

Deposit: 25%. Sixty days cancellation in winter, thirty days in summer

Minimum Stay: Fourteen nights at Christmas; seven nights in villas; applicable at other times, inquire.

Arrival/Departure: Transfer service on request

Distance from Airport: (Montego Bay Airport) 14 miles; taxi one-way, $35 for one to four passengers

Distance from Montego Bay: 12 miles; taxi one-way, $30 for one to four passengers

Accommodations: 13 one- and two-bedroom Great House villa suites; 56 estate villas with two to seven bedrooms

Amenities: Great House: Air-conditioning, ceiling fans; telephones; bath with tub and shower, hair dryer, basket of toiletries, bathrobe; beauty and massage salon, gift shop, cigar shop, art/craft gallery, convenience store; room with computer/Internet connection and fax for guest's use. For villas, inquire.

Electricity: 110 volts

Sports: Freshwater swimming pool; nine Nova cushion tennis courts (five lighted), equipment, resident pro; golf, caddies required, pro, pro shop; jogging trail; Sunfish, windsurfing, paddle boats, snorkeling; scuba diving, fishing, waterskiing, sailing, horseback riding arranged

Dress Code: Casual by day; elegantly casual for evening with long trousers and collared shirts for men year-round

Children: All ages; cribs, baby-sitters; Kids Club daily program

Meetings: Up to one hundred people

Day Visitors: Welcome

Handicapped: Limited facilities

Packages: All-inclusive, golf and other packages available

Rates: Great House, two persons, daily, EP. **High Season** (early January–March 31): $320-$360. **Low Season:** $200–$240. Inquire for villa prices.

Service Charge: Included

Government Tax: Included

COCO LA PALM

Negril, Jamaica, W.I.

Coco La Palm's five two-story buildings are set around a kidney-shaped pool surrounded by lush gardens along a pretty, tree-shaded beach in a tranquil corner of Negril's famous 7-mile beach. The hotel's open-terrace restaurant has an idyllic setting in front of the calm sea with light breezes softly caressing the air.

If there's a more pleasant place to start the day, I haven't seen it. What's more, you breakfast on some of the best food in Jamaica. In the evening the candlelit, open-air dining room becomes a romantic setting for dinner. The Beach Bar and Grill is open during the day for lunch and snacks.

Coco La Palm is for those who prefer a small, friendly, comfortable inn on the beach to the facilities and activities of Jamaica's well-known all-inclusive resorts. It's a modest,

quiet hotel—but many notches up from the typical laid-back Negril resorts.

In 2001, the resort almost doubled in size when it acquired Silver Sands, the property next door. The former oceanfront rooms have already been made into five suites overlooking the second swimming pool and the beach, now doubled in length. When a group, such as a wedding party, books the five suites together, it is given exclusive use of the pool. The additional twenty-three rooms acquired in the purchase are being called Coco Inn until they are brought up to the level of the La Palm accommodations. The required renovations and upgrading will take place over the next two years or so; in the meantime, these rooms are being priced at budget level.

The acquisition also gave Coco La Palm a sundries

shop, an art gallery, and a beauty salon that has limited spa treatments at reasonable prices (for example, an in-room massage is $20 for thirty minutes; $40 for an hour).

Across the road, Coco La Palm added a new building that houses a meeting room with audiovisual equipment and seating for thirty people; a laundry; a new bakery where all the resort's breads and pastries are made; and space for a future Internet center.

The Minnesota family-owned and -operated hotel has an easygoing, friendly atmosphere, set by the owner, John Vosika, and his son, Michael Marks, where guests feel an immediate camaraderie. You will meet the other guests at the poolside welcome cocktail party on Monday evening.

All the rooms at Coco La Palm are large—the standard rooms, for instance, are 450 square feet. They have tile floors and wooden ceilings; they're pleasantly, adequately furnished but not fancy. All are air-conditioned and have ceiling fans; a mini-kitchen unit with a refrigerator, sink, and coffeemaker; satellite television; a safe; and a large bath with his and hers showerheads.

Water-sports equipment is available from a vendor next door on the beach. The Negril Golf Course is about 3 miles to the east, and you can buy a reduced-price day pass to use Couples Swept Away's fitness center and sports facilities, a short distance away. Coco La Palm's particular area of Negril Beach is delightful for jogging, walking, strolling, or simply stretching out on the sand and watching the world go by or the sun sinking slowly in the west.

Coco La Palm ✱✱

Norman Manley Boulevard, Negril, Westmoreland, Jamaica, W.I.
Phone: (876) 957–4227, (809) 957–3460;
e-mail: cocolap@cwjamaica.com; www.cocolapalm.com

Owner/Manager: John Vosika
Manager/Sales Director: Michael Mark
Resident Manager: William "Ferron" Vassell
Open: Year-round
Credit Cards: Most major
U.S. Reservations: 7225 Hemlock Lane North, #104, Maple Grove, MN 55369; (800) 896–0987, (763) 493–5201, (703) 425–9022
Deposit: Three nights, or full payment if staying less than three nights
Minimum Stay: None
Arrival/Departure: Arranged for fee
Distance from Airport: (Montego Bay Airport) 56 miles (two-hour drive); bus one-way, $60; Negril Airport: 7 miles (fifteen-minute drive), taxi one-way, $10.
Distance from Negril: 2 miles
Accommodations: 71 (48 in Coco La Palm; 23 in Coco Inn) rooms and suites with ocean, pool, or garden view and patio, terrace, or balcony (17 junior suites with one king or two queens; one honeymoon suite with king; 14 superior rooms with two queens; 16 standard rooms with king; 23 budget rooms with twins or queen; one villa)
Amenities: Ceiling fan, air-conditioning; bath with large shower; safe; coffeemaker, refrigerator, wet bar; telephone, television
Electricity: 110 volts
Sports: Beach, swimming pool, Jacuzzi, water sports; golf nearby
Dress Code: Casual
Children: All ages; baby-sitting; up to two children under twelve free in room with parents
Meetings: Group conferences arranged; banquet services available
Day Visitors: No
Handicapped: One room available
Packages: Wedding
Rates: Per room, single or double, EP. *High Season* (mid-December–mid-April): $185–$250. *Low Season:* $145–$185. Coco Inn: *High Season:* $100. *Low Season:* Inquire.
Service Charge: 10 percent
Government Tax: 6.25 percent

COUPLES SWEPT AWAY
Negril, Jamaica, W.I.

If ten tennis courts, a fully equipped gym, two racquet courts, a squash court, an aerobics center, an Olympic-size swimming pool, unlimited golf, and yoga sessions hit the right buttons, you'll think you're in heaven when you arrive at this spiffy resort, which sweeps around the white sands of Negril Beach. And these marvels are part of an all-inclusive package: You pay nothing extra for meals, beverages, use of sports facilities, or even transfers and gratuities.

Couples Swept Away has found a niche within the niche of Jamaica's all-inclusive resorts. Not as frenetic or glitzy as the rest, but more romantic than some of its neighbors down the beach, Couples Swept Away enjoys a laid-back, serene ambience geared to people interested in keeping fit even when on vacation.

You don't really have to be a health and fitness nut to enjoy Couples Swept Away—mildly interested will do. No one will push you to rise at 7:00 A.M. and hit the courts before the sun gets too hot (besides, the courts are lit for night play) or if you don't show up for aerobics. The marvelous sports facilities are right here, on the premises, when—or if—you want to work out and use them.

Here you vacation in sync with nature. Wind chimes fill the air; flowers and tropical foliage dress the grounds. The Veggie Bar serves up incredible fresh fruit and vegetable drinks that look more like works of art than beverages.

The architecture and decor throughout show a sense of style. Low-key and in stellar good taste, the guest rooms as well as public areas make use of the best examples of Jamaica's superior-quality furniture, crafts, and art. Earth-toned fabrics, natural woods and ceramics, and rat-

tan pieces contrast well with the terra-cotta floors, which are practical as well as attractive.

The guest rooms, clustered tightly between the road and the beach, are in villa-style buildings of cream stucco trimmed with rich, dark hard wood and linked by a labyrinth of garden walkways. Floor-to-ceiling louvered doors and windows, helped by ceiling fans, encourage sea breezes to cool your suite. Spacious verandas with built-in divans and comfy rattan lounges lure you to laze away the hours gazing out to sea.

There are three categories of accommodations. Garden-view rooms are the farthest from the beach. Atrium suites, on or close to the beach, are in groups of four rooms that share a central garden. These can be a bit noisy if your neighbors have loud voices. (After complaints from guests about the traffic noises heard in villas toward

the back, these villas were soundproofed.) Both the garden and atrium rooms have huge verandas. The third type are villas directly on the beach. Each has two rooms upstairs with a separate veranda, and one suite on the ground floor, also with a private veranda.

Directly across the road from the resort's front entrance is the Sports and Fitness Complex, the most comprehensive facility of its kind in Jamaica—if not the Caribbean. In addition to the air-conditioned racquetball and squash courts and the lighted tennis courts (hard and clay), the fully staffed facilities include an exercise lap pool, a complete gym with Cybex, an aerobics center with an ExerFlex floor (it gives when you bounce), a basketball court, aquacise, saunas, steam rooms, whirlpools, bicycles, a jogging track, and a pro shop. The complex hosts

trendy fitness workout classes including "butts, guts, and thighs"; boxing and instruction; superabdominals, basketball clinics and games, Step 101; stretch classes; and a circuit cardio routine. All these are in addition to a mind-boggling daily schedule of exercise sessions and clinics, from aerobics and power walks to tennis and yoga. The center offers fitness assessments and evaluations and has personal trainers available by appointment.

Water sports include Sunfish sailing, windsurfing, waterskiing, snorkeling, and scuba diving—all with instruction. A dive resort course is included; PADI certification is extra. A free-form pool and a whirlpool are alongside a great beach. Unlimited golf at the Negril Hills Golf Club, a few miles from Couples Swept Away, is included; transportation is provided.

Couples Swept Away has two theme months, Spa or Wellness Month (September) and Tennis Month (October), with experts on hand to enhance the experience and give you the opportunity to interact with celebrities and learn from professionals.

The Oasis spa offers a full array of beauty and body services at an additional charge. Treatments include aromatherapy facials and massages, prenatal massages, and couple baths. Wedding spa packages are also available.

A commodious, two-level open pavilion next to the pool and beach houses the dining room and entertainment area. Regrettably, it is not in keeping with the great sense of style that characterizes Couples Swept Away.

Buffets feature international fare with a Jamaican flair, and table service is available. Pizza lovers might easily get swept away with the fresh renderings in the Sports Lounge, which has a big-screen television. Feathers, the resort's top restaurant, is open in the evening, offering sophisticated international and Caribbean selections with French influences. The Seagrape Cafe in a romantic, open-air setting by the beach features grilled fare with Jamaican flavors.

The piano bar is lively in the early evening, and a resident band plays nightly for dancing. Varied entertainment—a native floor show or a Jamaican band with a cabaret singer—is scheduled throughout the week. You'll find a game room with billiards and cable television. Couples Swept Away guests can connect to AT&T from their rooms for free (hotels often charge $1.00 or more) and now have an easy way to stay in touch at the resort's new computer room with twenty-four-hour e-mail facilities at no extra cost (some hotels charge $5.00 to $10.00 for use).

Most guests here come from the United States and Canada, but the number coming from Europe, other Caribbean islands, and Latin America is growing. In addition to its obvious appeal to fitness-oriented couples, Couples Swept Away has great charm for honeymooners and romantics of all ages. What's more, repeaters get the one-way arrival flight from Montego Bay Airport to Negril Airport free.

Couples Swept Away ✳✳✳

Norman Manley Boulevard, Box 3077, Negril, Jamaica, W.I.
Phone: (876) 957–4061, (876) 957–4040; Fax: (876) 957–4061; e-mail :couplesresorts@couples.com; www.couples.com

Owner: Lee Issa

General Manager: Jeffrey Boland

Open: Year-round

Credit Cards: All major

U.S. Reservations: (800) 545–7937

Deposit: One night; twenty-one days cancellation

Minimum Stay: Three nights

Arrival/Departure: Transfer included in all-inclusive package

Distance from Airport: (Montego Bay Airport) 60 miles, one-and-a-half hours by car

Distance from Negril: 3 miles; taxi one-way, about $8.00

Accommodations: 134 rooms in 26 two-story villas with verandas; 58 garden (24 with two double beds; 34 with king); 54 atrium (all kings); 20 beachfront (all kings)

Amenities: Air-conditioning, ceiling fans; bath with shower only, hair dryer, basket of toiletries; telephone, coffeemaker, television in lounge; room service for continental breakfast, ice service, nightly turndown service; spa (extra charge for treatments)

Electricity: 120 volts

Fitness Facilities/Spa Services: See text

Sports: See text

Dress Code: Casual by day; casually elegant in evening

Children: No

Day Visitors: $75 per day provides access to Sports Complex and Resort

Meetings: Up to 80 people

Handicapped: No facilities

Packages: All-inclusive, honeymoon, wedding (no extra charge)

Rates: Per person, per week, all inclusive. *High Season* (mid-December–mid-April): $1,855–$2,310. *Low Season:* $1,750–$2,205.

Service Charge: Included

Government Tax: Included

ROCKHOUSE HOTEL AND RESTAURANT
Negril, Jamaica, W.I.

Rockhouse was one of Negril's first hotels. Flower children put this then-undiscovered hideaway on the map in the early 1970s. But in 1995 Inhouse Hotels, owned by three enterprising young Aussies, purchased the old Rockhouse and renovated and upgraded it to such a degree that it's a new hotel.

Situated in the rocky area of the western coast on two and a half acres at the top of a cliff that drops precipitously to the sea, Rockhouse is comprised of fourteen thatched-roof, octagonal cottages of rock and wood in a jungle of exotic gardens. It reminds some people of a South Seas island and others of an African village.

Two particularly welcome amenities that the new owners added were a restaurant (the old hotel never had one) and a cliffside, freshwater swimming pool (which replaced a small, saltwater tidal pool).

The restaurant, built of stone with a thatched roof, has a cantilevered balcony suspended over the cove. It serves three meals daily and features local specialties, as well as a broad wine list. There is also a full room-service menu; with the installation of a new phone system, you can order from the restaurant to have food served in your room or anywhere on the property. During the winter season, the pool bar is open from 10:00 A.M. to sunset and serves grilled burgers, kebab, and fish.

The new pool, carved from rock at the edge of the cliff, pleases former guests who might not have cherished diving into the sea from the rocks, although the water here—aptly named Pristine Cove—is perhaps the cleanest and clearest in Negril. Ladders and stairs carved into the rock provide easy access to the water for swimming and snorkeling on the nearby reef. There is no beach but many more sunning places have been added. These cozy corners, built out over the rocks, have two lounge chairs and an umbrella and provide greater privacy and direct access to the sea. They also make a fine perch for watching dolphins or sunsets. Also near the pool, a new outside massage area has been added.

Even with all the changes, the resort maintains its seclusion and Jamaican flavor as a rustic escape with a primitive charm, light-years away from the action of Negril, or indeed, from civilization.

Regardless of how rustic the accommodations may look from outside, they are quite comfortable inside. The stone and wood, peaked-roof cottages have sliding glass doors that provide great vistas and lead outside to a terrace. They have an indoor toilet and sink and an enclosed outdoor shower open to the skies. The cottages are set far enough apart to offer privacy, too. Most are situated directly over the water so that you can fall asleep to the sound of the surf.

The original cottages are furnished with comfortable beds, and there is electricity to turn the ceiling fans and run the minibars. One cottage is divided into two studios; the others have queen-size beds. Four cottages have a sleeping loft with one double and a twin bed. Two of the cottages, #8 and #10, were upgraded completely, with stone facing on the outside and inside. New modern bathrooms are separated from the sleeping area by an attractive stone partition. Other cottages now have brightly painted exteriors and terraces repaved with cut stone. But perhaps the biggest change of all—air-conditioning has been added to

all the accommodations along with safes and CD players. Internet access comes next.

In 1998 the hotel doubled its capacity with the addition of fourteen more rooms in two two-story cement-block buildings (well disguised with colorful exteriors and wooden slat doors under thatched roofs). Less expensive rooms in the block farthest from the sea have small indoor bathrooms; more deluxe rooms are found in the building near the pool.

The latter has eight rooms with tiled baths and large patios at the front and back, each separated from the others by a bamboo-enclosed outdoor shower and tropical garden. The rooms are outfitted with furniture designed especially for Rockhouse and made from local woods. All rooms have ceiling fans, safes, and minibars. Rockhouse has also installed a pressurized water system with master tank storage, while power from backup generators ensures continuous service. The entire property runs on solar-heated water. There's also a new Rockhouse Shop.

Rockhouse has built a reservoir of loyal fans, particularly behind-the-scenes people from the movie and music world, such as producers and directors. But now, with the greater amenities, almost anyone who wants a close-to-nature experience, without giving up comfort and still being at the heart of the action in Negril, could be happy here.

Rockhouse Hotel and Restaurant *

P.O. Box 3024, West End Road, Negril, Jamaica, W.I.; Phone: (876) 957–4373; Fax: (876) 957–0557; e-mail: info@rockhousehotel.com; www.rockhouse.com

Owner: Inhouse Hotel, Ltd.
General Managers: Lisa Schnepf and Fabian Ippoliti
Open: Year-round
Credit Cards: Most major
U.S. Reservations: Direct to hotel
Deposit: Three nights
Minimum Stay: Three nights during U.S. public holidays
Arrival/Departure: Transfer by car $60, by bus $20, one-way
Distance from Airport: *(Montego Bay Airport)* 56 miles (two-hour drive); bus one-way, $60 up to four people. *Negril Airport:* 7 miles (fifteen-minute drive); taxi one-way, $10.
Distance from Negril: 2½ miles; taxi one-way, $5.00–$8.00.
Accommodations: 28 rooms (ten premium cottages, 12 studios of which two have bunk beds, six standard rooms), all with terrace or balcony and queen-size four-poster bed; four cottages with additional sleeping loft with double bed and twin
Amenities: Ceiling fan, stand fan, air-conditioning; safe, CD player; minibar; telephone; no television; bath with shower, hair dryer available; room service available
Electricity: 110 volts
Sports: Swimming pool; spa, horseback riding, tennis, golf; sailing, snorkeling, diving, windsurfing, and other water sports arranged
Dress Code: Informal
Children: Twelve years and older; charged at third-person rate
Meetings: Ten person conference facility
Day Visitors: Welcome
Handicapped: No facilities
Packages: No
Rates: Per room, double, EP. **High Season** (mid-December–mid-April): $120 (studio), $95–$195 (cottage). **Low Season** (mid-April–mid-December): $85 (studio), $65–$120 (cottage).
Service Charge: 10 percent
Government Tax: 6.25 percent

GRAND LIDO SANS SOUCI

Ocho Rios, Jamaica, W.I.

Romance *toujours*. It's always in the air at Sans Souci. Is it the gorgeous setting or the mellow air of tradition? Or is it the ambience of sans souci?

In French *sans souci* means "without a care," and you will not have many in this pink palazzo by the sea. One of Jamaica's oldest resorts, Grand Lido Sans Souci is nestled tightly between the mountains and sea on a bluff in terraced gardens. Enormous African tulip trees form umbrellas beside a mineral spring that spills down the rockbound cove to the sea. The springs, the centerpiece of the resort's spa, were known for their curative powers as far back as the 1700s. Recent tests found them to be on a par with the most famous spa waters in Europe.

The present resort, which became a member of SuperClubs in 1993, was born in the 1960s when a Jamaican company created a luxurious beachside residential complex to replace an earlier spa on the site. Stanhope Joel, one of Britain's wealthiest men, teamed up with well-known Caribbean architect Robertson "Happy" Ward to design Sans Souci with a charming blend of Georgian colonial and Italian Renaissance styles. At Ward's request Berger Paints created an exclusive color—Sans Souci Pink—for the hotel, which is still used.

Ward's plans, advanced for the times, put electrical and phone wires underground; an outdoor elevator from the lobby level to the mineral pool below for easy access; and an oversize outdoor chessboard on the terrace with 2-foot-high pieces (carved by a local Rastafarian who had never seen a chess set!). In all, forty-three apartments were built and sold to wealthy and titled British travelers.

The complex changed ownership several times over the years, but the major transformation came in 1984, when a Jamaican businessman formed the Sans Souci Hotel and Club. His wife, an interior designer, renovated the entire complex, dividing the apartments into deluxe rooms and one-bedroom suites. Her signature, the charming Balloon Bar with its tiny papier-mâché figures of famous balloonists, remains.

In 1991 a new complex, divorced from the older hotel, was added on a 400-foot private white-sand beach at the western end of the property. Its suites are a vision of pinks and corals with buff ceramic tiles and walls. They have folding French doors that separate the bedroom from the sitting room; other doors open onto the terra-cotta tile terrace. The bathroom, marbled from top to bottom, has twin sinks, a Jacuzzi tub, and a separate shower. Thirty-six more beachfront suites were added in 1998. Sans Souci has a clothing-optional beach where there's a pool with swim-up bar and a grill.

The units are convenient to the tennis courts, the pool, and Ristorante Palazzina, a casual air-conditioned indoor restaurant with covered terrace where buffet breakfast and lunch are served. The informal setting is convenient for sunbathers (often topless Europeans, who need only add a top for lunch). In the evening Palazzina serves Italian cuisine, with reserved seating from 6:30 to 9:30 P.M. Other options include the Beach Grill for snacks and traditional Jamaican specialties; the Terrace for afternoon tea; Bella Vista, where Jamaican cuisine is served in a casual setting under the stars less than 10 feet from the water's edge (no reservations required); and Casanova, serving gourmet cuisine in a sophisticated atmosphere (reservations required).

Accommodations in the older wings include veranda suites and one- and two-bedroom suites with large bedrooms and living rooms, most in soft yellow decor with custom-designed fabrics. Twenty-four-hour room service is available—an unusual feature for an all-inclusive resort.

The main lobby has elegant carved-wood furniture. A game room by the lobby has a pool table, backgammon, chess games, and various board games. From the lobby, several terraces (one for dining, another with a freshwater pool) shaded by pink-and-white-striped umbrellas and huge tulip trees step down to quiet lanes that wind through the gardens. They lead to the mineral pool, spa, and beachside pavilion with a gym and exercise room. Charlie's Spa, named for a giant green sea turtle that lives in the grotto of the mineral springs, is professionally staffed and offers massage, body scrubs, facials, reflexology, saunas, as well as manicures and pedicures in the beauty salon. Treatments are complimentary—one of each per person.

Live nightly entertainment showcases some of Jamaica's finest cabaret artists, musicians, and cultural shows. Weekly themed galas are also on the entertainment roster. And with a restaurant named Casanova offering candlelight-and-wine dinner and music for dancing under the stars, what else is there but romance in the air?

Grand Lido Sans Souci, like its sister resorts of the Lido group—Grand Lido Negril and Grand Lido Braco—is SuperClubs' top of the line. SuperClubs backs up its claims of a Super vacation with guarantees for credit or money back in case of a hurricane, days without sunshine, or other circumstances.

Grand Lido Sans Souci ★★★★

P.O. Box 103, Ocho Rios, Jamaica, W.I.
Phone: (876) 994–1353; Fax: (876) 994–1544;
e-mail: sslido@cwjamaica.com; www.superclubs.com

Owner: SuperClubs
General Manager: Pierre Battaglia
Open: Year-round
Credit Cards: All major
U.S. Reservations: (800) 859–7873; Fax: (305) 925–0334
Deposit: 50 percent per person to confirm reservation; balance due seven days prior to arrival; seven days cancellation; less than seven days results in $300 penalty, "No Show" $500 penalty
Minimum Stay: Three nights; seven nights during Presidents' Week, Easter, and Christmas
Arrival/Departure: Transfers included. SuperClubs has an air transfer arrangement with Air Negril from Montego Bay Airport to Ocho Rios (Boscobel Airport) for one-way $85 adult, which can be booked with your hotel reservations, (800) GO–SUPER.
Distance from Airport: *(Montego Bay Airport)* 60 miles; taxi one-way, $80; $30 round-trip in an air-conditioned minibus. *Boscobel Airport:* 10 miles; taxi one-way, $20
Distance from Ocho Rios: Two miles; taxi one-way, $18
Accommodations: 146 suites, most with terraces, in seven two- and three-story buildings (99 Jacuzzi suites; 72 beachfront; eight penthouses—all kings; twins available on request)
Amenities: Air-conditioning, ceiling fans; bath with tub and shower, hair dryer, basket of toiletries, bathrobe, slippers; radio, CD player, telephone, television; minibar, tea and coffeemakers; ice service, nightly turndown service, twenty-four hour room service
Electricity: 110 volts/50 cycles
Fitness Facilities/Spa Services: Charlie's Spa and gym with Universal equipment (see text); hair salon
Sports: Four swimming pools (three freshwater, one mineral water); three whirlpools; two lighted tennis courts; Sunfloats, snorkel gear, kayaks, windsurfing; diving, fishing arranged; complimentary green fees at SuperClubs Golf Club, Runaway Bay; Jacuzzi; clothing-optional beach
Dress Code: Casual by day, but cover-up and shoes required in Ristorante Palazzina for breakfast and lunch, and more elegantly casual in evening; jacket required in Casanova Restaurant
Children: No
Meetings: Up to 140 people theatre style; multimedia capability
Day Visitors: Yes, $75 per person day; $95 night
Handicapped: No facilities
Packages: Honeymoon, wedding, all-inclusive
Rates: Per person, per night, all inclusive. **High Season** (late December–late April): $325–$580. **Low Season:** $300–$510.
Service Charge: Included
Government Tax: Included

JAMAICA INN
Ocho Rios, Jamaica, W.I.

Located by a pretty beach on Jamaica's northern coast, Jamaica Inn is not fancy like a Ritz-Carlton and you might say it has strolled into the twenty-first century. Yet this unpretentious inn has an elegance and timeless grace that can only be acquired through years of not trying to be anything more than it is—simply the best.

From the moment you arrive, you can sense that Jamaica Inn is a very special place. Set on a six acre rise, it overlooks a cove with a crest of golden sand anchored by rocky fingers at each end. A reef, within swimming distance of shore, protects the waters and the beach, and a gentle breeze cools the air.

Built originally in 1949 as a four-room inn, Jamaica Inn is run by the second generation of Morrows from New England: Peter and Eric, who grew up here and consider it their home. They have inherited a fine tradition along with a fine inn, and their pride shows in every minute detail.

The staff, as polished as the silver with which you dine, is part of the attraction. Most have been here at least ten years and underscore the inn's continuity. When you have breakfast on your terrace—and don't even think of doing anything else—a courtly waiter will lay out a

starched white damask cloth, set the table, and provide fresh fruit and home-baked bread.

The inn's exterior is painted a distinctive blue—deeper than Wedgwood—mixed specially for the hotel. It's trimmed with snow-white balustrades and louvered win-

dows. Guest rooms are located in wings that extend from each side of the house to embrace the lawn, pool, and beach.

The hotel's crowning glory is its accommodations. Your bedroom opens onto a large balustraded balcony with a beautiful view. No hotel in the Caribbean has balconies quite like these. Fully furnished as a living room, each balcony has a sofa, wingback chair and ottoman, breakfast table, antique writing desk, rocking chair, window boxes with hanging vines, drying rack,

and large beach towels. It's like living in a villa.

The bedrooms are tastefully furnished with Jamaican antiques and period pieces. You can request king, queen, or twin beds. The guest rooms as well as the public rooms have recently been refurbished and a new phone system has provided direct-dial telephones with computer access in all guest rooms.

Room categories—premier, deluxe, superior—are determined by location: on the beach, on the water, or viewing the beach and sea. Each location has something going for it, but the rooms in the one-story West Wing (Rooms 16 to 20) are very special. They are right at the edge of the sea, with the water lapping the rocks at the foot of your balcony. The water is so clear that you can see to the bottom.

Adjacent to the reception area is a homey lounge furnished in English country style. Next door is a wood-paneled bar, reminiscent of an English club. The rooms open through louvered doors onto a large colonnaded terrace that runs the length of the main building and overlooks the gardens and beach. All meals and tea are served on the terrace—except in bad weather, when the Pavilion is used. If you prefer, meals can be served in your room.

A luxury beach cottage, next door to the west, is part of the hotel and named the Clearwater Suite. The cottage was built in the late 1950s as a hideaway by diamond magnate and champion racehorse owner Stanhope Joel. The cottage's broad terrace, paved with ballast stones brought in eighteenth-century sailing ships, hangs over an aquamarine cove; above it are three bedrooms (one in an annex) with private baths. It has a large living room and an indoor-outdoor dining area; it is furnished throughout with antiques. To one side is a private pool. A dedicated staff, including a gardener, cares for Clearwater guests. The suite provides privacy, luxury, and easy access to all the facilities of the inn.

The inn's other special suites include the Blue Cottage, directly on the beach, and the stylish two-bedroom Cowdray Suite on the second floor. Then there's the legendary White Suite, on a promontory with its own pool; over the years it has served as the haunt of European royalty, an occasional prime minister, a famous poet, a best-selling novelist, and a galaxy of media stars.

If you can pull yourself away from your comfortable room, you will find the beach to be one of Jamaica's finest. You can take up residence under a thatched umbrella; the pretty oval pool and sea are only a few steps away.

If you are more energetic, there's a croquet lawn, tennis next door, and terrific snorkeling off the beach. Sunfish, sea kayaks, and snorkeling equipment are available without charge. Arthur, the beachman, will take you sailing, or if you had something less strenuous in mind, the resort's brand new spa, KiYare, offers an eclectic menu of treatments from around the globe. Housed in thatched-roofed huts with hand-carved wooden pillars overlooking the sea, the spa is directed by Carolyn Jobson, who comes with extensive experience and an international following.

Dining at Jamaica Inn is a special experience, whether in the romantic ambience of evening or at the famous Sunday brunch. The resort's young chef has added lighter contemporary fare and Jamaican specialties to the traditional repertoire.

Guests gather for cocktails at 7:00 P.M. on the front terrace and dine at 8:00 P.M. on the lamplit lower terrace, where the soft music of the resident band sets the mood. The palms sway gently overhead, and the band serenades with quiet tunes for dancing under the stars. It's straight out of a Dick Powell or Myrna Loy late-night movie: the romance of the Tropics to the point of pure schmaltz. And it's wonderful.

While some might find Jamaica Inn a bit old-fashioned, most guests want it no other way. The Morrows frequently ask their guests—most of whom come from the United States—if they want less formality. The answer is always, "Don't change a thing." I agree.

Jamaica Inn ✫✫✫✫✫

P.O. Box 1, Ocho Rios, St. Ann, Jamaica, W.I.
Phone: (876) 974–2514, –2516; Fax: (876) 974–2449;
e-mail: jaminn@cwjamaica.com; www.jamaicainn.com

Owners/Managers: Eric and Peter Morrow

Open: Year-round

Credit Cards: All major

U.S. Reservations: Caribbean World Resorts, (800) 837–4608, Fax: (800) 404–1041

Deposit: Three nights in winter; one night in summer

Minimum Stay: None

Arrival/Departure: Transfer service arranged for charge

Distance from Airport: *(Montego Bay Airport)* One-and-a-half-hour drive by private car, with refreshments, one-way, $80; by shuttle bus, $20 per person

Distance from Ocho Rios: 2 miles; taxi one-way, $3.00; shuttle bus, $2.00 per person

Accommodations: 45 rooms and suites in one- and two-story wings with terrace; twin beds convertible to kings

Amenities: Air-conditioning, ceiling fans; bath with tub and shower, hair dryer; direct-dial phone with Internet access; nightly turndown service, ice service; room service at no additional charge 8:00 A.M.–10:00 P.M.

Electricity: 110 volts

Fitness Facilities/Spa Services: Fitness room with exercise equipment; beautician and masseur or masseuse on call

Sports: Freshwater swimming pool; free tennis at Shaw Park; water sports; special rates for golf at Upton Country Club; horseback riding arranged

Dress Code: Informal during day. After 7:00 P.M. in summer, shirt with collar required (jacket optional); December 16–April 15, jacket preferred. Occasionally, men wear black tie for dinner; women, long dresses; neither required.

Children: No children under twelve years old

Meetings: Off season, may book entire hotel

Day Visitors: No

Handicapped: Facilities

Packages: Honeymoon, weddings; winter Paradise

Rates: Two people, daily, MAP. *High Season* (mid-December–mid-April): $450–$745. *Low Season,* MAP: $275–$375. Suites: $695–$1,200 and $345–$555, respectively. Clearwater Suite: $1,100–$1,200 for two, up to $1,500–$1,800 for six. White Suite: $1,300–$1,400. Inquire for summer rates.

Service Charge: 10 percent

Government Tax: Included

SANDALS DUNN'S RIVER GOLF RESORT & SPA

Ocho Rios, Jamaica, W.I.

If you have never been to a Sandals resort, you need to understand what it is before you think of spending a week at one. Essentially, Sandals is a well-orchestrated, twenty-four-hour beach party for couples only.

More than a decade ago, Jamaican businessman Gordon "Butch" Stewart (Sandals's founder, owner, and number one asset) took a dying hotel, applied the all-inclusive Club Med concept (but with a Jamaican spin), limited the resort to couples only, and launched one of the Caribbean's biggest success stories. Sandals Dunn's River, which opened in 1991, is the chain's seventh and largest resort in Jamaica (others are in Antigua, the Bahamas, and St. Lucia).

The beachfront hotel, only seven minutes from Ocho Rios's famous Dunn's River Falls, typifies the Sandals experience and reflects Stewart's bounce and boyish enthusiasm. Here, as in all Sandals resorts, you have already paid for all your accommodations, meals, snacks, beverages (alcoholic included), sports (including equipment and instruction), entertainment, gratuities, taxes, and airport transfers in one package at one price. Now just dive in and enjoy it.

At Sandals Dunn's River there's such an array of attractions to enjoy that you'd need a month to do them all, unless you can manage twenty-four hours of nonstop action. Should you tire of this Sandals—which is unlikely—you can take advantage of the Sandals special "stay at one, play at seven" feature: Couples at any Sandals resort have access to all other Sandals at no additional cost. There is a free shuttle to Sandals Ocho Rios, but transfers to Montego Bay or Negril are not included.

Set on twenty-five tropical acres, the multistory Sandals Dunn's River is a complex of impressive structures in Italian Mediterranean style with Jamaican touches. They're painted a pale ocher with red tile roofs and wood-trimmed balconies, reminiscent of villas on the Italian Riviera.

You enter from a long garden driveway into an open colonnaded lobby furnished with rather grand divans; a welcoming-arms staircase with iron-filigree banisters leads to a mezzanine. The lobby opens onto a large tree-shaded terrace and two free-form swimming pools. One has a waterfall cascading over rocks, meant to resemble the resort's namesake, and a swim-up bar. The second pool, more sedate, has a wooden deck and a sunken bar on one side. The whirlpool at the water's edge is big enough to accommodate the neighborhood; two smaller ones are located elsewhere.

Guest rooms, in two midrise buildings and low-rise lanais, come in seven categories based on location: deluxe, premium, luxury, ocean view, grand luxe, grand-luxe ocean view, penthouse honeymoon, and one-bedroom oceanfront suites. The spacious rooms have a bright, cheerful decor. An arched doorway bordered with pretty tiles leads into a dressing area and the tiled bathroom. French doors open onto balconies with views of the sea and gardens or mountains.

The resort's main restaurant serves breakfast and lunch buffets but with an army of waiters on hand. A beach grill offers quick snacks such as hamburgers, hot dogs, popcorn, and fresh fruit. In the evening dinner at candlelit tables in the continental restaurant features an a la carte menu, which is changed daily.

You can also enjoy gourmet dining and white-glove service in three specialty restaurants: Windies, serving Jamaican cuisine; Teppanyaki, offering Oriental foods; and Ristorante d'Amore, featuring Italian fare. Reservations are required, but dining is at no extra cost. Alcoholic and nonalcoholic beverages are available anytime from any of the resort's seven bars and cocktail lounges.

Sandals's staff of young men and women, known as Playmakers, schedule activities on the beach and in and around the pool, as well as entertainment and special events throughout the day and evening. It's their job to make sure you don't have an idle moment—unless you want one, of course (though in this action-packed atmosphere, it may be a bit difficult to find many places to hide).

In addition to the white-sand beach and offshore reef, good for snorkeling, you'll find tennis courts (lit for night play), basketball, pitch-and-putt golf, billiards, shuffleboard, and complete water-sports facilities: diving, sailing, snorkeling, waterskiing, windsurfing, kayaking, and more.

If you're into fitness, you'll enjoy the bilevel health center with exercise and weight rooms, aerobics classes, two steam rooms, wet- and dry-heat saunas, and hot and cool Japanese tubs. The center has a full-fledged spa with Swedish massage, aromatherapy, reflexology, body wraps, facials, and other treatments. All carry an extra charge. A personal trainer is also available. In the past several years, similar spas have been added to other Sandals resorts in Negril, Ocho Rios, Antigua, Bahamas, St. Lucia, and the newest member, Sandals Plantation Inn in Ocho Rios, which is intended to mark a new level for the chain.

Other activities include croquet, billiards, horseshoes, table tennis, and outdoor chess; there's an indoor game room, movies, slot machines, a television room, a library, and a weekly crafts show. An excursion to Dunn's River Falls and round-trip transportation to Sandals Ocho Rios are included as well. Sandals' Golf and Country Club green fees are included, but rental of equipment is additional. A free shuttle is provided from Sandals Dunn's River.

Nightly entertainment features appearances by Jamaica's premier performers, theme parties, and staff-produced shows. There is dancing every evening and informal social gatherings at the poolside piano bar.

Most guests are from the United States. While Sandals is for couples, don't think that means only young couples. Every time I have been to a Sandals resort, I have seen couples of all ages. For anyone who wants a fun-filled, active vacation in a casual, friendly atmosphere, Sandals is a great deal.

Note: The Beaches chain is Stewart's answer for the many Sandals couples who now have children and want to bring them on vacation. Beaches Negril and Beaches Turks and Caicos were the first of the new chain, but you can look for others in the future.

Sandals Dunn's River Golf Resort & Spa ★★★★

Box 51, Ocho Rios, Jamaica, W.I.
Phone: (876) 972–1610, (800) SANDALS; Fax: (876) 972–2300; www.sandals.com

Owner: Gordon "Butch" Stewart
General Manager: Louis Grant
Open: Year-round
Credit Cards: All major
U.S. Reservations: Unique Vacations, (305) 284–1300, (800) SANDALS; Fax: (305) 667–8996
Deposit: $300 seven days after reservations; full payment thirty days prior to arrival; twenty-one days cancellation
Minimum Stay: Two nights
Arrival/Departure: Transfer from Montego Bay included
Distance from Airport: (Montego Bay Airport) 56 miles (one-and-a half-hour drive)
Distance from Ocho Rios: 5 miles; taxi one-way, $15
Accommodations: 256 rooms, including ten suites in five- and six-story buildings, two-story lanais; all with terrace and king-size beds
Amenities: Air-conditioning; television, clock-radio, telephone; safe; bath with tub and shower, hair dryer, basket of toiletries; minibar in five suites; ice stations; nightly turndown service; no room service
Electricity: 110 volts
Fitness Facilities/Spa Services: Fitness center and spa (see text)
Sports: Two freshwater swimming pools with swim-up bar; three Jacuzzis; hammocks; four lighted tennis courts and equipment; boating, snorkeling, diving (two-day resort course), windsurfing; horseback riding, deep-sea fishing, and golf arranged
Dress Code: Casual
Children: No
Meetings: Up to one hundred people
Day Visitors: Day pass, $85
Handicapped: Limited facilities
Packages: All-inclusive, three to seven nights; honeymoon, wedding ($750 additional charge or free with minimum five-night stay)
Rates: Per person, per night, all-inclusive. *High Season* (January–late March): $280–$645. *Shoulder Season* (late March–late June): $270–$635. *Low Season:* (late June–December 31) $250–$615.
Service Charge: Included
Government Tax: Included

SUPERCLUBS BREEZES RUNAWAY BAY

Runaway Bay, St. Ann, Jamaica, W.I.

A member of SuperClubs' Breezes group, this resort is set apart from its SuperClubs cousins and all-inclusive competitors by two major attractions: the Jamaica experience and an unusual golf program.

From the locally crafted furniture and art to the music and menus, the emphasis here is on celebrating Jamaica's culture. Unlike some resorts, which could be anywhere in the Tropics, when you stay at Breezes you know exactly where you are. It is also in keeping with the SuperClubs' policy of giving each of its resorts a strong distinguishing feature.

Fabrics from the island's mills, lessons in patois, Jamaican food specialties, and a lethal drink called a Mudslide are all offered to help you experience what is unique about Jamaica. (The headboards in the shape of palm trees and a setting sun are more than is necessary to make the point, but they were carved by local craftsmen, and that's what matters.)

Next to the resort is its other distinguishing feature and an enormous asset: an eighteen-hole golf course, which SuperClubs owns. Guests staying at Breezes enjoy free, unlimited green fees. Better yet, Breezes offers the Golf Academy, which, when it was inaugurated in 1990, was the first year-round golf school in the Caribbean. It is available to Breezes guests for free, non-Breezes guests pay $45 for half-hour instruction, $90 for one hour.

You can have up to forty-two hours of golf instruction weekly, and the school has a lecture room with video equipment and analysis facilities, ten practice bays, a practice sand bunker, and a chipping green. Golf clubs and carts are available for rent at the pro shop. On the western side of the resort's entrance is a nine-hole putting green; to the east is the golf clubhouse.

Travelers who don't know a wood from a five-iron need not fear: Breezes has a lot more going for it. The resort is located on a wide 2-mile stretch of golden sand on Jamaica's northern shore in Runaway Bay. It has two freshwater swimming pools and three Jacuzzis; a secluded corner of the beach is set aside for sunning in the buff.

Other sports facilities include four lighted tennis courts—and instruction; a full water-sports program including snorkeling, windsurfing, sailing, kayaking, and scuba for certified divers, plus a resort course for beginners. PADI certification is also available for a fee. The gym has Nautilus equipment and a daily aerobics and exercise program. There is a jogging track, cricket, volleyball, bicycles and bicycle tours, and a nature walk.

The resort has a game room, a croquet lawn, and table tennis, and there are enough scheduled activities daily to keep you busy into the night, even if you never get near a fairway. You might try your hand at arts and crafts, such as learning to carve wood. There are reggae and calypso classes, pool games, and glass-bottom boat rides. And when you want to take a break from all the activity, you'll find plenty of hammocks strung throughout the property.

The week starts on Sunday with an orientation, the introduction of the young, cheerful staff, and the manager's cocktail party. Buffet meals are served in the Beach Terrace, a large open-air pavilion conveniently located at the center of the resort by the beach. Martino's—an air-conditioned, casually elegant Italian restaurant—and the Starlight Grill are options for dinner.

The piano bar opens for cocktails, and different enter-

SuperClubs Breezes Runaway Bay ★★★

P.O. Box 58, Runaway Bay, St. Ann, Jamaica, W.I.
Phone: (876) 973–2436; Fax: (876) 973–2352;
e-mail: salesbzg@cwjamaica.com; www.superclubs.com

Owner: Innovative Resorts, Ltd.

General Manager: Cheddy Parchment

Open: Year-round

Credit Cards: All major

U.S. Reservations: SuperClubs, (800) 859–7873;
Fax: (954) 925–0334

Deposit: $250 per person within seven days of reservation;
balance due thirty days prior to arrival or on arrival

Minimum Stay: Three nights; five nights during Presidents'
Week, Easter, and Christmas

Arrival/Departure: Complimentary transfer service from
Montego Bay Airport

Distance from Airport: *(Montego Bay Airport)* 42 miles
(one hour by car)

Distance from Ocho Rios: 17 miles

Accommodations: 234 guest rooms, including four ocean-
view and four pool-view suites in three two-story wings; all
with terraces; all with twin or king-size beds

Amenities: Air-conditioning; bath with tub and shower,
hair dryer, toiletries; telephone, television, radio, CD player;
coffeemaker; iron and ironing board; room service for continental breakfast

Electricity: 110 volts/50 cycles

Fitness Facilities/Spa Services: Health club and gym
(see text)

Sports: See text

Dress Code: Casual; beachwear on Beach Terrace; no
shorts or T-shirts in Martino's

Children: Sixteen years and older

Meetings: Up to 250 people

Day Visitors: Day pass, $55; evening pass, $65; and disco
pass, $45

Handicapped: Facilities

Packages: All-inclusive, including green fees

Rates: Per person, per night, all-inclusive. ***High Season***
(late December–late March): $196–$209. ***Shoulder Season***
(late March–late April): $172. ***Low Season*** (late April–late
December): $163.

Service Charge: Included

Government Tax: Included

tainment is presented every evening: beach or toga party on one night; nightclub or folklore show on another; staff and guest talent night on another; and a cabaret featuring Jamaican performers on intervening nights (no artists are duplicated in a two-week stretch). The disco opens at 11:00 P.M. and goes until the last person leaves.

Guest rooms are located in three two-story buildings on both sides of the main building and the expansive gardens, connected by "Breezeways." The guest rooms are comfortable, with private balconies overlooking gardens and beach. The headboards aside, their decor is still not this resort's strong point. The craftsmanship is to be admired, but the designs are, well, hokey. More attractive are the gardens, which have their own "rain forest," and the fitness center, which is in a lovely open-air pavilion. Massages are available at an additional charge: $30, half-hour; $45, full hour.

Breezes is one all-inclusive resort that welcomes singles and even devotes a month to them in September. The resort is popular with honeymooners (weddings are offered without additional charge), and it's a bargain for any sports enthusiast. There are other Breezes resorts in Montego Bay and Nassau, Bahamas. As in the other resorts, SuperClubs backs up its claims of a Super vacation here with guarantees for credit or money back in case of a hurricane, days without sunshine, and other circumstances.

Martinique

As French as France and equally stylish, Martinique, the island of flowers, is a seductive beauty of savage mountain scenery and sophisticated resorts. From the north the land drops from razorback peaks covered with rain forests and an active volcano to flowing meadows and pastureland, to bone-dry desert. Whitecapped Atlantic waves crash against eastern shores; quiet, dreamy beaches hide in coves on the west. And it's all within a day's drive.

Fort-de-France, the pretty capital, is a shopper's favorite for French perfumes and designer fashions. La Savanne, the central square overlooking Fort-de-France Bay, is bordered by historic buildings and eighteenth-century town houses; it's graced with a statue of Napoleon's Empress Josephine, who was born on Martinique.

South of Fort-de-France the Caribbean coast is scalloped with white-sand beaches. Pointe-du-Bout, a finger in Fort-de-France Bay, is the island's main tourist center, with hotels, marinas, a Robert Trent Jones golf course, restaurants, bistros, and a casino. The two sides of the bay are connected by frequent ferries.

On the southern shore overlooking Diamond Rock, a 2-mile stretch of palm-shaded beach is popular for windsurfing. Sainte-Anne, an idyllic colonial village around a tree-shaded square, is known for its seafood restaurants. Grande Anse des Salines at the southern tip has the island's most idyllic beaches.

Dominating the northern profile of Martinique is 4,584-foot Mont Pelée, usually crowned with swirling clouds. Its eruption in 1902 was one of the most devastating ever recorded. A north-country tour often returns via the extraordinary memorial of St. Pierre, the town buried in seconds under Mont Pelée's ashes.

Route de la Trace, a central highland road between Fort-de-France and Mont Pelée, winds northward through rain forests; each hairpin turn looks across sweeping views of the capital and coast. On a hillside at 1,475 feet is Le Jardin de Balata, a private botanic garden with more than 1,000 varieties of tropical plants.

On the northern skirt of Mont Pelée, Grand' Rivière, an old fishing village of spectacular scenery, is reminiscent of a Gauguin painting. Big volcanic rocks from Mont Pelée rest at the edge of black-sand beaches where vertical cliffs carpeted with wind-sheared foliage drop to the sea and huge whitecaps roll in from the Atlantic.

Information

French West Indies Tourist Board, 444 Madison Avenue, New York, NY 10022; (212) 838–7800, (800) 391–4909; Fax: (212) 838–7855; www.francetourism.com

HABITATION LAGRANGE
Martinique, F.W.I.

Built into the ruins of a former sugar plantation dating from the early 1800s, Habitation Lagrange is a delight for travelers who prefer mountain vistas and tropical gardens to the beach and enjoy the ambience of old plantation days, complete with a somewhat colonial attitude.

Nestled in the hills above Marigot on the Atlantic coast, the centerpiece of the hotel is a restored two-story manor house enclosed in gardens profuse with bougainvillea, heliconia, and allamanda, against nearby hills dense with banana plantations and rain-forest lushness.

The estate house and surrounding buildings are so well done, you might think it was only yesterday that the sugar mill was grinding. But in fact when owner Jean-Louis de Lucy, whose ancestors came to Martinique to escape the French Revolution at about the same time the plantation began, undertook the restoration, the buildings were nothing more than dilapidated ruins. I first saw them at the inception of the renovation and, despite de Lucy's enthusiasm, could hardly believe the resort would turn out as well as it did.

The main house with fanciful turrets and curved corners has a wraparound veranda with slim wrought-iron columns reminiscent of Savannah houses. Grand mahogany doors lead into a hallway with parquet floors and a potpourri of objets d'art. To one side is a library and to the other a high-ceilinged bar with planter-style rockers that add to the colonial-era ambience and provide a comfortable nest to nod after a ti' punch or two, the island's famous—perhaps infamous is a better description—rum drink.

Directly ahead is the large drawing room, with one wall covered by a mural of plantation life, painted by the owner's uncle. The room, furnished in colonial style, has a pool table and an eclectic mix of antiques—ship models, a ship's telegraph, and Thai basketware. Large arched doors lead to a terra-cotta tile patio with inviting lounge chairs for more ti' punch or an easy place to relax, read, and forget the rest of the world.

The most charming guest rooms are on the second level of the manor house and what was once the stable; the latter faces the pool in the center of the bird-filled gardens. The rooms are furnished in Creole style with four-poster beds, rocking chairs, and armoires. Other guest rooms are found by the pool in a two-story building added for that purpose, but in keeping with the old style.

The rooms are traditional in decor, but have modern amenities: air-conditioning, television, VCR, radio, minibar, and direct-dial phones. In the modern bathrooms you will find Roger & Gallet toiletries and bathrobes.

The restaurant is housed in a thatched-roof pavilion, decorated with hanging plants and furnished with rustic tables and chairs. Meals are served by local women dressed in their traditional Creole costumes made from madras (a reflection of this island's large population of East Asians; they were brought here as indentured servants and probably worked these very cane fields after slavery was abolished).

Habitation Lagrange ★★

97225 La Marigot, Martinique, F.W.I.
Phone: (596) 53–60–60; Fax: (596) 53–50–58;
e-mail: habitation.lagrange@wanadoo.fr

Owner: Jean-Louis de Lucy
General Manager: Jean Sauvage
Open: Year-round
Credit Cards: American Express, MasterCard, Visa
U.S. Reservations: Caribbean Inns, Ltd., (800) 633–7411; or Martinique Select, (800) 823–2002
Deposit: Three nights; thirty days cancellation
Minimum Stay: None
Arrival/Departure: Transfer service not available
Distance from Airport: 23 miles (forty-five minutes); one-way taxi, $60 (for two people)
Distance from Marigot: 1 mile; one-way taxi, $8.00
Accommodations: 11 rooms, one suite
Amenities: Air-conditioning, ceiling fans; direct-dial telephone; minibar; mini-refrigerator (suites only); fax available; large marble bathrooms in manor house, others with tile; all have tub and shower, bathrobes
Electricity: 220 volts
Sports: Freshwater swimming pool; tennis court
Dress Code: Casual but chic
Children: Welcome; baby-sitting available
Meetings: No
Day Visitors: Welcome with reservations for lunch
Handicapped: No facilities
Packages: Honeymoon
Rates: Per room, daily, CP. *High Season* (mid-December–mid-April): $230–$300. *Low Season:* $180–$250.
Gratuity Charge: 10 percent
Service Charge: Included
Government Tax: Included

The French cuisine with Creole flair is one of the resort's attractions. And if Lagrange's tranquillity gets to you, you'll find any number of excellent restaurants in the vicinity—like mainland France, Martinique has good restaurants even in the smallest villages.

You might do some exploring of the countryside at the same time. The northeastern corner of Martinique is the least known, least traveled, yet most beautiful part of the island, with dramatic scenery of wind-shirred shores, the rain-forested slopes of Mont Pelée, and fishing villages like Grand' Rivière, which time has left behind. For hikers, many of the island's best trails are in the immediate vicinity of Lagrange.

Beautiful and romantic as it may be, Lagrange is not for everyone. Some may find it too quiet and remote, and they will certainly have second thoughts when they have to negotiate the terrible country road—it's only about a mile—to get there. But if you are looking for utter peace and quiet and are not put off by the romanticizing of the good ol' colonial days, then you will enjoy what some consider Martinique's best hotel.

HOTEL BAKOUA MARTINIQUE

Martinique, F.W.I.

The first time I visited Martinique, more than two decades ago, the Bakoua was the only hotel of any size or merit in the area of Pointe-du-Bout—all thirty rooms of it. Today the Bakoua has more than quadrupled in size, and Pointe-du-Bout has mushroomed into the center of Martinique's tourism industry, with many hotels, restaurants, cafes, marinas, and water-sports centers.

Of course, the ambience of the hotel and its environs has changed completely. If you like to be at the heart of the action rather than sequestered in a quiet retreat, and if you prefer the conveniences of a large resort to the intimacy of a small inn, you will be happy at the Bakoua.

The lobby captures a panoramic view of the Bay of Fort-de-France. The dining room, with its open-air Creole architecture, embraces the tropical setting that faces the cove of Anse Mitan. You can watch the yachts at breakfast and have a romantic view of the distant lights of Fort-de-France in the evening.

Accommodations are located in three large, long white stucco buildings topped by red roofs, all with balconies, overlooking either the gardens or the sea. Three of the buildings are constructed in the gardens on a rise above the bay; the fourth is a two-story block directly on the hotel's small beach, with the upper-story balconies shaded by coral-and-white-striped awnings.

The guest rooms and suites have a classic look with rich mahogany colonial style furniture—including some carved headboards on four-poster beds and cane-backed chairs accented by pretty pastel designer fabrics and ceramic tile floors.

In addition to its pretty, oval-shaped swimming pool perched on a terrace overlooking the beach and the bay, the Bakoua offers tennis, windsurfing, an introductory dive lesson, and exercise equipment and aerobics classes in the fitness center. Water sports such as sailing, diving, and waterskiing are available from a nearby dive shop for a fee.

The resort provides thrice-daily shuttle service to the nearby eighteen-hole golf course designed by Robert Trent Jones (the island's only one). Sailing excursions on the hotel's own boat, jeep excursions, hiking, deep-sea

Hotel Bakoua Martinique ★★★

La Pointe-du-Bout, 97229 Les Trois Ilets, Martinique, F.W.I.
Phone: (596) 66–02–02; Fax: (596) 66–00–41

Owner: Accor/Resort Hotels

General Manager: Yves Demptos

Open: Year-round

Credit Cards: All major

U.S. Reservations: (800) SOFITEL (763–4835); Fax: (914) 472 0451

Deposit: Three nights in winter, one night in summer, thirty days in advance; twenty-one days cancellation in winter, seven days in summer

Minimum Stay: None

Arrival/Departure: Meeting service at the airport

Distance from Airport: (Lamentin Airport) 10 miles; taxi one-way, $25 day, $40 night

Distance from Fort-de-France: 20 miles (forty-five minutes by road; twenty minutes by ferry); ferry one-way, $2.00

Accommodations: 139 rooms and suites (including 39 beachside, 53 ocean view, 39 garden view) in three three-story buildings and one two-story block, all with balconies or patios; king-size or twin beds

Amenities: Air-conditioning; direct-dial telephone, cable television, VCR, radio; safe; bath with tub and shower, radio, hair dryer, makeup mirror, basket of toiletries; mini-bar; room service when restaurants operating; concierge; shop

Electricity: 220 volts

Fitness Facilities/Spa Services: Fitness center with equipment and exercise sessions

Sports: Freshwater swimming pool; two lighted tennis courts (night-play charge); windsurfing, kayaks; putting green, table tennis; diving, waterskiing, sailing trips, deep-sea fishing, Sunfish, fishing dock; golf, horseback riding, biking, hiking arranged

Dress Code: Casual

Children: All ages; cribs; baby-sitters; one child under twelve years old can stay in garden room with parents free

Meetings: Up to fifty people

Day Visitors: Yes

Handicapped: No facilities

Packages: Summer

Rates: Per room, single or double, daily, FAB. **High Season** (mid-December–mid-April): $290–$420. **Low Season:** $157–$247.

Service Charge: Included

Government Tax: Included

fishing, and horseback riding can be arranged. The Bak-oua has its own dock where visiting yachts tie up and from which you can take an odyssey of a day or longer.

From the lobby and dining level at the top of the rise, steps lead down to the beach and water sports. Le Coco is the beach bar at the water's edge; La Sirène, a casual but not inexpensive beachside restaurant, serves snacks and a light lunch of salads, fish, and grilled meats. Le Châteaubriand, the main restaurant, serves a buffet breakfast and gourmet dining in the evening, featuring French Creole and international cuisine, as well as nightly musical entertainment. Guests can enjoy steel bands on one night, the Ballet de la Martinique on another, a salsa parade or a fashion parade on others.

Le Gommier, the open-air cocktail lounge off the lobby, offers a ringside seat for sunset along with music for listening. The cozy lounge, with its circular sunken bar, is something of the hotel's social center. The balmy tropical air, the convivial ambience, and the wonderful views of the sailboats in the bay impart the warmth and friendliness of the old Bakoua.

The Bakoua is essentially low-key. Its biggest attraction is its location at the center of Pointe-du-Bout resort life, yet quietly secluded in its own gardens. It's connected by frequent ferries to the heart of the capital directly across the bay and offers the services of a modern resort hotel in the French milieu of Martinique. You might want to brush up on your French.

Nevis

The lovely island of Nevis still typifies the Caribbean as many would like it to remain: gracious, innocent, and charming. Separated from St. Kitts by a 2 mile channel, Nevis rises in almost perfect symmetry from the sea to a dark green cone more than 3,000 feet high at its cloud-capped peak. Stretches of golden beach protected by coral reefs outline the coast.

Nevis was discovered by Christopher Columbus in 1493, and the first settlers came here from St. Kitts in 1628. Tobacco was their first export. By the eighteenth century sugar had replaced tobacco as the main crop, bringing with it large plantations and great wealth. Soon Nevis became the social hub of the Caribbean and developed an international reputation as the "Queen of the Caribbees."

Charlestown, on the western side of the island, is a West Indian colonial village lined with a medley of colorful old buildings so perfectly caught in time that the place could almost be a movie set. The Hamilton Museum was the home of Nevis's most famous native son, Alexander Hamilton, the first U.S. secretary of the treasury, who was born here in 1755.

North of Charlestown, Pinney's Beach is a 4-mile stretch of palm-fringed sands, where the Four Seasons Resort—the island's first large modern hotel and golf course—opened in January 1991, bringing with it jobs and a tourist boomlet.

Nevis and its sister island of St. Kitts have something of a monopoly on charming historic inns set in old sugar plantations, much as the plantations themselves cornered the market on sugar in their heyday. Morning Star, known locally as Gingerland, has several plantation inns located at about 1,000 feet in elevation on the southern slopes of Mount Nevis. Lanes and footpaths, ideal for hikers, run from one estate to the other.

Organized tours of Nevis with particular emphasis on the historical and natural attractions are available through The Nevis Academy, Box 493, Nevis, W.I.; (809) 469–5346.

Information

St. Kitts and Nevis Tourist Board, 414 East 75th Street, New York, NY 10021;
(212) 535–1234, (800) 582–6208; Fax: (212) 734–6511; www.stkitts-nevis.com

FOUR SEASONS RESORT NEVIS
Charlestown, Nevis, W.I.

Guidebook writers like me spend a lot of time thinking about what might have been. We are inclined to redesign hotels, rearrange room furniture, add a touch here and there—all in our heads, of course. My mind was working overtime when I first visited the Four Seasons on Nevis, the first Caribbean resort of that prestigious, luxury hotel group.

Located on Nevis's leeward coast, Four Seasons enjoys a glorious setting along a 2,000-foot stretch of golden sand on Pinney's Beach, where hundreds of stately palms grace the property from the sand to the foothills of lofty Nevis Peak. Arriving by boat from St. Kitts, you see the resort in the distance after twenty minutes at sea.

The Four Seasons literature describes the architecture as "plantation-style cottages," so I had expected to see colonial-type villas on the hillside, taking advantage of the view and breezes—the way smart plantation owners had done when they built their estate houses in colonial times. To my surprise I found twelve long, two-story buildings, devoid of any Caribbean character, strung out along the beach. They reminded me of army barracks. What might have been, I thought—Four Seasons missed a fantastic opportunity.

Why, if I was so disappointed, have I included it here? The answer is simple. The resort maintains the high standards for which Four Seasons is known, and its outstanding facilities go a long way toward overcoming the lousy architecture. Others think so, too: The resort was the first in the Caribbean to receive the highly coveted AAA Five Diamond rating.

The resort's commitment to hire and train local people is another plus. While the hotel was closed for almost a year to make major repairs and renovations following Hurricane Lenny in 1999, many employees worked at other Four Seasons properties around the globe. For many of them, it was their first working experience outside Nevis.

The modern Great House with lounges, bars, and restaurants anchors the complex. Its rather opulent lobby rises high to a mahogany-beamed ceiling with ornate lights; a wall of French doors opens onto flower-filled terraces. To one side is a mahogany-paneled library-bar.

Three restaurants offer a choice of casual or elegant dining. They highlight local fresh fruits, vegetables, and seafood, including lobster. The casual Grill Room is a large, open-air restaurant with colorful decor. The poolside Cabana restaurant, open for lunch, cocktails, and dinner was redesigned and a separate beach bar added during the recent renovations. The more formal Dining Room is set with candlelit tables, flowers, and linens. The room has a wide-plank hardwood floor, a high, beamed ceiling with ornate chandeliers, a cut-stone fireplace flanked by mahogany sideboards, and French doors on three sides.

The large, luxurious guest rooms are actually junior suites. Their decor has been enhanced with new stone tiles and a new Caribbean color scheme. But the huge bathrooms (with telephones)—marbled from top to bottom—are the real showstoppers.

All rooms have large verandas where you can dine. They are furnished with a teak dining table and chairs and

have a toaster so your room-service waiter can make fresh toast. Other nice touches include genuine down pillows, individual reading lights that clip onto books, and free laundry room facilities in each building. Dual-line phones have now been installed in all guest rooms.

The resort also has a group of thirty-two luxury two- to four-bedroom villas (some with private swimming pools) available for rent. These villas enjoy panoramic views of the sea, golf course, and nearby islands; they have fully equipped kitchens and spacious living and dining areas, along with full access to the resort and its services, including room service and catering. Villa rentals require a minimum five-night stay.

Four Seasons, with its spectacular eighteen-hole championship course designed by Robert Trent Jones, put Nevis on the map as a golf destination. The 6,766 yard course climbs from sea level up the volcanic slopes of Mount Nevis to an altitude of almost 1,000 feet at the signature fifteenth hole: an awesome 660-yard par five across a deep ravine with a breadth of 240 yards from the tee. From there the course descends quickly to the eighteenth hole at the ocean's edge. Throughout golfers enjoy breathtaking vistas.

The resort has two new vanishing-edge swimming pools and the court at the large tennis complex, managed by Peter Burwash International, have been resurfaced. The resort offers extensive water sports and a health club with Lifecycles, Stairmasters, and other equipment; locker rooms; a sauna; and massage. Exercise, aqua-aerobics, walks, and other fitness activities are offered daily. Demonstration sessions are free; lessons are not. Theme packages—family, nature, golf—enhanced with special activities are offered during the off season.

"Kids for All Seasons" is Four Seasons's program (free year-round) for children ages three to nine; it has a playroom with supervised activities and has been doubled in size. The resort provides children's beach toys, a bottle- and food-warming service, and supervised lunch, which is optional, as is early dinner. The program operates from 8:00 A.M. to 6:00 P.M. Several times weekly there is a snorkeling program for children ages eight to twelve. A new entertainment center for teens and preteens with Nintendo stations, billiards, and other activities was added during the recent renovations.

Also added is a new business center with computers with high-speed Internet access, while a new 800-square-foot conference room brings the resort's total conference facilities to almost 9,000 square feet.

Reminiscent of a Florida golf resort, the hotel is designed to attract groups: small meetings, golfers, and honeymooners. Guests, mainly from North America, range from tots to seniors, but most are active couples eager to enjoy the resort's sporting facilities.

Four Season Resort Nevis ★★★★

Box 565, Piney's Beach, Charlestown, Nevis, W.I.
Phone: (869) 469–1111; Fax: (869) 469–1040;
www.fourseasons.com

Owner: Nevis Hotel Development, Ltd.
General Manager: Robert Whitfield
Open: Year-round
Credit Cards: All major
U.S. Reservations: Four Seasons Resort Nevis, (800) 332–3442
Deposit: Three nights; twenty-one days cancellation
Minimum Stay: Ten nights during Christmas
Arrival/Departure: Transfers, $65 per person round-trip by land and sea. Most guests arrive by air in St. Kitts, where Four Seasons representatives meet and drive them to dockside lounge in Basse-Terre to board deluxe launch for thirty-minute zoom across channel to hotel. En route, staff completes check-in.
Distance from Airport: (Nevis Airport) 6 miles; taxi one-way, $18; $35 transfers from airport
Distance from Charlestown: 1 mile; taxi one-way, $8.00
Accommodations: 196 rooms and suites (43 with two double beds, 130 with king-size beds; 17 suites) all with verandas; 32 two- to four-bedroom villas, some with pools
Amenities: Air-conditioning, ceiling fan; telephone, clock-radio, television, VCR; baths with tub and shower, hair dryer, bathrobes, scales, lavish toiletries; stocked minibar; coffeemaker, icemaker; safe; no-smoking rooms; room service; hair salon
Electricity: 110 volts
Fitness Facilities/Spa Services: Health club (see text); air-conditioned exercise room
Sports: Golf (see text); ten tennis courts (three lighted), racquet rental; jogging, hiking, volleyball, croquet; two freshwater pools; snorkeling gear; abundant complimentary water sports.
Dress Code: Casual by day; cover-up and footwear in Great House; after sunset collared shirts, trousers, closed footwear for men; jacket and tie not required
Children: See text. Children's pool; baby-sitting; no charge for children under eighteen years old in same room with parents
Meetings: Up to 350 people
Day Visitors: Welcome with reservations
Handicapped: Facilities
Packages: Romance, honeymoon, golf, sports, tennis, Five-Diamond, family; wedding ($550); off-season theme
Rates: Two people, daily, EP. *High Season* (mid-December–mid-April): $600–$2,500. *Shoulder Season* (mid-April–May 31 and November 1–mid-December): $400–$2,350. *Low Season:* $250–$2,000. Prices include nonmotorized water sports. Villas: Inquire.
Service Charge: 10 percent
Government Tax: 8 percent

GOLDEN ROCK HOTEL

St. Georges Parish, Nevis, W.I.

High on the side of Mount Nevis, in an area known as Gingerland, is an unusual small inn 1,000 feet above the sea. It's on the grounds of an eighteenth-century sugar plantation operated by a direct descendant of the plantation's original owner.

Pam Barry, a Philadelphia native, came to Nevis on a visit in 1965 and stayed. She eventually became the owner-manager of Golden Rock and runs the inn as though she has invited you to her home. She sets the tone for Golden Rock in a chatty letter that guests find in their rooms.

The tireless innkeeper dines with her guests, organizes garden walks, hikes, and tours, shuttles them back and forth from town and the beach, and takes them to interesting folklore shows and other activities around the island. If you prefer to go off on your own, she can arrange car rentals at a very good rate.

Set in twenty-five acres of flower-filled gardens and surrounded by another seventy-five acres of tropical beauty, Golden Rock was built in the early 1800s by Edward Huggins, Pam's great-great-great-grandfather, a self-made man who was an estate overseer at only nineteen. Huggins built many other estates and is said to have owned seven.

As soon as you start up the narrow lane from the main road to the inn, you know you've arrived at a special place. Rooms with walls of century-old stone masonry, barely visible under curtains of brightly colored tropical flowers, have been converted into the living and dining spaces, with practical additions made only where needed.

The Long House, formerly the estate's kitchen and storeroom, contains the dining room, bar, and library and is the center of social activity. The rustic bar has a vaulted ceiling exposing the building's old walls. From it hang two large wicker baskets—lobster traps used by local fishermen—woven in a typical West Indian design that originated with the Carib Indians, who once inhabited the island. The congenial atmosphere at cocktails and after dinner makes it easy to be part of the family of new friends. Recorded classical music can be heard almost anytime, and musical entertainment is often provided by a staff member—or a guest.

The Courtyard, a flower-graced terrace with the bougainvillea-laden stone walls of the Long House as its backdrop, is the setting for lunch, afternoon tea, and cocktails, served to the musical accompaniment of birds and crickets.

The Sugar Mill, the original stone windmill tower pictured in the hotel's literature, was built in 1815 to supply power to the plantation. Today it houses the honeymoon suite but is large enough for a family of four or five. It has two floors connected by a winding wooden stairway and is furnished with two antique four-poster mahogany beds.

Accommodations are in cottages on the mountainside above the Long House. Each has white ceramic tile floors covered with rush throw rugs, a private bathroom, and a front porch with a grandstand view. The rooms are basic but comfortable, with island-made furnishings. The most noteworthy are the canopied four-poster bamboo beds made by the multitalented operations manager Rolston, who is also acclaimed for his rum punches. New amenities—shampoo, cream rinse, deluxe soaps, hair dryer, cof-

fee and tea makers, ice buckets, and ceiling fans—have been added in all rooms. Rolston and David (the head gardener, whose old-time string band plays on Saturday night) are typical of Golden Rock's gracious, friendly staff, most of whom come from the area and have been with the inn for a decade or more.

Dinner is served family-style in the Long House (tables for two are also available), which has gotten a new, more elegant look with French-colonial wood chairs and red table clothes and gold napkins You will dine on homemade soups and other specialties prepared with herbs grown in the estate's own gardens, fresh produce from village farmers, and fresh seafood caught by local fishermen.

In the gardens between the Long House and the cottages is a large spring-fed pool with a shaded terrace from which you'll find wonderful views across the southern part of the island and the sea. The estate has a strand of sand on 4-mile Pinney's Beach for its guests' use. The beach bar, open December to June, prepares a daily lunch of fresh seafood, cheeseburgers, and of course its famous lobster sandwiches. Golden Rock owns another sandy surf-washed beach on the windward side, where the snorkeling (gear provided) is good and the beachcombing excellent. When you go off on your own, the hotel will pack you a picnic lunch.

Conservationists will appreciate Pam's strong commitment to protecting the local environment. Golden Rock is a natural for nature lovers, with trails and unpaved roads in the immediate area for hiking. The Rainforest Trail, beginning from Golden Rock, leads up the mountain past several hamlets to the rain forest on the side of Mount Nevis. Pam has drawn a map for her guests to use. The trail is an easy hike. Keep a watchful eye and you are likely to see some wild monkeys observing you from behind a tree. There are also hikes that explore other areas of Nevis with excellent local guides.

A stay at Golden Rock is an unusual experience. The inn has a loyal clientele: an intellectually curious, well-traveled, eclectic group as likely to come from Europe as from the United States and Canada. Its historic setting is relished by romantics and history buffs alike. Its cozy, homey atmosphere makes everyone feel welcome, particularly someone traveling alone.

Golden Rock Hotel ✷ ✷ 🖉

Box 493, St. Georges Parish, Nevis, W.I.
Phone: (869) 469–3346; Fax: (869) 469–2113;
e-mail: gdhobson@golden-rock.com; www.golden-rock.com

Owner/Manager: Pam Barry
Open: Year-round except September
Credit Cards: Most major
U.S. Reservations: Direct to hotel
Deposit: Three nights; twenty-one days cancellation in winter, two nights deposit, fourteen days cancellation in off season
Minimum Stay: None
Arrival/Departure: Transfer can be arranged from St. Kitts for $25, from Antigua for $180; or a new 55-minute service from San Juan nonstop to Nevis on a new nineteen-seater Beechcraft that takes ninety pounds of luggage per person. Price is usually $300 round-trip but varies with time of year; inquire.
Distance from Airport: 7 miles, taxi one-way, $18
Distance from Charlestown: 5 miles; taxi one-way, $15
Accommodations: 16 hillside bedroom cottages with porches; all rooms with twin or king-size beds; Sugar Mill tower for up to four people
Amenities: Bath with shower, toiletries, hair dryer; coffee and tea makers, ice buckets; ceiling fans; no air-conditioning
Electricity: 110 volts
Sports: Freshwater pool, transport to two private beaches; mountain bikes, mountain hiking; tennis; waterskiing, scuba diving, sailing, windsurfing, sport fishing, kayaking, golf, horseback riding arranged
Dress Code: Smartly casual at night; informal in day
Children: All ages; baby-sitters available
Meetings: Small groups and wedding parties, up to thirty people
Day Visitors: Welcome
Handicapped: No facilities
Packages: Honeymoon, wedding
Rates: Per room, double, daily, EP. **High Season** (mid-December–mid-April): $210–$300. **Low Season:** $140–$175.
Service Charge: 10 percent
Government Tax: 8 percent

THE HERMITAGE

St. John, Nevis, W.I.

Hugging the forested southern slopes of Nevis Peak, 800 feet above sea level, this one-of-a-kind resort resembles a lilliputian village of dollhouses tucked into acres of tropical gardens. Its centerpiece is a small, 250-year-old great house, said to be the oldest all-wood house standing in Nevis. It is surrounded by traditional West Indian cottages with gingerbread trim, brought here from various locations around the island and reconstructed to serve as guest quarters.

The house was probably built about 1740—perhaps as early as 1680—by a family from Wales. Its longevity is attributed to the termite-resistant wood used for its heavy timbers, lignum vitae, which is highly prized for its strength and was perhaps taken from the original forest of Nevis.

room has a high, beamed ceiling constructed in the old style with dovetailed corners to strengthen the frame.

The northern and southern extensions have two stories, each with lounges on the first level and bedrooms above. The great house has a formal dining room, a bar, and, to one side, a small music room/library walled with books and a VCR—all comfortably furnished in antiques and Victoriana like your grandmother's parlor. The music room opens onto a pretty veranda, and the drawing room steps down onto a covered terrace with garden tables and chairs in a romantic setting with latticework and arches draped with flowering shrubs. The terrace is used for breakfast and lunch. An enchanting intimate dining room furnished with walnut

The house remained in the same family until 1971, when it was bought by Maureen and Richard Lupinacci, then newly arrived from Quakertown, Pennsylvania. The couple made extensive renovations and added the cottages before they opened the inn in 1985. Maureen runs the daily operation and oversees the kitchen; Richard, one of Nevis's most active hoteliers, is a director of the Bank of Nevis.

The great house is small (less than 2,000 square feet) even by Caribbean standards and built in the shape of a cross aligned to the points of the compass. The drawing

and mahogany antiques from Nevis's original Nelson Museum (there is a new museum near town) was added.

Guests stay in picturesque cottages—some old and some made to look old. The charming old ones have been carefully restored using original construction methods when possible. They are surrounded by tropical gardens brimming with flowers and exotic fruit trees. The guest rooms are furnished with romantic four-poster canopy beds with colonial-print coverlets; they have small bathrooms and private porches. In 1997 all the rooms were refurbished and upgraded with new fabrics and bedcovers. Most of the bathrooms were also redone and now have tubs and showers and pretty Victorian pedestal sinks with shiny brass fittings.

Another three cottages by the swimming pool are newer and more deluxe. They have large, airy rooms with a bath and dressing area and a patio or balcony with a hammock for taking in distant views of the sea. Six of the fifteen cottages have now been upgraded to a deluxe level. Each has a sitting room, kitchen, private porch, cable television, and telephone.

Mahogany Manor, a replica of a Nevis manor house, sits in private gardens at the top of the hill. It has two large master bedrooms with large baths and dressing rooms, a living room, a dining room, and a full kitchen with laundry as well as its own private pool. Cook and daily maid service can be arranged.

Among The Hermitage's most unusual features are its one-horse carriages pulled by 2,000-pound Belgian horses (originally used as Amish farm horses in Pennsylvania). They depart weekdays on trips through the countryside. The inn also has riding horses.

In the evening guests and island friends congregate in the parlor for cocktails and congenial conversation. Dinner, announced by ringing bells, is a family affair served in the dining room or on the cozy veranda, depending on the number of guests and the ambience they desire. If you prefer, you can dine romantically on your private balcony.

The Lupinaccis, known for their warm hospitality, usually dine with guests at a communal table. The couple have a reputation for serving some of the finest cuisine and wines on the island. A set menu, changed nightly, offers four courses of French, Italian, or Caribbean specialties stressing fresh local fish, vegetables, and fruit. On Wednesday evening there is a West Indian buffet with a string or "scratch" band (local musicians playing homemade instruments). Your companions are as likely to be English or European as American, and most will be in their midforties.

The Lupinaccis will drive guests the 4 miles to Pinney's Beach for swimming and water sports. They will also organize outings, prepare picnic baskets, and arrange car rentals. But The Hermitage is a homey, easygoing sort of place. You need not stir farther than the gracious gardens for afternoon tea or to a hammock strung between the breadfruit and mango trees, where gentle breezes will rock you to sleep.

Families are still important in Nevis, the Lupinaccis say. "We invite you to join ours at The Hermitage, a place where the cool breeze off the mountains meets the warm breezes from the sea . . . a special place where you make friends forever."

The Hermitage **

Figtree Parish, St. John, Nevis, W.I.
Phone: (869) 469–3477, (800) 682–4025; Fax: (869) 469–2481; e-mail: nevherm@caribsurf.com; www.hermitagenevis.com

Owners/General Managers: Richard and Maureen Lupinacci

Open: Year-round

Credit Cards: All major

U.S. Reservations: International Travel and Resorts (ITR), (212) 476–9444, (800) 223–9815; Fax: (212) 545–8467

Deposit: Three nights; twenty-one days cancellation in winter, fourteen days in summer

Minimum Stay: Four nights in winter

Arrival/Departure: Transfer service not provided

Distance from Airport: 12 miles; taxi one-way, $17

Distance from Charlestown: 3 miles; taxi one-way, $10

Accommodations: 15 units (six deluxe cottages with sitting room, kitchen, private porch, cable television, and telephone; other rooms in cottages with private bath; two guest rooms in stone carriage house, two in manor house); rooms have kings, queens, or twins that can be configured to suit

Amenities: Ceiling fans; most baths have tubs and showers, hair dryers; refrigerator, teakettle; room service 8:00 A.M.–10:00 P.M., nightly turndown service

Electricity: 110 volts

Sports: Freshwater pool; tennis; horseback riding; sailing, fishing, hiking with guide arranged

Dress Code: Informal

Children: All ages; cribs; baby-sitters available

Meetings: Small groups of up to twenty-four people

Day Visitors: Lunch and dinner with reservations

Handicapped: No facilities

Packages: Honeymoon, wedding

Rates: Per room, double, daily, EP. *High Season* (mid-December–mid-April): $325–$450. *Low Season:* $170–$265.

Service Charge: 10 percent

Government Tax: 8 percent

MONTPELIER PLANTATION INN

Nevis, W.I.

Nestled in lovely gardens and surrounded by sixty acres of rolling terrain, Montpelier Plantation Inn has an air of timeworn grandeur that gives the impression it has been there for three centuries, rather than a mere four decades.

Well, it has, and it hasn't.

The Montpelier Estate, in the interior hills at 650 feet above sea level on the southern side of Mount Nevis, was a prominent sugar plantation in the eighteenth century, belonging to the governor of the Leeward Islands. Here in 1787 the governor's niece, Frances Nisbet, wed Lord Nelson, the famous British admiral.

By the time James Gaskell acquired the property in 1964, the original great house was long gone, but remnants of the mill and other structures were enough to provide foundations to build a small inn. By reusing the original stones and retaining the traditional architecture, Gaskell achieved the inn's authentic appearance—at least in the main buildings.

An imposing brimstone structure that appears to be a great house was actually the old sugar boiling room, which was rebuilt into a grand drawing room where evening activities take place. Dinner is served on its western terrace. The attractive room has a high, vaulted ceiling that adds to its grandeur, and its antique furnishings are reminiscent of an English country manor, with portraits and old paintings on the walls and a mahogany bar.

The drawing room opens onto a colonnaded stone terrace on the east, where breakfast and lunch are served. It overlooks pretty gardens heavily laced with tropical foliage around a huge eighteenth-century windmill that once powered the sugar factory. Birds are everywhere, and the hotel has compiled a bird list, full of entertaining notes to help birders unfamiliar with Caribbean species locate them.

Beyond the mill is a modern spring-fed swimming pool with bright blue tiles and bordered by a masonry wall painted with murals. The poolside terrace has a bar with tables and chairs under a canvas awning.

The inn's guest rooms are in modest cottages beyond the main hall, all with patios overlooking Nevis's southern landscape and the sea. The cottage rooms have Italian ceramic tile floors and bathrooms renovated from top to bottom. All have high, beamed ceilings with ceiling fans, making them all the more spacious and airy.

Montpelier has a long-established reputation for good cuisine prepared by a staff of foreign and local chefs. Breakfast is a treat of local fruits and honey and homemade brown bread and johnnycakes. Lunch—a la carte—

and tea are served outdoors as well. The inn's charming historic setting attracts guests from other hotels for lunch or dinner.

In the evening guests gather in the bar or lounge for cocktails in an English weekend-in-the-country atmosphere; new and returning British and other European guests outnumber the Americans about four to one. Dinner is a candlelight affair with a set three-course menu offering a choice of entrees. You can dine at tables for two, or you may join others. The dining terrace offers views past the floodlit palm trees to the sea and the lights of St. Kitts. Montpelier and its neighboring hotels sponsor a local band and a dance once or twice a week during the winter season.

Montpelier provides free transportation once a day to and from its beach club on the northern end of Pinney's Beach, about twenty-five minutes away. The inn will prepare a picnic lunch for you, and in the winter season, there is a weekly beach barbecue lunch followed by a seaside game of cricket (yes, it's ever so British).

The informal retreat has a wonderful staff and a timeless, unspoiled quality, attracting nature lovers and couples of all ages as well as those traveling alone who appreciate its homey atmosphere. More English than other Nevis inns, Montpelier is like a gracious private house—private enough that when Princess Diana needed to escape from the public eye and the British press, this was the place she chose.

Montpelier recently acquired new owners, Lincoln and Muffin Hoffman; and the new general managers are their son and his wife, Tim and Meredith Hoffman. The new owners, who plan to operate the inn as a family affair, just as the Gaskell's did, have retained all the staff and expect to retain the inn's long-appreciated ambience as a country inn in the tropics. By the new winter season, they will have refurbished the public rooms and most of the guestrooms and introduced some new treats based on local products, such as fresh fruit juices for breakfast.

Montpelier Plantation Inn ✶✶

Box 474, Montpelier Estate, Nevis, W.I.
Phone: (869) 469–3462; Fax: (869) 469–2932;
e-mail: info@montpeliernevis.com; www.montpeliernevis.com

Owners: Lincoln and Muffin Hoffman
General Managers: Tim and Meredith Hoffman
Open: Year-round except mid-August–early October
Credit Cards: MasterCard, Visa
U.S. Reservations: Direct to hotel
Deposit: Three nights; forty-two days cancellation
Minimum Stay: Twelve nights during Christmas
Arrival/Departure: No transfer service
Distance from Airport: 12 miles; taxi one-way, $23
Distance from Charlestown: 4 miles; daily free transport to town and private beach; taxi, $15
Accommodations: 17 rooms in cottages (eight with two double beds, nine with king), all with inside sitting area and outside patios
Amenities: Ceiling fans; telephone with international direct dial; safe; tea and coffeemaker; bath with tub and shower, hair dryer; room service for continental breakfast; no radio, television, air-conditioning
Electricity: 220/240 volts; 110-volt shavers
Sports: Tennis, racquets and balls free, professional for extra charge; snorkeling equipment loaned; waterskiing, deep-sea fishing, windsurfing, golf, horseback riding, hiking, eco-rambles arranged
Dress Code: Informal but with style; men wear long trousers in evening; jackets and ties not required
Children: Eight years and older
Meetings: Small executive groups
Day Visitors: Welcome with reservations
Handicapped: Limited facilities; property has many steps
Packages: Honeymoon, on request
Rates: Two people, daily, CP. *High Season* (mid-December–mid-April): $350. *Low Season:* $240.
Service Charge: 10 percent
Government Tax: 8 percent

NISBET PLANTATION BEACH CLUB
St. James Parish, Nevis, W.I.

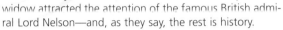

The keystone of the old windmill indicates that William Nisbet began building the great house of his sugar plantation on the northern shore of Nevis for his young bride, Frances, in 1778. Nisbet died a few years later; soon after the wealthy widow attracted the attention of the famous British admiral Lord Nelson—and, as they say, the rest is history.

Today Nisbet Plantation, which has an idyllic location at the foot of Mount Nevis on its own beach (most Nevis plantations were on the mountainside), is an antiques-filled plantation inn with a magnificent lawn that flows to the water's edge between double rows of stately palms and flowering gardens. With a little imagination you can easily picture the opulent life here in bygone days.

Nisbet continued as a sugar and coconut plantation until the 1950s, changing hands several times. In 1989 David Dodwell, a well-known Bermuda hotelier, acquired the inn and made extensive renovations, adding deluxe cottages and a handsome beach complex with a freshwater pool, a restaurant, and a bar.

An aura of the past continues to permeate the gracious inn, particularly its eighteenth-century Great House in classic West Indian architecture of gray volcanic stone. The resort's centerpiece, it houses the main dining room furnished with attractive antiques, the lounge with television and VCR, a library, a bar, and a veranda stylishly furnished with rattan sofas and chairs. It makes an inviting setting for afternoon tea and cocktails, when guests gather to socialize before dinner and to listen to a variety of musical entertainment.

Next to the Great House is an open pavilion with the reception desk and Treasures, a small gingerbread-trimmed cottage housing a boutique with imported Italian fashions from La Perla as well as souvenirs and handcrafts from local artisans.

Accommodations are in pretty, pale yellow Nevis-style cottages generously spaced in the 1/4-mile palm grove between the Great House and the beach, assuring ample privacy. The cottages, with louvered windows providing cross ventilation from the ever-present trade winds, are actually duplex suites, some with furnished screened patios serving as sitting rooms.

Other accommodations—three two-story villas near the beach—have four premier units each, more spacious and luxurious than those in the duplexes. Each unit has a king-size bed, a step-down living room, and an open patio with a wet bar and refrigerator. Bathrooms have a tub as well as a shower. All guest rooms are furnished and painted in white, with stylish, colorful fabrics accented with local paintings, terra-cotta pottery, and fresh flowers.

In 1998 the resort added a new telephone system, attached patios to the sixteen superior rooms, and improved the landscaping for more privacy. The premier rooms were spruced up and fitted with new bathrooms.

Nisbet's beautiful palm-studded beach is protected by reefs, but it can be windy, because it faces the Atlantic Ocean. It was the wind, however, that enabled William Nisbet to put the plantation here in the first place. Now, as then, the wind keeps the air cool and relatively insect-free—and gently rocks the hammocks strung between the palm trees. The resort has a croquet lawn, a large swimming pool, and a tennis court. Complimentary use of the court is limited to one hour at a time, and proper tennis attire is required.

During the season breakfast, lunch, and dinner are served several times a week in an informal setting at

Nisbet Plantation Beach Club ✱✱✱

St. James Parish, Nevis, W.I.
Phone: (869) 469–9325; Fax: (869) 469–9864;
e-mail: nisbetbc@caribsurf.com; www.nisbetplantation.com

Owner: David Dodwell

General Managers: Don and Kathie Johnson

Open: Year-round

Credit Cards: Most major

U.S. Reservations: Island Resorts Reservations, (410) 628–1718, (800) 742–6008; Fax: (410) 628–1732; e-mail: irr@worldnet.att.net

Deposit: Three nights; twenty-eight days cancellation in high season; fourteen days in low season

Minimum Stay: None, except during Christmas

Arrival/Departure: Airport transfer, $8.00; transfer package from St. Kitts, $30

Distance from Airport: 1 mile; taxi one-way, $8.00

Distance from Charlestown: 8 miles; taxi one-way, $15

Accommodations: 38 units with twin or king-size beds in 26 duplex cottages with screened patios; deluxe units have separate living room; twelve suites have living room, terrace, king-size beds, and couch that converts to queen

Amenities: Air-conditioning, ceiling fans; telephone; minibar, tea and coffeemaker; bath with tub in deluxe and premier rooms, shower only in superior rooms, hair dryer, bathrobes, basket of toiletries; nightly turndown service, complimentary laundry service, room service for continental breakfast

Electricity: 110 volts

Sports: Freshwater pool; free snorkeling gear and tennis; lawn croquet; golf, fishing, kayaking, windsurfing, scuba, horseback riding, hiking arranged

Dress Code: Informal by day; no beach attire in Great House and no jeans, shorts, or T-shirts after 6:00 P.M.; casually elegant in evening; jackets and ties not required

Children: All ages; children under twelve years old served dinner at 6:00 P.M. or by special arrangement; cribs, high chairs; baby-sitters

Meetings: No

Day Visitors: Welcome with reservations

Handicapped: No facilities

Packages: Honeymoon, anniversary, wedding, adventure

Rates: Per room, double, daily, MAP. *High Season* (mid-December–late March): $480–$645. *Shoulder Season* (April–May; November–December): $340–$450. *Low Season:* $290–$390.

Service Charge: 10 percent

Government Tax: 8 percent

Coconuts, the restaurant in the attractive beach pavilion. This is also the venue for the manager's weekly cocktail party and the beach seafood barbecue.

Dinner at the Great House, looking out across the avenue of royal palms to the sea, is the evening's highlight. The romantic candlelight setting in the antiques-filled room, with its original mahogany floors, is ideal for the leisurely five-course dinners of sophisticated European and Caribbean cuisine. During a full moon, when the light shines through the palm trees and reflects on the water, the scene is magical.

Nisbet is the Caribbean as it used to be, appealing to those who appreciate the island's serenity and want their space. In this relaxing setting you can choose privacy or the company of others, who are likely to be an even mix of Americans and British with a sprinkling of Europeans. Families with children are welcome and will appreciate the space. Brides will not find a lovelier wedding setting.

Some people say Nisbet's atmosphere is formal in an English manner, but I find the inn delightful. It's a bit tony, yes, but not stuffy.

Puerto Rico

American in tempo, Latin at heart, Puerto Rico is the gateway to the Caribbean. It has big-city action in San Juan and tranquillity in the countryside; glamorous resorts and friendly inns; golf, tennis, fishing, diving, horse racing, and baseball; and more history and scenic wonders than places many times its size.

Puerto Rico's two-year celebration of its 500 years of history in 1992 was centered around the exquisite restoration of Old San Juan, the oldest city under the U.S. flag. Along cobblestone streets, magnificent old mansions are alive with the city's smartest restaurants, shops, art galleries, and museums.

Only thirty minutes from San Juan, the Caribbean National Forest, commonly known as El Yunque, is the only tropical rain forest managed by the U.S. Forest Service. It has recreation areas and trails—and that's only the beginning. Across the center of Puerto Rico, a spine of tall green mountains divides the northern and southern coasts. The 165-mile Panoramic Route winds through the mountains and provides spectacular lookouts, hiking trails, swimming holes, and picnic areas.

Ponce, an architectural gem on the southern coast, is Puerto Rico's second largest town. It undertook a citywide restoration to mark the 300th anniversary of its founding in 1692. West of Ponce on the Caribbean coast, near La Parguera, is one of Puerto Rico's two bioluminescent bays, where microorganisms in the water light up like shooting stars with any movement.

Rio Camuy Caves Park near Hatillo is part of the Camuy River, the world's third largest underground river; you can see caverns as high as a twenty-story building. These are but a few of the attractions that enable Puerto Rico to claim it is the "Complete Island."

Information

Puerto Rico Tourism Company, 575 Fifth Avenue, New York, NY 10017; (212) 599–6262;
www.prtourism.com, www.discoverpuertorico.com

HYATT DORADO BEACH
Dorado, PR

The elegant Hyatt Dorado Beach has matured well. Built on a former coconut and grapefruit plantation in 1958 by Laurance Rockefeller, it was part of his ecologically oriented Rockresort group. Since then the resort has retained its quality and distinction despite changing times and owners and new competitors.

Set on Puerto Rico's northern shore near the town of Dorado, the resort is hidden under acres of palms and flowering gardens with more than 600 varieties of native plants. In its front yard are four of the best golf courses in the Caribbean, and in the back 2 miles of beach.

After thriving for years as a Rockresort, the resort passed through several owners before being purchased by Hyatt in 1985. Since the acquisition Hyatt has put millions into renovations to make it one of the chain's showplaces.

The Hyatt Dorado and its next-door sibling—the larger, more convention-oriented Hyatt Regency Cerromar—sprawl over 1,000 seaside acres. Together they offer so many options for recreation, dining, and nighttime activities that you don't need a car during your stay; shuttle buses make it easy to get from place to place.

Indeed, one of the beauties of the Hyatt Dorado is that it gives you the best of both worlds: the ambience of a small hotel with a main reception building that's a former plantation house, and the hustle-bustle and nightlife of Cerromar, only a short shuttle ride away. 1 mile, to be exact.

Certainly the quartet of Robert Trent Jones championship golf courses is one of the major draws. An entire wing of guest rooms has verandas overlooking the beautiful fairways for travelers who are passionate about the game. You can hone your skills with practice at Dorado's

driving range or putting greens, or take lessons and clinics from one of Hyatt's pros. A new addition is the Dorado Beach Golf Clubhouse with a well-stocked pro shop overlooking the East course and its outstanding new restaurant with a terrace facing the ocean. Located on the second level of the clubhouse, the restaurant, with its staff dressed in classic golf knickers, offers a menu of soups, salads, sandwiches, and a variety of Caribbean, Oriental, Middle Eastern, Mexican, and American entrees for lunch and dinner. It has a splendid show kitchen with state-of-the-art equipment blended with beautifully crafted European tiles and copper siding. Indeed, the restaurant is so delightful, you would enjoy it whether or not you play golf. Lunch on the breeze-filled terrace, overlooking a long stretch of palm-shaded beach, is as pleasant a setting as can be found in the Caribbean. And the food and service are good, too. A mile-long nature trail, suitable for hiking and biking, winds along Dorado's East course, the ocean, and through the resort's nature preserve.

Tennis is just as much of an attraction as golf. The sister resorts together have seventeen courts (four lighted for night play), of which seven are on Dorado's grounds. More extensive clinics and lessons are available at Cerromar's large complex, all under the direction of Peter Burwash International.

The 2-mile-long white-sand beach is sometimes better for sunbathing and viewing from your balcony than it is for swimming—the surf can be rough. But not to worry. Dorado has two swimming pools, one Olympic size; in addition, Hyatt's famous signature lagoon connecting six free-form swimming pools winds through almost five acres of the Cerromar next door.

The expanded Le Spa del Sol Health and Beauty Center at Cerromar offers a full range of beauty treatments, from Swedish massage to sports, neuromuscular therapy, herbal wraps, aromatherapy, and more. The fitness center features Trotter and Universal equipment, including treadmills, stationary bikes, dumbbells, and free weights. Le Spa is open from 7:00 A.M. to 9:00 P.M. weekdays, and 7:00 A.M. to 7:00 P.M. on weekends and holidays.

Dorado has its own placid lagoon, where gentle breezes offer a good place for fledgling windsurfers to try their boards. A team of instructors led by Lisa Penfield, a former world freestyle champ, teaches first-timers the sport. They also give an eight-hour certification course over three sessions.

Since it was first built, the Hyatt Dorado has more than doubled in size, yet it has never seemed like a big hotel. Its rooms have such variety, due to their style and location, that it avoids the cookie-cutter look of a large chain hotel. In addition to the guest rooms by the golf course, you have a choice of casita suites in three loca-

tions; all are in low-rise buildings extending from the large, graceful open-air lobby.

The spacious rooms have terra-cotta floors, marble baths with separate dressing rooms, and terraces; some have private lawns, sitting areas, and showers with skylights. They are decorated in soft Caribbean colors; some have four-poster beds, armoires, and other colonial-style pieces. Nine sets of connecting rooms are configured for families; eight rooms are designed to meet the Americans with Disabilities Act requirements. The crème de la crème is Casita Dorada, a Spanish-style hacienda on the ocean near the main building. It has two bedrooms, two baths, a parlor with a wet bar and two refrigerators, and its own private lawn.

The resort's newest additions are the Su Casa Cottages, thirty-six accommodations in three new buildings. Opened in December 2001, the low two-story structures overlooking the ocean are laid side by side on a piece of land known as "Rockefeller Point." Their design is meant to evoke the look of a Spanish hacienda and blends with their surroundings near the Su Casa restaurant, pool, the golf clubhouse, and the tennis facilities.

The guest rooms are decorated in traditional Spanish style with dark woods, terra-cotta tile floors, a pedestal bed, and Spanish upholstery and accents. The room layout consists of a sleeping area and separate living space with a sofa bed, lounge chairs, and coffee and end tables, accented by original artwork. The bathrooms have double sinks, a separate water closet with a second phone, and a Spanish tile shower and bathtub; the upper level has skylight baths. The rooms are furnished with double and king-size beds and are connected to the adjoining accommodations. All have a balcony or patio with a lounge chair, table, and chairs, only a step away from a private beach and a gazebo on the point—the prime spot for watching sunsets or holding a private wedding.

You can choose to breakfast on your terrace or at the Ocean Terrace Cafe overlooking the turquoise sea. The cafe also serves breakfast and dinner. The Beach Grill next to the Ocean Terrace serves sandwiches and light fare. Beach and golf bars offer light meals. The Surf Room, with dinner music, specializes in Caribbean dishes along with continental cuisine; it features a champagne brunch on Sunday.

The real dining treat at the Hyatt Dorado is Su Casa, an intimate, romantic restaurant housed in an authentic hacienda built in 1905. The elegant stucco house with terra-cotta tiles and iron-filigree trim is barely visible behind a jungle of tropical foliage. The gourmet menu features Spanish and Mediterranean selections, and there is live entertainment. Open in the winter season only, it is one of Puerto Rico's priciest restaurants. Costa del Mar is the Hyatt Dorado's sumptuous conference center.

The Hyatt Dorado has no casino, but if you want action, you will find plenty next door at the glitzy casino of the Hyatt Regency Cerromar and its nightclub. All the restaurants, bars, and entertainment lounges at Cerromar are available to Dorado guests—all you do is sign. The restaurants include the Swan Cafe, a three-level outdoor cafe by the edge of a lake; The Steak Company for steaks and seafood at dinner during high season; Zen Garden, a Japanese-Chinese restaurant; and Medici's for northern Italian cuisine.

Dorado guests also enjoy Cerromar's shops, barber and beauty salons, private airstrip, and Camp Hyatt, an activities program for children three to twelve years old. The camp operates daily year-round from 9:00 A.M. to 4:00 P.M. and 6:00 to 10:00 P.M.; the fee is $40 per child, per day for the daytime session. The program, supervised by bilingual, CPR-certified counselors, includes outdoor games, arts, crafts, Spanish lessons, swimming, biking, and mini-Olympics. It has a playground, an elevated pavilion connected by an arched bridge, slides, ladders, a sand pit, and a jungle gym. Cerromar's pool complex has a wading pool. Camp Hyatt has special room rates, check-in packet, children's menus, and room service.

The Hyatt Dorado is designed for experienced, affluent travelers who like large resort facilities with small-hotel charm. For those who can't decide between a resort vacation and a cruise, Hyatt makes it easy with Cruise Hyatt, a package that combines a Hyatt stay with a cruise on one of Royal Caribbean's ships departing from San Juan.

Hyatt Dorado Beach ★ ★ ★ ★ 🏖
Road 693, Km 12.6, Dorado, PR 00646
Phone: (787) 796–1234; Fax: (787) 796–2022; www.hyatt.com

Owner: Dorado Beach Hotel Corporation

General Manager: Fred Finden

Open: Year-round

Credit Cards: All major

U.S. Reservations: Hyatt Hotels, (800) 233–1234

Deposit: Three nights; fourteen days cancellation

Minimum Stay: Ten nights during Christmas; cancellation by October 31

Arrival/Departure: Transfers arranged for fee

Distance from Airport: *(San Juan International Airport)* 32 miles; Dorado Transport, available in baggage-claim area, offers transfers 11:00 A.M.–10:00 P.M. for $20 per person, one-way

Distance from San Juan: 22 miles; taxi one-way, $40–$50

Accommodations: 314 units with terrace or balcony: including 48 golf view; 28 pool view; 36 ocean view in Su Casa buildings; 168 beachfront; 18 casitas (all king); one two-bedroom casita—all with kings or doubles

Amenities: Air-conditioning, ceiling fans; telephone, television, radio, clock; bath with tub and shower, basket of toiletries; ice service, stocked minibar, coffeemaker; nightly turndown service, twenty-four-hour room service; concierge; iron and ironing board; safe; shops

Electricity: 110 volts

Fitness Facilities/Spa Services: See text

Sports: Two swimming pools; four golf courses; seventeen tennis courts; jogging and biking trails; water-sports center; windsurfing instruction and certification course

Dress Code: Casual by day; casually elegant in evening; jackets required in winter

Children: All ages; cribs; baby-sitting; Camp Hyatt at Cerromar (see text)

Meetings: Up to 800 people; additional facilities at Hyatt Regency Cerromar

Day Visitors: Yes

Handicapped: Facilities

Packages: Honeymoon, family, golf, tennis; Cruise Hyatt

Rates: Per room, single or double, daily, EP. *High Season* (mid-December– March): $395–$705. *Shoulder Season* (April 1–May 31 and October 1–December 21): $260–$470. *Low Season* (June 1–September 30): $175– $375.

Service Charge: 15 percent on food and beverages

Government Tax: 9 percent

EL CONQUISTADOR RESORT AND COUNTRY CLUB AND LAS CASITAS

Fajardo, PR

"Hi, there!" the big, muscular waiter with a smile as broad as his shoulders exclaimed, greeting a couple of Las Brisas breakfast patrons, pencil and order pad at the ready. So startled by the robust friendliness were these jaded New Yorkers that it took them a moment to recover their composure. As though on cue, they lifted their shoulders, straightened their travel-weary backs, and responded with smiling faces, "Good morning, buenos dias." Neither could remember when they had been greeted with such enthusiasm by a waiter in the Caribbean, not to mention New York.

Service with a smile is only one of El Conquistador's assets. Other attractions include the dramatic setting; the comfort and variety of accommodations, dining choices, and sports facilities; the stunning decor; a million-dollar art collection; and one of the most complete spas in the Caribbean.

Spread over 500 acres overlooking the fishing village of Las Croabas and Las Cabezas de San Juan National Park on the northeastern tip of Puerto Rico where the Atlantic meets the Caribbean, Puerto Rico's first true megaresort opened in October 1993. It is located 31 miles east of San Juan, about an hour's drive from San Juan International Airport.

Set at the edge of a 300-foot-high bluff and cascading down a heavily wooded cliffside to the shore, the multi-million-dollar resort is a reincarnation of a hotel of the same name built on the site thirty years ago. El Conquistador, now a Wyndham Resort, was so thoroughly remodeled and expanded that only those with exceedingly keen

memories are likely to recognize anything of its forerunner.

The resort is the creation of a fifteen-member design team that visited megaresorts in Hawaii and elsewhere to study their strengths and shortcomings. The results might be summarized in two words: *openness* and *options*.

To avoid the often sterile, homogenized character of megaresorts and to overcome their huge size, interior decorator Jorge Rosello, a master of space planning best known for his renovation of El San Juan Hotel, drew on Puerto Rico's Spanish heritage to give El Conquistador a distinctive local ambience.

Lounges, lobbies, patios, and plazas lead you from one space to another. Everywhere the eye is greeted with pleasing settings, dramatic vistas, or surprises. Around a corner or by an elevator where most hotels might have a table and mirror, Rosello has created a conversation nook; in lounges where guests might idly gaze up to a blank ceiling, he has occasionally added an interesting but unobtrusive fresco. Nothing, it seems, escaped Rosello's attention—even the chambermaid's cart is stylish.

Standard guest rooms, most with terraces, are as large as the mini suites of most hotels. Some have two double beds, but most are furnished with a king-size one. Rooms also include an easy chair, a coffee table, a loveseat that opens into a bed, handsome rattan chairs, a desk with a clock, and three phones, including one in the bathroom. All are air-conditioned and have ceiling fans. In early 2002, a complete refurbishment of all guest rooms was completed with new decor and furnishings, top-of-the-line Serta® mattresses, and the addition of two-line, high-tech cordless phones.

The sophisticated entertainment unit has a large television (there's also a small one in the bathroom), VCR, and stereo with CD player and tape deck. There is a stocked minibar in the bedroom and a small refrigerator in the bathroom.

The bathrooms are a triumph. Unusually large, the dressing rooms—separate from the bathtub or shower and toilet—have a long marble counter with a sink and a large mirror surrounded by theater lights, plus a separate vanity and chair.

Little things mean a lot. In the bathroom you will find a hair dryer, a coffeemaker, a bathroom scale, bathrobes, a loofah sponge, and plush towels. The walk-in closet has a safe and an iron and ironing board. Wall-mounted bedside lamps can be turned up brightly for reading or down low for—well, you decide.

El Conquistador is meant to be a destination in itself. It offers options in accommodations—five separate clusters, each with a different appeal, due to its location and layout; in dining and entertainment—eleven restaurants, several lounges and bars, and a casino; and in diversions—an eighteen-hole golf course, seven tennis courts, six swimming pools, a Golden Door Spa and fitness center, a shopping arcade, a marina, and an offshore beach-fringed island with water sports.

El Conquistador's impressive entrance, reminiscent of the courtyard of a grand palazzo, sets the style for the resort. Beautifully furnished with a casual feeling, the large yet inviting terrace sits under a high ceiling of staggered, peaked red tile roofs, suggesting houses in an Andalusian village. The tile and marble patio with conversation corners tucked in between the lush foliage has as its focus one of the resort's five large bronze sculptures by Angel Botello, the late Spanish-born artist who made Puerto Rico his home for almost forty years. From the sculpture at the edge of the patio there is an expansive view of the sea, with Palomino Island and other islets in the foreground and Culebra and Vieques in the distance. Below are bougainvillea-bedecked terraces, fountains, waterfalls, and three swimming pools that connect the main building wings.

Las Brisas, the northern wing, and La Vista, on the south, crown the crest of the bluff, providing most rooms with wonderful ocean views.

Cassave, named after the flat bread made from the cassava root of the Taino Indians, is open for lunch and dinner and serves "nuevo Latino" cuisine that fuses traditional Latin American and Caribbean flavors. The Amigos Lounge, a lobby bar near the casino, is the late-night hot spot with live entertainment by island bands. Club 21, a sports bar by the casino, has giant television screens, as well as a stage for nightly shows. Also off the main lobby is Casablanca, a dazzling, Moroccan-theme nightspot with nightly entertainment and dancing to the wee hours.

The main lobby is connected via a plaza to the convention center on the west and a V-shaped building with five floors of guest rooms on the north. The main floor is actually the fifth floor; guest-room floors are built down the hillside. Club Conquistador, an executive floor, is here too.

Next to the casino a duet of outside elevators, as well as a winding staircase, goes down to Las Brisas Restaurant, with casual indoor and outdoor dining terraces. Open from breakfast through late evening, it offers continental and American fare, including "fitness first" menus and Domino's pizza. The terrace overlooks the swimming pool complex. Along with three pools—one with a swim-up bar—there are five whirlpools, lanais, lounge chairs with small red flags to signal an attendant, and the Gazebo, an outdoor bar.

La Vista, the hotel's southern wing, is near the golf and tennis facilities. It is a modern rectangular building around a tropical garden. Rooms on the eastern side overlook the pool complex and spectacular sea views; those on the west look out over the golf course with the rain forest of El Yunque and the bay of Luquillo in the background.

Additional accommodations are found in three distinct "villages." Each cluster has its own manager. Las Olas, midway down the cliff, has a private setting intended mainly for honeymooners. Built in a half moon around a large swimming pool, the units have large balconies overlooking the marina and coast. Las Olas and La Marina by the shore are reached from the hilltop Las Brisas via a funicular that runs regularly throughout the day and evening.

La Marina, a waterfront village that resembles a Mediterranean fishing village with a boat-filled harbor and waterfront shops, offers accommodations in town houses. It is designed for families and those who want to be near water sports. Its restaurants include the Sting Ray Cafe, serving seafood specialties, and the casual Ballyhoo Bar and Grill with pizza, salads, sandwiches, and a raw bar of fresh oysters, grilled shrimp, and conch fritters.

From La Marina, where sailing and deep-sea fishing can be arranged, water taxis ferry guests in fifteen minutes to Palomino, the resort's hundred-acre tropical island rimmed with white-sand beaches. The island offers swimming, sunning, snorkeling, sailing, windsurfing, kayaking, horseback riding, and more. All equipment is nonmotorized. Scuba diving can be arranged, and there is a hiking trail that leads to pristine beaches on the opposite side of the island. The island's snack bar, Iguana's, serves drinks and tropical dishes.

El Conquistador has a new fleet of sixteen vehicles costing more than $1.6 million to transport guests between the airport in San Juan and the resort. Four of the motorcoaches are equipped with recliner seats and minibar. Wyndham has also added a new custom-designed 149-passenger water ferry, *Conquistador II*, for the shuttle to Palomino Island. The state-of-the-art ferry transports guests between the island and the resort in seventeen minutes. Other improvements in the works are the redesign of all three resort pools and a new water slide at the main pool.

LAS CASITAS

On the bluff beyond La Vista is Las Casitas, a resort-within-a-resort where exclusivity is the keynote. It combines the privacy and personalized service of a small hotel with the facilities of a large resort. Designed to resemble a colonial village complete with cobblestone streets, a bell tower, fountains, a public plaza, and villas in the style of Old San Juan, it is the most luxurious part of El Conquis-

tador, offering lovely villa accommodations and outstanding personal service—enough to win a AAA Five Diamond rating, one of only three resorts in the Caribbean to get the highly coveted award. The ninety pastel-colored villas, intended for affluent travelers who want privacy and a tony ambience, have one to three bedrooms, a living room, and a fully equipped kitchen. Those poised on the edge of the cliff have balconies that embrace spectacular views.

Concierge service and private butlers are on hand to pamper guests and fill their every request. They will unpack bags, make reservations, arrange parties, and even cook special meals if asked. The service begins before you leave home with a pre-arrival call to determine your preferred drinks, meals, and other details so that your casita can be stocked accordingly. The royal treatment continues on arrival, when each guest is met at the airport by a resort representative who assists with baggage and transfers. For stays of four nights or more, complimentary private transportation to the resort is provided.

At the resort Las Casitas guests are personally welcomed by a village host and escorted to their villas, which are fitted with casually elegant, comfortable furniture specially designed for Las Casitas and accented by textured fabrics. All units have entertainment centers in both the living room and bedroom with television, VCR, and CD player. You'll also find a fully stocked bar, multiline telephones, a safe, a hair dryer, and an iron with ironing board. The kitchen has an oven, a microwave, and a coffeemaker, and it's stocked with dishes and cutlery. Las Casitas guests enjoy housekeeping service twice daily and exclusive use of the village swimming pool, Jacuzzi, terrace, and library lounge.

Las Casitas village has an exclusive restaurant, Le Bistro, where fine French cuisine is served nightly except Sunday. Recently, it added a new a la carte menu. The intimate restaurant, which accepts no outside reservations, seats eighteen guests in one candlelit room and sixteen in another. Las Casitas guests also enjoy a complimentary deluxe continental breakfast daily at the pool area.

Las Casitas village is convenient to the golf course and tennis facilities, and next to the resort's fabulous Golden Door Spa, which offers the most complete fitness and beauty programs of any resort in the Caribbean. You can begin with a personal trainer who will analyze your needs, discuss your goals, and design a fitness program that you can take home. Then you have a wide range of treatments—from massage to aromatherapy to hot stones—from which to select to help you relax and feel pampered. A fitness center with a full range of equipment will help you keep in shape. The spa has added outdoor cabanas for treatments in three locations—at the Marina,

Palomino Island, and the T'ai Chi lawn. Inspired by the original Golden Door, the spa entrance is being enhanced with a signature golden door and a Zenlike garden.

Las Casitas has begun a $37-million expansion that will add seventy-six units—fifty-five ocean view, sixteen overlooking the golf course—and two new swimming pools. The villas, situated on 156 acres next to the present ones, will be available for individual sale, with the owner deciding whether or not to join the rental program. Seventeen units are one-bedroom; 25, two-bedroom; and 25, three-bedroom. They will have large living rooms and balconies, marble bathrooms, and Italian kitchens with granite counter tops.

El Conquistador's eighteen-hole golf course (6,700 yards, par seventy-two), designed by award-winning architect Arthur Hills, is a beautiful spread across hills and valleys with four small lakes, one with a waterfall. Rain-forest-clad El Yunque is in the background; views of the Atlantic are to the north and of the Caribbean to the east. Six holes with water hazards and tight greens of Bermuda grass challenge a player's accuracy rather than strength. There's a practice putting green and free golf clinic daily. The course was recently renovated and has new car paths, sand bunkers, and landscaping. An additional nine holes are being added to the course. It now has a fleet of ninety new golf carts and new Callaway and Ping golf clubs. El Conquistador is one of three Wyndham resorts operated by Troon Golf, a leading firm in luxury golf course operations.

The tennis complex has seven courts, including a stadium court. A daily clinic is conducted by one of the two Peter Burwash pros. The clubhouse for the golf and tennis complex has a pro shop, locker rooms, and the Grill, an outdoor terrace where breakfast, lunch, and cocktails are served. Bogey's is a snack bar on the golf course; a refreshment wagon circles the course during the day.

Camp Coqui offers daily supervised activities for children ages three to twelve for $38 per day. The kids are separated into two groups: ages three to nine and nine to thirteen. Named for the *coqui,* Puerto Rico's indigenous tree frog, Camp Coqui offers a wide range of educational and fun-filled diversions, from Spanish lessons and nature hikes to a marine biology session before snorkeling. There's specially designed kid-size equipment, such as mini-windsurfers, tennis, and golf gear. The camp boasts an average of one certified counselor for every six children. Activities are held at Camp Coqui's facilities on Palomino Island daily from 9:00 A.M. to 3:00 P.M. and include lunch and a signature T-shirt. Beds are available for naps. Private baby-sitting services are available. The resort also offers weeklong summer camps for ages seven to twelve. Children under twelve may stay free in a room with their parents.

The El Conquistador has the most beautiful convention facilities in Puerto Rico, if not the Caribbean, with four elegant ballrooms, four smaller rooms, terraces, and gardens. Fine furnishings are enhanced by original art and antiques, marble and rich woods, and magnificent crystal chandeliers. The center has a separate entrance and its own activities desk. A helicopter pad is located to its west.

Make no mistake, El Conquistador is large—very large. You will sense its dimensions upon arrival and when you first walk through the various lounges and levels to your room. But you will quickly forget about its size when you begin to see the details—and that's the beauty of it.

El Conquistador Resort and Country Club and Las Casitas ✴ ✴ ✴ ✴

1000 El Conquistador Avenue, P.O. Box 70001, Fajardo, PR 00738
Phone: (787) 863–1000; Fax: (787) 863–6500.
Las Casitas: (787) 863–6746; Fax: (787) 863–6758;
www.wyndham.com

Owner: Patriot American Hospitality
General Manager/El Conquistador: Robert Gunthner
Hotel Manager/Las Casitas: Jose Negron
Open: Year-round
Credit Cards: All major
U.S. Reservations: (800) 468–5228. Las Casitas: (800) 452–2274.
Deposit: Three nights; seven days cancellation, except thirty days at Christmas
Minimum Stay: Seven nights during Christmas, from December 24
Arrival/Departure: At San Juan International Airport, guests are met and board a motor coach to the resort. The cost is $25 one-way, billed to your hotel account. For Las Casitas, see text.
Distance from Airport: *(San Juan International Airport)* 31 miles
Distance from Fajardo: 2 miles
Accommodations: 926 rooms and suites with terraces in five locations. Las Casitas: 90 casitas (144 deluxe rooms and suites). Las Olas village: 73 deluxe rooms. La Marina village: 168 rooms and suites. Las Brisas: 229 deluxe rooms and suites. La Vista: 304 deluxe rooms and suites. Either two double beds or one king.
Amenities: Air-conditioning, ceiling fans; safe; bath with tub and shower, hair dryer, his and hers robes, iron and ironing board; two televisions with movie channels, VCR, stereo with tape deck and CD player, three multiline phones; stocked honor bar, small refrigerator; desk with clock; nightly turndown service, room service; casino; spa; shopping arcade. Las Casitas: See text.
Electricity: 110 volts
Fitness Facilities/Spa Services: See text
Sports: Six swimming pools; seven lighted tennis courts; golf course, clubhouse, pro shop, locker room, bar; thirty-two-slip marina, sailboats, catamarans, yacht charters; deep-sea fishing arranged; Palomino Island with snorkeling, diving, hiking, volleyball, kayaking, windsurfing, horseback riding, and more
Dress Code: Casual by day; casually elegant in evening
Children: Camp Coqui with supervised activities; cribs, high chairs; baby-sitters (see text)
Meetings: Large convention center
Day Visitors: Yes
Handicapped: Limited facilities
Packages: Adventure, golf, tennis, honeymoon
Rates: *High Season* (January–April): $350–$545. **Low Season:** $250–$350. Christmas rates higher; inquire.
Service Charge: 10 percent
Government Tax: 11 percent

PARADOR HACIENDA GRIPINAS

Jayuya, PR

A restored nineteenth-century coffee plantation in the central mountains near the town of Jayuya, Parador Hacienda Gripinas is a working plantation that evokes the atmosphere of bygone days more than any other of the island's *paradores,* or "country inns."

Named for the tangy-sweet flavor of its coffee, Gripinas is perched at 3,000 feet on twenty-three acres where the coffee aroma lingers in the air. A narrow, country road (Route 527) overhung with mango trees winds up to the parador through pastoral settings that are light-years from the glitter of San Juan.

The 200-year-old hacienda, which opened to guests in 1975, is a traditional, gracefully simple island home built of wood with a wide veranda and shuttered windows. Painted white with green trim, it is surrounded by gardens of tropical flowers and shaded by large fruit and flowering trees. Inside, the parlors are furnished with some quality carved-wood pieces.

Most of the accommodations are set in a separate wing and furnished simply with bare wood floors. Arrangements differ, but all rooms have modern baths. (Guest rooms in the original great house are more attractive.) They also have lovely views of the countryside. If you are a light sleeper or unaccustomed to the sounds of the Caribbean country, you will need to use a pair of earplugs. A chorus of coquí, minuscule Puerto Rican tree frogs, sings nonstop through the night, and at 4:00 A.M. a neighborhood rooster begins trumpeting loud enough to wake the dead.

The dining room is made up of three rooms, one of which has a small interior patio with pretty greenery. Gripinas is counted among Puerto Rico's gastronomic inns. All meals are served at set hours and feature Puerto Rican cuisine and regional specialties. The Sunday buffets are popular with local people; the seafood and lobster are especially good. You will also enjoy fresh local fruits and juices and sample the rich Tres Picachos coffee grown here.

Guests, mostly from the U.S. mainland and Puerto Rico and occasionally some Europeans, pass the time reading to the accompaniment of the frequent rain, lazing in the hammocks and rockers on the veranda looking out

Parador Hacienda Gripinas *

P.O. Box 387, Road 527, Km. 2.5, Barrio Vegita, Jayuya, PR 00664
Phone: (787) 828–1717 or (787) 828–1718; Fax: (787) 828–1719; e-mail: gripinas@excite.com; www.haciendagripinas.com

Owner/Manager: Edgardo Dedos

Open: Year-round

Credit Cards: Most major

U.S. Reservations: Direct to hotel

Deposit: One night

Minimum Stay: Two nights on weekends; three nights on holiday weekends

Arrival/Departure: No transfer service; must have car

Distance from Airport: *(San Juan International Airport)* Two-and-a-half-hour drive

Distance from Ponce: One-hour drive on winding road; no taxi; local bus only

Distance from San Juan: Two-and-a-half-hour drive; local bus only

Accommodations: 19 rooms

Amenities: Air-conditioning; bath with shower only; television; no room service

Electricity: 110 volts

Sports: Freshwater swimming pool; walking and hiking trails; birding

Dress Code: Casual

Children: All ages

Meetings: Up to forty people indoors; up to 150 people in open-air facilities

Day Visitors: Welcome

Handicapped: Limited facilities

Packages: Honeymoon

Rates: Per person, daily, MAP. *Year-round:* $92 single; $63 double

Service Charge: 15 percent on food; energy charge $2.00 per room per day

Government Tax: 7 percent

over the countryside, and conversing with other guests. There is a tiny room with a television set that receives CNN and other cable services, in addition to local broadcasting.

Footpaths along a riverbed bordered by stands of bamboo and tree ferns lead to a large swimming pool fed by a pretty waterfall and an outdoor bar in a beautiful setting. The inn has a basketball court, and if you are really energetic, you can take hikes in the woods and perhaps pick your fruit for breakfast along the way.

The homey, unpretentious parador, with its quiet rural setting, typifies the "other Puerto Rico" and appeals mainly to outdoor enthusiasts, nature lovers, birders, history and culture buffs, and people who simply want to escape from the city.

THE HORNED DORSET PRIMAVERA HOTEL
Rincón, PR

With its inviting lobby, sculpted archways, and stunning views of the Mayaguez coast and the sea, The Horned Dorset Primavera has what the Spanish would term *tremendo cache*, that indefinable blend of grace and good taste seen only in the best of Caribbean hostelries.

Ever since former academics Harold Davies and Kingsley Wratten opened it in May 1988, an elite list of islanders and mainland Americans and Europeans have been discovering the special charms of this unique hideaway on Puerto Rico's western end. The intimate European-style inn was a welcome addition to Puerto Rican shores, heretofore known primarily for the miles of high-rise hotel-casinos on metropolitan beaches.

As longtime proprietors of the small, highly acclaimed Horned Dorset Inn in upstate New York (named for a breed of sheep the men once raised there), Davies and Wratten were no strangers to the hotel business when they began scouting the Caribbean for a second property in the early 1980s. They settled on a hilly four-acre site at the foot of the Cordillera Central in the "middle of nowhere," as they describe it.

Working closely within the context of its luxuriant garden setting, leading Puerto Rican architect and naturalist Otto Octavio Reyes-Casanova created a graciously proportioned Spanish colonial manor house complete with classic arches, black-and-white marble floors, and a fountain-splashed lobby. Nearby, a cluster of whitewashed, red tile-roof buildings, called Villas de Las Mesas, house the villa suites, all with private balconies.

Throughout the public rooms massive carved mahogany pieces, terra-cotta floors, and Portuguese decorative tiles add richness and depth to the airy, tropical decor, along with abundant arrangements of exotics plucked from the surrounding botanical gardens. From the floral prints covering commodious rattan sofas and chairs to the Chinese porcelain lamps, the profusion of shapes, colors, and designs blends harmoniously.

The suites, varying somewhat in individual character,

are given equal thought and attention with an eye toward comfort. Handsome armoires and mahogany-pillared queen beds, made by well-known woodworkers from Ponce, are equipped with firm mattresses and soft down pillows. Italian marble lines floors and walls in the generous bathrooms fitted with brass fixtures and old-fashioned footed tubs, bidets, and toilets from Lille, France. Louvered doors open onto a balcony with a view of the small beach; a wicker settee and tables complete the adjoining sitting room. Behind the four highest suites of the Villas de Las Mesas are another swimming pool and a small gym.

Casa Escondida, a separate addition opened in March 1995, is a seafront guest house with meeting facilities. Also designed by Octavio Reyes-Casanova, along with his associate, Oswaldo Colon, it is meant to resemble a nineteenth-century Puerto Rican hacienda. The house has eight guest rooms, with butler service. Four rooms have private plunge pools, while the others have private roof terraces or balconies. There is a large central room with a 30-foot-high ceiling and space to accommodate twelve people in an informal living room seating arrangement or thirty people as a meeting room. The second floor has a private dining room where twelve can breakfast, lunch, or conduct a private meeting around a large oval table; electronic and other business equipment is available.

Mirador Villa is the hotel's most secluded, luxurious accommodation. The freestanding building perched high above the resort is a one-bedroom suite with an airy living room furnished with antiques, a king-size bed, a large marble bath, a large wraparound terrace, and a small pool. Dinners can be arranged in the hotel's private dining room in the main building. When Casa Escondida is not functioning as a meeting facility, the rooms can be rented by other hotel guests or family groups who want the extra luxury these rooms provide.

The hotel has added twenty-two deluxe sea-view villas in five two-story buildings on a cliffside facing the sea and framing a new lap pool. The decor—imported wood, marble tiles, and antiques—is consistent with The Horned Dorset's style. The first level of each unit has a separate living room, dining area, bath, and rear-view terrace. The hotel's main entrance has been moved to a new hilltop, beam-ceilinged reception building. Electric carts will be available to take guests to their rooms in either the new and old sections of the hotel. Guests have two options for dining: the Primavera Restaurant, serving five-course gourmet meals, and the new outdoor terrace by the sea specializing in grilled fare. Both restaurants are directed by executive chef Aaron Wratten.

True to the culinary precedent established by its North American sibling, The Horned Dorset Primavera serves a classic French menu but showcases a wealth of regional flavors and products as well.

Shopping outings are the ongoing occupation of both proprietors and son Aaron Wratten, who trained at such famous New York restaurants as Danie and Aurora and is now the resort's executive chef. They hit the streets of neighboring Rincón, Mayaguez, and Aguadilla for the freshest goods. Breakfast includes such delights as hearty Yauco coffee from the island's mountain slopes, crusty French bread, and delicious finger bananas, papayas, and pineapples from the fertile fields of nearby Lajas. Luncheon selections feature fresh grilled fish along with a variety of salads and sandwiches.

Breakfast and lunch are served poolside or on the veranda of the Great House. Dinner is in the air-conditioned, formal waterfront dining room draped with Italian linens and lighted by turn-of-the-century wrought-iron chandeliers. The menus have several prix-fixe dinners for $68, created by Aaron Wratten. There is also a chef's tasting menu of seven courses for $92 and a sophisticated wine card. Little wonder the hotel wants to be known as a "food destination."

The Horned Dorset Primavera promotes itself as "a place without activities," which is the owners' way of saying their hotel is not for everyone. It's geared for travelers who want a quiet vacation away from crowds. Most guests seem to welcome this respite, spending entire days about the pool, in the lounge filled with classical music, or the library brimming with books, breaking the pace with an occasional walk on the beach. The sea can be rough here, and the narrow beach is not the hotel's strong suit. Arrangements can be made for golf, diving, deep-sea fishing, or whale-watching.

Come early evening the expansive front terrace beckons guests for drinks, tapas tasting, and a last tantalizing view of the molten tropical sun dissolving by inches into the Mona Straits beyond. As the horizon dims and waves lap at seawalls just below, far off to the south the lights of Mayaguez begin to twinkle.

The Horned Dorset Primavera Hotel ★★★★

Rincón, PR 00677
Phone: (787) 823–4030, (800) 633–1857; Fax: (787) 823–5580; e-mail: hdp@coqui.net; www.relaischateaux.fr/horneddorset

Owners/Managers: Harold Davies, Kingsley Wratten, Willhelm Sack

Open: Year-round

Credit Cards: All major

U.S. Reservations: Direct to hotel, (800) 633–1857; or Relais et Châteaux, (212) 856–0115

Deposit: Reservation secured with credit card

Minimum Stay: Four–seven nights in winter

Arrival/Departure: Transfer arranged by hotel for fee

Distance from Airport: (Mayaguez Airport) 3 miles (ten minutes); taxi one-way, $40. San Juan International Airport: Two-and-a-half-hour drive; taxi one-way, $180

Distance from Rincón: 5 miles; taxi one-way, $20

Accommodations: 30 ocean-view villa suites with terrace in six buildings, all with queen-size beds; eight rooms in Casa Escondida; Mirador Villa with pool (one bedroom with king); 22 deluxe villas added in 2002.

Amenities: Air-conditioning, ceiling fans; bath with tub and shower, basket of toiletries; hair dryers available; ice service; room service for breakfast; no phone, television, radio

Electricity: 110 volts

Sports: Freshwater swimming pool; golf, snorkeling, diving, deep-sea fishing, hiking, birding nearby

Dress Code: Casual chic; trousers for men at dinner

Children: None under twelve years old

Meetings: No

Day Visitors: Yes

Handicapped: Limited facilities

Packages: Honeymoon

Rates: Per person, daily, EP. **High Season** (December 15–April 15): $380–$800. **Low Season:** $280–$650. Add $76 per person per day for full breakfast, prix-fixe dinner excluding gratuity; must be taken for length of reservation.

Service Charge: 15 percent on food and beverages

Government Tax: 9 percent general tax; 6 percent service tax

EL SAN JUAN HOTEL & CASINO
Carolina (San Juan), PR

Stylish, luxurious, and fun, the El San Juan lets you have your cake and eat it, too. It's a complete beachside resort only a few miles from the airport but within easy reach of the city center. It's large enough to offer all the facilities you could possibly want but not so large that it loses its personality.

Indeed, the El San Juan is so distinctive you could never confuse it with another hotel. Walk through its lavish lobby, brimming with art and activity, or stroll over to the poolside veranda with its 1930s decor and gardens, and you'll know immediately that this is like no other place.

The El San Juan does have its quiet corners, but this hotel is really for people who want to be in the center of the action, day or night. It has nine restaurants (each with a different cuisine), nine bars, a casino, a nightclub, a disco, three swimming pools, three tennis courts, water sports, a health club and spa, a daily children's program, an arcade of chic boutiques, and a staff of more than 1,000 who make sure it hums around the clock.

Set in fifteen acres of tropical gardens on the Atlantic northern coast, the El San Juan is located on the eastern

ideas, working more than a decade apart but resulting in a remarkable duet.

In the 1960s New York designer Alan Lanigan traveled through Africa, Asia, and Europe collecting artwork, relics, balustrades, and other decorative and architectural elements to embellish the hotel. He acquired storefronts to design a shopping arcade, and shipped heavy wooden doors, many more than a century old, from North Africa; oil paintings and art deco lamps from Europe; statues and jardinieres from the Orient; as well as mahogany from the Dominican Republic. In the 1980s Puerto Rican interior designer Jorge Rosello recognized the uniqueness of Lanigan's work and built on it, essentially keeping the old intact. He enlivened the interior with a more cheerful environment, creating a more tropical feeling. More recently the hotel has undergone a complete renovation from top to bottom, with new restaurants and shops and a new beachfront wing with twenty-one deluxe suites and a private pool. The building, set at the edge of the beach and surrounded by tropical gardens, is situated in such a way that the suites have ocean views from their bathrooms as well as

edge of the city. The landmark hotel reigned as the grande dame of Caribbean hotels in the 1960s, but by the decade's end, when Puerto Rico's fortunes had tumbled, the El San Juan closed and the Isla Verde area deteriorated. Williams Hospitality bought the hotel in 1984 and reopened it one year and $50 million later, launching Puerto Rico's tourism renaissance. In 1997 El San Juan—along with its sister hotel, El Conquistador—were bought by Patriot American and folded into the Wyndham group.

The El San Juan actually underwent two transformations by two interior designers, with completely different

their verandas. The suites —as large as some New York apartments—are furnished in period-style mahogany pieces with colorful fabrics and pillows and a convertable sofa. Each has a minibar, a safe, three multiline telephones, voice mail, fax-modem outlets, and an iron and ironing board. The huge bathrooms have a double-sink vanity, separate shower, and six-foot-long whirlpool bathtub.

At one end of the complex is the Monarch Suite, a fabulous one-bedroom layout with a master bath, guest bath, dining room that seats twelve, bar, baby grand piano, and full kitchen.

The famous, fabulous, action-center lobby is the hub of the hotel and the best people-watching spot in San Juan. To one side is the Wine Bar, where caviar, foie gras, sushi, and cheese are served. It's the only Cruvinet wine bar in the Caribbean and offers twenty-two champagnes and wines by the glass. To the other side is the casino, where Rosello added the Winners Circle, a plush lounge that serves as both a piano bar and a sports bar.

El San Juan was one of the first hotels in the Caribbean to add a cigar bar. And what a bar! Situated in the lobby by the entrance to the casino, the elegant, clubby corner has as its backdrop a wall of private humidors—each with its own lock and key—which rent for $1,250 per year.

Live entertainment is featured until the wee hours at El Chico, a nineteenth-century-style saloon, where you can hear Latin music; and at Babylon, one of San Juan's "hot" discos and a mecca for the under-twenty-three crowd. The roof has the Tequila Bar and Grill and an outdoor Mexican restaurant where the margaritas are fabulous. The newest rooftop addition is The Ranch at El San Juan, Puerto Rico's first country-western bar and grill, complete with a mechanical bull and the Nashville sound.

Back Street Hong Kong, a Chinese restaurant, is approached through a replica of a Hong Kong street (created for the 1964 New York World's Fair). Other dining choices include La Veranda Cafe, a casual outdoor terrace overlooking the pool and gardens; The Palm, a replica of the famous Manhattan steakhouse; the new Bistro, a sidewalk cafe—indoors; La Piccola Fontana, for northern Italian dishes; and Yamato, a Japanese restaurant.

Guest rooms are posh and contemporary, offering great variety: casitas with Roman baths; poolside, ocean, and garden suites, and moderate, standard, and superior rooms and suites in the tower. Some suites have kitchenettes.

The hotel has a rooftop health club and solarium, tennis, and a comprehensive water-sports program. It also has an unusual complimentary service: a computer-customized vacation. You select your preferences from a menu of activities as varied as merengue classes and deep-sea fishing.

The computerized service can work in conjunction with Kids' Klub, a supervised program for children ages five to twelve offered daily from 10:00 A.M. to 4:00 P.M., with children divided into groups for activities appropriate to their ages and interests. A printed program of activities, which change daily, is available in advance. Kids' Klub costs $28 per day per child, including lunch. There is a trained counselor for each ten children.

Paradise Club is El San Juan's place for teenagers. Its most popular activities are lessons in salsa and sampling the exotic sundaes at Scoops, a poolside ice cream parlor.

El San Juan Hotel & Casino *****

6063 Isla Verde Avenue, #187, Carolina (San Juan), PR 00979
Phone: (787) 791–1000, (800) WYNDHAM; Fax: (787) 791–6985; www.wyndham.com

Owner: Patriot American Hospitality
Management: Wyndham International
Managing Director: Rich Cortese
Hotel Manager: Jose Suarez
Open: Year-round
Credit Cards: All major
U.S. Reservations: El San Juan Hotel & Casino, (800) 468–2818, (212) 755–9030; Fax: (787) 253–0178
Deposit: One night; three days cancellation
Minimum Stay: None
Arrival/Departure: No transfer service
Distance from Airport: (Luis Marin Muñoz International Airport) 5 miles; taxi one-way, $8.50
Distance from Old San Juan: 10 miles; taxi one-way, about $16
Accommodations: 389 rooms and suites, most with verandas (261 in main building, 128 in gardens and on beach)
Amenities: Air-conditioning, ceiling fan; cable television, VCR, clock-radio/cassette player, CD player; three telephones; safe; iron and ironing board; bath with tub, shower, vanity, bathrobes, toiletry basket, 5-inch TV, hair dryer; nightly turn-down service on request; ice service, stocked minibar; twenty-four-hour concierge, room service; business services
Electricity: 110 volts
Fitness Facilities/Spa Services: Fully equipped fitness center and spa on tenth floor of main building
Sports: Beach, three freshwater swimming pools, three Jacuzzis, three lighted tennis courts, equipment, daily clinics free; snorkeling, scuba, windsurfing for fee; golf, boating, fishing, horseback riding, hiking arranged
Dress Code: Casual by day; elegantly casual in evening
Children: All ages; Kids' Klub, Paradise Club (for teenagers), supervised activities; game room; cribs, high chairs, baby-sitters; children's pool
Meetings: Up to 1,500 people
Day Visitors: Welcome
Handicapped: Limited facilities; wheelchairs; dedicated rooms
Packages: Honeymoon; Caribbean Magic
Rates: Two people, daily, EP. *High Season* (late November–April 30): $395–$545 (rooms), $595–$1,225 (suites). *Low Season:* $285–$430 (rooms), $480–$925 (suites).
Service Charge: None
Government Tax: 18 percent

THE GALLERY INN/GALERIA SAN JUAN

Old San Juan, PR

Artists don't usually have the temperament for managing a hotel, but for Jan D'Esopo, it's only one of several things on her plate—or palette, in this case. This is an art-gallery-cum-inn, as the name implies, and there is nothing quite like it in the Caribbean. But what really sets the Gallery Inn apart is that it occupies three of the oldest buildings in Old San Juan.

La Cueva del Indio, as one of the rambling old buildings was known, faces north to the Atlantic Ocean from the topmost crest of the old city. Strategically located between the two large forts, the structure is the oldest military residence (built about 1750) on the northern side of the old walled city. Historians believe it served as the captain's quarters for the Spanish Artillery.

New York–born Jan and her husband, Manuco Gandia, a native of Puerto Rico, acquired their first building in 1961, and the restoration took two years. Today the complex of three buildings has more than fifty spaces: a maze of rooms, passageways, courtyards, balconies, and gardens. You need a map to find your way around.

The art gallery and its exhibit rooms occupy most of the ground floor and double as the inn's lobby. The entrance is marked only by a street-number sign, but you will know you are in the right place when you see a row of sculpted heads on the windowsill of the silk-screening studio at the front of the house. The gate leads into a small bricked courtyard filled with plants and more sculpture. You may need to step over a sleeping dog to get into the gallery.

The guest rooms are situated in every nook of the three story white stucco buildings, and you make your way along narrow steps, around tight corners, and under broad arches. You will discover that the old stone, brick, and wood floors are seldom even, and steps go up and back down to reach some rooms. The handsome, beamed ceilings of ausubo wood (a termite-resistant native tree) are high in most places, but occasionally you might need to bend slightly to make your way. And everywhere plants and flowers overflow their bases, some hanging from upper balconies of the inner courtyard to the ground.

Every wall and surface, bookshelf and ledge, is enlivened with sculpture and paintings, either by Jan or a young artist she is helping to get established, or by acclaimed artists who come to give seminars or simply to visit. Special rates are extended to artists—who are often seen painting in a courtyard—depending on season and availability (inquire in advance if you qualify).

No two guest rooms are alike in size, decor, or amenities, except that now all have new Tempur-Pedic® mattresses—an unusual extravagance for a small, modest inn. Some have terraces; all have their own bath with shower,

except two adjacent rooms that share a private bath. A third-floor suite has a living room and an extra bed for a third person and two terraces with views over Old San Juan and the sea.

Basically, the rooms are furnished in Spanish colonial decor, but the artist in Jan has enabled her to mix contemporary pieces, art, and antiques in an eclectic way without being funky. Well, maybe not too funky. To be honest, the entire house, from workshops to the sundeck on top, has a musty-dusty chaotic order to it—and that, of course, defines a great deal of its charm.

The Gallery offers a continental breakfast, and occasionally Jan creates one of her famous dinners. (In addition to being an artist and innkeeper, she is an accomplished chef and caters elegant dinner parties for local businesses and visiting VIPs. She says she can seat as many as ninety people for dinner, but I haven't figured out where.) Old San Juan now has many super restaurants, all within walking distance; they are among the pleasures of visiting the Old City. The Gallery has a refreshment bar in the main gallery that works on the honor system. You keep tabs and pay upon checkout.

The guests who come here—as many from Europe as from the United States—are a group as eclectic as the house. If you are exacting or need orderly surroundings to feel comfortable, pass up this one. On the other hand, if being amid art and artists is stimulating for you and you are flexible, undemanding, and willing to forgo some of the usual amenities of a hotel, you could enjoy a stay here immensely.

The inn is homey as well as historic, but there's no one to pamper you. The owners and their staff will try to accommodate you but essentially, you fend for yourself. You are welcome as part of the family and encouraged to explore the house, enjoy the paintings and sculpture, ask questions—even pick up a paintbrush if you feel so inspired.

The Gallery Inn/Galeria San Juan (S)

204 Calle Norzagaray, Old San Juan, PR 00901
Phone: (787) 722– 1808, 723–6515; Fax: (787) 977–3929; e-mail: reservations@thegalleryinn.com; www.thegalleryinn.com

Owner/Manager: Jan D'Esopo
Open: Year-round
Credit Cards: All major
U.S. Reservations: Direct to hotel
Deposit: One night, payable by credit card
Minimum Stay: Two nights during high season (November–April)
Arrival/Departure: No transfer service
Distance from Airport: 12 miles; taxi one-way, $16
Distance from Condado Beach Area: 3 miles; taxi one-way, $10
Accommodations: 24 rooms including 11 suites, some with terrace or balcony
Amenities: Honor bar; room service on request
Electricity: 110 volts
Sports: Horseback riding, tennis, boating, snorkeling, scuba, windsurfing, deep-sea fishing, hiking arranged
Dress Code: Informal
Children: Age nine and older
Meetings: Up to forty people for meetings, ninety for dinner
Day Visitors: Yes, by appointment
Handicapped: No facilities
Packages: No
Rates: Two people, daily, CP. *Year-Round:* $145–$350.
Service Charge: 9 percent
Government Tax: 9 percent

HOTEL EL CONVENTO

Old San Juan, PR

This sixteenth-century convent in the heart of Old San Juan has been transformed into a lovely, small hotel, with its historic architecture maintained throughout while the facilities behind its imposing facade have been modernized. By the time the present owners acquired the building, it had had so many incarnations that the fact that they could complete the renovations successfully was nothing short of a miracle.

Originally built in 1651 to house the first Carmelite convent in the New World and occupied by them until 1903, the building stood vacant for a decade until it was finally bought by the Church from the Carmelite sisters for $151. Subsequently, the building was rented as a dance hall and a flophouse without electricity, running water, or sanitary facilities. By 1953 it had become a parking lot for garbage trucks.

To save the historic building from the wrecking ball, Robert F. Woolworth (of the Woolworth family) bought it in 1959 from the Catholic Church for $250,000, and after three years of renovations and restorations, opened it in 1962 as the elegant, hundred-room El Convento Hotel.

The hotel was a triumph socially but couldn't earn back what had been spent on it, and in 1971 the owner gave El Convento as a gift to the Puerto Rican government in lieu of back taxes. Over the next twenty-five years, the hotel deteriorated slowly as a succession of management companies operated it. Finally in 1995 it was sold to a group of San Juan business interests that spent two years and more than $15 million (about $275,000 per room) to create the present fifty-seven-room hotel.

The renovations, which kept the architectural integrity of the original convent, were done by Jorge Rosello, an enormously talented Puerto Rican interior designer and space planner best known for the handsome interiors he created for El San Juan Hotel and El Conquistador Resort.

Partially covered during previous renovations, the spacious interior courtyard of the former convent—its arches and balconies hidden for centuries behind its 30-foot-thick walls—is again open to the sky. It has three different street entrances. The lower two floors of the building house specialty shops, along with three informal cafes: Cafe Nispero, which takes its name from a huge tree whose spreading arms shade the courtyard; Cafe Bohemio, a sidewalk cafe; and El Picoteo, operated by the same group as Cafe Bohemio, which has a new chef who has expanded the tapas menu.

The newest addition is the Blue Agave Grill, a new

restaurant in the oldest part of El Convento. Situated in the lower ground level beneath the hotel's main entrance, the restaurant was dug—literally—out of 500 years of history. With no architectural or building plans to go by, owner Deborah Morales says her team had to feel their way through the ancient structure. Among their finds was the original cistern—a large structure that will become a cozy side room for twelve diners. The restaurant specializes in authentic Mexican cuisine with infusions of Puerto Rican and Caribbean flavors and light fare. Blue Agave is named for the cactus plant from which tequila is made; 100 percent Blue Agave tequila is one of the restaurant's specialties. A hit from opening day, the unusual restaurant draws San Juan's fashionable crowd.

The hotel occupies the third to fifth floors and is reached by a private entrance and keyed elevator. Guests check in at the concierge and reception desk next to a guest lounge on the third floor. The wide corridors and rooms, decorated with handcrafted furniture from Spain, have retained their ancient tile floors, previously covered by carpeting, and their mahogany ceiling beams, which have been either restored or replaced. All rooms are air-conditioned and have a multiline telephone with dataport, remote control television, VCR and stereo entertainment center, an iron and ironing board, coffeemaker, refrigerator, safe, hair dryer, and robes. The hotel has a new junior suite (Room 404), which is an ideal family suite with two double beds in the main bedroom and a pull-out couch in the living room. Located adjacent to the pool terrace, it enjoys great views, too.

Hotel guests enjoy a complimentary "eye-opener" breakfast of juice, coffee, and pastries, along with the morning newspaper delivered on request to the room prior to breakfast. In the evening are complimentary wine and hors d'oeuvres.

The rooftop Mirador Terrace has a small swimming pool, a Jacuzzi, and an indoor fitness center with massage facilities—all added in the recent renovation. La Vista Terrace has a music room and library, and wonderful day and night views overlooking Old San Juan and the coast. The hotel offers a full-service business center and conference center for up to twenty-four people.

El Convento, an Old San Juan landmark, is located on historic Cristo Street across from San Juan Cathedral, where Ponce de Leon is entombed, and within easy walking distance of the important historic sights, museums, art galleries, shopping, and some of the top restaurants in the city. It is twenty minutes from San Juan International Airport and five minutes from the cruise piers, making it convenient for pre- and postcruise stays.

Hotel El Convento ✷✷✷

100 Cristo Street, P.O. Box 1048, Old San Juan, PR 00902
Phone: (787) 723–9020; Fax: (787) 721–2877;
e-mail: elconvento@aol.com; www.elconvento.com

Managing Company: Puerto Rico Hospitality Group, Inc.
General Manager: Consuelo MacMurray
Open: Year-round
Credit Cards: All major
U.S. Reservations: (800) 468–2779
Deposit: One night; three days cancellation prior to arrival, otherwise one-night penalty will apply
Minimum Stay: Three nights December 27–January 1
Arrival/Departure: No transfer service
Distance from Airport: (San Juan International Airport) 5½ miles
Accommodations: 59 rooms and suites
Amenities: Air-conditioning; television, VCR, stereo entertainment center; refrigerator; multiline telephones with dataport; hair dryer; iron and ironing board; safe; nightly turndown service
Electricity: 110 volts
Fitness Facilities/Spa Services: Fitness center
Sports: Plunge pool, Jacuzzi; tennis, golf, water sports arranged; historic walking tours
Dress Code: Casual by day; smartly casual in evening
Children: All ages; baby-sitting available; no charge for crib in room; children under thirteen free in room with parents
Meetings: Up to 300 people
Day Visitors: Yes
Handicapped: Facilities
Packages: Discover Old San Juan, Romance, Pre/Post Cruise, Town and Country
Rates: Per room, single/double, EP. **High Season** (December 24–March 31): $265–$375; suites, $500–$1,200. **Low Season** (April–December 23): $150–$240; suites, $500–$1,200.
Service Charge: 10 percent
Government Tax: 11 percent

THE RITZ-CARLTON SAN JUAN HOTEL & CASINO

Isla Verde, Carolina, PR

Located in Isla Verde on eight beachfront acres less than ten minutes from the international airport, this hotel is a Ritz-Carlton inside and out, with signature architecture and design. But check the details and you will see that it has a style and character all its own.

First there is the lobby, whose windows span the first and second floors and look out on the gardens to the swimming pool and the sea. It's very impressive. Here, in the pleasant surroundings of the lobby lounge from 3:00 to 5:00 p.m. daily, tea is served with a harpist providing background music. It sets the tone for the hotel. And does this hotel have tone!

From the moment you step into the rosy beige marbled lobby, you see and sense a refinement that no other hotel in San Juan can match. To the right is the front desk—it's marble; to the left is the concierge's desk—it's marble, too. And the floors, here and throughout the hotel, are covered with the most handsome hotel carpets ever to grace a hallway. Wonderful works of art by Puerto Rican artists enliven the walls throughout the hotel.

The building is in the shape of a U around a bilevel swimming pool and gardens that stretch to a wide beach. To one side of the pool is a large Jacuzzi under a pretty gazebo; to the other you'll find the Ocean Bar and Grill

(which serves lunch and daytime snacks), a spa and fitness center, and two lighted tennis courts.

The spa, housed in an elegant marble and stone bilevel building, has eleven treatment rooms for facials, massages, manicures, pedicures, hydrotherapy, and body wraps. The fitness center offers yoga, aerobics, and other strength and fitness activities.

Tucked out of sight around the corner from the lobby is a large casino—the first for a Ritz-Carlton—with its own separate entrance and parking for 1,000 cars. Across the gardens in the opposite wing are the bar and restaurants on the ground level; upstairs is a huge, elegant ballroom that extends to an outdoor terrace overlooking the gardens and the pool.

En route to the restaurants, you pass The Bar, a cigar and martini bar with lovely wood-paneled walls and built-in humidors (available for rent) that keep 2,000 cigars at the proper temperature. You can also enjoy seventy different rums (after all, it's Puerto Rico), including thirty-year-old rum at $18 a shot.

The intimate Vineyard Room is designed in the style of a Napa Valley or Spanish hacienda, with a wood-beamed ceiling, wooden floors, and an open kitchen. It has become the hotel's gourmet restaurant and one of San Juan's top eateries with its own dedicated chef, Stephen

Trojahn, who creates new, innovative dishes, often using Puerto Rican cuisine and produce as inspiration and, other times, simply using his fertile imagination. The Caribbean Grill, the main restaurant, has indoor and outdoor seating by the gardens and pool. It seems to have won a big vote of approval from San Juan residents, judging from the crowds at Sunday brunch. Next to the restaurant is a sushi bar that takes advantage of the variety of fish coming fresh from San Juan waters.

The guest rooms seem a bit small by Ritz-Carlton standards, but they are tastefully appointed with lively tropical prints and have large marble bathrooms with separate toilets. The rooms are air-conditioned and have stocked mini-bars, a television, three telephones with dual lines and dataport, a clock-radio, a safe, a hair dryer, scales, signature bathrobes, and deluxe toiletries. There is twice-daily maid service and twenty-four-hour room service. Nonsmoking floors are available.

The Ritz-Carlton Club floor, accessible only by a key-activated elevator, has larger, deluxe rooms, a private lounge, and gracious, truly helpful concierge staff and offers complimentary continental breakfast, light lunch, afternoon tea, hors d'oeuvres, cordials, and truffles.

The Ritz Kids Club, for ages four to fourteen, operates Sunday to Thursday from 9:00 A.M. to 4:00 P.M., Friday and Saturday from 9:00 A.M. to 9:00 P.M. This is the first Ritz-Carlton to offer a Ritz Kids Day at the Spa.

The Ritz-Carlton San Juan Hotel & Casino ✶✶✶✶
6961 State Road, #187, Isla Verde, Carolina, PR 00979
Phone: (787) 253–1700, (800) 241–3333; Fax: (787) 253–0700

Owner: Green Isle Partner Ltd. S.E.
Management: The Ritz-Carlton Hotel Company, L.L.C.
General Manager: Mark Stevenson
Open: Year-round
Credit Cards: Most major
U.S. Reservations: Direct to hotel, (800) 241–3333
Deposit: One night, fourteen days after booking; three–seven days cancellation in high season, depending on week
Minimum Stay: Four to seven nights in winter
Arrival/Departure: Transfer arranged for fee
Distance from Airport: 1½ miles; taxi one-way, $10
Distance from Old San Juan: 3 miles
Accommodations: 414 guest rooms, six executive suites, 34 superior kings, four grandview suites
Amenities: Air-conditioning; safe; cable television, three telephones with dual lines and dataport, clock-radio; baths with tubs and showers, hair dryers, bathrobes, scales, deluxe toiletries; honor bar; twice-daily maid service, twenty-four-hour room service; nonsmoking floors available
Electricity: 110 volts
Fitness Facilities/Spa Services: Full-service spa
Sports: Swimming pool, water sports; golf, diving, deep-sea fishing, horse racing, sailing, horseback riding arranged
Dress Code: Casual chic; trousers for men at dinner
Children: All ages
Meetings: Up to 1,300 people
Day Visitors: Yes
Handicapped: Facilities
Packages: Spa, summer, honeymoon
Rates: Per room, EP. *High Season* (mid-December–early January and mid-January–early April): $400–$1,000. *Low Season:* $300–$825. Ritz-Carlton Club rooms: $500–$3,000 and $360–$2,000, respectively; two-bedroom suites: $1,250–$3,500 and $1,050–$2,500, respectively.
Service Charge: 19 percent
Government Tax: 11 percent on room

THE WATER CLUB

Isla Verde, Carolina, PR

Sensual, stylish, and sophisticated, the new Water Club is Puerto Rico's first urban boutique hotel with the trendy cool look meant to define today's young sophisticates. Here, however, Puerto Rican designers—they're young too—Pedro Rosario and Anny Falgas of Designworks, have taken the hard edges that typify many of the boutique prototypes in New York, South Beach, and other urban centers and softened the decor with indirect and recessed lighting, waterfalls, and a lot of creativity.

The Water Club is the $4-million remake of the former Colonial Beach Hotel located on the beach in San Juan's Isla Verde district near the international airport. The aim has been to create a hip hotel with interesting, innovative design in a clubby atmosphere, offering the kind of personal service that only a small hotel can provide.

Both in size and decor, The Water Club is the antithesis of the large convention-casino resorts typical of San Juan's beachfront. By comparison, The Water Club's decor is austere, using beige to suggest San Juan's sandy beaches; blue for the sea washing its shores; and white, the minimalist trademark.

Taking the hotel's name as the theme, water in one form or another—by name, color, sound, or in reality—greets you from the front door to the top floor. At the entrance, you pass through a door of aqua-tinted glass sculpted in a modern wave design. It opens onto a small, cool—very cool—minimalist two-story atrium lobby.

To one side is the reception desk set off by soft indirect lighting and to the other, Liquid, the lobby bar with waterfalls behind glass at the entrance. (There's another bar, Wet, but more about that later). Overhead, elongated, sheer white curtains—a Philippe Starck inspiration, no doubt—cover the upper walls of the atrium, completing the dramatic effect.

Step into an elevator and be dazzled by another waterfall rushing down behind glass panels with blue lights overhead, creating a deep-in-the-ocean environment. It takes a bit of getting used to, but it's very effective.

The water theme continues on the nine guest-room floors. Step out of the elevator and look toward one end of the hall to see the soft flicker of votive candles and, at the other end, a whimsical water mural. Miniature lights with blue filters give off a soft light and hidden ceiling speakers in the corridors emit the sounds of gently breaking waves.

The guest rooms with minimalist decor in white and beige—some call it functional chic—are light and airy with a comfortable feel more like a bedroom at home than a hotel. Among several innovative features, the custom-made king-size bed is set at an angle from the wall to capture ocean views through a wall of windows. Behind the headboard is a glass writing table, suspended from the back of the headboard by thin wires. The desk has its own light and telephone with dual ports. There is a portable phone on the nightstand by the bed.

A six-foot-high, three-panel screen with canvas pockets holds newspapers and magazines—mostly fashion magazines and helpful tourist publications. The rear wall of the guest room is covered by a sexy sheer white curtain. At night, blue fluorescent, recessed lighting sets a seductive mood. When all the rooms are illuminated, the lights cast a blue glow on the building, making it a show-stopper for passersby, near and far.

But the most ingenious feature of the guest rooms is the Rosario-designed entertainment center. The television, VCR, and radio sit on shelves extending from a single floor-to-ceiling pole that turns on its axis, making it easy to rotate the television shelf, for example, toward any direction in the room.

The room's one discordant note is the space for hanging clothes (it's only a recess in the wall, open to view and too short to accommodate long dresses). The redeeming features are an iron and ironing board and white waffle-weave robes.

Items you will be tempted to take home are the DO NOT DISTURB sign that reads DON'T EVEN THINK ABOUT IT on one side and WE'RE OUTTA HERE on the other; and the DESIRES write-on board just inside the door where guests can leave messages for hotel staff.

The open-air rooftop on the eleventh floor is action-central by day if you want to work out in the fitness center, swim in the small pool, relax in the whirlpool, and enjoy a wide-angle view of the city and the ocean. It's also a nice perch for sunset.

At the entrance to the rooftop is an illuminated fossil-stone wall; to one side is the lounge, topped with a white canopy and furnished with long, overstuffed futons covered in white canvas, plus some conversation starters—a large, unusual chair by Charles Eames (costing a cool $6,000) and a fireplace—yes, a fireplace in balmy San Juan. Candles and indirect lighting set a sensual ambience.

Wet, the casual rooftop bar, has handsome panels of Indonesian wood carvings for a backdrop and an unusual bar counter with a gully full of ice where you can set your drink to keep it cool.

Liquid, the bar by the lobby entrance, was designed to be the hottest (or should I say the coolest) spot on the San Juan nighttime radar, attracting a fashionable local crowd that wants to be part of the high-energy scene, along with tourists who want to be there, too. It seems to be succeeding in its mission. From the time the hotel opened, Liquid has been the trend-setting night place to be.

Liquid is open in the morning for breakfast from 6:00 to 11:00 A.M., when the bar becomes a buffet table with full service and when you can actually see the decor. The bar area is slightly elevated, two steps up with a curved rail, and has high tables and stools shaped somewhat like cocktail glasses and surprisingly comfortable. A waterfall running the length of the bar ripples down the back wall of slate.

Tangerine, a restaurant serving Pacific Rim cuisine, is located on the second floor and open for dinner from 7:00 P.M. to midnight. The only public space not suggesting water, Tangerine is decorated in stark white, except for one tangerine-colored chair at each table and orange tiles on the floor. It has an outdoor terrace for smokers overlooking the palm-shaded beach. By day, the restaurant becomes Ocean, a meeting room, and next to it is Oxygen, a twelve-person boardroom.

The Water Club is the brainchild of the personable, hands-on manager David Kurland, a well-known hotelier who was formerly the president and managing director of the El San Juan Hotel & Casino down the street. Kurland, the late Michael Chadwick, and Puerto Rican entrepreneur Joaquin Bolivar, who founded the forerunner of American Eagle Airlines, purchased the Colonial Beach and Excelsior hotels in San Juan to develop a chain of boutique hotels in Latin America.

The Water Club is designed for business travelers and vacationers alike. Both will be happy. The hotel has the advantage of being near the city, near the airport, and on the beach.

The Water Club (N)

2 Tartak Street, Isla Verde, Carolina, Puerto Rico 00979
Phone: (888) 265–6699, (787) 728–3666; Fax: (787) 728–3610;
e-mail: info@waterclubsanjuan.com;
www.waterclubsanjuan.com or wwwdesignhotels.com

Owner: Chadwick Hospitality Group

Managing Partner: David Kurland

Open: Year-round

Credit Cards: Most major

U.S. Reservations: Design Hotels or direct to hotel

Deposit: Confirmation with credit card; forty-eight hours cancellation

Minimum Stay: None

Arrival/Departure: No transfer service

Distance from Airport: 3 miles; taxi, $10

Accommodations: 84 rooms, including four with balconies; six one-bedroom suites; king or double beds

Amenities: Air-conditioning; telephone; safe; down comforters and pillows; iron and ironing board; two-line dataport, cordless phone and wireless Internet access, television and CD player; twenty-four hour room service; turndown service

Electricity: 110 volts

Fitness Facilities/Spa Services: Open-air fitness center; massage on request

Sports: Beach, rooftop swimming pool; snorkeling, tennis, deep-sea fishing, diving arranged.

Dress Code: City casual

Children: All ages but not recommended

Packages: Get Wet, Power Meeting, Romance, Honeymoon, Pre/Post Cruise

Rates: Per room, per day. *High Season* (late December–April 30): $199–$695. *Low Season:* $169–$695. Christmas/New Year's, inquire.

Service Charge: 3 percent

Government Tax: 9 percent

St. Barts

Tiny St. Barts is an Eden of 8 square miles with green hills and rolling terrain edged with pretty white-sand beaches and ringed by shallow reefs ideal for snorkeling. The darling of sophisticates and others who can afford it, this haven was discovered four decades ago by the Rockefellers and the Rothschilds, who wisely kept it a secret as long as they could.

A ten-minute flight from St. Martin, St. Barthélémy (as it is properly named), is one of the French West Indies. The language is French, the currency is the franc, and the boutiques are stocked with famous French designer perfumes and accessories. It is also the gastronomic capital of the Caribbean, with sixty gourmet restaurants at last count.

Arawak Indians, Christopher Columbus (who named the island for his brother's patron saint), French settlers from St. Kitts, the Knights of Malta, Carib Indians, Frenchmen from Normandy and Brittany, the British, and the Swedes all were here. Those who left a permanent mark were the Swedes, who named the tiny harbor and capital, Gustavia; and the French from Normandy, from whom most of the population are descended.

At Corossol, the most traditional of the tiny fishing villages, shy elderly women still don the calèche, a stiff-brimmed bonnet derived from a seventeenth-century Breton style, and make hand-woven straw hats and other products from the supple straw of latania palms' fan-shaped fronds.

The tiny island is a beguiling beauty on which every turn in the road—and there are many—reveals striking panoramas. It is easy to tour by car on its roller-coaster roads.

Gustavia, the miniature port on the western coast, is a yachting mecca. On the north St. Jean Bay is the center of resort and water-sports activity. Grand Cul-de-Sac, a large reef-protected bay on the northeast, is another resort center. On the northwestern end, Colombier is a pretty cove accessible by foot or boat.

Anse des Flamands to the north is one of the island's most beautiful beaches; Governor's Cove and Anse de Grande Saline, to the south, are the most secluded. Signs banning nude bathing abound but are not always obeyed: Teeny monokinis are the fashion.

Information

French West Indies Tourist Board, 444 Madison Avenue, New York, NY 10022;
(212) 838–7800, (800) 391–4909; Fax: (212) 838–7855;
www.stbarthonline.com, www.st-barths.com

EDEN ROCK
St.-Barthelémy, F.W.I.

Perched on a great crag of quartzite splitting the splendid beach of St. Jean Bay, the historic Eden Rock was St. Barts's first hotel—a diamond in the rough recently polished and returned to stardom.

Designed and built in 1953 by pioneer-aviator-turned longtime-mayor Remy de Haenen, who first landed his tiny plane on a grassy field nearby, the stone structure where he made his home sprouts dramatically from a rock base that has long been an island landmark. The property gradually became run-down on an island increasingly chic, until it was sold in 1995 to a British couple armed with the resources and sense of style to set the jewel properly. And did they ever! David and Jane Matthews completely restored and upgraded their tropical stone inn, adding new rooms on the beach, a pool, a water-sports center, and three restaurants.

The original six clifftop rooms, with names such as the Greta Garbo Suite, are the breezy best choices, although every room is different. Some have four-poster beds, mosquito netting, antiques, and panoramic terraces; some are awash in tropical colors with watercolors and gouaches by Jane and her children; others are old-fashioned with whimsical touches such as steamer trunks and family heirlooms from the owners' Surrey estate. All rooms are air-conditioned and have a ceiling fan, a direct-dial telephone, a safe, minibar, and satellite television and VCR. Fax

Eden Rock ✳ ✳ ✳

Baie de Saint-Jean, 97133 St.-Barthelémy, F.W.I.
Phone: (590) 590–29–79–99; Fax: (590) 590–27–88–37; e-mail: info@edenrockhotel.com; www.edenrockhotel.com

Owners: David and Jane Matthews

General Manager: Pamela Parker

Open: Year-round except September 1–October 17

Credit Cards: All major

U.S. Reservations: Karen Bull Associates, (888) 576–6677

Deposit: High season, three nights, thirty days cancellation. Christmas holidays, ten nights, full prepayment, sixty days cancellation. Low season, one night, fifteen days cancellation.

Minimum Stay: Ten days during Christmas; five days in February; three days off season

Arrival/Departure: Complimentary transfers included

Distance from Airport: 1 mile; taxi one-way, $7.00

Accommodations: 16 units (eight beachfront suites; two deluxe rooms; four beach cottages; two cabins) with king, queen, or two single beds; some with four-poster beds; Harbour House (the owners' house)

Amenities: Air-conditioning, ceiling fan; direct-dial telephone, cable television, VCR; safe; minibar; hair dryers; fax and e-mail facilities available

Electricity: 220 volts/60 cycles

Fitness Facilities/Spa Services: Outdoor mini-spa with seawater rock pools; exercise machines on beach

Sports: Swimming pool, water sports

Dress Code: Casual

Children: All ages

Meetings: No

Day Visitors: Yes

Handicapped: No facilities

Packages: Summer, honeymoon

Rates: Per room, daily, FAB. *High Season* (early December–mid-May): $340– $1,970. *Low Season:* $275–$670. Harbour House: $1,550 and $1,200, respectively.

Service Charge: Included

Government Tax: Included

and e-mail facilities are available from the front desk. More recently, the resort has added two new beach cottages.

Also available for rent is Harbour House, the owners' home, when the couple is away for extended periods in Europe. The house has a large balcony overlooking the bay, a private courtyard garden, a plunge pool, a kitchenette, a bath and shower, and a sitting area. The bedroom, decorated in white and gold, is furnished with a hand-carved king-size bed, antiques, and original oil paintings.

The Sand Bar and Eden Beach Restaurant, known popularly as The Beach, are busy all day and into the evening with casual, moderately priced a la carte dining. The Eden Rock Restaurant Gastronomique—The Rock—on the hilltop terrace has spectacular views over the coral reef directly below and over the grand stretch of St. Jean Bay. This is a more elegant (and expensive) venue.

The inn has added a small, open-air spa at the water's edge with seawater pools carved from the rock and an outdoor treatment room; the services of a physiotherapist are available, based on your needs. There's also exercise equipment by the beach.

The Eden Rock manages to combine elegance and just plain funky fun into a small package on one of St. Barts's prime locations.

FILAO BEACH HOTEL

St.-Barthelémy, F.W.I.

Location, location, location. What's true for real estate is just as true for hotels, and the Filao has the location at the heart of St. Jean Beach in the elbow of Eden Rock, the resort that launched St. Barts's tourism less than three decades ago. You cannot get closer to the action.

Opened originally in 1981, the Filao Beach makes the most of its St. Jean Beach location. Its convivial, laid-back atmosphere attracts the neighbors—and almost everyone else on St. Barts—to its bar and pleasant open-air beachfront restaurant.

Set in a jungle of tropical flowers and flowering trees, the hotel is comprised of one-story white stucco, red-roof bungalows, each with two units. They are arranged close to the sea in more or less a tight U around the central beachfront pavilion. There is a restaurant, bar, and swimming pool where the faithful, the onlookers, and the newcomers come throughout the day (it's the best people-watching spot in town).

The rooms, each named for a French château, are identical in size and layout but may vary in furnishings. The rooms are comfortable with white wood-beamed ceilings, white bamboo furnishings, and nice Italian tiles. The rooms have king-size beds, twins, or a queen-size bed and sleep sofa, particularly suited for a family with a child. Sliding glass doors open onto a front porch, but the dense vegetation that gives you privacy all but blocks any view of the sea. All the bathrooms were renovated and upgraded with new fittings in 2000 and now all rooms have been refurbished with a clean, fresh look of bright coral and white.

One of Filao's most convenient features is its entrance. Set back from the main road, the hotel can provide a parking area for guests' cars—a blessing in the most heavily traveled part of the beach. You don't need a car for transportation in the immediate environs, but you may want to rent one to explore the island.

From the small lobby, which has a Caribbean feeling,

Filao Beach Hotel ✳✳✳

P.O. Box 667, 97099 St.-Barthelémy, F.W.I.
Phone: (590) 590–27–64–84; Fax: (590) 590–27–62–24;
e-mail: filao.st.barth@wanadoo.fr; www.filaobeach.com

Owner: S.A.I.T., S.A.
General Manager: Pierre Verdier
Open: Year-round except September–mid-October
Credit Cards: All major
U.S. Reservations: Direct to hotel or via e-mail
Deposit: Three nights in winter; one night in summer
Minimum Stay: Ten days during Christmas; five days in February; three days off season
Arrival/Departure: Complimentary transfers included
Distance from Airport: 1 mile; taxi one-way, $7.00
Distance from Gustavia: 4 miles; taxi one-way, $10
Accommodations: 30 rooms in 15 bungalows, all with terraces (two corner deluxe beachside; eight deluxe beachside, all with kings except two with twin beds; ten superior garden with queen plus sofa that converts to single bed; ten deluxe with king or twin beds)
Amenities: Air-conditioning, ceiling fans; telephone, cable television with English and French films; bath with tub and shower, bidet, hair dryer, basket of toiletries, makeup mirrors, bathrobe in deluxe units; small refrigerators; safes; nightly turndown service, room service when restaurant in operation
Electricity: 220 volts/60 cycles
Sports: Freshwater swimming pool; tennis, boating, snorkeling, scuba, windsurfing, deep-sea fishing, other water sports arranged
Dress Code: Casual
Children: All ages; cribs; baby-sitters
Meetings: No
Day Visitors: Yes
Handicapped: No facilities
Packages: No
Rates: Per room, daily. **High Season,** FAB (mid-December–early April): $350–$613. **Shoulder Season,** FAB (April–May and mid-October–mid-December) $245–$425. **Low Season,** CP (June–August): $189–$358. Winter rates include airport transfer and American breakfast; rates at other times are CP and include transfers.
Service Charge: Included
Government Tax: None

you pass directly into the gardens and then the open-air dining pavilion and bar, right on the beach. The Filao is the place to be, particularly at lunch. Along with sunbathers from the beach, the town's businesspeople (who close shop for lunch) are found socializing at the bar and enjoying salads, grilled fish, and the specialties of the day. The restaurant serves breakfast, lunch, and dinner; it's closed on Monday.

Swimming, snorkeling, and windsurfing are good here. Windsurfers, scuba diving, and other water sports are available from a nearby concessionaire on the beach. When you want to stay in for the evening, you will find two films—one in English, another in French—shown nightly on your television, along with CNN.

A member of the Small Luxury Hotels of the World, the Filao Beach is relaxing, sociable, and fun. Its friendly staff, unpretentious environment, and lack of the self-conscious chic that afflicts some other St. Barts resorts enable everyone to feel welcome and comfortable here. If any one person is responsible for this invitation to enjoyment, it is Pierre Verdier, one of the most hospitable hoteliers in the islands. Filao Beach is the laid-back Caribbean at its easiest. It appeals to travelers who care less for what their digs look like and more for where they are: directly on the beach and at the heart of the action.

GUANAHANI

St.-Barthelémy, F.W.I.

Gingerbread-trimmed creole cottages in Easter-egg colors sit in baskets of flowering gardens on fifty hillside acres sloping down to inviting beaches. Overlooking Grand Cul de Sac to the east and Marigot Bay to the west, Guanahani is an exclusive luxury oasis of refined simplicity.

But this stylish haven has more to it than simply a touch of class. It's *très sympathique*. Friendly, not intimidating, this charmer manages to be classy and cozy at the same time. Since it opened in 1986, Guanahani has been a hit among an international array of celebrities and well-heeled sophisticates in search of privacy and comfort in a quiet setting of tropical luxury.

Guest rooms and suites are situated in colorful one-story cottages, each with one or two units, at various levels of the hillside. Due to their location, some afford a greater sense of privacy and better views than others. They also differ in size, layout, and decor.

For all the exuberant colors of the exterior, Guanahani's guest rooms are marked by the elegance of simplicity: a soft, light, fresh decor in white with pastel accents rendered in the finest of fabrics and linens. All rooms face the sea and have their own covered wooden veranda secluded in a garden.

Most have the high, beamed ceilings typical of Creole architecture, which make them seem spacious, and are furnished with a king-size bed (some four-poster) or twins, a sitting area with a desk, a stocked minibar, and a large tiled bath. Some suites have kitchenettes, some have whirlpools, others splash pools. The landscaping is impeccable and the housekeeping immaculate. Guanahani completely renovates some rooms each year on a rotating basis.

The newest, deluxe villa rooms and suites are a little funky but elegant in their clean lines—and comfortable and practical at the same time. They hug the hillside with a second swimming pool and a reception cottage whose interior resembles the large parlor of a private home, furnished in handsome wicker with stylish fabrics of tropical colors. There's also a small meeting room.

Early on, Guanahani established a reputation for fine, albeit expensive, cuisine in both of its restaurants. L'Indigo, the informal open-air restaurant, has a delightful setting beside one of the Caribbean's prettiest swimming pools, with a wide wooden deck overlooking the grove of palm trees that lines the beach. Like everything else about Guanahani, it has style. Breakfast is served here, or you can dine on tropical fruit and freshly baked croissants on your terrace. L'Indigo serves lunch until late afternoon.

Bartolomeo is a more formal (but only slightly) restaurant serving gourmet French cuisine and Mediterranean specialties at dinner. Actually, the only "formal" elements are the crystal and china glowing in the candlelight and the five-star service.

The resort has a rather unusual way of taking care of children. Breakfast and lunch are offered daily with a special menu for children six and under at Indigo at specific hours. A kindergarten for children between ages two and six is provided on the beach from 9:00 A.M. to 5:00 P.M. and

Guanahani ✶✶✶✶

Grand Cul de Sac, 97133 St. Barthelémy, F.W.I.
Phone: (590) 590–27–66–60; Fax: (590) 590–27–70–70;
e-mail: guanahani@wanadoo.fr; www.leguanahani.com

Owner: Société Hotelière des Antilles Françaises, a subsidiary of Colony Capital

General Manager: Marc Thézé

Open: Year-round

Credit Cards: All major

U.S. Reservations: Leading Hotels of the World, (800) 223 6800, (212) 838–3110; Fax: (212) 758–7367; or WIMCO, (800) 932–3222, (401) 849–8012; Fax: (401) 847–6290

Deposit: None; only credit card number

Minimum Stay: Ten nights during Christmas; five nights in February; three nights balance of year

Arrival/Departure: Airport transfers included

Distance from Airport: 3 miles; taxi one-way, $20

Distance from Gustavia: 5 miles; taxi one-way, $25

Accommodations: 75 units (12 one-bedroom pool suites; nine one-bedroom suites; 33 deluxe rooms; 21 standard rooms); all suites have sitting room, terrace; some have private pool

Amenities: Air-conditioning, ceiling fans; telephone, cable television, VCR; bath with shower, hair dryer, Hermes toiletries, bathrobe; safe; stocked minibar; nightly turndown service, twenty-four-hour room service; boutique, hairdresser; car rental service

Electricity: 220 volts

Fitness Facilities/Spa Services: Fitness center with exercise equipment; masseuse

Sports: Two freshwater swimming pools; private plunge pools; two lighted tennis courts and equipment; free use of snorkeling gear and nonmotorized water-sports equipment; scuba for fee; boating, fishing, horseback riding arranged; two beaches; Mistral windsurfing school property

Dress Code: Casual but chic at all times; no shorts, tank tops, swimsuits, T-shirts, or similar attire in dining room after dark

Children: See text; cribs, high chairs; baby-sitters

Meetings: Up to twenty-two people

Day Visitors: Welcome

Handicapped: No facilities

Packages: Dive, honeymoon, weekend; five-night Spree; seven-night Romance through October 31, 2003

Rates: Per room, daily, CP. *High Season* (mid-December–early January): $650–$1,650. *Shoulder Season* (mid-January–late April; November–mid-December): $470–$1,180. *Low Season* (late April–October 31): $290–$820.

Service Charge: Included

Government Tax: None

offers a taste of French culture and language through various interactive activities and games. For children ages seven to twelve, there is a $95 supplement when sharing parent's room that includes breakfast and lunch daily as well.

Guanahani has two beaches (neither as inviting as the pretty freshwater swimming pool or Jacuzzi) and tennis courts, as well as a tennis pro for private instruction. A wide range of water sports is available. Horseback riding and trips by private planes or yachts can be arranged.

You can get your exercise walking between the upper sections and the beach pavilion, reception area, tennis courts, restaurants, boutique, and beauty salon; a road barely wide enough for a car winds through the property, connecting the facilities. The fitness center has a treadmill, step machine, rowing machine, cycle machine, multistation, Olympic bar and bench, and free weights.

Consider the setting, the style, the panache, then add to these excellent service—and you have what Guanahani is truly about.

Although it's the island's largest hotel, Guanahani doesn't seem big, but that's the secret of St. Barts. Its hotels are on the same scale as the island, the ambience low-key. Gracious and romantic, Guanahani is glamorous in an understated way.

HOTEL CARL GUSTAF
St. Barthélémy, F.W.I.

Climbing the steep hill above Gustavia's harbor, the Hotel Carl Gustaf is a refined adaptation of local architecture, tucked neatly in perfect symmetry into gardens above the delightful hodgepodge of sturdy Swedish stone buildings and typical French Creole houses comprising the capital. The hotel seemed to be a jolt to the eye when it opened in December 1991, changing the look of the little historic harbor. But over time this pale pink hillside haven (suitable only for the most ambulatory) has blended into its verdant landscape. Now it's scarcely noticed.

What may be something of a puzzle is why—on an island famous for its beaches and seaside resorts—the owner of the resort chose this locale for one of St. Barts's priciest hotels. After a few days' stay, though, you'll have your answer.

The location is a plus for people who do not like to drive on St. Barts's narrow, winding roads, particularly at night, yet want a choice of restaurants in town; who don't need a beach at their front door and don't mind an eight-minute walk to the nearest one; and who relish sunsets and charming vistas.

Named in honor of the present king of Sweden, whose forebears owned St. Barts briefly a couple of centuries ago, the Carl Gustaf has only a dozen units, all self-contained one- and two-bedroom suites. They climb the hillside on either side of a multitiered staircase divided down the middle by a vertical row of palms and flanked by planters of blooming brilliant hibiscus, oleander, allamanda, and other tropical flora. Perched at the top of the complex is a small reception area and the panoramic poolside restaurant and bar with incomparable views of the postage-stamp harbor, roller-coaster hills, and turquoise sea beyond.

Built by a successful French developer, a longtime habitué of St. Barts with plans to retire here, the Carl Gustaf was designed for busy businesspeople like himself in search of a refuge from civilization—but one with all the conveniences and electronic connections necessary to maintain contact with it.

No expense—absolutely none—was spared, and the filthy rich and famous, especially those Type As who work to keep themselves so, may welcome the luxury of such amenities as fax machines, direct-dial phones, Internet access, televisions, and video and stereo systems in every suite—and they all work! Why you need two of everything (his and her televisions, perhaps) remains a mystery.

Each unit has its own private plunge pool on a wooden deck with its own spectacular view of the harbor, wonderfully framed by slim white columns and elaborate fretwork. Other amenities include twenty-four-hour room service, a conference room, and a fitness center with sauna. Anchored in the harbor below is a luxurious cabin cruiser, available exclusively to hotel guests for fishing excursions or day trips to offshore islands.

Given the hotel's location, space is at a premium and rooms are relatively small (or perhaps the furniture is a bit too large and makes the space seem small). Still, from your airy private terrace with its enchanting view, who cares? At the front of the partly canopied deck is the wide-open sitting and dining salon, tastefully furnished in pale Italian rattan with pastel Swiss fabrics, a handsome heavy wood and stone table and chairs from France, and paintings of old sailing vessels (for which the rooms are named). Recently, doors and screens were added between the living/dining room and the terrace to keep the mosquitoes and other small creatures of the Tropics at bay. The kitchenette comes equipped with an ultramodern halogen double-burner stove, a full fridge, and Limoges china.

Each bedroom has French doors opening onto the deck as well as the living room, and each has its own phone, fax machine, and television-VCR. There's a small three-room bath—a dressing room with a well-lighted double vanity (limited counter space but hair dryer and magnifying mirror), a separate shower, and a separate toilet. Some guests settling in at these prices might miss a bidet, not to mention a tub.

Beds (two singles that can be pushed together) have lovely shaped wooden headboards and cushioned banquettes at the foot, which open for storage. Closet doors and trims everywhere are elaborate hand-carved wood filigree, giving the decor a special charm; door handles and bath fixtures are brass and add to the look of quality.

You will love the privacy of an early morning plunge into your own petite pool, followed by a breakfast of warm croissants delivered for you to enjoy on your private deck while you watch Gustavia come to life below and the early boats leave the harbor. At sunset you can return to see the lights of the lilliputian harbor flicker on and luxury yachts tie up for the night.

Hotel Carl Gustaf ✴✴✴

P.O. Box 700, Gustavia, 97133 St. Barthélemy, F.W.I,
Phone: (590) 590–27–82–83; Fax: (590) 590–27–82–37;
e-mail: carlgustaf@compuserve.com; www.carlgustaf.com

Owner: Jacques Laurent
General Manager: Emmanuelle Bourgueil
Open: Year-round
Credit Cards: All major
U.S. Reservations: WIMCO, (401) 849–8012, (800) 932–3222; Fax: (401) 847–6290
Deposit: Three nights; forty days cancellation high season, fifteen low season
Minimum Stay: One night; ten nights during Christmas
Arrival/Departure: Airport transfer included
Distance from Airport: 2 miles; taxi one-way, $15
Accommodations: 14 rooms (seven double rooms with two king-size beds and small extra room with bunk beds; six rooms with king-size bed; one honeymoon suite with king-size bed and Jacuzzi); all with plunge pools
Amenities: Air-conditioning, ceiling fans; telephone, fax, Internet access, television, stereo; bath with shower, bathrobes, hair dryer; fully equipped kitchen, minibar; safe; twenty-four-hour room service; bottle of champagne, basket of fruit, and bouquet of flowers in room upon arrival
Electricity: 220 volts
Sports: Pool, shuttle to beach; fitness room, sauna; 46-foot motorboat; snorkeling gear, water sports arranged
Dress Code: Casually elegant
Children: All ages
Meetings: No
Day Visitors: Welcome
Handicapped: Not recommended
Packages: Honeymoon, summer
Rates: Per room, daily, CP. *High Season* (early January–mid-April): $897 (one bedroom); $1,227 (two-bedroom). *Shoulder Season* (mid-April–May 31 and November–mid-December): $632 and $897, respectively. *Low Season* (June–October): $538 and $689, respectively. Prices include airport transfers and bottle of champagne on arrival.
Service Charge: Included
Government Tax: Included

HOTEL SAINT BARTH ISLE DE FRANCE
St.-Barthelémy, F.W.I.

Flanking Anse des Flamands, a wide strand of fine white sand described by *Paris Match* as "la plus belle" of St. Barts's fourteen beaches, and sprawling into a magnificent latania palm grove across the way, the Isle de France (as it is locally known) is a prime beach resort and elegant retreat. Opened in 1991 and rebuilt four years later after Hurricane Luis battered Baie des Flamands, it reopened in 1996 with an airier restaurant, La Case de l'Isle, and a spectacular pool (now separated from the beach by a green railing, which somewhat obstructs the glorious vista).

The property is divided into two separate areas, each with a large pool and its own charm. On the beach side are a dozen rooms in a large, two-story colonial-style plantation house: six upstairs, six down, all facing the water and unusually spacious by St. Barts's standards.

The enormous ground-floor junior suites have French doors opening onto patios facing the pool and beach. Huge marble bathrooms have separate shower and tub and dual sinks. Upstairs rooms come with seafront terraces.

Furnishings are eclectically mixed with an obvious French flair. There are assorted antique pieces, mainly from England; some splendid hand-carved four-poster wooden Creole beds from Barbados with romantic mosquito netting; a smattering of smart wicker and rattan; and everywhere precious old French and English books begging to be borrowed (perhaps forever, one would fear).

The resort has just been totally redecorated. All guest rooms have new furniture, upholstery, and curtains. All units have a mini-fridge, tea and coffeemaker, cable television, and safe. Large, elegant marble baths sport huge tubs (some with whirlpools), separate showers, bidets, double vanities, hair dryers, bathrobes, Signoricci soaps, and other amenities.

Also in the main building are a small reception area, a charming Old World veranda with conversation areas, and a vast marble breezeway leading to the pool, beach, and restaurant.

On the other side of the road are sixteen woodsy cot-

tages carefully etched into the palm grove in a secluded retreat, quite unlike any other resort on the island. A few of the latania bungalows are designed for family use: Some are suites; some have one entrance to two separate bedrooms, each with its own bath.

Others are intended for couples, particularly those with large oval bathtubs for two beside a blooming planter and a tinted picture window with mini-blinds. During the day, bathers see out, but at night . . . well, it may be best to bathe in the dark or close the blinds. Some units face the pool directly, but with no screens on the windows or doors, the tendency on hot days is to close up and turn on the air-conditioning.

The resort has undertaken a modest expansion with one room in a new hillside bungalow and is building a two-bedroom fisherman's cottage and a two-bedroom beach suite. In autumn of 2002, a Molton Brown Spa is scheduled to open.

The hillside bungalow, with the best view of the sea and the resort's only accommodation with a private plunge pool, is less expensive than a beach room. It offers lots of privacy. Ah, but there are fifty stairs up or down, no room service, and housekeeping only once a day in the morning—all elements that could be a disadvantage for some people. The room is furnished with a king-size bed and has a bathroom and a terrace with a kitchenette and the private plunge pool.

Also tucked among the palms are two lighted tennis courts, an air-conditioned squash court, and an exercise room with treadmill, Stairmaster, Lifecycle, rowing machine, and free weights. Massage is also available.

La Case de l'Isle, the hotel's beachfront restaurant, is designed after a traditional island house or case and serves breakfast, lunch, and dinner by candlelight, with light French island fare such as *loup de mer à la citronnelle*.

Service and style both come with smiles under general manager Evelyn Weber, formerly at St. Martin's La Samanna, who brings reassurance in English to the hotel's largely North American patrons and her truly Gallic flair and savoir-faire to the European guests.

Hotel Saint Barth Isle de France ✳✳✳

P.O. Box 612, Baie des Flamands, 97098 St.-Barthelémy, F.W.I. Phone: (800) 810–4691, (590) 590–27–61–81; Fax: (590) 590–27–86–83; e-mail: isledefr@saint-barths.com; www.isle-de-france.com

Owner: Patrick Pilzer

General Manager: Evelyn Weber

Open: Year-round except September–mid-October

Credit Cards: All major

U.S. Reservations: Crown International, (800) 628–8929; or direct to hotel, (800) 810–4691

Deposit: Three nights; thirty days cancellation; except sixty days December–May

Minimum Stay: None

Arrival/Departure: Round-trip transfers included

Distance from Airport: 3 miles; taxi one-way, $15

Distance from Gustavia: 3 miles; taxi one way, $15

Accommodations: 35 rooms and suites with terraces or patios (beach, garden, or hillside), all with king or twins, seven with four-poster king

Amenities: Air-conditioning; telephone, VCR, cable television with remote control; safe; tea and coffeemaker, stocked mini-fridge; marble bath with tub (some with Jacuzzi tub), separate shower, bidet, double vanities, hair dryer, bathrobes, basket of toiletries (three garden rooms with shower only); room service, nightly turndown service; boutique

Electricity: 220 volts

Fitness Facilities/Spa Services: Fitness room with exercise equipment

Sports: Two freshwater swimming pools; one lighted tennis court, one air-conditioned squash court; snorkeling; sailing, windsurfing for fee; deep-sea fishing, boating, scuba, horseback riding arranged

Dress Code: Casual chic

Children: All ages; cribs; baby-sitters

Meetings: No

Day Visitors: Yes

Handicapped: No facilities

Packages: Honeymoon; getaway; two-week, three-week packages available May 1–October 31

Rates: Per room, double, daily, CP. *High Season* (December 20–April 30): $595–$1,090. *Low Season* (late April–August 31 and mid-October–mid-December): $410–$535.

Service Charge: At discretion of guests

Government Tax: Included

LE TOINY

St.-Barthelémy, F.W.I.

If you like grand vistas, privacy, and exclusivity; appreciate planning and detail; don't give a whit about beaches; and can handle steep hills and steeper prices—then you are probably a good candidate for Le Toiny.

Perched on a hillside on the windy, rocky southeastern region of St. Barts, the tony cottage complex is the only upscale resort in this corner of the island; heretofore, tourism development had not been seen. Designed in the style of Creole houses, each cottage is a large self-contained deluxe suite with a living room, kitchen, pantry, large bedroom, walk-in closet, furnished covered terra-cotta terrace and 20- by 10-foot private pool overlooking the sea, all designed with exquisite attention to detail. The cottages are staggered along the hillside so as to ensure maximum privacy.

Although the decor evokes the colonial era with

Le Toiny ✻✻✻

Anse de Toiny, 97133 St.-Barthelémy, F.W.I.
Phone: (590) 590–27–88–88; Fax: (590) 590–27–89–30;
e-mail: letoiny@saint-barths.com; www.letoiny.com

Owner: Michael Shen
General Manager: David Henderson
Open: Year-round
Credit Cards: All major
U.S. Reservations: WIMCO, (800) 932–3222
Deposit: Three nights; thirty days cancellation; full repayment with package
Minimum Stay: Ten nights during Christmas
Arrival/Departure: Airport transfers included
Distance from Airport: 4 miles (fifteen to twenty minutes); taxi one-way, $20
Distance from Gustavia: 5 miles (fifteen to twenty minutes); taxi one-way, $25
Accommodations: 12 cottages with private pools (each with one bedroom, central living room/dining room/kitchen, large bathroom, terrace); one cottage with three bedrooms
Amenities: Air-conditioning, ceiling fans; three direct-dial telephones, two cable televisions with VCR, fax machine, exercise equipment; hair dryer, bathrobe; safe; stocked minibar; nightly turndown service, twenty-four-hour room service; boutique; car rental service
Electricity: 220 volts
Fitness Facilities/Spa Services: Exercise bicycle or Stairmaster in room; in-room massage
Sports: Freshwater swimming pool; twelve private pools; water sports, boating, fishing, horseback riding arranged
Dress Code: Casual but chic at all times
Children: Yes
Meetings: No
Day Visitors: Welcome
Handicapped: No facilities
Packages: Summer (late April–late October)
Rates: Per room, double, daily, CP. *High Season* (mid-December–mid-April): $800. *Low Season* (late April–mid-December): $575.
Service Charge: Included
Government Tax: None

mahogany furniture, including large armoires and four-poster beds crafted in Martinique, the kitchens have the latest high-tech equipment. The gleaming white tile bathrooms—largest in the French West Indies—are ultraposh, with separate tub and shower, double sink, hair dryer, bathrobe, and designer soaps and toiletries. The resort has added two new cottages that will come on stream in December 2002.

The air-conditioned suites have three two-line phones, two cable televisions, a VCR, a desk, a fax machine, and a safe. A main building holds a reception room elegantly decorated in Oriental antiques, along with a bar-lounge. It opens onto the restaurant, La Gaiac, set on an open-air terrace, which embraces a large swimming pool and overlooks extensive sea views. The restaurant is considered one of the best on an island noted for its abundance of good restaurants.

The hotel has no sports facilities, other than swimming in your private pool or using the exercise equipment in your suite, but water sports can be arranged. A footpath leads down to the shore, but the sea here is generally too rough for swimming.

Le Toiny is a member of the prestigious Relais et Châteaux.

LE VILLAGE ST. JEAN HOTEL
St.-Barthelémy, F.W.I.

This cluster of hillside cottages is the best-kept secret on St. Barts. Set high on the side of a steep hill overlooking St. Jean Bay at the heart of St. Barts, Le Village St. Jean combines quiet villa living with hotel facilities and amenities. It's all within walking distance of popular restaurants, shops, and the island's liveliest beach.

For years this unpretentious resort has attracted an impressive list of distinguished guests, including the Zabars of New York deli fame; the late well-known food critic Craig Claiborne, who came annually at Christmas, and who kept a set of pots and pans here; an occasional French or American movie star; and an array of smart people from eighteen to eighty who know a good value when they see it.

But even with its great location, grand views, sensible accommodations, and moderate prices, its biggest assets, many habitués will tell you, are the friendliness and care that its savvy family owners convey.

Created in 1970 by André and Gaby Charneau, who came to St. Barts from Guadeloupe, the resort is now

operated by their daughter Catherine and son Bertrand and his wife, New York–born I. B. Their youthful energy and commitment add that extra sparkle to this hilltop gem. One or all will greet you upon arrival with a welcome drink.

The white stucco cottages trimmed with wood and native stone are designed to resemble a hillside village with a variety of styles and accommodations: hotel rooms, one- and two-bedroom suites with covered sundecks in two-story cottages, a three-bedroom house, and a new deluxe villa with a private pool. The units are large for this island, and comfortably furnished with twin or king-size beds and tile floors and baths. Some rooms have sea views; others look over the gardens.

The four hotel rooms are spacious, high-ceilinged bedrooms with a balcony overlooking the sea and furnished with twin beds and a mini-fridge; continental breakfast is included in the rate. The cottages have kitchens screened behind louvered doors on terraces. Those in the deluxe cottages are larger than the regular ones and have the best views. Four units have second

bedrooms suitable for children. One suite with a Jacuzzi and kitchenette is actually a tiny villa with a wraparound terrace in a secluded garden with an outdoor shower. Recently, Le Village added Villa Iguana, a two-bedroom, two-bath cottage with a private swimming pool and a magnificent view. Designed in contemporary style by Jinnie Kim, a noted Korean-American designer, the deluxe Villa Iguana is a combination of luxury and simplicity as well as practicality with such conveniences as a modern stainless steel kitchen—all at a reasonable price.

La Terraza, managed by Bertrand and wife, I.B., is an indoor-outdoor terrace restaurant and bar serving northern Italian and southern French fusion cuisine. The kitchen makes its own pizzas and pasta, which are available as takeout if you want to enjoy dinner on your own terrace. La Terraza is open nightly, except Wednesday, during the winter season and closed in June and July. Just down the hill is Kiki-é Mo, an Italian gourmet food market offering lunch in a casual setting as well as take-out and catering.

One level up from La Terraza is the attractive freshwater swimming pool with cascading waters on one side and a terrace and Jacuzzi overlooking the bay on the other. Further diversions include a lounge with satellite television, a video and reading library, and a business center with Internet access.

It's about a three-minute spill down the hill to the beach (though a ten-minute climb on the return), with restaurants, shops, other hotels, and water-sports centers along St. Jean Bay. You don't need a car, but you might want one for exploring the island, checking out the other beaches, and sampling some of the expensive temples of haute cuisine (with the money you save staying at Le Village).

Le Village St. Jean Hotel *

P.O. Box 623, 97098 St.-Barthelémy, F.W.I.
Phone: (590) 590–27–61–39, (800) 651–8366; Fax: (590) 590–27–77–96; e-mail: vsjhotel@wanadoo.fr; www.villagestjeanhotel.com

Owners: The Charneau family
General Managers: Catherine Charneau
Open: Year-round
Credit Cards: Most
U.S. Reservations: Direct to hotel
Deposit: Three nights; forty-five days cancellation in winter, thirty days in summer, $60 penalty for cancellation year-round; $100 penalty for February cancellation
Minimum Stay: Twelve nights during Christmas
Arrival/Departure: Complimentary airport transfer
Distance from Airport: 1½ miles; taxi one-way, $10
Distance from Gustavia: 3 miles; taxi one-way, $15
Accommodations: 25 units in 14 cottages and three villas (six hotel rooms, 16 one-bedroom units, one Jacuzzi suite, four one-bedroom units with small guest bed, two two-bedroom villas and one three-bedroom villa); with twin, queen-size, or king-size beds
Amenities: Air-conditioning, ceiling fans; direct-dial telephone with voice mail, stereo with CD player, bath with shower only, hair dryer; refrigerator; room service for breakfast; television and VCR in lounge; in-room massage; business center with Internet access; concierge
Electricity: 1/0 volts

Sports: Freshwater swimming pool, Jacuzzi; tennis, boating, snorkeling, scuba, windsurfing, deep-sea fishing, horseback riding arranged for charge
Dress Code: Casual
Children: All ages; cribs, high chairs; babysitters
Meetings: Up to fifty people
Day Visitors: Yes
Handicapped: No facilities
Packages: Summer, honeymoon
Rates: Per room CP or cottage EP, daily. *High Season* (January 8–mid-April): $165–$499. *Low Season:* $95–$299.
Service Charge: 10 percent
Government Tax: None

St. Kitts

Located in the heart of the Leeward Islands, St. Kitts has a beauty and grace that enchants visitors, taking them back to another era when life was more genteel. From all the Caribbean islands he saw, Christopher Columbus selected St. Kitts to name for his patron saint, St. Christopher.

It's something of a newcomer to Caribbean tourism, but St. Kitts was the first island settled by the English in 1623, giving England great wealth from the land that produced the highest-yielding sugar crop in the world. From their base in St. Kitts, the English settled Nevis, Antigua, and Montserrat, but not before battling the French, who arrived in 1624 to stake out their claim. St. Kitts remained a British possession until 1983, when full independence was established.

Shaped like a paddle with an area of 65 square miles, St. Kitts rises from intensively cultivated lowlands and foothills to a central spine of mountains covered with rain forests. The northern part of the island is dominated by Mount Liamuiga, known in colonial times as Mount Misery, a dormant volcano that rises to almost 4,000 feet. A coastal road makes it easy to drive—or bike—around the island and provides access to the splendid hiking of the mountainous interior. There are no cross-island roads through the central mountains, but there are footpaths.

The Southeastern Peninsula, a hilly tongue of land different in climate and terrain from the main body of St. Kitts, is covered with dry woodland and salt ponds and scalloped with the island's best white-sand beaches. It has a new magnificently engineered highway of about 7 miles that has made this part of the island accessible by land for the first time.

St. Kitts and its sister island of Nevis are separated on the surface of the sea by a 2-mile-wide strait known as the Narrows, but they're joined below the surface by a subterranean rock base on which their volcanic mountains were formed eons ago. Daily ferry service connects the two islands.

Information

St. Kitts and Nevis Tourist Board, 414 East 75th Street, New York, NY 10021;
(212) 535–1234, (800) 582–6208; Fax: (212) 734–6511;
e-mail: www.info@stkitts-nevis.com; www.stkitts-nevis.com

THE GOLDEN LEMON INN AND VILLAS

Dieppe Bay, St. Kitts, W.I.

If you are looking for a definition of style, you will find it at The Golden Lemon, one of the most fashionable small inns in the Caribbean. To be sure, this is style as defined by the resort's owner, Arthur Leaman, but a more practiced arbiter you could not find. One look at this "country inn in the Caribbean" and you might say he invented the word.

On the northern coast of St. Kitts at Dieppe Bay, The Golden Lemon is set in a seventeenth-century stone and wood structure draped in tropical splendor and shaded by a grove of coconut palms. Leaman bought the historic building in 1961 and renovated it to resemble an island plantation house with a second-story balcony where you can enjoy breakfast along with sea views. The ground floor of the gracious old manor—dressed in bright lemon yellow (what else?) with white trim—contains a cozy lounge and bar and the dining room, which has an outside terrace, where lunch is served. To one side is a greenery-cloaked patio and swimming pool.

As he tells the story, Leaman came to St. Kitts by accident on a freighter headed for South America. The ship developed mechanical trouble, and since this was 1950, long before St. Kitts had an international airport, the passengers waited a week or more while repairs were completed. Young and handsome, Leaman soon caught the eye of the island's leading social maven, who took him under her wing.

Leaman had been scouting the Caribbean for a hideaway for himself. Smitten with St. Kitts, he decided there was no need to look farther. He bought the remote building—with a damaged roof and no water or electricity—and combed the island for antiques and objets d'art to furnish his (then) seven-room inn.

Leaman's friends told him he had bought a lemon, so he named it The Golden Lemon. For more than three decades it has garnered praise for its stylish accommodations, good food, and fine service, attracting an international set of urbane and sophisticated devotees.

The Golden Lemon has rooms in the historic building and rooms and suites in modern buildings that blend with the old remarkably well. The Lemon Court, a small complex, has spacious superdeluxe one-and two-bedroom villas, each with a pool and private terrace at the water's edge. The Lemon Grove, a cluster of condominiums by the sea, adds ten one-and two-bedroom villas set in walled gardens, giving them a great deal of privacy. Each villa has steps leading from one of the rooms directly into a private swimming pool, a feature first used in The Lemon Court.

The decor throughout The Golden Lemon has the mark of "style by Leaman," a former decorating editor at *House & Garden* magazine. The spacious rooms, always accented with fresh flowers, are extremely comfortable and more like those in a private home than a hotel.

Each room is different but all are decorated with fresh, clean lines—no fuss, no frills—and furnished with Leaman's eclectic collection of antiques, objets d'art, island crafts, original art, wicker, and wrought-iron furniture. Some have high four-poster or canopied beds; others are highlighted with antique chests, armoires, or an unusual piece of furniture or interesting fabrics.

The quiet inn fronts a palm-shaded black-sand beach that might have been a drawback for some; for Leaman, it was just another element to make his resort unique. Good snorkeling can be enjoyed on a reef fronting the beach, and the resort has a tennis court.

Those who enjoy a congenial cocktail hour join Leaman in the front gallery at 7:00 P.M. and dine at 8:00 P.M. Dinner by candlelight in the antiques-filled dining room is the real treat at The Golden Lemon. Leaman seats his guests, sometimes hosting one of the tables,

The Golden Lemon Inn and Villas ✳ ✳ ✳

Dieppe Bay, St. Kitts, W.I.
Phone: (869) 465–7260, (800) 633–7411; Fax: (869) 465–4019;
e-mail: info@goldenlemon.com; www.goldenlemon.com

Owner/Manager: Arthur Leaman
Open: Year-round except September–October 15
Credit Cards: Most major
U.S. Reservations: Caribbean Inns, Ltd., (800) 633–7411;
Fax: (843) 686–7411; www.caribbeaninns.com
Deposit: Three nights; twenty-one days cancellation in high
season, fourteen days in low season
Minimum Stay: Four nights in high season, villa policy differs
Arrival/Departure: Transfer can be arranged; taxi one-way,
$20
Distance from Airport: 14 miles (thirty-minute drive)
Distance from Basseterre: 16 miles; taxi one-way, $25
Accommodations: 32 units with double, twin, and queen-
size beds (eight rooms in main building with balcony; six
suites in Lemon Court with pool; ten villa condos with private
pools and terraces)
Amenities: Ceiling fans; Internet access; bath with shower,
hair dryers, basket of toiletries; telephones; room service
available for all meals; boutique; no radios, television, air-con-
ditioning
Electricity: 110 volts
Sports: Freshwater pools, tennis, snorkeling on premises;
deep-sea fishing, diving, rain-forest nature walks, hiking with
guide on nearby Mount Liamuiga arranged
Dress Code: Casual but chic
Children: No
Meetings: Small groups
Day Visitors: Welcome for lunch and swim with reservations
Handicapped: No facilities
Packages: Honeymoon, wedding, all-inclusive
Rates: Two people, daily, CP. **High Season** (mid-Decem-
ber–mid-April): $300–$465. **Low Season:** $245–$390. Sin-
gle: $200–$300 and $160–$220, respectively.
Service Charge: 10 percent
Government Tax: 7 percent

and rotating them so they meet one another, unless
they prefer a private table. The dinner menu offers soup
and a choice of appetizer, main course—fresh fish or a
classic European dish served with local vegetables that
you might not recognize—and dessert served with quiet
attention and grace.

Rarely is it possible to say that a place is unique, but
The Golden Lemon is. Leaman's personal management is
omnipresent, down to the last flower and tea biscuit. That
The Golden Lemon is not everyone's cup of tea would be
good news to Arthur Leaman, since he's worked hard to
ensure its singular style.

The inn's distinctive flavor generally appeals to writers,
actors, and artists, although a surprising number of young
lawyers and doctors seem to have found their way here,
too, along with some seasoned sophisticates—some
famous, many just with style. Leaman says he designed
The Golden Lemon for people who "enjoy being pampered in an ambience of informal elegance . . . people
who enjoy doing nothing in grand style."

OTTLEY'S PLANTATION INN
Basseterre, St. Kitts, W.I.

Fashion magazines from California to the Champs Elysées have been using this gorgeous Caribbean "lara" as a backdrop almost from the day it opened. Perched on a hillside overlooking St. Kitts's eastern coast, the elegant inn is built into the historic ruins of a sugar plantation. It is set in ten magnificent acres of manicured lawns, with another twenty-five acres of rolling sugarcane fields edged by palm trees in the front and rain-forested mountains to the rear.

Established about 1703 when the Ottley family came to the island, it continued to operate as a plantation—under different owners—until the 1960s. In 1988 Americans Art and Ruth Keusch bought Ottley's with their daughter and son-in-law, Martin and Nancy Lowell; they've since been joined by a sister, Karen Keusch. After making extensive renovations and adding a second floor to the great house, they opened the inn in 1990.

The drive from the main eastern coast road climbs through cane fields and along columns of royal palms to

lawns so well tended you'll think they are the fairways of a swank golf course. Upon arrival you will be greeted by a member of the family—all hands-on managers. Marty, a congenial host whose horticultural training is evident everywhere, will offer you a welcome drink and show you to your room.

The great house, dating from 1832, is a majestic brimstone structure with two tiers of wraparound balconies trimmed with white railings, yellow shutters, and Brazilian hardwood doors. On the ground floor is a formal living room, beautifully appointed with antiques and period furniture, and a mahogany bar. It provides an elegant setting for afternoon tea, cocktails, and evening socializing. A small side room has the library, with a television set and VCR.

The first floor has three guest rooms, and upstairs are six wonderfully spacious ones with high, beamed ceilings—Scarlett O'Hara would have loved them. Each room is different, but all are delightfully furnished with antiques and white wicker. Plush bedspreads and chair covers of handsome floral prints are set against white walls with island prints and white wooden floors with Portuguese scatter rugs. The spacious bathrooms have separate dressing areas, well-lit vanities, tubs, and showers.

Large bedroom windows with dark wood louvers let in the breezes and open onto views of the exquisite gardens and surrounding countryside flowing to the sea. In front of the window are a table and chairs where you can enjoy breakfast and take in the view. And everywhere there are enormous bouquets of fresh tropical flowers.

Near the entrance the English Cottage, once a cotton storehouse, has a large bedroom and a separate sitting room that can be converted into a bedroom; each has its own patio and bathroom— one with a Jacuzzi bath and a plunge pool.

Recently the inn added five luxury cottages, each with two large guest rooms. These spacious cottages have elegant Italian tile baths, minibars, hardwood doors, and louvered shutters; they are handsomely decorated in Caribbean colonial style. The larger of the two rooms has a king-size bed, a Jacuzzi in the bathroom, and a private plunge pool on the ocean-view patio. The slightly smaller second room, furnished with either a king or twin beds, has a romantic corner tub in the bathroom. It can be furnished with a sofa and used as a sitting room. Thus, as a private cottage, it has a bedroom and sitting room, two bathrooms, two private patios (one with a plunge pool), and magnificent views.

A tennis court and official-size croquet court have also been added; an exercise and spa facility, to be housed in exotic thatched huts at the forest's edge, is planned for the coming year. Meanwhile manicures, pedicures, massages, and other spa services may be had in your room.

On the southern side of the great house, steps lead down to garden terraces and the beautiful stone ruins of the boiling house, now converted into a spring-fed swimming pool with a bar and stone terrace at the far end. One wall of the boiling house, with arched windows opening onto the swimming pool, forms a backdrop for the Royal Palm, the inn's open-air restaurant, popular with Kittitians and guests from other hotels as well. The Sunday brunch is a particular favorite.

Next to the great house is the remnant base of the windmill. Now encircled by allamanda bushes, it is a popular setting for outdoor weddings—a more romantic spot would be hard to imagine. Behind the great house is a mango orchard with wonderful old trees. All of Ottley's fruit-and-flower-filled gardens attract birds by the dozens.

Farther on, a bridge leads to footpaths along a gully and stone walls to trails through the rain forest that borders the property. The vegetation is fabulous, with enormous mahogany trees, gigantic elephant ears, and other rain-forest species. Self-guided tours are available, but Marty is a wonderful guide, too.

Ottley's historic, romantic setting, coupled with its informal, friendly atmosphere, will appeal both to singles and couples who seek a quiet vacation in gracious surroundings. The numbers—twenty-four rooms for forty-eight guests, on thirty-five acres, attended by a staff of forty-five—all but guarantee space, grace, and peace.

Ottley's Plantation Inn ✦✦✦

Box 345, Basseterre, St. Kitts, W.I.
Phone: (869) 465–7234, (800) 772–3039; Fax: (869) 465–4760; e-mail: ottleys@caribsurf.com; www.ottleys.com

Owners/Managers: Art, Ruth, and Karen Keusch; Martin and Nancy Lowell

Open: Year-round

Credit Cards: All major

U.S. Reservations: Direct to hotel

Deposit: Full prepayment; thirty days cancellation, except forty-five days for Christmas/New Year's

Minimum Stay: Seven nights during Christmas/New Year's

Arrival/Departure: Airport transfer included for stays of seven nights and longer

Distance from Airport: 6 miles (fifteen minutes); taxi one-way, $15

Distance from Basseterre: 10 miles; taxi one-way, $20; daily free shuttle to town, two beaches, and golf course

Accommodations: 24 rooms (nine in great house; six two-room cottages; one three-room villa), all with verandas; king- or queen-size beds (four with twin or king-size beds, two with two queens); nine with Jacuzzi and plunge pool. Villa with full kitchen can accommodate up to eight people.

Amenities: Air-conditioning, ceiling fans; telephone; safe; umbrella, flashlight; bath with tub and shower, hair dryers, basket of toiletries; coffeemaker; iron and ironing board; room service on request; some with minibar; no television

Electricity: 110 volts

Sports: Tennis court; croquet; daily free shuttle to beach with water sports; hiking on trails adjacent to property; golf, fishing, boating, snorkeling, scuba, windsurfing, horseback riding arranged

Dress Code: Informal

Children: Year-round in royal suites and grand villa

Meetings: Up to thirty-five people

Day Visitors: Restaurant open to outside guests; reservations required for dinner and Sunday brunch

Handicapped: No facilities

Packages: Honeymoon, wedding, golf, diving, five to ten days or longer custom-tailored

Rates: Per room, double, daily, FAB. *High Season* (mid-December–mid-April): $295–$725. *Low Season:* $225–$515. Single: deduct $25.

Service Charge: 10 percent

Government Tax: 7 percent

RAWLINS PLANTATION

Mount Pleasant, St. Kitts, W.I.

Near Dieppe Bay on the northwestern coast of St. Kitts, at 350 feet above sea level, is one of the Caribbean's most delightful small inns, Rawlins Plantation. With cloud-capped Mount Liamuiga rising 4,000 feet to form the backdrop, this quiet country inn is located on twelve acres in a pastoral setting that looks across acres of gently sloping cane fields to panoramic views of the Caribbean and neighboring St. Eustatius.

The former sugar plantation was established about 1690 and operated for almost 300 years. In 1968 Phillip Walwyn, a descendent of the family that took possession in 1790, returned to St. Kitts to live on the estate. He cleared the overgrown ruins of the sugar factory, removing tons of rock and rubble; rebuilt the main building, which had been destroyed by fire; restored others; and landscaped the surrounding grounds. He opened the inn in 1974.

In 1989 the inn was purchased by Walwyn's friends Paul Rawson, an English hotelier, and his Kittitian-born wife, Claire, who shared an unusual appreciation of the plantation. Two months later Hurricane Hugo hit the island; undeterred, the Rawsons repaired the damage and took the opportunity to upgrade the inn.

From the main road, a bumpy (much-maligned) country road, improved by the new owners, trails up along royal palms to the main buildings, which are set in open lawns and flowering gardens. The main house, built into the former boiling house—still with its 40-foot-tall rock chimney—has a living room and library, a formal dining room, and some guest quarters, all with attractive mahogany antique furniture. The dining room extends onto a veranda that overlooks the swimming pool, fed by Rawlins's own mountain stream, and a latticework gazebo.

Pieces of the old machinery such as the coppers—round-bottom vats used for boiling cane—are placed here and there around the grounds. Historic notes that interest guests, they also make decorative props for the flower-festooned gardens. Fresh flowers grace the rooms and dining tables as well.

Most accommodations are in cottages built on the ruins using the salvaged rock and designed to blend with the plantation setting. Homey and personal, the rooms have pitched roofs and are individually decorated in light, fresh, English country prints and furnished with four-poster beds and other antiques. All have modern bath-

rooms. The old windmill, dating from 1690, was made into a charming split-level unit of yellow and white decor, which is often used as the honeymoon suite.

Rawlins's outstanding cuisine, featuring produce grown in the inn's own gardens, is created with great care by Cordon Bleu–trained Claire Rawson, who combines French discipline with her West Indian heritage. Lunch, a buffet of West Indian specialties, draws guests from throughout the island. Paul, a wine connoisseur, stocks fine vintages that are stored in an old, naturally cool cellar.

While lunch is casual, dinner is a more stylish, candlelit affair, with four courses served on fine English china and crystal surrounded by old family silver and antiques, evoking the life of a planter in bygone days. You may choose to dine alone or with other guests. Service by the attentive staff is laudable.

Life at Rawlins is very low-key and easy paced, intended for people who can get along on their own. Days are spent sunning by the pool, lazing in a hammock, playing tennis or croquet, reading in the library, and enjoying afternoon tea or one of the inn's famous rum punches on the veranda at sunset.

Those with more energy can hike up the rain-forested slopes of Mount Liamuiga. The inn will pack you a picnic lunch and help you engage a guide. (Bring good walking shoes.) Nature lovers, particularly bird-watchers, will enjoy the gardens and nearby woods. The closest beach, a palm-shaded stretch of black sand at Dieppe Bay, is fringed by a reef good for snorkeling.

At the foot of the property, Phillip Walwyn has restored another seventeenth-century building of the plantation and turned part of it into an art gallery that is operated by his wife, Kate Spencer, herself an artist.

A stay at Rawlins is like being a guest in someone's country home—which, of course, you are. Rawlins's guests, many of whom are annual visitors, are more often English than American.

Rawlins Plantation ★★

Box 340, Mount Pleasant, St. Kitts, W.I.
Phone: (869) 465–6221; Fax: (869) 465–4954;
e-mail: rawplant@caribsurf.com;
www.rawlinsplantation.com

Owners/General Managers: Paul and Claire Rawson
Open: Year-round except September
Credit Cards: All major
U.S. Reservations: Direct to inn, or JDB Associates, (800) 346–5358; Fax: (703) 548–5825
Deposit: Three nights; twenty-one days cancellation
Minimum Stay: Four nights in season
Arrival/Departure: Transfer can be arranged for fee
Distance from Airport: 16 miles; taxi one-way, $25
Distance from Basseterre: 16 miles; taxi one-way, $25
Accommodations: Ten double rooms in cottages with verandas (five with twin beds; one with double; three queens; one king)
Amenities: Ceiling fans; bath with tub, hair dryer, basket of toiletries; nightly turndown service; laundry service, afternoon tea included in rates; room service available on request; no air-conditioning, television, radio, telephone
Electricity: 220 volts (110 for shavers); transformers available
Sports: Freshwater swimming pool; croquet lawn, grass tennis court; hiking with guide, golf, deep-sea fishing, boating, diving, biking arranged
Dress Code: Informal by day; casually elegant in evening
Children: Over twelve years of age accepted, but not encouraged
Meetings: No
Day Visitors: Welcome for lunch with reservations
Handicapped: No facilities
Packages: No
Rates: Per room, daily, MAP. **High Season** (mid-December–mid-April): $450. **Low Season:** $295. Single, $340 and $200, respectively.
Service Charge: 10 percent
Government Tax: 7 percent

St. Lucia

Lush, mountainous St. Lucia, the second largest island in the Windwards, is a nature lover's dream with scenic wonders on a grand scale. Every turn in the road—and there are many—reveals spectacular landscapes of rain-forested mountains and valleys covered with fruit and flowering trees. Mostly volcanic in origin and slightly pear shaped, St. Lucia is only 27 miles in length, but its mountainous terrain rising to more than 3,000 feet makes it seem much larger.

On the northwestern coast Castries, the capital, overlooks a deep natural harbor sheltered by an amphitheater of green hills. On the northern tip Pigeon Point, an island connected to the mainland by a causeway, has been made into a national park. It has a historic fort and museum and is the venue for St. Lucia's annual international jazz festival.

Soufrière, south of the capital, is the oldest settlement on St. Lucia. At its prime in the late eighteenth century, there were as many as one hundred sugar and coffee plantations in the vicinity. The quaint little port has a striking setting at the foot of the magnificent Pitons, sugarloaf twins that rise dramatically at the island's edge.

Soufrière lies amid a wonderland of steep mountain ridges and lush valleys, and it is the gateway to some of St. Lucia's most celebrated natural attractions: a drive-in volcano with gurgling mud and hot springs, pretty waterfalls, sulfur baths with curative powers that were tested by the soldiers of Louis XVI, and a rain forest with a trail across the heart of the island.

St. Lucia has some of the best and the worst roads in the Caribbean. None encircles the island completely, but you can make a loop around the southern half, which has the main sightseeing attractions. A new road along the western coast from Castries to Soufrière has made one of the most scenic drives in the Caribbean a joy to travel again. An alternative is a forty-five-minute motorboat trip available daily between Castries and Soufrière.

Information

St. Lucia Tourist Board, 820 Second Avenue, New York, NY 10017;
(212) 867– 2950, (212) 867–2795, (800) 456–3984;
e-mail: slu.tour@candw.lc; www.stlucia.org

ANSE CHASTANET BEACH HOTEL

Soufrière, St. Lucia, W.I.

On the northern side of Soufrière, facing the twin peaks of the Pitons, is one of the Caribbean's most enchanting resorts. Anse Chastanet, built along a steep hillside of tropical splendor overlooking a secluded cove, has a setting so idyllic that you will forgive (if not forget) the atrocious road leading there. If you prefer, you can also reach this hideaway by boat, arriving directly on Anse Chastanet's golden beach.

There are hillside rooms in octagonal, gazebo-type cottages, all with grandstand views of the Pitons or the sea and the unforgettable St. Lucian sunsets. The rooms are comfortable but not fancy—why compete with nature? They have wood-beamed ceilings and walls of louvered windows and doors leading to wraparound verandas draped in brilliant bougainvillea and hiding under some of the flowering trees for which the cottages are named. Near the beach are three two-story villas, which harmonize so well with their natural setting that they can hardly be seen. The villas house twelve spacious, deluxe suites.

All Anse Chastanet's rooms have rattan furnishings and other pieces in local woods—mahogany, wild breadfruit, and purple heart—designed by owner Nick Troubetzkoy, an architect, and crafted by local woodcarvers. Woven grass rugs (a St. Lucian specialty) are on the earthen tile floors; original art by local and international artists decorates the walls; and bright plaid madras cotton is used for the bed- and cushion covers. (Madras is used by St. Lucian women for their traditional dress.)

Troubetzkoy's most dazzling creations—eleven huge suites of bold, sensational design—put Anse Chastanet in a league of its own when they were added in 1993. These handsome architectural wonders, perched high above the first cottages, offer luxury and space. Some rooms have atrium gardens; others are built around trees, much like a tree house. Each suite has a different arrangement, and all have breathtaking views. But don't expect them to look like an *Architectural Digest* spread. Rather, they are rustic and sparsely furnished.

The best are six premium suites in Cottage 7, where the Pitons are the centerpiece. The enormous bedroom/sitting room extends to a terrace with no windows or walls; in the upper-story suites, ceilings soar to 20 feet.

Anse Chastanet requires you to be something of a mountain goat. Nothing but your legs gets you up and down the one hundred or more stone steps that climb from the beach to the topmost rooms. But it's worth every heart-pounding breath for the magnificent scenery. There is also an easier way, at least for part of the climb: If you rent a car (as most guests do), you can drive on the service road to the beach.

The reception pavilion contains an open-air bar, a library, the Pitons Restaurant where breakfast and dinner are served, and the Treehouse terrace, another dining area.

Trou-au-Diable, the beach restaurant, features Creole specialties at lunch; an ice cream cart patrols the beach in the afternoon, and the beach bar is open all day. You can also have lunch under your thatched umbrella on the more secluded northern end of the beach.

The resort has a fitness center, a tennis court, and a spa with several massage therapists who provide an extensive variety of facials, therapeutic massages including reflexology and aromatherapy, and other treatments in the privacy of your room or in the new and larger beachside spa center with six treatment rooms and a wide array of treatments. It is open daily from 9:00 A.M. to 8:00 P.M. On the second floor is an art gallery. There are also two boutiques and a water-sports center.

Anse Chastanet fronts some of St. Lucia's best reefs, which are protected as a marine park. They are close enough for snorkelers to reach directly from the beach. Some divers call the stretch between Anse Chastanet and the Pitons the best diving in the Caribbean.

Scuba St. Lucia, the resort's SSI (Scuba Schools International) Platinum PADI Gold Palm training facility, is directed by SSI-PADI master trainer Michael Allard, along with his wife, Karyn, and a ten-member professional team. Also open to nonhotel guests, it offers beach and

boat dives four times daily, night dives, and courses for beginners, certification, and underwater photography. The resort's 37-foot O-Day sailing vessel is available for half- and full-day trips, as well as for introductory lessons.

A more secluded strand of sand is a ten-minute walk (or a few minutes' motorboat ride) north of Anse Chastanet at Anse Mamin. Here you can also explore the extensive eighteenth-century ruins of Anse Mamin, one of the earliest sugar plantations on St. Lucia.

Anse Chastanet is close to some of St. Lucia's main natural attractions and offers guided hikes on the property at no charge to guests. Off-property hikes start at $55 per person and include a guide, transportation, and sometimes a picnic lunch. In connection with the St. Lucia National Trust, the inn has developed nature, bird-watching, and botanical tours.

The resort's newest addition, Bike St. Lucia, is a mountain-biking facility offering guided excursions on custom-designed rain-forest trails, clearly marked for levels of difficulty and patrolled by Bike St. Lucia staffers. Each rider is issued a Bell helmet, souvenir water bottle, and trail map. The resort has bike rentals: a half day $49, and a full day $69.

You'll dine in the magical, romantic setting of the Piton Restaurant on cuisine that makes generous use of fresh seafood, vegetables, and other local ingredients. The manager's wine party on Monday starts the week's evening activities. There is live music nightly and a beach barbecue with a reggae band on Tuesday and Friday. But Anse Chastanet is not a place for nightlife; most guests are back in their "tree houses" by 10:00 P.M.

That Anse Chastanet, with its romantic ambience, attracts honeymooners comes as no surprise. It is also the setting for about eight weddings per month. But you don't have to fall into either category to fall in love with this corner of paradise. And yet, Anse Chastanet isn't for everyone. But if you are a sporting enthusiast or something of an escapist, yearn for tranquillity, relish beauty, and are refreshed by remarkable tropical landscapes, you will love every minute at this friendly, unpretentious resort.

Anse Chastanet Beach Hotel ✶✶✶✶ 🍃

Box 7000, Soufrière, St. Lucia, W.I.
Phone: (758) 459–7000; Fax: (758) 459–7700;
e-mail: ansechastanet@candw.lc; www.ansechastanet.com;
www.bikestlucia.com; www.scubastlucia.com

Owners/Managing Directors: Nick and Karolin Troubetzkoy
Open: Year-round
Credit Cards: All major
U.S. Reservations: Ralph Locke Islands, Inc., (000) 223–1108; Fax: (310) 440–4220
Deposit: Three nights in winter, two nights in low season; thirty days cancellation
Minimum Stay: Three nights in winter, five nights during Christmas/New Year's
Arrival/Departure: Airport transfer arranged for fee; hotel runs scheduled boat to Castries
Distance from Airport: (Hewanorra International Airport) 18 miles (forty-five minutes); taxi one-way, $55. Vigie Airport: 20 miles (two hours); taxi one-way, $75
Distance from Castries: 20 miles; taxi one-way, $75; by sea, $36
Distance from Soufrière: 1½ miles; taxi one-way, $10
Accommodations: 49 units with twin or king-size beds (three standard, four premium, 12 deluxe beachside, and 29 hillside gazebo-cottages; one- and two-bedroom suites), all with verandas
Amenities: Ceiling fans; bath with shower only, hair dryers, basket of toiletries; tea and coffeemakers, minibars with optional provisioning plans; room service for breakfast; no radios, telephones, televisions, air-conditioning
Electricity: 220 volts/50 cycles
Fitness Facilities/Spa Services: See text
Sports: Tennis court (no lights); free snorkeling, Sunfish, windsurfing; no pool; superior dive facilities with full range of equipment, three dive boats and 36-foot trihull flattop for up to twenty-four divers, film lab for underwater photography; changing rooms, freshwater showers
Dress Code: Casual; men wear slacks or long-cut Bermuda shorts and shirts in evening
Children: None under four years of age; baby-sitters on request
Meetings: Up to seventy-five people
Day Visitors: Individuals with advance notice
Handicapped: No facilities
Packages: Honeymoon, scuba diving, wedding, spa
Rates: Per room for two people, daily. **High Season,** MAP (mid-December–mid-April): $425–$760. **Shoulder Season,** EP (mid-April–May and November 1–mid-December): $235–$520. **Low Season** (June–October 31): $200–$475. Single and triple rates available, EP; inquire.
Service Charge: 10 percent
Government Tax: 8 percent

THE BODY HOLIDAY AT LESPORT
Cariblue Beach, St. Lucia, W.I.

Sporting a new name to better reflect its nature, The Body Holiday at LeSport is a sports and spa resort offering an organized but unregimented vacation. Unique in the Caribbean (although its sister property, LaSource in Grenada, is a near copy), it is designed for today's professionals, striking a middle ground between the rigorous regime of a health spa and a sports-intensive vacation. For active and fitness-minded people, it's the best buy in the Caribbean.

LeSport is the ultimate all-inclusive resort. For one price you get all meals, tea, and snacks; full use of the extensive spa and sports facilities with instruction; all drinks and beverages; nightly music and entertainment; all gratuities, taxes, and round-trip airport transfers.

Set on a secluded beach on the northwestern tip of St. Lucia, LeSport climbs through fifteen hillside acres of tropical gardens. It has guest rooms in two-, three-, and four-story buildings. Except for twenty-nine with garden views, all have terraces or patios looking west to the sea—and what a treat. Sunsets are magnificent.

Recently, LeSport completed a $9 million project that added fifty-two rooms and suites, along with refurbishing and enhancing of public areas. A highlight was the creation of singles' rooms, priced as singles with no supplement, one of the very few hotels in the Caribbean with accommodations for singles. Each is a generous 280 square feet; a second person can be accommodated at a reduced rate. All of the new grand luxury rooms and suites are oceanfront with a terrace and marble bathrooms.

The original guest rooms are furnished in white rattan with king-size, four-poster canopied beds and have salmon-colored walls and fresh new curtains and floral bedspreads; bathrooms are faced with white Italian and salmon Portuguese marble.

In a spectacular hillside setting high above the resort is the Manderley, LeSport's fabulous Victorian fantasy with West Indian gingerbread and New Orleans filigree, offering privacy in luxurious accommodations. The house has a large living room and dining room that open onto a wrap-around balcony; three bedrooms, some with four-poster and some with canopied beds; and a wood-paneled library. All the rooms are attractively decorated with antiques and period furniture. On the terrace of the gar-

den swimming pool, you can enjoy breakfast along with a stunning view of St. Lucia. A house-keeper, butler, vehicle, and all LeSport facilities are included in the price. The villa can also be rented on its own, exclusive of the resort.

LeSport's spa facilities are in the Oasis. The name is exactly right. Perched seventy-eight steps up from the main resort, this heavenly two-story haven with graceful colonnaded courtyards, keyhole arches, reflecting pools, and fountains is designed in the Moorish style of Spain's Alhambra Palace.

The facility has thirty-nine exercise and treatment rooms where you are pampered and rejuvenated from head to toe in a program of thalassotherapy, which, for the uninitiated, involves baths and treatments using seaweed, seaweed products, and seawater. Also included are jet hose shower, Swiss needle shower, jet-stream pool, seaweed wraps, algae baths, loofah rubs, massage, facial, and hair care, as well as sauna and hot and cold plunge pools—all complimentary. A few treatments come with a minimal charge. Reflexology, for instance, costs $60.

You begin with a health questionnaire and visit to the resident nurse. Treatments are individually tailored, and you'll receive a printout of your schedule. The staff members are versed in all the treatments and, like the entire LeSport team, they have a pleasant, gentle manner and are eager to please.

All meals include a wide choice of dishes and are served in the Terrace, an open-air, beach-side restaurant encased in tropical gardens. Breakfast and lunch are lavish buffets, along with a la carte menus.

Dinners are served a la carte, except for a Caribbean buffet and a barbecue and beach party. Wines at lunch and dinner and all other beverages (except for French champagne) are included. Tao, a second, gourmet restaurant, added in 1999, almost immediately gained a well-deserved reputation for extraordinarily fine cuisine created by the talented Filipino chef Jun Agad (now with LaSource in Grenada), who specializes in East-West fusion dishes. Tao's decor, which also blends Asia and the New World, is as handsome as the cuisine is remarkable. And best of all, dining here is included in the resort's basic rates.

The air-conditioned piano bar, the gathering spot for

cocktails and after-dinner socializing, was enlarged and refurbished with red terra-cotta walls, white wicker furniture, and red and white fabrics. It features music by the resort's pianist nightly from 7:00 P.M. until the last guest retires. On the Terrace music by a live band is heard nightly, and jazz by a terrific local combo, a local dance troupe, a West Indian show, and a staff show are staged weekly.

Sports facilities are fabulous. Topping the list of water sports are trips for certified divers; you can snorkel directly off the beach. Windsurfing and Sunfish sailing instruction are offered daily. The resort has three pools—one for water volleyball, one for swimming, and the spa lap and exercise pool—as well as a tennis court (lighted), bicycles, aerobics, yoga, fencing, archery, volleyball, and weight training, all with instruction.

The fitness instructor will interview you and calculate your lean body mass (muscle, water, and bone), body fat (stored calories), body water, and metabolic rate. From this data you learn your calorie requirements, and a fitness program is adapted to your needs. You then get personal, individualized training for the duration of your stay. LeSport has daily tai chi and yoga classes, and daily walking and hiking excursions. Golf, including green fees, is available at a nearby course. Walk on the Wild Side offers daily hikes in the rugged interior of St. Lucia led by a certified mountaineer. Turtle-watching, which might include overnight camping on the beach, is often available from about March through June.

With its lush, secluded setting and body pampering (lots of pampering), LeSport has a sensual, romantic quality. In winter Americans and Europeans come in equal numbers, but in summer there are more Europeans. Although most guests are couples, this is one of the few Caribbean resorts where singles feel comfortable and find it easy to make friends.

Remember, LeSport is not a regimented spa. It's better. You design your own schedule.

The Body Holiday at LeSport ✦✦✦✦ 🌊

P.O. Box 437, Cariblue Beach, St. Lucia, W.I.
Phone: (758) 450–8551, (800) 544–2883; Fax: (758) 450–0368; e-mail: lesport@candw.lc; www.lesport.com.lc

Owner: The Barnard Group, St. Lucia

General Manager: Allen Stocker

Open: Year-round

Credit Cards: All major

U.S. Reservations: Direct to hotel or (800) 544–2883

Deposit: $300 per person within ten days of booking

Minimum Stay: Six nights during Jazz Festival in May

Arrival/Departure: Transfer included for seven-night stay

Distance from Airport: *(Vigie Airport)* 7 miles (twenty minutes). *Hewanorra International Airport:* 28 miles (ninety minutes)

Distance from Castries: 8 miles; taxi one-way, $50

Accommodations: 154 rooms including 29 singles (most with four-poster king-size beds, terraces, and ocean or garden views)

Amenities: Air-conditioning; bath with tub and shower, marble vanity with two sinks, hair dryer, bathrobe, basket of toiletries; mini-refrigerators in all except single rooms; telephones, Internet access; room service for continental breakfast; boutique; hair salon; no television or VCR

Electricity: 220/110 volts

Fitness Facilities/Spa Services: See text

Sports: See text

Dress Code: Sports and beachwear during day; only slightly dressier in evening

Children: Minimum age, ten years old during high season; children ten to fifteen get 25 percent discount when sharing room with parents; however, spa treatments are not included. For remainder of year, inquire.

Meetings: Up to thirty-five people

Day Visitors: Welcome with reservations; packages range from $31 noon–3:00 P.M. with lunch and drinks to $56 full day with lunch, dinner, and drinks; treatments subject to availability and priced separately

Handicapped: Limited facilities

Packages: Honeymoon, wedding

Rates: Per person, daily, all-inclusive. *High Season* (mid-December–late March): $375–$535. *Shoulder Season* (early April–mid-May and mid-October–November): $330–$400. *Low Season:* $240–$315. Single rates available; Plantation House priced separately.

Service Charge: Included

Government Tax: Included

ROYAL ST. LUCIAN
Castries, St. Lucia, W.I.

Brisk and efficient check-in at a fountain-spouting atrium lobby, a personalized suite tour by a member of the management, a phone and piped-in Muzak—in the bathroom—are typical accoutrements you would find in a plush New York or Tokyo hotel. But on laid-back St. Lucia?

Opened in late 1990 on Reduit Beach on St. Lucia's leeward shores, the Royal St. Lucian was the island's first all-suite luxury hotel. The three-story structure, designed in rather grand Georgian Palladian style, hugs a lavish pool and bar area; all suites face the sea. The hotel is meant for the discriminating few (read rich, fast-track Type As) who expect a full spectrum of services—from room service to turndown service—all delivered at lightning speed, even in the Caribbean where a slow pace, many would say, is meant to be not only accepted but savored.

What's amazing is that at the Royal St. Lucian, it works. After registering in the open-air lobby, cool with marble and tropical greenery, the royal treatment at the

Royal begins when guests are whisked off to their suites by a member of the management staff. What they find is pure luxury.

All suites boast tile floors and plush carpeting in the bedroom and separate sitting area (some with sleep sofas), along with a full lineup of luxury amenities—air-conditioning, room safe, phones, fully stocked minibar, cable and local television, ceiling fans, bathrobes, and radios that run local stations in addition to the hotel's background music channel. The spacious marble bathrooms have separate shower and tub, phone, radio, scales, and hair dryer. Ceramics from Santo Domingo and original works by internationally acclaimed artists are showcased throughout the property.

All suites have private patios or balconies overlooking the gardens, pool, and beach. Eight beachfront suites feature larger sundecks and loggias with terrace bars; three grand deluxe suites boast extra-spacious interior rooms, and lounge and dining terraces. The Presidential Suite has

a two-tiered terrace; the upper terrace is for sunbathing and dining, and the lower one, with a Jacuzzi, is for shaded relaxation.

You may be tempted to loll in the luxury of your suite till late morn, but there's plenty to do when you venture out. The resort's centerpiece, La Mirage—an expansive pool with a waterfall and bridge—invites you to sunbathe at its shallow end or have a drink at the swim-up bar. On mile-long Reduit Beach you can windsurf, sail a Sunfish, and snorkel. Waterskiing and windsurfing lessons cost extra. You can take advantage of the complimentary tennis facilities at the Rex St. Lucian Hotel next door, or golf at the newly renovated St. Lucia Golf Course nearby. Scuba diving and deep-sea fishing can be arranged for an extra fee. Reduit Beach's white sands are also perfect for a stroll, perhaps to nearby Rodney Bay Marina, the departure point for day sails and yacht charters.

Overlooking the beach, the breezy L'Epicure restaurant, offering all-day dining, specializes in Caribbean fare and seafood. For more elegant dining in the evening, the sophisticated restaurant Chic! has an a la carte menu featuring nouvelle Caribbean and continental fare. The soft music of early evening in the Mistral Lounge is followed by light jazz nightly. You can sip rum-and-coconut-laden concoctions like the Lucian Lush and the Smooth Talker with views of the moonlit sea providing a romantic backdrop.

The royal treatment awaits you at the Royal Spa, too, provided you just won the lottery. But then, if you can afford the hotel, the spa might not seem expensive. Located at the edge of the beach, this serene sanctuary offers a full range of therapies, beauty treatments, and fitness programs. It has a Jacuzzi, cold plunge pool, sauna, steam room, hydrotherapy room, three treatment rooms, and a fitness center with Cybex equipment. Professionals are available daily to put you through your exercise paces, tailor an individual fitness program for you, and provide instruction in use of the equipment.

Treatments include hydrotherapy baths, body wraps, scrubs, massages, and facials. Therapeutic mud and algae are imported from Europe—Fango from Italy and Moor mud from Hungary, algae from Turkey and Greece. Different massage styles are used, such as the Swedish technique and Oriental shiatsu. You can have massages on the beach or in the privacy of your suite. The spa is limited to those over age sixteen.

The atmosphere at the Royal St. Lucian is sedate, but if you want to step up the pace, limbo, lambada, and crab racing are daily occurrences at neighboring hotels. The Royal St. Lucian is for travelers who appreciate efficiency, luxury, and serenity—and don't mind some hints of pretension.

Royal St. Lucian ★★★★

Reduit Beach, Box 977, Castries, St. Lucia, W.I.
Phone: (758) 452– 9999; Fax: (758) 452–9639;
e-mail: royalslu@candw.lc

Owner: Royal St. Lucian Hotel Ltd.

General Manager: Ross Stevenson

Open: Year-round

Credit Cards: All major

U.S. Reservations: MRI, (305) 471–6170, (800) 255–5859; Fax: (305) 471-9547

Deposit: Three nights

Minimum Stay: three nights

Arrival/Departure: Transfer arranged for fee

Distance from Airport: *(Vigie Airport)* 6 miles, taxi one-way, $15. *Hewanorra Airport:* 39 miles; taxi one-way, $62.

Distance from Castries: 6 miles; taxi one-way, $15, shuttle to town, $15

Accommodations: 96 luxury suites, all with terraces, and all with two twins or king; some with sofa beds

Amenities: Air-conditioning, ceiling fans; bath with tub and shower, hair dryer, basket of toiletries, scales, bathrobe; direct-dial telephones (including sitting room and bath), cable television, radio; safe; stocked minibar; ice service, nightly turndown service; room service daily until 10:00 p.m.

Electricity: 220 volts

Fitness Facilities/Spa Services: See text

Sports: Freshwater swimming pool, children's pool; free use of two tennis courts at Rex St. Lucian, with pro, lessons, equipment for fee; complimentary snorkeling gear, Sunfish, windsurfers; diving, deep-sea fishing, horseback riding, waterskiing arranged for fee

Dress Code: Elegantly casual

Children: All ages; cribs, high chairs; baby-sitters; Children's Club for ages four to twelve with supervised activities available weekdays at Rex St. Lucian

Meetings: Conference room seats up to 150 people

Day Visitors: Welcome with dinner reservations and at bar

Handicapped: Two suites fully equipped

Packages: Honeymoon, spa, tennis, golf, deep-sea fishing, dive, family

Rates: Two people, daily, EP. **High Season** (mid-December–early April): $500–$870. **Low Season** (mid-April–mid-December): $400–$660. Spa packages priced separately.

Service Charge: Included

Government Tax: Included

St. Maarten / St. Martin

This small island in the heart of the Caribbean is Dutch on one side and French on the other. How an island of only 37 square miles became divided hardly seems to matter anymore except to history buffs and tax collectors.

Columbus discovered the island in 1493 and claimed it for Spain; several centuries later a young Dutchman, Peter Stuyvesant, lost a limb wresting the island from Spain. Still later the French got into the fray, and somewhere along the way, the Dutch and the French agreed to stop fighting and to divide the island instead.

Today there are no border formalities, because there are no real boundaries. The only way you can tell you are crossing from one country to the other is a welcome sign at the side of the road. A short twenty-minute drive separates Philipsburg, the capital of Dutch St. Maarten, and Marigot, the capital of French St. Martin. The two flags nonetheless give the island an unusual international flair.

Philipsburg is the main port for cruise ships and the commercial center. The international airport is also on the Dutch side. Until recently Marigot was a village, but with new development it has become as busy as its Dutch counterpart. Yet it is unmistakably Gallic.

St. Maarten is intensively developed—overdeveloped is more accurate—for tourists. Still, it remains one of the Caribbean's most popular islands: It has something for everyone, whatever the style, and offers as much to do as places ten times its size.

The island has excellent sports facilities for tennis, golf, horseback riding, sailing, diving, wind-surfing, and sport fishing. There's nightlife at discos and casinos. You can shop in trendy boutiques or air-conditioned malls for goods from around the world.

St. Maarten has a well-deserved reputation as a food lover's haven; and you can find restaurants serving Italian, Mexican, Vietnamese, Indonesian, Chinese, French, Dutch, and West Indian cuisine. The truly gourmet ones are in the village of Grand Case, near Marigot, but be prepared when the bill comes: Some of the French restaurants are very expensive.

St. Maarten is a transportation hub for the northeastern Caribbean. Its location makes it an ideal base for exploring nearby Anguilla, Saba, Statia, St. Barts, and St. Kitts/Nevis.

Information

St. Maarten Tourist Office, 675 Third Avenue, New York, NY 10017;
(212) 953– 2084, (800) 786–2278; Fax: (212) 953–2145; www.stmaarten.com

LA SAMANNA
St. Martin, F.W.I.

Snow-white villas draped in brilliant magenta bougainvillea sit between sea and sky on fifty-five tropical hillside acres stretching along one of the Caribbean's most gorgeous beaches.

Small and exclusive, La Samanna was designed with the international sophisticate in mind, to provide unpretentious luxury far from the real world. Set on the crest of a hill overlooking a 3,500-foot arc of deep white sand on Long Bay, the resort combines striking Mediterranean-Moorish architecture and colorful decor with a sophisticated Riviera ambience. When it opened in 1974, it set a new style in casual elegance in the Caribbean.

La Samanna was conceived by the late James Frankel, a New York businessman who was inspired to bring the flavor of the Mediterranean to the Caribbean. He equated luxury with privacy and asked noted Caribbean architect Robertson "Happy" Ward to design a private oasis that would be more like a collection of villas on a secluded estate than a hotel. Organized activities and manager's cocktail parties were verboten; nothing would intrude on the resort's peace. La Samanna was named for Frankel's three daughters—Samantha (who's married to tennis great Ivan Lendl), Anouk, and Nathalie.

Today, in contrast to St. Martin's unbridled growth, La Samanna is an oasis of untrammeled beauty, appreciated even more now than when it first burst onto the scene. Upon entering the gardens, walled from the outside world, you find classic white stucco structures recalling a Greek island village. Stone steps wind down a multilevel sweep of balconies, arches, terraced gardens, and shaded walkways to the beach below.

At the entrance to the main building, you will find a reception desk, a concierge, and a small lounge. They open onto The Restaurant to one side and on the other, step down to La Samanna's signature bar with its colorful Indian wedding-tent canopy. The hotel's bartender remains on duty as long as guests linger. Below the bar a flower-encased terrace overlooks a pretty swimming pool smothered in tropical gardens. Lunch on the terrace is available for guests who do not want to leave the informal comfort of the pool for the dining room.

La Samanna has a surprising variety of accommodations for its size. Standard guest rooms are located in the three-story main building. Rooms open onto balconies that capture the fabulous view of curving Long Bay. The top floor has the Terrace Suite with three bedrooms and

wraparound terraces with grandstand views of Long Bay.

Six second-floor guest rooms were enhanced by adding balconies and stairs for direct beach access. The interiors, created by Vision Design of Dallas, draw on St. Martin's Creole heritage and La Samanna's Moorish architecture. Natural textures with rich cotton prints in deep blue, red, and gold colors are set against mahogany and teak furniture with bamboo accents. All guest rooms have been given similar decor plus televisions and VCRs.

One- to three-bedroom suites in two-story units (some with rooftop terraces) and villas dot the hillsides that spill down to the beach. Most guest rooms and villas have individual entrances and private terraces or patios, and are separated by a jungle of flowering hedges and trees that provide maximum privacy. Suites and villas have kitchens, dining areas, large living rooms, and patios. All guest rooms have air-conditioned bedrooms; appointments include custom-designed, hand-carved furniture and colorful fabrics.

All meals are served in The Restaurant, an open-air terrace with an eagle's-nest view of Long Bay. It has long had a reputation as one of the Caribbean's best and most original—and very expensive. The chef maintains the tradition of combining French tradition with Caribbean influences. From time to time the resort offers a celebrity guest chef program. The restaurant has an extensive wine list—a collection begun by Frankel, who was a connoisseur.

La Samanna has a fitness center with exercise equipment, a certified fitness trainer, and morning aerobics classes. In 2001, it opened a new spa that proved to be so popular it had to be expanded before year's end. Also available are three tennis courts with night lights and a watersports center. Other new facilities include a game room with a pool table, table tennis, and board games, including some for children; and a meeting pavilion with state-of-the-art audiovisual equipment, a private dining room, a kitchen, and a lounge. It can be used for weddings, too.

The resort has a helicopter landing pad as well as a new boutique. The latter, built into a coral knoll across from the resort's main building, stocks designer jewelry, perfume, fine clothing, and La Samanna's signature line.

La Samanna caters to a sophisticated, affluent clientele. Through the years the privacy and elegant informality have pleased a roster of stars, celebrities, and captains of industry, most from North America, some from Europe. The romantic resort is an ideal honeymoon spot, but its seclusion and villa facilities also make it desirable for couples and families with young children.

Among the services the hotel offers is airport check-in on departure. Your luggage and formalities are handled in advance, and your boarding pass obtained. All you have to do it show up. In my book, that's service.

La Samanna ★★★★

P.O. Box 4077, Marigot 97064, St. Martin, F.W.I.
Phone: (590) 590–87–64–00; Fax (590) 590–87–87–86;
www.orient-expresshotels.com

Owner: Orient Express Hotels

Managing Director: Bernard de Villele

Open: Year round except September–October

Credit Cards: All major

U.S. Reservations: La Samanna, (800) 854–2252, (212) 319–5191; Fax: (212) 832–5390

Deposit: Three nights; twenty-one days cancellation, except ninety days for Christmas/New Year's

Minimum Stay: Fourteen nights during Christmas holidays; five nights over high-season weekends and some holidays

Arrival/Departure: Airport meet-and-assist service

Distance from Airport: 1½ miles; taxi one-way, $15

Distance from Philipsburg: 2½ miles; taxi one-way, $14

Distance from Marigot: 5 miles; taxi one-way, $15

Accommodations: 81 rooms (eight deluxe; four suites in main and hillside buildings; 24 one-bedroom and 16 two-bedroom apartments; six three-bedroom villas), all with kings or twins

Amenities: Air-conditioning, ceiling fan; telephone; bath with tub and shower, bathrobe, hair dryer, deluxe toiletries; nightly turndown service; minibar or refrigerator with beverages, twenty-four-hour room service, food order service; boutique

Electricity: 220 volts

Fitness Facilities/Spa Services: Fitness center; spa treatments arranged

Sports: Freshwater swimming pool; three lighted tennis courts, tennis pro; waterskiing, windsurfing, Sunfish, snorkeling gear free; waterskiing lessons available; golf, horseback riding, fishing, sailing charters arranged; fitness center

Dress Code: Casual; no jacket or tie required at dinner

Children: All ages; cribs; baby-sitters; children under age twelve free in room with parents

Meetings: Up to sixty people

Day Visitors: With reservations for lunch or dinner

Handicapped: No facilities

Packages: Honeymoon; three or seven days

Rates: Per room, daily, FAB. *High Season* (mid-December–mid-April): $675– $1,345. *Shoulder Season* (November 1–mid-December and mid-April–May 31): $500–$1,125. *Low Season* (June 1–early September): $360–$935. Two- and three-bedroom suites priced separately; inquire.

Service Charge: Included

Government Tax: 5 percent

PASANGGRAHAN ROYAL GUEST HOUSE
Philipsburg, St. Maarten, N.A.

With its back on Front Street and its front on the bay, Pasanggrahan Royal Guest House combines a bit of island beauty and city bustle with a touch of history and a lot of charm—and all at budget prices.

The name (pasanggrahan is Indonesian for "guest house") reflects this landmark's history as the former government guest house, after serving as the governor's mansion in the late 1800s. Its distinguished guests included the Dutch queen Juliana (she was Princess Juliana at the time), who stayed here for a time during World War II. (Both Indonesia and St. Maarten were then Dutch colonies.) In 1983 the Pasanggrahan was acquired by Oli de Zela, a native of American Samoa, and her late husband.

Now hidden under tall palms in a tropical garden in the heart of Philipsburg, between the main street and the beach, the Pasanggrahan is a casual and friendly hotel that many would rank as the best bargain in the

Caribbean. A wood-frame building painted white with green trim, it has an antiques-filled reception area and lounge presided over by a portrait of Queen Wilhelmina. A long white veranda extends the length of the front, overlooking the beach and the activity in the harbor.

It's the perfect setting for a Sidney Greenstreet movie. No doubt that's why the bar was given his name. It is located in an area that was once part of the room occupied by the royals. Happy hour here is especially popular with local dignitaries and the business community—and everyone who knows about the great strawberry daiquiris.

There is one guest room on the second floor of the main building; the rest are in a pair of two-story beachfront buildings adjacent to the main building and in one cottage. The most spacious and appealing, the Queen Room—what else?—is directly above the Greenstreet Bar

Pasanggrahan Royal Guest House *

Front Street, P.O. Box 151, Philipsburg, St. Maarten, N.A.
Phone: (599) 542–3588; Fax: (599) 542–2885

Owners/General Managers: Oli Ale de Zela Tinitali and Tini Tinitali

Open: Year-round except September

Credit Cards: MasterCard, Visa

U.S. Reservations: Direct to hotel

Deposit: Three nights in winter; one night in summer

Minimum Stay: Inquire

Arrival/Departure: No transfer service

Distance from Airport: 5 miles; taxi one-way, $15

Accommodations: 31 rooms, including the Queen Room and cottage (28 have terrace or patio)

Amenities: Air-conditioning, ceiling fans; bath with tub and shower; refrigerators, ice service; nightly turndown service; twenty-four-hour security; telephone, television, radio, clock; no room service

Electricity: 110 volts

Sports: None on premises; tennis, golf, boating, snorkeling, diving, windsurfing, deep-sea fishing, horseback riding arranged

Dress Code: Casual

Children: Off season only, all ages; cribs, high chairs

Meetings: Up to 200 people in garden

Day Visitors: Welcome

Handicapped: Facilities

Packages: No

Rates: Per room, daily, EP. *High Season* (mid December–mid-April): $147– $175. *Low Season:* $88–$125.

Service Charge: 15 percent

Government Tax: 5 percent

and terrace. It is reached by a private spiral staircase. Pleasantly furnished, the room is cozy rather than queenly. It was once occupied by Juliana, and it does have a queen-size bed, although not the same one Her Highness used.

There are two types of rooms in the annex: standard, which are rather small, and superior, which are larger and deluxe. All rooms have air-conditioning, telephone and television; superior rooms have small refrigerators.

All rooms are furnished with either twin or king-size beds and have white tile and wood bathrooms. Beach-front rooms have balconies, shared in some cases. The furnishings are simple—basic wood furniture and some wicker. Colorful prints by local artists and Indonesian batik hangings decorate the walls, but they must compete with the colors of the Caribbean and the picturesque sailboats in the harbor outside your window.

Meals are served at the Oceanview Restaurant with seating either on the beachside veranda or in the garden dining area, particularly enjoyable at sunset. The restaurant features California and Pacific Rim cuisine at moderate prices. The garden area, with a gazebo bar, is also a popular venue for cocktail parties and special events held by the business community. Afternoon tea for guests is served here. A folklore show is performed on Friday and Sunday evening.

The beach in front of the Pasanggrahan stretches the length of Front Street. The inn doesn't have a water-sports center, but at either end of the beach you'll find diving, sailing, and water-sports shops where almost anything can be arranged; they have scheduled activities daily.

St. Vincent and the Grenadines

Nature's awesome power and exquisite beauty live side by side in this chain of idyllic islands. Mountainous and magnificent, St. Vincent is the largest of the multi-island group. Its lush terrain, thick with tropical forests and banana plantations, rises quickly from the sea to more than 4,000 feet in the smoldering volcanic peaks of La Soufrière in the north.

The Botanic Gardens in Kingstown, the capital, are the oldest in the Western Hemisphere. Among their prized species is a breadfruit tree from the original plant brought from Tahiti by Captain Bligh of the *Bounty.*

St. Vincent has a series of mountain ranges up the center of the island. The Buccament Forest Nature Trail is a signposted loop through the fabulous rain forest where gigantic gommier and other hardwoods make up the thick canopy towering more than 100 feet.

La Soufrière has erupted five times since 1718, most recently in 1979. The crater, about a mile across, smolders and emits clouds of steam and sulfur fumes. The Falls of Baleine tumble 70 feet in one dramatic stage through a steep-sided gorge of volcanic rock at the foot of the Soufrière Mountains. From Kingstown the falls are accessible only by sea; excursions depart almost daily.

The Grenadines, stretching south from St. Vincent more than 65 miles to Grenada, are a chain of three dozen islands and cays often called by yachtsmen the most beautiful sailing waters in the world. Only eight are populated.

Bequia, the largest and most developed of The Grenadines, is known for its skilled sailors and boatbuilders. The island's laid-back lifestyle has made it a favorite of artists, writers, and old salts who never found their way back home.

Young, Palm, and Petit St. Vincent are private island resorts; Mustique is a celebrity mecca. Other islands with resorts are Mayreau, Canouan, and Union, all with remarkable beaches and small resorts with facilities for sailing, diving, fishing, and other water sports. Tobago Cays are four uninhabited islets scalloped with seemingly untouched white-sand beaches and beckoning aquamarine waters.

Dive aficionados call St. Vincent the sleeper of Caribbean diving; reef life normally found at 80 feet in other locations grows here at depths of only 25 feet and includes an extraordinary abundance and variety of tropical reef fish.

Information

St. Vincent and The Grenadines Tourist Office, 801 Second Avenue, New York, NY 10017; (212) 687–4981, (800) 729–1726; www.svgtourism.com. The area code for St. Vincent is 784.

YOUNG ISLAND

St. Vincent, W.I.

If painter Paul Gauguin had stopped here after leaving Martinique, he might not have pressed on to the South Seas in his search for the totally exotic. The lush, volcanic terrain of undeveloped St. Vincent is a dead ringer for Tahiti fifty years ago, and it's still teeming with mystery.

But there's no mystery about Young Island. This thirty-five-acre private-island resort only 200 yards off St. Vincent's southern shore is luxury amid tropical profusion, a fantasy version of Polynesia in miniature. Your adventure begins when you board a Grenadine version of the *African Queen* for the five-minute ride across the narrow channel to Young Island.

One of Young Island's longtime staff members meets guests at the dock, usually preceded by a waiter carrying a tray of hibiscus-decorated rum punch. (You'll need a drink after the daylong journey—two plane rides, taxi, and boat—it takes to reach Young's tropical shores.) From the dock you will be led along stone paths through a maze of greenery to your island quarters—one of two dozen or so thatched bungalows of Brazilian hardwood and volcanic stone tucked away on the beach or hidden on a hillside. What they lack in telephone and television, they more than make up for in comfort and lush surroundings.

Guests partial to bird's-eye views and aerobic hikes always choose the hillside aeries. These feel like tree houses but offer great comfort and enchanting island decor as well as unexpected amenities: a huge bowl of local fruits and, for guests on a return visit (often couples who honeymooned here), a bottle of champagne. Two of the beachside cottages have plunge pools.

Inside the bungalow you feel as if you are outside. Vertical wooden louvers let in the outdoors, and sliding glass doors open onto a huge balcony suspended above the bush. A seductive hammock for two awaits, along with a splendid view of the mountainous mainland or The Grenadines, dribbling south toward Grenada. Even the shower, cleverly appended to the dressing quarter with its jungle canopy and shoulder-high wooden "curtain," is alfresco.

Somewhere down below, a free-form pool and tennis court hide amid the breadfruit and banana trees. Water spirits head for the dock to go snorkeling, windsurfing, or sailing. Dive St. Vincent is headquartered directly across Young Island Cut. Young also keeps a couple of yachts at the ready, along with a captain and chef, for day or overnight sailing trips; it offers a year-round package that

Young Island Crossing, P.O. Box 211, St. Vincent, W.I.
Phone: (784) 458–4826; Fax: (784) 457–4567;
e-mail: y-island@caribsurf.com; www.youngisland.com

Owners: Dr. Frederick Ballantyne and Vidal Browne
General Manager: Bianca Williams Porter
Open: Year-round
Credit Cards: All major
U.S. Reservations: Ralph Locke Islands, Inc., (800) 223–1108;
Fax: (310) 440 4220
Deposit: Three nights in winter, two nights in summer;
$1,500 for packages
Minimum Stay: Ten nights during Christmas
Arrival/Departure: Transfer service arranged for fee
Distance from Airport: *(St. Vincent Airport)* 1½ miles; taxi
one-way, $8.00
Distance from Kingstown: 3 miles; taxi one-way, $10
Accommodations: 30 in bungalows, all with patio (26 with
king-size beds; five one-bedroom suites)
Amenities: Ceiling fans; garden shower, hair dryer, basket of
toiletries, bathrobe; ice bucket, small refrigerator; safe; nightly
turndown service, room service for breakfast
Electricity: 220 volts/60 cycles
Sports: Saltwater swimming pool; one lighted Har-Tru tennis
court; free use of pedal boats, snorkeling gear, windsurfing
equipment, and instruction; sailing, deep-sea fishing, diving
arranged at additional cost
Dress Code: Casual
Children: All ages; cribs, high chairs; baby-sitters available at
prevailing rates
Meetings: Up to fifty people
Day Visitors: For meals
Handicapped: Limited facilities
Packages: Honeymoon; Sailaway
Rates: Per room, double, daily, MAP. *High Season* (mid-
December–February 28): $475–$710. *Shoulder Season*
(March 1–31): $390–$655. *Low Season* (April–mid-December):
$345–$560.
Service Charge: 10 percent
Government Tax: 7 percent

combines a stay at the resort with a two- or three-day
cruise of The Grenadines.

But most guests tend to plop on the beach in hammocks under one of the *bohios,* the thatched-roof gazebos that enhance the island's South Pacific appearance.
Occasional thirst may propel some to paddle a few strokes
from shore to the Coconut Bar, a swim-up bar in a
thatched hut that seems to float atop the Caribbean
waters. Breakfast, lunch, and dinner are served in shaded
garden nooks, some bounded by a moat, overlooking the
beach.

By night guests gather in the wood-beamed bar and
enjoy a variety of local entertainment several times a
week. A cocktail party is held by the pool on Friday night
with the Bamboo Melodians.

Young offers a proper wine list, and the menu
changes daily according to the whim of the chef (and
what's available). The results might be such tempting
choices as papaya soup laced with garlic or an island-
grown avocado brimming with caviar, perhaps followed
by just-caught lobster or a fillet of red snapper in cream-
and-pepper sauce.

It's only when you hike back into the bush and up the
hill that you might regret the many-course dinner, nur-
tured with spirits of cane and grape.

THE FRANGIPANI HOTEL
The Grenadines, Bequia, St. Vincent, W.I.

You've heard it said that if you stand long enough in Times Square, sooner or later you'll see the whole world go by. In its own (decidedly more laid-back) way, the beach bar at the Frangipani Hotel can make a similar claim. Okay, maybe not the whole world—but surely a good slice of its more interesting and eccentric citizens.

Bequia's Admiralty Bay is one of the finest deep-water harbors in the Caribbean, and often the first landfall for yachts cruising from the Mediterranean to these warm waters. The Frangi, as it is known to habitués, is smack in the heart of the waterfront, surrounded by flowering bushes and trees.

Once the family home of the former prime minister of St. Vincent and The Grenadines, James "Son" Mitchell, it has been welcoming yachties and tourists for so many years that it has achieved legendary status throughout the Caribbean.

The Frangi has never tried to be anything other than what it is—a simple guest house—and there, in its utter

lack of pretension, lies its charm. Mere steps from the yacht-filled bay, the hotel has been described in a novel this way: "Like the white hunter bars in Kenya, it's a pickup place, social headquarters, news central, information booth, post office and telegraph [and now phone and fax] office, in short, the nerve center of the permanently-in-transit charter-boat trade."

Here you can gossip or flirt with serious salts who have circumnavigated the globe often, with boat bums and beach bunnies, Washington lawyers on bare-boat charters, college professors and freelance backpackers, couples with unpublishable biographies, locals and winter residents, dreadlocked Rastafarians in Batman T-shirts, expatriate Inuits, billionaire Arabs on zillion-dollar yachts, minor celebrities, older men with younger women, younger men with older women, and trios and combos of every age, nationality, and color imaginable.

On Thursday night the Frangi holds its weekly jump-up (barbecue and steel band), so called because the music does make it difficult not to jump up and dance. Around the bar, people are generally so chatty (and, as sundown turns the sky mauve, so full of rum) that Attila the Hun could make friends here. Needless to say, solo travelers love it, though most guests are couples.

Breakfast, lunch, and dinner are served in an open-air dining room by the lobby. The food is simple and very good, mostly West Indian fare cooked in mass quantities by local women who obviously enjoy their work. The drinks are good, too, once you've caught Harold's eye. Harold, you will quickly learn, has been tending bar here for two decades or so, and has no plans to adjust his inner clock to anything but Caribbean time.

Rooms at the Frangipani are simple, period. People stay here for what can honestly be called one of the last few "true Caribbean experiences" still available. If you're looking for professionally decorated, five-star polish, don't give this one even a thought.

The rooms are airy and adequate but have no amenities such as phone or television, and you will need to bring your own shampoo. Rooms in the old house that face the water are simple to the point of bare—bed, tabletop or ceiling fan, sink, mosquito netting. Most have no private bath, and some have no hot water (but how cold does water get in 82-degree weather?). The view—and the people-watching—make up for it. The nicer stone units with terraces

are in the back of the main house, and therefore have no view of the bay. Be aware, too, that you'll be living in close proximity to geckos and other island critters as well as lush foliage.

The tile-floor lobby is small but has maps and a take-one-leave-one paperback library. Anything you need, if it's humanly possible to obtain, will be provided cheerfully by Lou Keane, a Canadian woman who has been running the Frangi for decades. (In return, satisfied repeat guests happily run a supply train of everything from New York bagels to hard-to-find plumbing supplies.)

Noise isn't much of a problem; little happens past 9:00 p.m. on the island, and dinner is nearly impossible to find after 7:00 P.M. But on Thursday, the barbecue, jump-up revelry, and the band (playing the same five amplified songs nearly every night at a different hotel) assault the eardrums till midnight or later.

Pack light; a T-shirt thrown over your swimsuit borders on formal attire here. Serious resort wear and high heels will cause muffled giggles (if not a sprained ankle). There's some nice shopping, but the island offers no glitz, gambling, or Gucci. And with any luck, locals and longtime visitors pray, it never will.

The Frangi has a tennis court, and full water sports (diving, snorkeling, windsurfing) are available at The Clubhouse next door; two gorgeous beaches are a half-hour stroll or a short land- or water-taxi ride away.

The Frangipani Hotel ✳

Box 1, Bequia, St. Vincent, W.I.
Phone: (784) 458–3255; Fax: (784) 458–3824;
e-mail: frangi@caribsurf.com; www.frangipani.net

Owner: James "Son" Mitchell
General Manager: Sabrina Mitchell
Open: Year-round except September–mid-October
Credit Cards: Most major (except American Express)
U.S. Reservations: Direct to hotel
Deposit: Three nights; twenty-one days cancellation less 10 percent
Minimum Stay: None
Arrival/Departure: No transfer service. If arriving by yacht, tie your dinghy to Frangi's dock; if by air, land at airstrip—however, landing could be chancy due to winds on eastern side of island. There's beautiful twenty-minute roller-coaster drive across southern half of Bequia to hotel. Ferry daily between St. Vincent's Kingstown and Bequia, one-way, $4.00.
Distance from Airport: (Bequia) 3 miles; taxi one-way, $10
Accommodations: 15 rooms (five in main building, ten in garden units), eight with terrace or patio
Amenities: Ceiling fans; bath with shower only; breakfast service in garden units
Electricity: 220 volts
Sports: Tennis free; boating, snorkeling, diving, windsurfing instruction for fee; hiking, birding; sunset cruises; no pool
Dress Code: Very casual
Children: All ages; cribs; baby-sitters
Meetings: No
Day Visitors: Welcome
Handicapped: No facilities
Packages: Dive
Rates: Per room, double, daily, EP. **High Season** (mid-December–mid-April): $55–$150. **Low Season:** $40–$120.
Service Charge: 10 percent
Government Tax: 7 percent

THE COTTON HOUSE
Mustique Island, St. Vincent, W.I.

More charming than grand, the Cotton House is neither intimidating nor formal, despite its role as snooty Mustique's only hotel of note. Rather, it has the appeal of an English country inn set on manicured shores, where everything is veddy nice.

Opened in 1977, almost two decades after Colin Tennant bought Mustique and began developing it as a private tropical paradise for his royal and ritzy pals, The Cotton House was created out of the ruins of the stone and coral buildings of an eighteenth-century sugar and cotton plantation. The lovely two-story stone main house, originally the warehouse, was the brainchild of the famous British theater designer Oliver Messel, whose genius created many of the posh houses on Mustique.

The main house, with its refined proportions, is highlighted by cedar shutters and arched louvered doors. It's ringed with wide, breezy verandas where afternoon tea and candlelit dinners are served. A handsome horseshoe-shaped wooden bar is at the entrance to the large salon with high-peaked, wood-beamed ceilings; the salon, or Great Room, is lavished with antiques and amusing accoutrements. There's a piano for occasional entertainment and guests' enjoyment. About a third of the lounge is given over to the dining room so that guests have a choice of dining inside or out on the veranda. In either case they enjoy the fine creations of French-born executive chef Jean-Jacques Uge, who spent several years at famous European restaurants and was the personal chef of the French prime minister at his residence before coming to The Cotton House.

The lounge, bar, and dining veranda have been rejuvenated as part of a major renovation of the entire property. The furnishings were painstakingly preserved, and the original fabric designs by Oliver Messel copied and freshened.

A small reception area at the back of the house is flanked by a bulletin board bearing various announcements and ads for charter boats offering day (and longer) sails. Just above and behind the main complex is the Messel-designed swimming pool area, nestled in what appear to be Romanesque ruins or perhaps a theater backdrop (actually the former site of nothing grander than a chicken coop).

Here, lunch is served during the off sea-son alfresco under a covered colonnade that's only somewhat protected from the bold black-birds (West Indian grackles) by a nearly invisible net, which they negotiate easily. Entire slices of toast are spirited away while guests gaze over the pool or more distant countryside. A breezy bar in the corner, separating the lounge from the eating area, serves fresh and surprisingly powerful papaya and mango punches until late afternoon, when the main house's bar opens.

Accommodations are in two Georgian-style buildings, and known as the Grenadine Suites, with two upper and two garden-level deluxe accommodations with private verandas, which look out at the ocean and the gardens colored with hibiscus and bougainvillea, and are connected by French doors from the bedroom and living room. Two other buildings, each with four deluxe Messel rooms, are furnished with the original Oliver Messel furnishings; and three newer Grenadine cottages climb the steps to the pool. Most of the rooms and suites are furnished with a king-size bed draped in mosquito netting and have large marble bathrooms, usually with tub and shower.

The attractive and understated interior decor uses earth tones and white pickled-wood furniture; rooms are equipped

with CD stereos, fully stocked minibars, and air-conditioning and ceiling fans. For many people the ceiling fans and cross ventilation provided by the louvered windows suffice. Most rooms have cream-colored tile floors and marble-composite bathrooms. Some of the smaller rooms were joined to create suites. All rooms have a terrace or patio.

Five rooms and suites opened in 1997 in the restored Coutinot House add more variety to the resort's accommodations. This house, a short way from the main house, is only steps from the sea, with a private path leading to a secluded beach. The rooms, offering the ultimate in privacy and panoramic sea views, contain writing desks, armoires, full dressing rooms, and wrought-iron, four-poster beds. The large bathrooms have separate tubs and showers; the landscaped gardens directly outside add privacy and an indoor-outdoor effect. Tubs are strategically positioned for great views of the Caribbean and Grenadine Islands beyond. Each guest room has a wraparound terrace, ideal for watching the fabulous sunsets. The Tower, a suite on the second floor, has two oversize sundecks and a private entrance via the original house tower. You can book rooms in Coutinot House individually or book the entire house. Prices include all meals, beverages (including wine, champagne, beer, and house cocktails), afternoon tea, water sports, tennis, and Cotton House amenities and services.

The Cotton House has two tennis courts and is set between two of the white-sand beaches that scallop the island. It has Sunfish, windsurfers, and other water-sports equipment, and the dive shop offers a resort course and PADI certification. Snorkeling within swimming distance from shore at Endeavor Bay Beach is terrific. Deep-sea fishing and sailing excursions to nearby islands can be arranged. Only a short walk from the main house is a bird sanctuary; hiking almost anywhere on Mustique rewards you with outstanding views. The latest addition is a spa offering facials and massage and a selection of body treatments.

Cotton House guests are greeted by a resort representative in Barbados for their air transfer to Mustique. Upon arrival on the island, they are welcomed by the resort's director of guest relations, who escorts them to the resort and to their rooms. The housekeeping staff will unpack and press all clothing on your day of arrival at no charge. For those traveling with children, there's a full-time nanny.

The Mustique Company, the island's development concern, which also handles the rental and sales of homes, usually hosts a party for homeowners—often prospective ones—and guests to meet. Some of the other guests will be honeymooners; others will be globetrotters, as likely to hail from Europe and South America as from the United States.

The Cotton House ✱✱✱

Box 349, Mustique Island, St. Vincent, W.I.
Phone: (784) 456-4777, (877) 240-9945; Fax: (784) 456-5887; e-mail: cottonhouse@caribsurf.com; www.cottonhouse.net

Owner: The Mustique Company
General Manager: Olivier Sevestre
Open: Year-round except late August–mid-October
Credit Cards: All major
U.S. Reservations: Direct to hotel, (877) 240-9945, or Crown International, (800) 628-8929
Deposit: Three nights; twenty-one days cancellation
Minimum Stay: Seven nights during Christmas with 50 percent deposit upon reservation confirmation; five nights in February
Arrival/Departure: Complimentary transfer arranged
Distance from Airport: 1 mile; transfer included in hotel rate
Accommodations: 20 rooms and suites
Amenities: Air-conditioning, ceiling fans; telephone; bath with tub and shower, hair dryer, basket of toiletries; ice service, minibar; nightly turndown service, room service 7:00 A.M.–11:00 P.M.; television on request; unpacking/pressing service upon arrival
Electricity: 220 volts
Fitness Facilities/Spa Services: European mini-spa
Sports: Freshwater swimming pool; hammocks on beach; free use of two tennis courts; snorkeling gear, windsurfing, kayaks, deep-sea fishing, horseback riding, diving arranged for charge
Dress Code: Casual by day; casually elegant in evening
Children: All ages; none under eight in dining room after 7:30 P.M.; children's menus; baby-sitters
Meetings: Up to fifteen people
Day Visitors: No
Handicapped: No facilities
Packages: Dive; honeymoon; resort and sail combination
Rates: Per room, double, daily, MAP. *High Season* (mid-December–mid-April): $750–$1,250. *Low Season* (late April–mid-December): $530–$1,000.
Service Charge: 10 percent
Government Tax: 7 percent

PALM ISLAND BEACH CLUB
Palm Island, St. Vincent, W.I.

In March 1999 Palm Island was purchased by Rob Barrett, the owner of Galley Bay and the St. James Club in Antigua, who closed the hotel for renovations. By the time the hotel reopened in January 2000, Palm Island was practically a new resort.

The 135-acre private island, located at the southern end of The Grenadines, was originally turned into a resort by the late John Caldwell, the Johnny Appleseed of the Caribbean. When he came upon the island, it was an uninhabited, mosquito-infested swamp that Caldwell remade as his own private paradise. But then probably anything seemed easy after he had sailed 8,500 miles alone in a small boat from Panama to Australia to find and marry his Mary, separated from him by World War II—a story he described in his book *Desperate Voyage*.

Caldwell obtained the island from the government of St. Vincent for a $1.00 annual fee and a ninety-nine-year lease and promptly changed the name from Prune (who would believe an island called Prune was paradise?). Over the course of several decades, he planted thousands of coconut palms all over the island (and neighboring islands), earning himself the title of Coconut Johnny. The palms grew into the magnificent specimens that sway in everyone's daydreams and dot the resort's pure white beaches and undulating interior. Caldwell also planted every species of Caribbean tree that blossoms or bears fruit—all attracting an enormous variety of birds and turning Palm Island into a veritable, if not an official, nature preserve and wildlife refuge.

Palm Island, scalloped with five white-sand beaches, has a new free-form freshwater swimming pool with waterfalls, a game room, two restaurants, two bars, and a boutique. There are twenty-eight newly constructed deluxe guest rooms and four Ocean Palms rooms; all are decorated to reflect the laid-back ambience of The Grenadines. All have balconies or patios, air-conditioning, ceiling fans, and louvered windows, and most have a king-size bed. The custom-designed rattan and bamboo furniture is accompanied by brightly colored bedspreads and curtains and original artwork created by a resident Palm Island artist. The amenities include a safe, mini-fridge, basket of toiletries, bathrobes, nightly turndown service, and room service for continental breakfast and afternoon tea.

The resort has several types of rooms. Palm View rooms, located a few yards from the beach, overlook the tropical gardens. The Plantation House, a two-story building with wraparound balcony, has four suites (two upstairs and two down). Each is furnished with two queen-size beds plus a pullout couch, and has a large balcony or patio and a private bath. These rooms are particularly suited for a small family. The spacious Beach Front

rooms have an additional living area and patio, only steps from the clearest, purest aqua stretch of Caribbean water ever to lap a beach; mountainous Union Island and other nearby islands float on the horizon.

The Grenadines Restaurant serves breakfast, lunch, and dinner, while the smaller Yacht Club Restaurant, with its own bar, offers grilled fare in a casual beachside setting. Also, you should know that Palm Island has long been a popular stop for yachties, who enliven the social scene at the bar and often stay for dinner. Some guests might object to the intrusion, but most welcome the new faces and old salts, so long as there aren't too many of them.

Topping the list of activities is the superb snorkeling for which the island is known. It is surrounded by reefs, most within wading distance or a short swim from shore. A day trip to the nearby Tobago Cays National Marine Park is an absolute must and is included in the inclusive price. These uninhabited islets, surrounded by water so brightly turquoise it almost hurts your eyes, offer some of the best snorkeling in the Western Hemisphere. The water is shallow and so clear that snorkeling gear isn't even necessary to see most of it.

Palm Island operates as an all-inclusive resort, one of the few on its own private island in the Caribbean. Breakfast, lunch, dinner, and all drinks are included in the rates, as is the use of sports facilities, equipment, and instruction—table tennis, horseshoes, open-air fitness center, walking trails, tennis, bicycles, and nonmotorized water sports such as kayaking, windsurfing, sailing, snorkeling, and reef fishing. Scuba excursions, deep-sea fishing, and boat charters can arranged for an additional charge.

The new Palm Island is different from its predecessor. Some will be happy with its updated rooms and amenities; others may long for the basic old Palm. Yet all would likely agree that this pristine island has a spectacularly beautiful setting.

Palm Island Beach Club ★★★

St. Vincent, W.I.
Phone: (784) 458–8824; Fax: (784) 458–8804;
e-mail: res@palmislandresorts.com; www.palmislandresorts.com
Mailing address: 6401 Congress Avenue, Suite 100, Boca Raton, FL 33487

Owner: Rob Barrett

General Manager: Julian Waterer

Open: Year-round

Credit Cards: All major

U.S. Reservations: (800) 345–0356; (954) 481–8787; Fax: (954) 481–1661, (561) 994–6344

Deposit: Three nights; twenty-one days cancellation

Minimum Stay: None

Arrival/Departure: Fifty-minute flight (daily) from Barbados to Union Island (complimentary with seven-night stay); there guests met by Palm Island representative and transfered by golf cart to dock to board Lady Palm for ten-minute boat ride to island. Air reservations handled by Palm Island's reservation office.

Distance from Airport: *(Union Airport)* 1 mile

Accommodations: 40 rooms with balconies or patios and king-size beds; four suites with two queen-size beds in two-story building with wraparound balcony

Amenities: Air-conditioning, ceiling fans; radio; mini-fridge, coffeemaker; bath with shower only, hair dryer, toiletries

Electricity: 110 volts

Sports: Five beaches, free-form freshwater swimming pool, tennis, nature trails, nonmotorized water sports

Dress Code: Smartly casual

Children: All ages

Meetings: No

Day Visitors: No

Handicapped: Limited facilities

Packages: Honeymoon

Rates: Per room, two people, daily, all-inclusive. *High Season* (mid-December–mid-April): $680–$910. *Low Season* (mid-April–mid-December): $560– $690.

Service Charge: Included

Government Tax: Included

PETIT ST. VINCENT RESORT

Petit St. Vincent, St. Vincent, W.I.

If you've ever fantasized about owning your own private tropical island—complete with invisible elves to cook, clean, and bring you drinks in your ultracomfy abode—start packing.

Haze Richardson is one of those rare individuals who did more than fantasize: He reclaimed what was basically an uninhabited 113-acre speck of land in the middle of nowhere and over twenty years turned it into one of the premier private-isle resorts in the Caribbean.

Other resorts may be more stylish and manicured, prettier and more lush, but only on Petit St. Vincent (pronounced PET-ty St. Vincent, or just PSV to cognoscenti) can you live out your dream of being all alone, in casual luxury, beyond the reach of time and care in the middle of an aqua sea. You and your significant other can easily spend a week on PSV without ever having to see another human being. You can even miss the manager's cocktail party and no one will bat an eye. But you might not want to miss the local string band from Petit Martinique, or the little band from Carriacou that comes with fiddle, guitars, quatro, and steel pans, or the steel band from Union on Saturday nights.

Then, too, what is paradise to some could drive others to the brink within twenty-four hours. PSV has no town, there's no local bar to repair to, and your fellow guests—while nothing if not well bred and polite—won't be around to socialize. You'll spot other houses, but only in the distance. So be sure you can handle it. PSV is a haven for honeymooners and harried tycoons (few others can afford it) who expect superior service, security, peace, and privacy—and private beaches outside their widely spaced stone houses.

Yes, houses. The accommodations on PSV aren't suites or even bungalows: They are full-size houses. Built of bluebitch stone with wood-beamed roofs and large windows, they have a spacious living room with two daybeds; oversize bathrooms with large vanities, dressing room, and rock showers; big bedrooms with two queen-size beds; ceramic tile floors; and patios. Large windows and sliding doors look out on foliage and sea views. The houses are furnished with tasteful, very comfortable couches and chairs, upholstered in neutral tones. All of the accommodations are renovated with new fabrics and furniture from time to time to keep them fresh and, recently, some entryways were made more attractive by replacing the concrete with patterned brick. Also, greater emphasis has been placed on the gardens, with flowering plants by every cottage and in public areas.

Small, secluded beaches are only steps from the door of most houses, but be warned: Windy Point is aptly named—the wind gusts can be enough to awaken even heavy sleepers.

Though room rates do not vary by type, there are definite variations among rooms. Those on hills and promontories are more secluded and offer the grandest views, while those on the beach are closer together. Six cottages are especially suited to families or groups of friends, because they offer larger living rooms separated from bedrooms by patios, with baths off both living rooms and bedrooms.

Meals are served in The Pavilion, the open-air dining and bar area near the dock, or in the smaller pavilion, but many guests prefer room service—and it is room service like no other. You signal your needs by raising the yellow flag outside your door; staff members, who putt-putt continuously around the island in mini-mokes, take your written or spoken order for food, drink, or whatever else you fancy.

Guests are the only ones on Caribbean time; service is swift (there is a ratio of two staff members per guest), assuming you haven't raised your red flag mistakenly in the interim. Red flags mean "leave me alone," and PSV

personnel have strict orders not to bother you for any reason when they see one.

Should you care to venture beyond your own patch of paradise, there is a lighted tennis court, newly resurfaced with Astroturf, and a jogging and fitness trail that winds around the island. When that becomes too tiring, you'll find hammocks under thatched canopies thoughtfully placed every 100 yards or so along the beach. A day by the beach has proven so popular with guests that they can order a box lunch and thermos of cold water to be brought to them. A new building with shower and toilet has also been added there for guests' convenience. The thatched canopies on the west beach each have a dining table, two chairs, and two chaise lounges, and a small cocktail table.

PSV does not have a spa, but it will call in an esthetician from neighboring Carriacou for facials and massage upon request.

Water sports? Most—windsurfers, ocean kayaks, "spyaks" for reef viewing, Sailfish lessons—are included in the rates. Scuba diving and waterskiing are extra. If island living has gotten into your blood and even a house seems too civilized, you can live out your shipwreck fantasies in style. PSV will arrange a boat to drop you on a tiny island of blinding white sand, in turquoise water even more blinding. It looks unreal, with nothing on it but a thatched umbrella for shade. The islet's official name is Mopion; guests prefer to call it Petit St. Richardson.

PSV serves some of the best food in the Caribbean, occasionally with a West Indian flavor. Richardson imports supplies almost daily from the States (filets mignons, duck, wines, fresh produce), and the chef does wonderful things with them. After dinner, brandy, Scrabble, conversation, or a bit of music on the resident piano, a moke will drive you home. Or you can stroll your way home, flashlight in hand, perhaps accompanied by one of Haze's many yellow Labrador retrievers. Then enjoy a moonlight swim—and don't forget to hoist the red flag, darling, while I open the champagne.

Petit St. Vincent Resort ✱✱✱

Petit St. Vincent, St. Vincent, W.I.
Phone: (784) 458–8801; Fax: (784) 458–8428;
e-mail: psv@fuse.net; www.psvresort.com

Owner/Manager: Haze Richardson
Open: Year-round except September–October
Credit Cards: All major, but cash, personal checks preferred
U.S. Reservations: Petit St. Vincent, P.O. Box 12506, Cincinnati, OH 45212; (513) 242–1333, (800) 654–9326; Fax. (513) 242–6951; e-mail: psv@fuse.net
Deposit: Three nights; thirty days cancellation
Minimum Stay: None
Arrival/Departure: Complimentary transfer arranged by boat only; on Union Island PSV picks up guests who arrive by small plane from Barbados or St. Vincent or private charter.
Distance from Airport: *(Union Airport)* 4 miles
Accommodations: 22 in villas with patios; doubles with two queen-size beds
Amenities: Ceiling fans; bath with shower, hair dryer, basket of toiletries, bathrobe; minibar; beach bags, umbrellas; flashlights; ice service, nightly turndown service, room service 7:30 A.M.–9:30 P.M.; no air-conditioning, telephone, television
Electricity: 110 volts
Fitness Facilities/Spa Services: Masseuse from nearby Carriacou by appointment for fee
Sports: One tennis court; Sunfish and Hobie Cat sailing, snorkeling gear, ocean kayaks, spyaks, windsurfing free; diving, waterskiing, deep-sea fishing, charter boat sailing for charge
Dress Code: Casual by day; elegantly casual in evening
Children: All ages; cribs; high chairs; baby-sitters
Meetings: No
Day Visitors: No
Handicapped: Limited facilities
Packages: Summer
Rates: Per room, two people, daily, FAP. *High Season* (mid-December–mid-March): $915. *Shoulder Season* (mid-March–mid-April): $745. *Low Season* (November 1–mid-December and mid-April–August 15): $585.
Service Charge: 10 percent
Government Tax: 7 percent

Trinidad and Tobago

Different yet similar, this island duet is the ultimate Caribbean kaleidoscope: A mélange of Europeans, Africans, and Asians has woven intricate cultural patterns into a tapestry of fabulous flora and fauna.

The birthplace of calypso and steel bands, Trinidad is the country's banking and trading center; its visitors are more interested in business than beaches. Twenty-two miles to the northeast lies tiny Tobago, an island so lavishly beautiful and serene that it makes even the most severe Caribbean cynic smile.

The mating of Trinidad and Tobago is a bit of a historical irony. Columbus discovered Trinidad on his third voyage and named it for three southern mountain peaks symbolizing to him the Holy Trinity. The Spaniards held the island for three centuries until they were unseated by the British in 1797. But Tobago, because of its strategic location, was so prized by Europeans that it changed hands fourteen times. Finally, in 1889, Tobago asked to become a part of Trinidad; they became independent in 1962.

Trinidad has gone through the oil boom and bust. At the heart of Port-of-Spain, the capital, Victorian architectural relics give it a distinctive character. It has an interesting zoo, botanic gardens, and restaurants featuring local cuisine that reflects the country's West Indian, East Indian, and Chinese components.

Trinidad explodes once a year in Carnival, the granddaddy of all Caribbean Carnivals. The balance of the year, it offers tennis, golf, art galleries and museums in historic buildings, antiques in offbeat shops, and a music- and dance-filled nightlife.

The most southerly of the Caribbean island states, Trinidad is only 7 miles off the coast of Venezuela and was originally part of the South American mainland. As a result its flora and fauna include many South American species not seen elsewhere in the Caribbean. It also has such strange natural features as mud volcanoes and an asphalt lake.

But of all its natural wonders, the most spectacular is the bird life. More than 425 species from North and South America and the Caribbean meet here in the forested mountains and mangroves. Of special note is the nightly sunset arrival of hundreds of scarlet ibises, the national bird, to roost in a sanctuary of the Caroni Swamp only 7 miles south of the capital. Guided boat trips through the swamp end where the birds return daily.

Information
Trinidad and Tobago Tourism Development Authority,
(888) 595–4TNT; www.visitTNT.com

ASA WRIGHT NATURE CENTRE
Port-of-Spain, Trinidad, W.I.

Deep in a rain forest on the slopes of the Northern Range at 1,200 feet overlooking the Arima Valley is the Asa Wright Nature Centre, a bird sanctuary and wildlife reserve with an inn. Built about 1906, the inn is in the Victorian estate house of the former coffee, citrus, and cocoa plantation, now mostly returned to the wild. It is surrounded by dense tropical vegetation; sitting on its veranda is like being in an aviary, except that the birds come and go freely from the surrounding rain forest.

The Centre, a private institution unique in the Caribbean, was established in 1967 on the Spring Hill Estate by its owner, Asa Wright, an Icelandic-born Englishwoman whose rugged manner may have helped give rise to many tall tales about her. She acquired the 197-acre property upon the death of her husband and was persuaded by naturalist friends to create a nonprofit trust to preserve the area and make it a study and recreation center.

The inn is rustic but comfortable; services are minimal. Most of the rooms are in bungalows, furnished with a bureau, desk, chair, and reading lamp and have attractive bedcovers and curtains; all have private bath. The rooms also have screened porches or outside areas where you can enjoy the birds and the great outdoors in privacy.

At the entrance to the manor house, beyond the office where useful nature books can be purchased, are the main house's two bedrooms. Directly on, a hallway leads into the parlor and, to one side, the dining room. Both rooms are comfortably furnished in a traditional, homey manner as they might have been in their plantation days. On the veranda outside the parlor, guests gather for afternoon tea and at other times to watch birds, as well as nightly before dinner for the inn's complimentary rum punch.

All meals, fresh and hearty, are served in the dining

room family-style. The tables even have lazy Susans in the center for diners to help themselves. The kitchen will prepare picnic baskets if you want to spend the day hiking and birding or drive to the beach on Trinidad's Caribbean northern coast.

Natural history programs with slides, lectures, and videos are usually scheduled in the evening. But by evening, after an active and exhilarating day with nature, you will probably be happy to go quietly off to bed.

The Centre has its own guides and five hiking trails, which day visitors may also use for a small fee. The trails, ranging from half-hour strolls to difficult three-hour hikes, are designed to maximize viewing of particular species. Maps are available for self-guided forays into the rain forest.

With ease you will see tanagers, thrushes, trogons, blue-crowned motmots, many species of hummingbirds, the beautiful crested oropendola, and dozens of other bird species. The trails pass through magnificent rain forest; the upper-story canopy is often more than 100 feet above you. North of the Centre are other trails at 1,800 feet, where you can spot species that prefer high elevations. Generally the best time to see the greatest variety of birds is from December to March.

The most celebrated species at Asa Wright is a nesting colony of oilbirds, which make their home in a cave located on the property. This rare bird is found only here and in northern South America. The site can be visited only with a guide.

While the inn takes guests on an individual basis, most people staying here are likely to be part of a natural history or birding group from the United States, Canada, Britain, or Germany. The Asa Wright Centre is unique, though obviously not for everyone. For bird-watchers, naturalists, and hikers, it's nirvana. And I believe this quiet, friendly inn should also appeal to anyone—age fourteen to ninety-four—who is a true nature lover.

Asa Wright Nature Centre (S)

P.O. Box 10, Port-of-Spain, Trinidad, W.I.
Phone: (868) 622–7480 (for messages only); Fax: (868) 667–0493;
e-mail: asawright@caligo.com; www.asawright.org

Owner: Asa Wright Nature Centre
General Manager: Louis Julien
Open: Year-round
Credit Cards: None
U.S. Reservations: Caligo Ventures, 156 Bedford Road, Armonk, NY 10504; (914) 273–6333, (800) 426–7781; Fax: (914) 273–6370
Deposit: $100 per person
Minimum Stay: None
Arrival/Departure: Transfer service arranged for fee
Distance from Airport: One-and-a-half-hour drive; taxi one-way, $20
Distance from Port-of-Spain: Two-hour drive. From Arima: 71/2 miles (thirty minutes); taxi one-way, approximately $10
Accommodations: 25 rooms, most with terraces (two in main building, 21 in bungalows; 19 with twins, two with kings, three singles)
Amenities: Ceiling fans; bath with shower only; no room service, phones, television, radios, air-conditioning
Electricity: 110 volts
Sports: No facilities; natural pool for wading; Caribbean coastal beaches less than an hour's drive
Dress Code: Very casual
Children: Over fourteen years of age
Meetings: Up to fifty people
Day Visitors: Yes
Handicapped: Very limited facilities
Packages: Natural history and birding tours
Rates: Per person, daily, AP. *High Season* (mid-December–mid-April): $105 (double), $139 (single). *Low Season:* $80 and $106, respectively.
Service Charge: Included
Government Tax: Included

HILTON TRINIDAD
Port-of-Spain, Trinidad, W.I.

A Port-of-Spain landmark since it opened in 1962, the upside-down Hilton has the best views in town and ringside seats for Trinidad's famous Carnival staged at the Queen's Park Savannah, which stretches at the hotel's feet.

Built into a hillside, the dramatic design climbs the hill to the top where you will find the lobby after you, too, have climbed the circular driveway that leads to the entrance. From the lobby at the top, the rooms step down the hillside. It may be a bit confusing when you get into the elevator and push the down button to go to your room on the eighth floor, or push the up button to return to the lobby. But it doesn't take long to get adjusted, particularly when you discover the rewards of the innovative architecture. From the terrace of the lobby, en route to the guest-room wings, you get a spectacular view over Port-of-Spain and the Gulf of Paria.

Business travelers make up the majority of guests at the Trinidad Hilton, as is the case of most city-center Hiltons, and the hotel is geared to them. But this hotel is also the preferred place for tourists who can afford it—although given the price of comparable Caribbean hotels, it would be unfair to leave the impression that the Trinidad

Hilton is expensive. What's more, it is one of the few hotels in the Caribbean that does not raise its rates during the winter months, except for five days during Carnival week. In addition to its hillside perch, the Trinidad Hilton has a wonderful central location within walking distance of many of the capital's main attractions. Steps through the gardens on the park side take you directly to the Savannah, and from there you can walk to a museum and art gallery, botanic gardens, and the zoo, among other attractions. The staff throughout the hotel is pleasant and helpful, and the convenient hotel shops include branches of the main duty-free stores at the port and airport.

The Trinidad Hilton may have the best seats in town for Carnival, but that's really not the ideal time to be a guest here, and certainly not the time to judge it. During Carnival week the hotel is bursting at the seams with revelers, and unless you are as revved up as they are, you may not think it's much fun at all.

At other times, however, the Trinidad Hilton is truly an oasis in the city, with twenty-five acres of beautiful gardens under the spreading arms of huge flamboyants, poui, jacaranda, and other flowering tropical trees. It has

a large swimming pool in a garden setting, tennis courts, and a small health club.

The rooms, which were updated over the last several years, now sport a new look with pastel, Caribbean-print bedspreads and curtains. They have been equipped with safes and voice mail phones, along with the comforts people have come to expect from the international chain. Eco-friendly soap and shampoo dispensers were installed in the bathrooms. Four Presidential Suites were created, each with a Jacuzzi, private kitchen, and bar. All rooms have balconies, most with good views either of the Savannah, the gardens and pool, the Northern Mountains, or the Gulf of Paria. Some on the lower floors (lower to the ground, that is) are up against the hill and heavy foliage and don't look out at much of anything. Rates do vary with the view.

Two executive floors with a lounge cater to business travelers with extra amenities, including an airport meeting service, preregistration, rapid check-in and check-out, and complimentary continental breakfast and cocktails. The hotel has the best meeting facilities in the city and twenty-four-hour taxi service.

A staircase in the lobby winds down into an informal restaurant, a high-ceilinged, airy, and air-conditioned room where breakfast buffets and a la carte menus are available. La Boucan, the main dining room, is more formal and serves local and international fare. Be sure to try callaloo soup, a Trinidad favorite. Every Monday night a poolside fiesta buffet features local cuisine along with local entertainment including steel band and calypso music.

The Gazebo Bar poolside and the Carnival Bar are popular rendezvous spots for Trinidadians as much as for visitors. The Carnival Bar features live bands and dancing on the weekends. Trinidad, should you forget, was the birthplace of calypso and the steel drum.

Hilton Trinidad **

P.O. Box 442, Port-of-Spain, Trinidad, W.I.
Phone: (868) 624–3211; Fax: (868) 624–4485;
e-mail: hiltonpos@wow.net; www.hilton.com

Owner: Trinidad and Tobago government
General Manager: Ali Khan
Open: Year-round
Credit Cards: All major
U.S. Reservations: Hilton Reservation Service, (800) HILTONS
Deposit: One night; inquire for Carnival.
Minimum Stay: None; inquire for Carnival.
Arrival/Departure: Airport meeting service available on request
Distance from Airport: 17 miles; taxi one-way, $20 day, $30 night
Distance from Port-of-Spain: 1 mile to port; taxi one-way, $7.00
Accommodations: 394 rooms and suites with balconies (including 23 king, 236 twins, 175 queen; 57 executive-floor rooms)
Amenities: Air-conditioning; direct-dial telephone, cable television, radio; bath with tub and shower; minibar in some rooms; safes; executive floor and lounge, business services; room service 6:00 A.M.–11:30 P.M.; shops; business center
Electricity: 110 volts
Fitness Facilities/Spa Services: Health club with sauna and massage
Sports: Freshwater swimming pool; two lighted Chevron Cushion tennis courts, free to hotel guests during day, nominal charge for evening, proper tennis attire required, racquets for rental, instruction available; golf, boating, snorkeling, scuba, deep-sea fishing, hiking, birding arranged; botanic gardens and zoo nearby
Dress Code: City casual
Children: All ages; cribs, high chairs; baby-sitters; no charge for children sharing room with parent, with maximum three people occupying room
Meetings: Up to 1,200 people
Day Visitors: Yes
Handicapped: Facilities and two rooms
Packages: Golf, Carnival
Rates: Per room, double, daily, EP. *Year-Round* (except during Carnival), standard, $195–$236; deluxe, $205–$246; Executive Floor, $226–$267. Carnival (February 28–March 4, 2003), $290–$340.
Service Charge/Government Tax: 21.5 percent
Utility Surcharge: $1.95 per day

Turks and Caicos Islands

A diver's paradise lying at the end of the Bahamas chain, the Turks and Caicos (pronounced KAY-kos) have been dubbed the Caribbean's Last Frontier. A British Crown Colony made up of eight islands and several dozen cays, the islands stretch across 90 miles in two groups separated by the Turks Island Passage, a deep-water channel of 22 miles.

To the east is the Turks group, which has Grand Turk, the capital with about half of the colony's population of 8,000; and neighboring Salt Cay, an old settlement with windmills and salt ponds, declared a Heritage Site under UNESCO's World Heritage program.

To the west are the Caicos Islands—South, Middle, North—which form an arch on the northern side of Caicos Bank. The small archipelago is surrounded by virgin reefs, most uncharted. Provo, as Providenciales is known, is the commercial center and the site of most of the resort and commercial development. North of Provo is Pine Cay, home of the Meridian Club.

The islands are not richly blessed with tropical vegetation, but they do have a surprising variety of flora. Coconut palms, casuarinas, sea grapes, and palmettos give them a rugged, windswept beauty. Middle Caicos and North Caicos have fertile soil with lush patches of citrus and fruit trees.

The islands have some exceptional natural attractions: almost 200 miles of untouched beaches, acres of tropical wilderness and wetlands, and magnificent seas with some of the most spectacular marine life in the world. Several locations are national parks and bird sanctuaries (two islets in the Turks and eight locations in the Caicos), and a nature lover's paradise.

Grand Turk is a long, skinny island of 9 square miles along the Turks Island Passage. This and Salt Cay are great places for whale-watching in spring and autumn, when the passage becomes a thoroughfare for migratory humpback whales and giant manta rays.

Information

Turks and Caicos Islands Tourist Board, 11645 Biscayne Boulevard, Suite 302, North Miami, FL 33181; (800) 241–0824, (305) 891–4117; Fax: (305) 891–7096; e-mail: tci.tourism@caribsurf.com; www.turksandcaicostourism.com

GRACE BAY CLUB
Providenciales, Turks and Caicos Islands, B.W.I.

Situated on one of the most beautiful beaches in the world—powdery porcelain sands that run for 12 uninterrupted miles washed by gorgeous, reef-filled turquoise waters, with slightly more than six acres fronting 750 feet of the pristine shore—the Grace Bay club designed a hideaway that is elegant yet casual, sumptuous yet understated and refined.

The Grace Bay Club is designed for affluent, sophisticated international travelers who appreciate quality along with tranquillity. It was the first luxury resort to open on Provo (Providenciales on the map), and although there are others popping up on this newly discovered island, there's little likelihood that any of the new ones will match this impeccably designed and superbly maintained beauty by the bay.

Set in gardens on the beach, the Grace Bay Club suggests a gracious Spanish village in stucco the color of the late-afternoon sun. Red tile roofs at staggered levels, terra-cotta floors, stone balustrades, wrought-iron balconies, and shaded terraces are interlaced with lush courtyards, splashing fountains, and arched pathways framed in bright bougainvillea. The graceful setting is enhanced by elaborate landscaping and hidden corners heady with exotic fragrances.

No two suites are alike, and little seems squared or symmetrical in the free-form, three-story main building. The accommodations range from 700-square-foot studios to 1,700-square-foot two-bedroom penthouses, some with lofts and roof terraces.

The most extraordinary are the vast, pie-shaped luxury suites with wraparound views to die for. Ground-floor units boast patios with private solariums and paths leading to the beach, all hidden from view in a fragrant feat of tropical landscaping.

One-bedroom suites contain two bathrooms, and two-bedroom suites have three, all done up in decorative Mexican tile. Master baths are replete with dual vanities, marbled Roman tubs, and separate toilets. The suites are self-contained retreats in every respect—oceanfront terrace or patio, full kitchen with sit-down bar, refrigerator with icemaker, microwave, dishwasher, and washer and dryer (and even detergent!). All accommodations have air-conditioning and a ceiling fan, a direct-dial phone, cable television with thirty-two channels, and a VCR.

Part of the resort's allure is its entirely distinctive decor. Furniture in rattan and wicker comes from Thailand and the Philippines; handcrafted wooden armoires, tables, and mirrors hail from Mexico and Guatemala; carpets are imported from Turkey and Spain; and art and pottery are products of Haiti, Mexico, Brazil, and Thailand. Most paintings were framed by a Cuban in Florida, who often matched the wooden frames to the exact colors from the works. Such attention to detail adds to the charm of Grace Bay, a charm that most resorts never achieve.

The resort's boutique is in a separate building, which also houses the Grace Bay offices and an attractive open-sided reception area where guests sign in at a massive Brazilian desk—one that you would love to take home.

Another design masterpiece is the Anacaona Restaurant, named for the Lucayan Indian goddess (her name means "flower of gold"). It consists of patrician palapas strung along the beach. In the evening, tiki torches cast a romantic glow, enhanced by flickering candlelight from each table. The rustle of palm fronds is punctuated by the jungle cry of tree frogs and the occasional coo of a ground dove.

The main palapa's thatched roof (built by Seminole Indians from Florida) is supported by a ring of classic white columns, reminiscent of a sort of tropical Temple of the Vestal Virgins, and arranged on four levels. Some are tiled, some wooden, so that diners on each have front-row views of the tranquil turquoise-turned-lavender-turned-silver waters of Grace Bay, framed by floodlit palm trees and smoke from the flaming torches.

A well-stocked bar, including a Danish aquavit to accompany the kitchen's smoked fish, occupies another circular palapa next to the restaurant—a favorite haunt of visitors and Provo town residents alike. The "grill" palapa on the other side of the main palapa also serves as a conference room for those who simply must do business.

The restaurant continues to bring to Provo a level of fine dining that few places in the Caribbean can match. Eric Brunel, whose experience includes The Ritz in Paris under chef Guy Legay, offers menus that combine light Mediterranean cuisine with a Caribbean flair. The resort also has a fine wine reserve.

Grace Bay's other amenities include a freshwater swimming pool and Jacuzzi overlooking the beach and two lighted tennis courts. There is a small video and book library as well as backgammon, chess, and other games.

Serenity Spa at Grace Bay Club is the newly designed facility for beauty and health treatments, situated on the second floor of the reception lounge. The spa, operated by two British professionals, has two treatment rooms and offers a wide variety of services, including aromatherapy, massage, reflexology, and some creative ones, such as a Jettison Jet Lag package and numerous ionithermie treatments.

Complimentary windsurfing, Sunfish sailing, and snorkeling gear, along with a full range of water sports and bone-, bottom-, and deep-sea fishing are available. Day sails and small-boat excursions to nearby uninhabited islands are popular. Scuba—some of the best in the Tropics—and golf just across the road can also be arranged.

Grace Bay Club ✶✶✶✶

P.O. Box 128, Providenciales, Turks and Caicos Islands, B.W.I. Phone: (649) 946–5757, (800) 946–5757; Fax: (649) 946–5758; e-mail: www.gracebayclub.com

Owner: Fair Enterprises of Denver

General Manager: Martein van Wagenberg

Open: Year-round except September

Credit Cards: MasterCard, Visa, American Express; personal checks by prior arrangement only

U.S. Reservations: Direct to hotel

Deposit: Three nights; for December 16–January 1, cancellation must be received before November 1

Minimum Stay: Ten nights during Christmas/New Year's

Distance from Airport: 10 miles; airport transfer included

Distance from Business Center: 3 miles

Accommodations: 22 oceanfront suites, all with one or more private terraces or balconies; all with king-size beds (convertible to twins) and queen-size pullout sofa beds

Amenities: Air-conditioning, ceiling fans; direct-dial telephone, thirty-three- channel cable television including CNN, VCR; safe; complete kitchen facility; washer and dryer; twice-daily maid service, nightly turndown service; daily New York Times; bath with tub and shower, bathrobes, hair dryers, and exclusive bath amenities; room service; fax machine on request

Electricity: 110 volts

Fitness Facilities/Spa Services: Massage and beauty treatment services at hotel spa

Sports: Freshwater swimming pool and Jacuzzi; two soft-surface, lighted tennis courts; complimentary water sports including windsurfers, Sunfish sailboats, kayaks, bicycles, snorkeling; scuba diving and private sailing trips aboard the Beluga, a 37-foot catamaran, arranged for additional charge; free shuttle to Provo Golf Club, where guests receive reduced green fees and priority tee times

Dress Code: Casual sportswear by day; elegantly casual in restaurant for dinner; long pants, collared shirts

Children: No children under twelve years old

Meetings: No

Day Visitors: Welcome

Handicapped: No facilities

Packages: Honeymoon, wedding, golf

Rates: Per room, double, daily, CP. *High Season* (mid-December–mid-April): $640–$1,450. *Low Season:* $390–$950. MAP: Add $65 per person.

Service Charge: 10 percent

Government Tax: 9 percent

THE MERIDIAN CLUB ON PINE CAY

Pine Cay, Turks and Caicos Islands, B.W.I.

Since it does not have a telephone and the only way to reach it is by boat or private plane, you could say the Meridian Club is remote and exclusive. But what really sets the resort apart and makes it one of the truly great hideaways is its refreshing simplicity and its wild natural setting along one of the world's most gorgeous beaches.

The small, unpretentious resort belongs to the homeowners of an exclusive residential development on Pine Cay, a privately owned 800-acre Island—about the size of New York's Central Park—floating on spectacularly beautiful aquamarine water between Provo and North Caicos.

Set on 2 uninterrupted miles of pristine white sand washed by clear, languid water, the club is comprised of a clubhouse and clusters of cottages less than a stone's throw from the beach. Some of the private homes also are available for rent. No cars are allowed on the island; you get around on leg power by walking or biking or, when available, by golf cart.

The clubhouse is the reception and social center, with an indoor-outdoor dining room on the first floor and an attractive upstairs lounge with a bar, corner library, and veranda. Guests and homeowners—a well-traveled, well-heeled, and somewhat intellectual group—mingle here nightly for cocktails hosted by the manager and for after-dinner socializing.

The clubhouse opens onto the pool, which has a wide terrace used for breakfast, lunch, and tea, and for barbecues on Wednesday and Saturday night. Dinner, served family-style, is an informal affair in the dining room. The food is good, not gourmet. The resort has a visiting chef program during the season.

The beachfront cottages, powered by solar energy, are connected by a walkway lined in bougainvillea. Most guest rooms are large junior suites, tastefully furnished with off-white rattan and colorful prints. They have a king-size or twin beds, a separate sitting area, a large bathroom with shower, and screened porches facing the beach. Every year the resort does some sprucing up, adding fresh decorating touches to the cottages.

At the end, a bit separate from the group, is a hexagonal cottage that honeymooners like for its privacy. The rustic cottage has stone floors and a tiled bath with an enclosed outdoor shower. It has its own barbecue area and a thatched beach hut just large enough to shade two.

Use of water-sports equipment and daily excursions to

nearby cays for snorkeling are included in the room rate. The snorkeling, with the reefs rich in marine life, is some of the best you will ever find. Bonefishing, which is said to be outstanding in May, is also available, as is deep-sea fishing. The resort also arranges for golfers to play at the Royal Turk Golf Club on Provo.

Several features set the Meridian Club apart from other retreats. The untamed appearance of Pine Cay is the most apparent and the one the homeowners are determined to maintain. Strong-willed environmentalists, they have resisted the temptation to expand and, instead, have converted about two-thirds of the island into a national park. They are equally vigilant about the coral reefs protecting the island.

Covered mostly with dry scrub, Pine Cay has freshwater lakes and gets its name from a type of tree that covers vast areas of the Caicos. It has a nature trail, and any dirt road can be used by birders to spot some of the 120 bird species found here.

The camaraderie between owners and guests is unusual, too. (In most resort developments the residents and resort guests seldom see one another.) The congeniality and high number of repeat visitors are also reflected in the warm relationships between guests and staff members, who, if not polished to Savoy shine, are attentive and caring.

Although the Meridian Club is barefoot living most of the time, it maintains a certain gracious style and civility. Its small size makes it easy for guests to feel at home quickly. In addition to homeowners and their affluent friends, your companions are likely to be professionals, business executives, eastern establishment types, and a titled European or two. Times may be changing, but not on Pine Cay; there are still no cars, and cellular phones are not permitted.

The Meridian Club on Pine Cay ✱✱ 🦋

Pine Cay, Turks and Caicos Islands, B.W.I.
Phone: (212) 696–4566, (800) 331–9154; Fax: (649) 946–5128;
e-mail: rmiresorts@juno.com; www.meridianclub.com

Owner: The Meridian Club
General Managers: Walter and Beverly Plachta
Open: November 1–late June
Credit Cards: None; personal checks accepted
U.S. Reservations: RMI Marketing, (800) 331–9154, (203) 602 0300; Fax. (203) 602–2265
Deposit: Three nights; thirty days cancellation
Minimum Stay: Seven nights during Christmas
Arrival/Departure: For stays of five nights or more, the club provides either boat- or air-taxi transfer at its discretion between Provo and Pine Cay. To have transfers included in room rate, arriving/departing guests must use certain American Airlines flights; inquire from reservations.
Distance from Airport: *(Provo Airport)* 10 miles; taxi to boat dock one-way, $25 (included in room rate); resort has 2,800-foot airstrip used by private planes, small charters, and interisland carriers.
Distance from Provo Town Center: 15 miles
Accommodations: 12 suites in beachfront bungalows; eight one- to four-bedroom cottages, all with terrace or patio; twin beds or king
Amenities: Ceiling fans; bath with shower, basket of toiletries; ice service, nightly turndown service, room service for breakfast; afternoon tea; no air-conditioning, telephone, television, VCR, radio, clock
Electricity: 110 volts/60 cycles
Sports: Freshwater pool; tennis and equipment, bikes, boating, snorkeling and equipment, sailboats, windsurfing included; wilderness trails and birding; deep-sea fishing, bonefishing, tarpon fishing, reef fishing, scuba, and golf on Provo arranged
Dress Code: Always casual
Children: No children under twelve years of age; those under eighteen not allowed in bar after 6:00 P.M. unless accompanied by an adult family member
Meetings: Up to twenty-six people
Day Visitors: No
Handicapped: No facilities
Packages: Hideaway, Shell Seeker
Rates: Two people, daily, AP. *High Season* (mid-December–March 31): $825. *Shoulder Season* (April): $650. *Low Season* (May 1–late June and November 1–mid-December): $585.
Service Charge: 10 percent
Government Tax: 9 percent

PARROT CAY
Providenciales, Turks and Caicos Islands, B.W.I.

Opened for the Christmas holidays in 1998, this secluded, exclusive, private-island hideaway zoomed to the top of the charts as the place to see and be seen almost from the first day, thanks to its well-known, well-heeled owners who have a loyal, and often royal, following, and prices likely to make everyone take notice.

Parrot Cay actually began in the late 1980s, when a wealthy Kuwaiti constructed the resort on the uninhabited islet that came to be known as Parrot Cay. The resort was completed in 1991, furnished, and scheduled to open, but just before the first guests were to arrive, the Gulf War erupted.

Parrot Cay remained shuttered and desolate for the next seven years, when it was purchased by an unlikely twosome, Singaporian Christina Ong—owner of London's Metropolitan and Halkin, two Four Seasons on Bali, and the Four Seasons on London's Canary Wharf—and British entrepreneur Robert Earl, founder of the Hard Rock Cafe and Planet Hollywood restaurants.

They realized the potential and lure of this abandoned getaway rapidly approaching a state of decay, with its almost 3-mile-long ribbon of powdery white-sand beach, bordered by constantly changing hues of crystalline azure waters. The infrastructure was already there; all that was needed was some imagination and an infusion of millions.

And have they ever. When the word got out, the beautiful people and celebrities came running. On a single day in its first spring, Bruce Willis, the Saatchi family of advertising fame, and noted fashion designer Jean Galliano were all in residence in their respective beach suites.

Located on an almost inaccessible 1,000-acre island in the Turks and Caicos, Parrot Cay is elegant in its simplicity. It is designed for those who demand anonymity, yet want to be in the company of trendsetters who must be the first to discover the newest playground.

Aside from the absolute privacy, the lure—especially when you're luxuriating in a beach suite or being indulged by the mainly Malaysian staff—is the aura of casual elegance achieved by British interior designer Keith Hobbs of London's United Designers. His other work includes the Metropolitan Hotel, Nobu Restaurant, and the Armani store in New York.

Hobbs took the elements of traditional colonial decor and artfully blended them with Asian simplicity—four-poster beds and a lavish use of white fabrics, especially gossamer-thin netting around the beds and as closet "doors" and curtains. The effect is romantic and soothing, not to mention sensuous. Teak furniture with woven reed seats and backs in the simplest of Asian lines is everywhere. Decks have a deep teak daybed with a unique tray that brings the coffee table up close, making it ideal to snuggle effortlessly in a corner with a good read.

The main building is an updated version of Caribbean colonial architecture, set high on a hill overlooking the Atlantic on one side and the inlet that separates the cay from the larger island of North Caicos on the other. Hobbs gave the original dark-wood building a lighter look by painting the railings of its multilevel terraces white, set off by the blues and aquas of the water.

From the main building, sited at the top of a 50-foot rise (the highest point of the island), the rooms and suites in two-story, red-tile-roof buildings cascade down the hill toward the sea. Along the beach are the newest cottages, all with one- and two-bedroom suites and by far the most

desirable—and expensive—of Parrot Cay's 116 rooms.

The original swimming pool was covered over and now serves as gigantic flowerpot with five palm trees shading the new zero-entry pool. Alongside are the beach restaurant and bar—and all are only steps from the water's edge. The gentle slope of the pool's bottom along its long side gives you the illusion of walking into the sea. A few steps away near the beachside suites is the fitness center, with a full complement of weights and exercise equipment.

Beyond lie the new duplex one- and two-bedroom beach suites, each with direct access to the beach. The two-bedroom units also have private pools. The most private of all is Pirate House, a three-bedroom villa on a high hill, rebuilt from the ruins of a house once occupied by Parrot Cay's only known resident. It has a private pool and comes with a dedicated staff.

If you must stay in touch with the outside world, multiple international direct-dial phones with dataports are strategically placed in each room and suite, while the daily *New York Times* fax is presented at breakfast. Televisions and VCRs are in the suites and can be placed in standard rooms upon request at no additional charge. Those who desire more entertainment might have an after-dinner drink at the bar or a stroll along the beach in the moonlight. And those who crave unabashed solitude can simply dial up for room service regardless of the hour.

Wending your way to Parrot Cay, like all good things, isn't easy. Scheduled service is available from Miami to Providenciales, or Provo, as it's known by aficionados. After being met by the resort's greeter and assisted into a waiting van, you'll have a ten-minute cab ride to the marina, where the resort's 48-foot high-speed cruiser is ready to whisk you over smooth, translucent, inside-the-reef waters to Parrot Cay, about twenty to thirty minutes.

At the dock you're greeted by the staff and driven in Parrot Cay's version of a stretch limousine—an elongated golf cart (there are no cars on the island)—to the main building, where a chilled face towel and cold drink await you. You'll immediately sense that you've chosen well. From here it's on to your suite or room, where your luggage is already in place.

Life on Parrot Cay is as you please. There are two lighted tennis courts, an armada of small watercraft, a well-stocked library and lounge, and a large, circular bar attended by a twenty-five-year veteran of New York's famed Peacock Alley, Rupert Francis, who will regale you with stories of his experiences with the glitterati before and after dinner—which, by the way, is served in the dining room one floor below.

Add to this Parrot Cay's Asian-style spa, Shambala—where you can be pampered with body treatments of imported herbs, spices, and flowers and enjoy massage techniques and other spa rituals to induce deep relaxation and promote revitalization, along with such Eastern-inspired therapies as chi balancing, Thai and Chinese massage, body realignment, and yoga—and you've got a winner less than two hours from Miami. The prices preclude the wanna-bes, and the location eliminates day trippers. But isn't that what life on a private island is all about . . . privacy, peace, pampering, and, of course, price?

Parrot Cay ★★★★

P.O. Box 143, Providenciales, Turks and Caicos Islands, B.W.I
Phone: (649) 946–7788, (877) 754–0726; Fax: (649) 946–7789;
e-mail: parrot@tciway.tc

Owner: Caicos Holdings
Resident Manager: Nicolas Simmonds
Open: Year-round except September–mid-October
Credit Cards: All major
U.S. Reservations: Crown International, (800) 628–8929
Deposit: 30 percent prepayment; thirty days cancellation
Minimum Stay: Fourteen nights during Christmas season
Arrival/Departure: Transfer from Providenciales Airport included (see text)
Distance from Airport: *(Providenciales Airport)* 5 miles
Accommodations: 55 rooms (14 deluxe garden-view rooms, 29 deluxe ocean-view rooms, four ocean-view suites, six one-bedroom beach house suites, two two-bedroom beach houses with private pools, one three-bedroom villa with pool); four-poster beds
Amenities: Air-conditioning, ceiling fan; direct-dial telephone with dataport; safe; bath with tub and shower, hair dryer; tea and coffeemaker; room service; television, radio, CD players in suites, and in rooms on request; library

Electricity: 110 volts
Fitness Facilities/Spa Services: See text
Sports: Hobie Cats; lighted tennis courts; air-conditioned gym; mountain bikes, nature trail; snorkeling, windsurfing, waterskiing, diving; golf in Provo at additional cost
Dress Code: Smartly casual; trousers requested at dinner
Children: All ages; babysitting
Meetings: No
Day Visitors: No

Handicapped: No facilities
Packages: Romantic getaways; spa
Rates: Per room, per night, FAB. *High Season* (early January–late April): $530–$1,450. *Shoulder Season* (April 17–May 31 and October–December 16): $430–$1,250. *Low Season* (June 1–August 31): $360–$1,150. Two- and three-bedroom villas, inquire.
Service Charge: 10 percent
Government Tax: 9 percent

POINT GRACE

Grace Bay, Providenciales, Turks and Caicos Islands, B.W.I.

Located on Grace Bay at the center of Twelve-Mile Beach, Point Grace fronts one of the most beautiful beaches in the world, protected by the Princess Alexandra Park, a marine reserve on the northern coast of Providenciales. The resort is named for its location, which, in turn, was named for Grace Hutchings, who spent her honeymoon in a cottage here over one hundred years ago.

Point Grace, opened in 2000, is an unusual boutique hotel with thirty ultraluxurious one-, two- and three-bedroom suites and two spectacular one-of-a-kind penthouses. The hotel, designed by Simon Wood, is comprised of two four-story beachfront buildings, each with ten units of two- and three-bedroom suites. All have air-conditioning, ceiling fans, a full kitchen, safe, and washer/dryer. Sliding glass doors lead to large terraces with extensive sea views.

Behind the beachfront buildings in a crescent around a cloverleaf pool are four yellow cottages with white gingerbread trim—replicas of Grace's original honeymoon cottage. One, known as Grace's Cottage, houses the hotel reception and concierge and a lounge where a continuous supply of hot and iced cappuccino, espresso, tea, and fruit are available throughout the day and wine and hors d'oeuvres are served in the early evening. The other cot-

tages have one- and two-bedroom suites, steps away from the pool.

What sets Point Grace apart is the exquisite furnishings—the best money can buy—and the extraordinary attention to detail. Finishes are the highest quality and include large mahogany entry doors to the suites, Turkish marble floors, unusual rust-colored marble vanity tops in the bathroom, and Italian granite countertops in the kitchen.

When you see the kitchens, you may want to move in permanently. Although they are unlikely to see much use by guests, the kitchens have top-of-the-line halogen stoves, two stainless-steel wall oven units, refrigerator with icemaker, stainless steel sink, garbage disposal, and coffeemaker. In the wood-paneled cabinets is a complete set of Villeroy and Bosch tableware plus glass- and stemware for ten. Kitchens can be stocked with groceries in advance.

The interior design, created by Teri D'Amico Interiors and Kraton Gallery, varies from suite to suite, room to room. All have Indonesian hardwood and teak furniture—designed for the hotel and different in every room—brightened with colorful Thai silk and Indonesian batik accents. All have king-size beds (some four-poster), cable television (in several rooms of a suite), as well as CD and DVD players. Color notes against the white walls—usually Impressionist paintings and African tribal art—are well placed.

Spacious bathrooms are finished with hand-painted tiles and mahogany vanity cabinets. Most have a separate shower and bath and double sinks. All have a hair dryer, robes, complimentary Indonesian sarongs, and Ednae bath amenities. Bathrooms have a large supply of thick towels and you sleep on the highest quality Frette cotton sheets and bedcovers. The nightly turndown service is unlike any other—a romantic oil lamp glows to light your way.

Point Grace's latest addition is a beachfront, full-service European-style spa, modeled after the Thalgo Spas in France and featuring thalassotherapy, which uses seawater and seaweed properties in treatments. Also available are aromatherapy, reflexology, and facials.

Meals—early morning coffee, continental breakfast (included in the rate), lunch and dinner—are served poolside or on the veranda of Grace's Cottage. An afternoon sorbet is offered to those lounging by the pool or beach. The hotel provides a free shuttle to take guests to dinner

at restaurants in the Grace Bay area. On twenty-four- to forty-eight-hours notice private chefs are available to prepare meals in the guest's suite or villa, and room service is available from select local restaurants. Grace's Cottage has a small wine cellar. Hutchings, the pool bar, provides waiter service poolside and at the beach. on Monday evenings, a barbecue dinner is served by the pool.

Adjacent to the main lounge is a small business center with computer facilities for e-mail and Internet access; a television; and the beginnings of a small library of books, CDs, DVDs, and board games. Secretarial services are available. The *New York Times* fax is delivered every morning to your suite or villa along with breakfast.

Point Grace offers water sports and bicycles (and helmets) for adults and children and provides complimentary transportation to the Provo Golf and Tennis Club about 1 mile away. Excursions to enjoy some of the finest diving in the Caribbean; deep-sea, bottom-, and bonefishing; and day sails can be arranged. Sunfish, snorkel gear, kayaks, and windsurfers are available for guests. Point Grace's "Fun Playhouse in the Sand" offers children four years and older a small, unsupervised playground. Baby-sitting is available.

On the northeastern point of Providenciales in the swanky gated community of Leeward, Point Grace has three four-bedroom villas available for rent. Lavish in an understated way, the large villas are set in lovely landscaped gardens with a large swimming pool and a guest house only steps away from the ocean. One villa has a tennis court, gym, and massage room. The villas are staffed for housekeeping; butlers, chefs, and personal assistants are available upon request.

Point Grace ✳✳✳

P.O. Box 700, Grace Bay, Providenciales, Turks and Caicos Islands, B.W.I.
Phone: (649) 946–5096; Fax: (649) 946–5097;
e-mail: reservations@pointgrace.com; www.pointgrace.com

Owner: Point Grace L.P.
Managing Director: Andre Niederhauser
Open: Year-round
Credit Cards: American Express, Visa, MasterCard, Discover
U.S. Reservations: (888) 682–3705; Fax: (649) 946–5097
Deposit: Three nights within ten days of confirmation, thirty days cancellation
Minimum Stay: Five nights; seven at Christmas; penthouse, two weeks; three villas, one week
Arrival/Departure: Guest met at airport and transferred to hotel
Distance from Airport: Fifteen-minute-drive by taxi
Accommodations: 32 units (one- to three-bedroom beachfront suites, with large terraces; nine poolside suites; two penthouse suites)
Amenities: Air-conditioning, ceiling fans; full kitchen, washer/dryer; safe; twice-daily maid service (see text)
Electricity: 100 volts
Fitness Facilities/Spa Services: See text
Sports: Beach, swimming pool, some water sports; golf, tennis, deep-sea fishing, diving arranged
Dress Code: Casual
Children: All ages; cribs, high chairs
Packages: Gulf, family, three and five nights, weddings, spa
Rates: Per suite, per day, CP. *High Season* (mid-December–mid-April): one bedroom $525–$795; two-bedroom, $895–$1,120; three-bedroom, $1,410–$1,765. *Low Season:* $395–$545; $625–$795; $970–$1,200, respectively.
Service Charge: 10 percent
Government Tax: 9 percent

U.S. Virgin Islands

Topside or below, few places under the American flag are more beautiful than our corner of the Caribbean. Volcanic in origin, the Virgin Islands are made up of fifty green gems floating in a sapphire sea; only three are developed. They are only a short distance apart, yet no islands in the Caribbean are more different from one another than are our American trio.

St. Croix, the easternmost point of the United States, is the largest. A low-lying island of rolling hills, it was once an important sugar-producing center. Many plantation homes and sugar mills have been restored as hotels, restaurants, and museums; Christiansted and Frederiksted, the main towns, are on the National Register of Historic Places.

St. Croix offers an impressive variety of activities, from hiking in a rain forest to turtle-watching, but its most popular sports are snorkeling and scuba diving. The island is surrounded by coral reefs; off the northeastern coast is Buck Island Reef National Monument, the only underwater park in our national park system.

St. John, the smallest of the trio, is truly America the Beautiful. Almost three-quarters of the mountainous island is covered by the Virgin Islands National Park. Around its edges lovely little coves hide some of the most alluring porcelain-white beaches and aquamarine waters in the Caribbean.

The National Park Service Visitor Center in Cruz Bay schedules ranger-led tours, hikes, and wildlife lectures and publishes a brochure outlining twenty-one trails. Cruz Bay, the island's main town, is booming from new popularity and rapidly losing its tiny-village charm to traffic and tacky T-shirt shops. The island is reached by ferry from St. Thomas in twenty minutes.

St. Thomas floats on a deep turquoise sea with green mountains and an irregular coastline of fingers and coves sheltering idyllic bays and pretty white-sand beaches. Only 13 miles long and less than 3 miles wide, it seems larger because of its dense population and development. Its capital, Charlotte Amalie, is the busiest cruise port in the Caribbean.

St. Thomas offers good facilities for water sports and for tennis and golf, but it is best known for its smart boutiques with clothing, accessories, perfumes, and jewelry from world-famous designers.

The Virgin Islands, as U.S. territories, have a special tax status that gives returning U.S. residents a $1,200 exemption from customs duty rather than the $600 applied to visitors from other places.

Information

U.S. Virgin Islands Division of Tourism, 1270 Avenue of the Americas, #2108, New York, NY 10020; (800) 372–8784, (212) 332–2222; Fax: (212) 332–2223; www.usvi.net, www.stjohnusvi.com. Offices also in Atlanta, Chicago, Los Angeles, Miami, Coral Gables, Washington, D.C., and San Juan, Puerto Rico.

THE BUCCANEER
Gallows Bay, St. Croix, U.S.V.I.

At The Buccaneer you could roll out of bed to play golf or take a swim at one of the two pools before breakfast, explore some of the Caribbean's best reefs fronting three white-sand beaches before lunch, and then enjoy a game of tennis before dinner—all within eyeshot of the pink palazzo whose history stretches back 300 years.

Spread over 300 tropical acres near Gallows Bay on St. Croix's northern coast, The Buccaneer was opened in 1948 as an eleven-room inn in a seventeenth-century estate house by a family whose origins on the island date from the same period. The building's thick walls and graceful bonnet arches are still visible in the French Wing; the Cotton House serves as administration space; and the eighteenth-century sugar mill is the venue for the manager's weekly cocktail party (and makes a romantic setting for weddings). The party is hosted by the resort owners.

Now greatly enlarged and developed into a complete resort, the main building sits on a rise with commanding views. The roadside entrance passes along a drive lined with royal palms and well-kept gardens bright with bougainvillea and a great variety of tropical trees.

Some of the accommodations are in the main building, while others are housed in a variety of cottages and bungalows near the fairways and tennis courts and in terraced gardens cascading from the main building to the sea. All have terraces. If you are a beach body, you may prefer the rooms that snake along the seashore. They have high, cedar-beamed ceilings and stone terraces overlooking the sea and pretty sunsets. Oceanfront rooms have marble floors and bathrooms. Two deluxe one-bedroom suites, Ficus and Frigate, are furnished with four poster beds, two baths, and a living room. They connect to make a two-bedroom suite.

The most luxurious accommodations are twelve beachside units, called Doubloons, in keeping with the resort's tradition of naming rooms for gold coins rumored to have been buried by the buccaneers who sailed these islands. The large rooms are housed in a marble terraced villa that echoes the island's Danish colonial architecture. Each has king-size four-poster beds or two queen-size beds, wide terraces or balconies with beach and sea views, picture windows with window seats, walk-in closets, and spacious bathrooms with whirlpool tubs and double showers.

To get ready for its fiftieth anniversary in 1998, The Buccaneer got a face-lift in almost every part of the resort. Thirty-two rooms on the second floor of the main building were given marble floors, new furniture, carved four-poster beds, and new doors made of solid mahogany. Originally known as the Hamilton Wing—for Alexander Hamilton, who spent his childhood here when the property was called Estate Shoys—the second story follows the contour of the original seventeenth century foundation, which results in a group of rooms that each have a different shape and size; all have great views of the island, the sea, or both.

Another historic group, the four Widow's Mite rooms—originally built in the 1700s and so named because their expansive sea views recall rooms used by a ship captain's wife awaiting her husband's return from a long voyage—now have marble floors, newly outfitted bathrooms, all-new furniture, and a window seat tucked into the panoramic bay window.

The Buccaneer's tennis complex is the largest on the island. The nearby accommodations, recently renovated and refurbished, have brand-new bathrooms; they were designed for families. The eighteen-hole golf course (5,810 yards, par 70) dips and dives from hilltops to the water's edge. For fitness folks a 2-mile, eighteen-station parcours jogging and exercise path winds through the hilly terrain. Those with something less strenuous in mind can join the weekly art class or check their e-mail in the new Business Center.

At the newly renovated and improved Hideaway spa you can iron out the kinks and enjoy a massage, sauna, seaweed wrap, or other pampering while your kids participate in a free program that includes crafts, supervised snorkeling, sing-alongs, parties, their own daily newsletter, a beachside playground, and a video game room.

One of The Buccaneer's two pools is by the main building, set into seventeenth-century foundations. The second is a free-form pool on quiet Beauguard Beach next to The Grotto, where burgers and snacks are available.

The Beach Shack, the water-sports center, offers staffled snorkel, kayak, and Sunfish tours. Lunch is served daily at The Mermaid, a breezy beachside restaurant, which is also the setting for the weekly evening Surf and Turf buffet featuring local specialties and steel band music.

At breakfast in the open-air Terrace in the main building, you'll enjoy views of the fairways and the sea; in the evening the lights of Christiansted twinkle in the distance. Dinner offers a continental menu with West Indian selections. The Brass Parrot, a separate air-conditioned restaurant adjacent to the Terrace, has a more casual bistro-style menu at moderate prices, especially suited for families. Nightly the Terrace bar hosts live musical entertainment by different combos.

The Armstrong family, now the third generation to operate the hotel, is a family of naturalists. General manager Elizabeth Armstrong leads free weekly nature walks. The golf course is a popular birding spot.

A quiet, self-contained, family-owned and -operated resort with a casual and friendly ambience, The Buccaneer is suitable for all ages and all situations, from singles to families. It appeals most to travelers who want an active vacation with a wide range of sports. Many guests are repeaters; some are from families that, like the owners, are into the third generation.

The Buccaneer ★★★★ 🏖

Box 25200, Gallows Bay, St. Croix, U.S.V.I. 00824-5200
Phone: (340) 773–2100; Fax: (340) 778–8215;
www.thebuccaneer.com

Owner: The Armstrong family

General Manager: Elizabeth Armstrong

Open: Year-round

Credit Cards: All major

U.S. Reservations: Direct to hotel, (800) 255–3881

Deposit: Seven nights during Christmas/New Year's

Minimum Stay: Two nights

Arrival/Departure: Transfer service included in honeymoon packages

Distance from Airport: 10 miles (forty minutes); taxi one-way, $14.00 for two, $7.00 each additional passenger; private car, $30.00 for up to four people.

Distance from Christiansted: 2 miles; taxi one-way, $6.00; hourly hotel shuttle to town, $3.00 per person, one-way, $4.00 round-trip

Accommodations: 138 rooms and suites, all with terraces (50 oceanfront, 34 Great House, 12 Doubloons, 12 ridge rooms, 12 tennis units, eight family cottages, five suites, and five units in various locations); 54 with kings, 84 with two queens

Amenities: Air-conditioning, ceiling fan; safe; telephone, satellite television; refrigerator; dressing area; bath with tub and shower, basket of toiletries, most with hair dryer; ice service, nightly turndown service, room service at specific hours; boutiques

Electricity: 110 volts

Fitness Facilities/Spa Services: Health club; spa treatments (see text)

Sports: Two freshwater pools; parcourse exercise path. Tennis: Eight Laykold tennis courts (two lighted), pro shop, fee for courts, lessons, equipment. Golf: Green fees, charge for equipment, caddies, carts, lessons. Snorkeling, Sunfish, kayaking: Free lessons and equipment. Charges for sports facilities and equipment generally waived in packages. Day and evening cruises, fishing, horseback riding arranged.

Children: All ages; activities program; cribs; baby-sitters; during summer children eighteen and under stay free in room with parents

Meetings: Up to fifty people

Day Visitors: Yes

Handicapped: Limited facilities

Packages: All-inclusive, golf, tennis, honeymoon, wedding, family, water sports, ecology

Rates: Per person, double, daily, FAB. *High Season* (mid-December–March): $265–$630. *Low Season* (mid-April–mid-December): $195–$390. Weekly rates available in summer; inquire.

Energy Surcharge: 4 percent

Government Tax: 8 percent

HIBISCUS BEACH HOTEL
St. Croix, U.S.V.I.

Situated on a 2,000-foot white-sand beach fronting Pelican Cove the Hibiscus is the best value to appear in St. Croix in years—and only 3 miles from Christiansted.

The small, quiet resort is made up of seven two-story buildings—painted in hibiscus pink with white gingerbread trim—clustered around an open-air pavilion, bar, and swimming pool. To one side another building houses the front office and an air-conditioned dining room.

The air-conditioned guest rooms, all with patios or terraces and sea views, are nicely and comfortably furnished in cheerful colors with one king-size or two double beds, and all about 60 yards from the beach. Each has a fully stocked minibar, safe, telephone, radio, color television with cable, and ceiling fan. Bathrooms are small and have showers only. Recently, they were upgraded by adding glass shower doors and new vanity tops with built-in tissue holders.

Two rooms are designed for disabled people and each has an adjoining guest room for a traveling companion. The buildings, connected by wooden boardwalks at ground level, are fully ramped for wheelchair accessibility. There is one two-bedroom suite with a kitchenette.

General manager and part owner Wendall Snider, who describes himself as a Silicon Valley burnout, escaped California in the late 1980s for a peaceful life in the Caribbean and selected St. Croix, which he and his wife, Nan, had known from frequent diving trips.

Snider and his partners built Hibiscus from scratch, opening it in 1992. It enjoyed an immediate success due to its location, its price, and the friendly, homey, neighborhood feeling that Snider and his staff provide.

Days at Hibiscus are easily spent doing as little as possible in the beach chairs and hammocks strung between palm trees along the crescent beach cooled by the steady breezes. You can simply listen to the surf lap the sand and watch the pelicans dive for their lunch. And if you're so inclined, the beach isn't bad for a morning jog or evening stroll, either.

There is a shallow reef on the western side for some good snorkeling; equipment is available for use without charge. For the more ambitious, diving is good beyond the reef, where the sea drops off quickly. And if you are really energetic, the resort will arrange horseback riding, golf, and sailing for an additional fee.

You can change the scenery a little by moving over to the freshwater pool that's next to the beach bar and bordered by stately palms, colorful hibiscus, and sea grape trees. Quiet by day, the bar and beachfront restaurant become something of a local hangout at happy hour, gathering in the neighborhood for drinks and quickly making guests feel at home.

The Hibiscus has become something of a cultural mecca, with weekly entertainment by an eclectic mix of jazz and steel pan musicians, as well as other island artists. The resort features the sounds of Trinidad native Bill Blass and his steel pan band on Wednesday at 6:30 P.M. Happy hour might have songs of sea adventure and Irish chants during an electric mandolin show by Tony Romano on Thursday at 5:00 P.M., while jazz trios perform on Saturday at 8:00 P.M. During Sunday brunch, from 10:30 A.M. to 2:00 P.M., former Broadway producer, director, and actor

David Richards entertains with a medley of popular show tunes. Snider says his aim is to offer guests an array of performers who reflect the multicultural nature of St. Croix.

The Hibiscus Beach Hotel offers golf and dive packages as well as an all-inclusive plan, which covers all meals, a rental car for a week, admission to the Whim Plantation Museum and the St. George Botanical Gardens, plus a daily choice of golf, a two-tank dive, a snorkeling cruise to Buck Island, or parasailing.

But don't be too hard on yourself if your resolve for an active next day fades easily into one of those unforgettable Caribbean sunsets.

Hibiscus Beach Hotel ✱✱

4131 La Grande Princesse, St. Croix, U.S.V.I. 00820-4441
Phone: (340) 773–4042, (800) 442–0121; Fax: (340) 773–7668;
e-mail: hibiscus@viaccess.net; www.1hisbiscus.com

Owner: Hibiscus Partners
General Manager: Wendall Snider
Open: Year-round
Credit Cards: All major
U.S. Reservations: Direct to hotel, (800) 442–0121
Deposit: Three nights, 50 percent deposit for packages; thirty days cancellation for December 21–March 31, fourteen days cancellation for April 1–December 21
Minimum Stay: None
Arrival/Departure: No transfer service
Distance from Airport: 8 miles; taxi one-way, $6.00 per person, $12.00 minimum per taxi
Distance from Christiansted: 3 miles; taxi one-way, $4.00 per person, $8.00 minimum per taxi
Accommodations: 36 rooms and one two-bedroom efficiency apartment in seven two-story buildings; two rooms designed for disabled people; all have patio or balcony and a king or two double beds
Amenities: Air-conditioning, ceiling fans; fully stocked mini-bar; coffeemakers; safe; fresh flowers daily; telephone, cable television, radio; bath with shower only, hair dryers
Electricity: 110 volts
Sports: Freshwater swimming pool; complimentary snorkeling gear; golf, sailing, fishing, horseback riding arranged for fee
Dress Code: Casual
Children: All ages; children under twelve years old may stay free with parents in room; cribs, high chairs; baby-sitters
Meetings: Up to seventy people
Day Visitors: Welcome
Handicapped: Two rooms; property ramped
Packages: Honeymoon, anniversary, golf, dive, all-inclusive
Rates: Per room, double, daily, EP. **High Season** (mid-December–April): $180–$190. **Low Season:** $130–$140. Single rates available; inquire.
Service Charge: At discretion of guests
Government Tax: 8 percent

CANEEL BAY

St. John, U.S.V.I.

Consider these numbers: 166 rooms on 170 acres and a staff of 450. Not bad odds, you could say. But these are only some of the elements that have made Caneel a legend.

Opened in 1955 as Laurance Rockefeller's first Caribbean venture, Caneel was the first of the ecologically built hideaways of the Rockresort style. Caneel is built into the ruins of an old sugar plantation within the Virgin Islands National Park. It's sprawled on a peninsula scalloped with seven flawless beaches protected by coral reefs that are also part of the national park. Indeed, the fact that Caneel is framed on all sides by the national park forever ensures its pristine quality.

The Caneel appeal is immediately apparent, with acres of carpetlike meadows, artfully arranged shrubbery, and gardens of tropical flowers. Guest rooms and suites are clustered in cottages of natural rock and weathered wood. They're all but hidden in the vegetation and are widely scattered. Some cottages are in the hillside tennis gardens, but most are set directly on the beaches.

The Cottage Point area on a bluff facing the water is the most requested honeymoon spot for its seclusion. Paradise Beach is next to the famous Cottage Number 7, formerly the Rockefeller home and now luxury digs for visiting bigwigs. Scott Beach, where units are in single-story buildings, is popular for its afternoon sun and lengthy beach. And cozy Turtle Bay Beach boasts the best snorkeling.

Regardless of locale, Caneel's rooms are airy and spacious and remain no-nonsense affairs with walls of louvered and screened windows for cross ventilation, and private patios. There are no telephones or televisions—

only the twitter of birds, the chorus of mating tree frogs, and the rhythmic lull of the sea. However, Caneel has made several nods to the twenty-first century. Air-conditioning has been added to all units, and most of the bathrooms have been renovated and upgraded. There are outdoor phones with AT&T direct at each of the clusters of buildings, and you can now get a complimentary cellular phone from the front desk if you really must stay connected to the outside world. A business center with a computer, printer, Internet access, and telephone has been added in a private room by the front lobby.

Breakfast and lunch buffets indulge guests with many choices. If you prefer a light lunch, the open-to-the-breezes bar by the central building is a delightful setting in the shade by day and popular for drinks in the evening. If you prefer quieter, air-conditioned comfort, Turtle Bay Estate House serves a midday meal during the winter season. You can also return there for afternoon tea or for the weekly wine tasting in The Wine Room, where 2,000 bottles of wine are displayed.

Caneel is at its most magical at night, when the grounds are aglow with low "mushroom" lamps, and Polynesian-style torches hidden in the thick foliage light the paths near the activities building. A laid-back combo completes the mood with light dance music.

Dinner is served in three locations, all with a view of the twinkling lights of St. Thomas in the distance. The casual Beach Terrace on Caneel Bay Beach has an open kitchen with a wood-burning stove and rotisserie. It was recently renovated and upgraded and serves a buffet breakfast and

lunch plus table service dinner. Equator, in the flower-fes-tooned ruins of an eighteenth-century sugar mill, offers a cornucopia of Caribbean and other specialties and a fun Caribbean carnival decor in which to enjoy it—but all, nat-urally, in the low-key style that is Caneel's trademark. The third venue is the enormous eighteenth-century mill, site of the more formal, romantic Turtle Bay Estate House, where it's time to dress up and sit down to a five-course meal.

Caneel offers a host of water sports and a variety of sail excursions and charter cruises, available from the Beach Hut staff members are trained to give lessons in the use of snorkeling equipment and in windsurfing, Sunfish sailing, kayaking, and aquafins. The resort has eleven ten-nis courts and tennis pros who arrange round-robins, hold clinics, and are available for lessons. You'll find jogging paths (and hiking trails in the national park) and an air-conditioned fitness center with cardiovascular training equipment. Aerobics classes are one of a changing selec-tion of daily activities. You'll also find The Self Centre, where yoga, meditation, and relaxation techniques are offered for $25 per session. Three-hour watercolor lessons are also on the roster.

Caneel is trying to handle a growing demand from guests who want to bring their children, and at the same time accommodate those who come to Caneel to get away from children—theirs and anyone else's. All ages are welcomed year-round. The Peace, Quiet, Kids at Caneel program is designed for families; others are not. Second, the resort has created The Teen Center, which is equipped with Ping-Pong, a pool table, computer with Internet access, and a juke box. The hours are 9:00 A.M. to 10:00 P.M.; the cost for a half day is $35, a full day $50, dinner and a movie $25.

Finally, Turtle Town, a children's center at one end of the property, has a designated group of cottages as fam-ily units. Turtle Town has a full-time director and a staff of one counselor to every five children. Each day's program has a theme with special stress put on environmental appreciation of the resort and of St. John. The center is open from 9:00 A.M. to 4:00 P.M. and costs $50 per child per day (with lunch), or $35 for a half day. Parents may join in the activities. Children may register in advance or on arrival. The resort also offers a baby-sitting service for $10 per hour with a three-hour minimum.

Whether you fall into the with-kids or no-kids group, contact the manager in advance and be specific about your needs. Fortunately, Caneel is large enough and so spread out that it can accommodate guests of all ages without anyone trampling on others, provided the resort is informed of guests' needs in advance. If you wait until you are there to complain about kids or noisy neighbors, the resort's options for solving the problem may be lim-ited, particularly when there's a full house.

Caneel Bay ★★★★

P.O. Box 720, St. John, U.S.V.I. 00831-0720
Phone: (340) 776–6111; Fax: (340) 696–8280;
e-mail: www.rosewood-hotels.com or www.caneelbay.com

Owner: Deutsche Bank
Managing Director: Brian Young
Open: Year-round
Credit Cards: All major
U.S. Reservations: Rosewood Hotels and Resorts, (888) ROSE-WOOD, (214) 871–5454; Fax: (214) 871–5444; (340) 776–6111
Deposit: Three nights; twenty-eight days cancellation for Decem-ber 19–April 15, fourteen days for balance of year
Minimum Stay: Ten nights during Christmas
Arrival/Departure: Transfer on Caneel Bay's cruiser from St. Thomas five times daily and Little Dix in Virgin Gorda twice weekly
Distance from Airport: (St. Thomas Airport) 12 nautical miles (see Arrival/Departure, above)
Distance from Cruz Bay: 3 miles; taxi one-way, $2.50 per person
Accommodations: 166 rooms in one- and two-story cottages with terrace (44 ocean view, 55 beachfront, 27 premium junior suites, five in Cottage 7, ten courtside, 25 tennis/garden)
Amenities: Air-conditioning, ceiling fans; bath with shower (few with tub), hair dryer, toiletries, iron and ironing board; safe; cof-feemaker, minibar, sodas and ice service; nightly turndown, room service with charge for breakfast; no telephone; television in Estate House Lounge and Beach Bar; nightly movies; business cen-ter, Internet
Electricity: 110 volts
Fitness Facilities/Spa Services: Fitness center (see text); massage on request
Sports: Freshwater swimming pool; eleven tennis courts; use of tennis and nonconcession water sports included in rate; deep-sea fishing, boating, golf in St. Thomas arranged; dive shop offers resort course, certification; clinic; jogging path, hiking trails
Dress Code: Casual by day; in evening men required to wear col-lared shirts and trousers; December 19–April 15 jackets also required for dinner in Turtle Bay Estate House
Children: Year-round (see text)
Meetings: Up to 100 people
Day Visitors: Welcome in certain areas only
Handicapped: Limited facilities
Packages: Dive, tennis, sailing, honeymoon, wedding; Island Hop-per (with Little Dix)
Rates: Per room, daily, CP. *High Season* (December 19–March 31): $425–$1,020. *Shoulder Season* (April 16–May 31 and mid-November–mid-December): $375–$820. *Low Season:* $300–$675.
Service Charge: 10 percent
Government Tax: 8 percent on room only

MAHO BAY CAMP AND HARMONY
St. John, U.S.V.I.

Folks, we're talking camp here. Camp as in *camping*—no private baths, no hot water, not even running water, except in the communal bathhouses.

This escape to paradise means tented cabins, which you'll probably share with friendly little lizards, mosquitoes, and other bugs. Getting to this heavenly rest takes seven hours or more via plane, taxi, ferry, and another taxi. On the last stretch—a bone-cracking ride on the wooden seats of a converted flatbed truck—self-doubt may set in. At Maho's reception area you'll be checked in by a friendly attendant, who'll give you the dos and don'ts about Maho and about protecting paradise. Then you'll lug your luggage up (or down) the hill to your abode.

It's obvious that Maho Bay Camp is not for everyone. What may be less obvious is why I have included Maho in this book in the first place. But, you see, many people think Maho offers the greatest vacation in the Caribbean. They come from all over the United States and all walks of life. Maho has a year-round occupancy rate of 80 percent, among the highest in the Caribbean, with a waiting list in winter. The majority of guests are repeaters, and the staff is made up mostly of folks who came as guests and decided to stay.

Maho Bay, a private campground in the Virgin Islands National Park, is unique in the Caribbean. It was created in 1976 by engineer-ecologist Stanley Selengut, who is now teaching the world that being an environmentalist can be good business. The camp enjoys a gorgeous setting on a wooded hillside that falls to a small beach and overlooks an exquisite bay of reef-protected turquoise waters and expansive scenery of mountainous green neighboring islands. Maho Bay has none of the amenities of a typical tropical retreat. On the other hand, true campers call it luxurious.

Accommodations are in tented cabins, all but hidden in the thick foliage that climbs the hillsides, and are connected by a network of boardwalks and wooden steps. The dense woods help ensure privacy but sometimes obscure the view. Each cabin, made out of a translucent water-repellent fabric, is built on a 16-by-16-foot wooden platform suspended above the ground on wooden pilings, like a tree house. It is surprisingly roomy and quite comfortable.

The tent has a sleeping area with twin beds; a sitting area just large enough for a trundle couch that sleeps two; a small kitchen unit with a two-burner propane stove, electrical outlets, cooler, dishes, and utensils; and an outside deck, which makes a great perch for watching the sunset or counting the stars.

There are five bathhouses with sinks, toilets, and showers at various locations around the property; a grocery store, which is neither nonprofit nor cheap; a multipurpose outdoor community center for meetings, seminars, and weddings; barbecue areas; and a cafeteria style restaurant and bar in an outdoor pavilion with spectacular vistas where breakfast and dinner are available.

If you are more a beach person, you might prefer the camp's lower reaches, but if you don't mind the hike to heaven, the tents higher up are the most desirable, both for their wonderful views and because they have high ceilings with ceiling fans, which stir the air and help keep away mosquitoes.

But Maho's greatest innovations are at Harmony—perfect for people who love the idea of camping but can't hack the inconvenience. It's also fabulous for people interested in the newly developing science of building with recycled materials—old tires, newspapers, plastic bottles, that sort of thing. Located high up the hillside above Maho, Harmony is, in fact, an experiment in environmental living and it's wonderful. Selengut, in conjunction with the U.S. National Park Service, built six units, each with two large guest rooms, following the *Guiding Principles of Sustainable Design*. The units are built totally from recycled materials,

partly to prove that it can be done and partly to test products in the school of hard knocks of the Caribbean.

If no one had told you, you probably would not realize that these units were anything other than attractively furnished hotel rooms with a kitchen and dining area, a bath, and a large terrace. Each has an outdoor cooking grill powered by the sun. Indeed, the entire unit is powered by sun and wind. Remember, Harmony is an experiment. Some nights you might not have lights; some days you might not have hot water. But if you go with the spirit of adventure and curiosity and if you truly care about the environment, you will enjoy your stay. And you'll come away asking, why doesn't everyone build this way?

More recently, Maho has added a craft center, focused principally on glassmaking as part of its Trash to Treasures recycling program, with demonstrations twice daily by artists-in-residence. Other crafts, such as pottery and printmaking, are offered from time to time.

Another program, Learning Vacations, is operated in conjunction with Omega Institute and offers a series of weeklong workshops in January and February focusing on personal enrichment.

As St. John beaches go, Maho's isn't much, but there are two longer white-sand stretches a short walk or swim away. All three beaches are great for snorkeling. The resort offers scuba, sailing, windsurfing, and kayaking at an additional charge. But the highlight is hiking on any of the national park's twenty-one trails.

Maho protects the environment with missionary zeal—and with the national park's rules. Evening programs are usually eco-oriented and may feature presentations by staff from the national park service or a visiting expert. Maho also hosts conferences on ecology.

Maho has a taxi service, which makes five trips into Cruz Bay during the day, but if you want to take in the town's nightlife, transportation in the evening can be a problem unless you rent a vehicle. Jeeps are recommended. Cab drivers do not like the rough road into the camp, about 1/2 mile from the main road.

If you understand that Maho is a campground, and that's the type of vacation you want, you will not find better facilities in a more beautiful setting in the Caribbean. Unfortunately, many people not suited for Maho—perhaps having a romanticized notion of what it is, go there anyway—attracted by the low price and the illusion that they can hack it.

As a postscript, Selengut has another tented resort, Concordia, that is something of a combination of the first two—not as basic as Maho and not as deluxe as Harmony. It's located on a hillside at the eastern end of St. John near Coral Bay. Details on facilities and prices are available from Maho Bay Camps.

Maho Bay Camp and Harmony * (S) 🍃

Cruz Bay, St. John, U.S.V.I. 00830
Phone: (340) 776–6240; Fax: (340) 776–6504;
e-mail: mahobay@maho.org; www.maho.org

Owner: Stanley Selengut

General Manager: Maggie Day

Open: Year-round

Credit Cards: Most major

U.S. Reservations: Maho Bay Camps, Inc., (800) 392–9004, (340) 776–6240; Fax. (340) 776–6504

Deposit: Half of reserved stay; fourteen days cancellation less 50 percent of room cost

Minimum Stay: Seven nights holiday weeks

Arrival/Departure: No transfer service; twenty-minute ferry ride from Red Hook dock on St. Thomas to Cruz Bay, $3.00; forty-five-minute ferry from Charlotte Amalie to Cruz Bay, $7.00

Distance from Cruz Bay: 8 miles; taxi one-way, $11.00 for one, $9.00 shared; Maho's service, $5.00

Accommodations: 114 tent cabins, all with twin beds and trundle couch for two; 12 guest rooms in six Harmony units

Amenities: Fans (seven with ceiling fans), showers in communal bathhouses. For Harmony, see text.

Electricity: 110 volts

Sports: Hiking in national park; boating, snorkeling, diving, windsurfing, kayaking, deep-sea fishing available

Dress Code: Informal

Children: None under four years of age

Meetings: Up to 125 people

Day Visitors: Welcome

Handicapped: No facilities at Maho; one unit at Harmony

Packages: No

Rates: Two people, daily, EP. Maho, **High Season** (mid-December–April 30): $108–$115; $15 each additional person; **Low Season** (May 1–mid-December): $75. Harmony, **High Season** (mid-December–April 30): $185–$210; **Low Season** (May 1–mid-December): $110–$145.

Service Charge: None

Government Tax: 8 percent

WESTIN RESORT ST. JOHN
Great Cruz Bay, St. John, U.S.V.I.

It looks like a Hollywood film set: Broad steps lined with royal palms leading down through landscaped gardens to the resort's centerpiece, an enormous swimming pool with waterfalls and islands under tall, graceful palms.

Tucked in a cove on forty-seven hillside acres, this deluxe resort fronts a 1,200-foot white-sand beach on yacht-filled Great Cruz Bay. Thirteen guest-room buildings are terraced on the hillside between the reception area at the top and the pool and beach below. Most guest rooms have a patio or balcony with views of the sea. All sport pretty, fresh Caribbean decor.

There are six categories of guest rooms, from garden view to two-bedroom suites. Each has a hair dryer, a coffeemaker, a safe, cable television, telephones, an iron and ironing board, and a minibar. The one- and two-bedroom suites have whirlpool baths—right in the bedroom!

The Westin St. John has a variety of restaurants and bars amid its garden splendor. The informal Beach Cafe is the main restaurant, set in a large open-air pavilion by the beach. It serves breakfast and dinner daily, offering a la carte menus and buffets. Sunday brunch is as popular with town folks as it is with guests. The Beach Bar, adjacent to the restaurant, makes a pleasant outdoor terrace setting for predinner cocktails or to linger with friends in the evening.

For the ever-thirsty and casual nibblers, there is Snorkel's Pool Bar & BBQ by the pool for lunches, afternoon snacks, and drinks; the bar is open daily until midnight. Another unusual attraction is the Mango Deli, where you can find sandwiches, salads, hot food, wines, fresh meat, cold drinks, and ice cream. Box lunches and complimentary coolers are available for day trips. Chloe and Bernard, an expensive gourmet restaurant, is located above the main lobby.

The manager's evening cocktail party is a popular occasion for guests to meet and mingle. Most are from the United States, but some come from South America and Puerto Rico; on a recent visit I met a couple from as far away as Australia.

At the Westin the use of the six Astroturf tennis courts is free, and regular clinics provide a chance to pep up your game. A full array of water-sports equipment, including all you need for snorkeling, kayaking, and windsurfing, is available for rent; lessons can be arranged. The hotel's dive shop holds beginner courses as well as others for certification at an additional charge. Certified divers can enjoy excursions one- and two-tank dives, wreck and night dives—departing daily from the hotel's dock.

The resort has a splendidly equipped health club with two exercise rooms filled with the latest weight-training and cardiovascular equipment, plus showers, a sauna, and a steam room; it also offers aerobics and massage therapy.

Many guests are content to spend their days by the beach, occasionally trying out the yellow-and-blue-striped trampoline—yes, trampoline—or by the beautiful tree-shaded freshwater swimming pool, which covers a quarter acre. If you wander by it in the evening, you'll get a surprise—slim strands of pink, purple, blue, green, and yellow neon lights rim the pool's edge just below the water level and shimmer on the surface. It sounds hokey, but it works.

If you have never snorkeled, you could not find more beautiful waters than those around this island to make your first discovery. St. John's coastal reefs are part of the Virgin Islands National Park. The Westin offers sailing excursions to secluded beaches, where you can snorkel from the boat or shore. Deep sea fishing, sunset cruises, and private charters are available from the dock, too.

The Westin Kids Club for children age three to twelve offers indoor and outdoor activities, play areas, and year-round supervised fun. In addition to the traditional arts and crafts, there is storytelling and daily themes—Our Island Home, for instance, teaches youngsters what it's like to live in the Virgin Islands. U-Wanna Iguana allows them to discover island wildlife such as iguanas, mongooses, and birds. Our Island, Our World introduces Roary the Westin Eco-Saur to teach children about recycling, reusing, and reducing to save the earth's resources. Campers can also enjoy volleyball and supervised beach activities. The club is open daily from 9:00 A.M. to 4:00 P.M. and 6:00 to 10:00 P.M. Prices range from $25 for a half day to $45 for a full one (with lunch); evening sessions can also include dinner. Baby-sitting is available upon request.

Getting to the resort is made easy starting with the lounge at the airport on St. Thomas, which the hotel maintains for guests. On arrival you are met at the airport, then taken by van to Red Hook on St. Thomas to board the hotel's boat, which speeds you across the waters to the resort's private dock. Your hotel registration is completed in the airport lounge, and upon arrival at the Westin dock you are greeted dockside by a Marina Ambassador with a rum punch and a room key. and escorted directly to the room. It's an efficient way of handling arrivals, since the lobby is at the front of the hotel at the top of the hill. A new 149-passenger ferry, the *Westin Breeze,* debuted in April 2002. "Iguana Stops" is the resort's shuttle that makes a round of the property every fifteen minutes.

The combination of a casual ambience and a romantic setting makes the Westin a natural for honeymooners. At the same time, its services and facilities have much to offer families with children—as well as couples of all ages.

Westin Resort St. John ★★★★

P.O. Box 8310, Great Cruz Bay, St. John, U.S.V.I. 00831
Phone: (340) 693–8000; Fax: (340) 693–8888; www.westin.com

Owner: Westin Hotels & Resorts
General Manager: Gregg Lundberg
Open: Year-round
Credit Cards: All major
U.S. Reservations: Direct to hotel; or Westin Reservations, (800) WESTIN–1
Deposit: Three nights, within fourteen days of reservation; cancellation for Christmas by October 1; fourteen days cancellation remainder of year
Minimum Stay: Six nights during Christmas
Arrival/Departure: Guests met at St. Thomas Airport by hotel representative for transfer to Red Hook dock and boat directly to hotel dock; cost is $65 round-trip, including tips; $45 for children age four–twelve; three and under, free.
Distance from Airport: *(St. Thomas Airport)* 20 miles; taxi to Red Hook dock one-way, $10.00 shared
Distance from Cruz Bay: 1½ miles; taxi one-way, $2.50 per person
Accommodations: 285 rooms, including seven one-bedroom and 14 two-bedroom suites in 13 two- and three-story buildings, all with two double beds or kings, most with terrace
Amenities: Air-conditioning; telephone, cable television, in-room movies; bath with tub and shower, hair dryer, deluxe toiletries; coffeemaker, minibar, refrigerator; safe; nightly turndown, room service; business services; iron and ironing board; concierge
Electricity: 110 volts
Fitness Facilities/Spa Services: See text
Sports: Freshwater swimming pool; two outdoor Jacuzzis; whirlpool in suites; six tennis courts, equipment for rent, resident USPTA pro, lessons for fee, pro shop; trampoline; kayaks; watersports equipment; diving and sailing excursions; deep-sea fishing, golf in St. Thomas arranged; hiking on park trails
Dress Code: Casual by day; elegantly casual in evening
Children: Westin Kids Club; cribs; baby-sitters
Meetings: Up to 300 people; audiovisual equipment
Day Visitors: Yes
Handicapped: Limited facilities
Packages: Honeymoon, dive, wedding, family, all-inclusive
Rates: Per room, daily, EP. *High Season* (mid-December–mid-April): $425–$850. *Shoulder Season* (mid-April–May 31 and mid-October–mid-December): $320–$675. *Low Season* (June 1–September 30): $245–$475.
Service Charge: None
Government Tax: 8 percent

MARRIOTT FRENCHMAN'S REEF
AND MORNING STAR BEACH RESORT
St. Thomas, U.S.V.I.

A $50 million renovation in 1998 transformed this old white fortresslike structure into a pretty pink edifice with white trim and natural stone accents set in landscaped, flowering gardens. And the transformation is in much more than the facade.

Frenchman's Reef and Morning Star, its adjacent sister resort on the beach—both Marriott franchises since 1992—were badly damaged by Hurricane Marilyn in 1995, but remained open throughout the crisis to house rescue workers and hotel staff who had lost their homes. Finally, after St. Thomas had fully recovered, the hotel closed for eight months to make the transformation.

A palm-lined driveway leads to the entrance where you step into a beautiful lobby, open and airy with views that extend all the way out to the sea. A double stairway leads down to bars and restaurants on the first level, which overlooks a pool area that wraps all around the building's sea side. On the lower level are two adjacent swimming pools with a waterfall at one end, a fountain at the other, a swim-up bar at the center, and views to infinity at every turn.

At the far side of one pool, another set of steps leads down to a third level with another waterfall and an extension of land along the rocky coast at the edge of the cliff, where there are two Jacuzzis. To one side of the pool complex is a fitness center with steam rooms, spa treatment rooms, and a sauna; and on the other side you'll find Sunset Terrace and the new Sunset Grill and Bar. It's amusing to be here in the late afternoon, watching the cruise ships sail out of the harbor at sunset: The passengers on the ships are taking as many pictures of the resort as the hotel guests are of the ships.

A pretty gazebo on the southern side of the pools is used for weddings (the hotel does such a huge wedding business that it has a special department, Weddings in Paradise, to handle them). Here, too, steps lead down to Morning Star Beach; another swimming pool; two lighted Omni-turf tennis courts; the two- and three-story Morning Star Villas; a beachfront snack bar, Coconut Joe's; and Star, a small convenience store.

Other Frenchman's Reef eateries are Windows on the Harbor, the main dining room, with a popular Friday-night seafood buffet and Sunday brunch; the Captain's Cafe, serving light fare; and Espresso/Presto, a snack bar and convenience shop by the lobby. The Pirates Den is a nightclub with live entertainment and a sports bar. Another wing of

the restaurant level houses a brand-new ballroom and meeting rooms, a separate area for group check-in, and a business center.

Twenty-two rooms of the old Frenchman's Reef were eliminated to make way for eighty-eight new luxury suites in the redesigned resort. A new floor was added on the top of the hotel to create twenty-one bilevel suites with living rooms and loft bedrooms, along with seventeen royal suites with cathedral ceilings, Jacuzzis, and a spiral staircase that winds up to the bedroom. Eight new lanai suites were added on the ground floor of the Sunset Wing overlooking the pool and ocean.

All the guest rooms were totally renovated with new

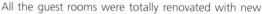

Marriott Frenchman's Reef and Morning Star Beach Resort ★★★

Marriott Beach Resorts, P.O. Box 7100, St. Thomas, U.S.V.I. 00801
Phone: (340) 776–8500; Fax: (340) 715–6191;
e-mail: resorts@marriott.vi; www.marriotthotels.com/sttfr;
www.offshoreresorts.com

Owner: Marriott International
General Manager: John Peck
Open: Year-round
Credit Cards: Most major
U.S. Reservations: (800) 223–6388
Deposit: Two nights; seven to fifteen days cancellation, depending on season
Minimum Stay: None
Arrival/Departure: Transfer arranged upon request
Distance from Airport: *(Cyril E. King Airport)* 6 miles; taxi one-way, $7.50 for one person, $4.50 each for more than one
Distance from Charlotte Amalie: 3 miles; taxi one-way, $6.00 for one person, $4.00 each for more than one
Accommodations: 408 rooms and suites at Frenchman's Reef; 96 villa units at Morning Star
Amenities: Air-conditioning; direct-dial telephone; safes; cable television, movies; icemaker; refrigerator; twenty-four-hour room service; bath with tub and shower, hair dryers, toiletries; iron and ironing board; shops; beauty salon; full-service business center; wedding service
Electricity: 110 volts
Fitness Facilities/Spa Services: See text
Sports: Three freshwater swimming pools; two tennis courts; free clinics; water sports
Dress Code: Casual
Children: All ages; under eighteen years old stay free in room with parents
Meetings: Up to 1,000 people; audiovisual facilities
Day Visitors: Yes, with reservations
Handicapped: Facilities
Packages: Golf, family, honeymoon, wedding, dive
Rates: Per room, single or double, EP. *High Season* (late December–mid-April): $299–$529. *Shoulder Season* (mid-April–June 1): $265–$385. *Low Season:* $155–$275.
Government Tax: 8 percent on room

bathrooms and refurbished in bright, attractive decor. Each room has a mini-fridge, separate icemaker (the only one I've seen in a Caribbean hotel), hair dryer, coffeemaker, iron and ironing board, telephone with voice mail and data lines, safe, television, chaise lounge, desk, balcony, and twenty-four-hour room service. The clifftop location of the hotel affords most rooms spectacular views.

The new water-sports center offers snorkeling, diving, kayaking, windsurfing, parasailing, sport fishing, and sailing excursions. Free clinics for tennis, snorkeling, and diving are offered, as are aerobics and jazzercise. A ferry shuttle departs from a special dock several times a day for Charlotte Amalie, eight minutes away by boat.

Best of all, there's a new attitude among the staff to go along with the new hotel. From the front desk to the restaurants to housekeeping, all personnel participated in a special training program that has raised the service to a level not seen in a St. Thomas hotel before. That transformation was every bit as significant in creating the new Frenchman's Reef as the new facade, the new suites, or the three waterfalls.

RENAISSANCE GRAND BEACH RESORT

St. Thomas, U.S.V.I.

This deluxe, full-service resort on a great beach is grand in the eyes of many. Spread across thirty-four hillside acres on the northeastern shore of St. Thomas, the Renaissance Grand Beach Resort fronts 1,000 feet of pearly sands, beautiful turquoise waters, and a horizon filled with a host of neighboring islands.

The Renaissance Grand Beach is approached by a long, palm-lined, landscaped driveway leading to the reception building. Upon arrival you get an inviting view straight through the lobby to the beach and the sea. On the second floor of the building are several shops, including a hair salon.

The resort's architecture—straight out of Akron, Ohio—was never one of its strong points. Built in stucco of contemporary design with sharply angled shingled roofs, the structures appear too modern and too massive for their Caribbean setting. Fortunately, the masses of palm trees, oleander, and bougainvillea soften the setting and all but hide many of the buildings. Indeed, the gardens around the entire property give this tropical haven a romantic quality—one of its biggest assets, along with the beach, of course.

Guest rooms are located in two separate areas: poolside and hillside. Bougainvillea, the area by the beach, has seven two-story buildings around the huge, beautiful pool; they are staggered to provide each unit with a garden or sea view. In Hibiscus, the area where most rooms are located, the buildings are tiered up the steep hillsides. All have grand views of the Caribbean and neighboring Virgin Islands.

Transportation is on call to shuttle you up and down the hills when you prefer not to make the climb. All the one- and two-bedroom suites are in the hillside buildings, all with panoramic views.

The decor of the rooms calls on a rainbow of pastels to provide a quiet, inviting look. There are marble foyers and bathrooms, and the master bedrooms of suites and town houses have whirlpools. The stocked minibar of the past has been replaced by a mini-refrigerator. At High Tide Market in the lobby, you can order a basket of items or individual items to be charged to your bill and sent to your room.

The Renaissance has two freshwater pools, one overlooking the beach and a second one toward the back of the property, next to one of the resort's main restaurants and near the fitness center. There is also tennis, along with racquets and clinics; a full range of water sports operated from the hotel's private dock; and a dive center offering day and night dives for beginners and certified divers. All nonmotorized water sports, snorkeling gear, and introductory pool lessons for snorkeling and scuba are complimentary.

The fitness and spa center is impressive. It has LifeFitness equipment, including treadmills, Lifecycles, LifeStep, free weights, and weight machines. The men's and women's locker rooms are each equipped with changing rooms, showers, sauna, and steam rooms. Complimentary exercise classes are offered six times a week, including aqua aerobics, and beach aerobics. A weekly yoga class is offered for a small fee. Two rooms in the fitness center are reserved for massages, facials, body wraps, and waxing.

Of course, if you have something less taxing in mind, you'll find hammocks (roomy enough for two) stretched between the palm trees.

Dining at the Renaissance takes in views and breezes, too. Baywinds on the Beachfront, the oceanfront dining room and bar, offers American cuisine with a Caribbean accent in an a la carte menu and buffet breakfast daily, plus a "lite bites" menu from 10:00 P.M. to midnight and nightly

entertainment. The Palm Cafe, a poolside snack bar, serves light meals and drinks in an outdoor setting during the day.

Smugglers Steak and Seafood Grille, in an open pavilion by the garden pool, is the resort's main dinner venue; it features seafood, including a live lobster tank, and black Angus beef. Its grilled specialties are prepared in an open "exhibition" kitchen. It's especially popular for its award-winning Sunday brunch, when a grand buffet with a dozen or more choices for every course is there to tempt you, along with a make-your-own Bloody Mary bar—all for only $24.95 ($11.95 for children). No wonder it's popular! Piano music fills the room during Sunday brunch.

The Renaissance encourages families to bring their children by providing Club Gecko, a program of supervised activities for age four to twelve, during holidays. It operates daily, except Sunday, for four hours and costs $35 per child, per day, including lunch. The activities are as varied as face painting, iguana hunts, pool games, and nature hikes or a movie and pizza party. Also, the resort's restaurants offer a children's menu for those age twelve and under.

The Renaissance Grand Beach's facilities and relaxing, casual atmosphere offer broad appeal to honeymooners, couples of all ages, and families. The majority of guests are from the United States, and at least some are part of a group; they are usually people who have been high scorers in their company's incentive program. A week at this resort is considered quite a prize.

Renaissance Grand Beach Resort ✳✳✳

P.O. Box 8267, Smith Bay Road, St. Thomas, U.S.V.I. 00801
Phone: (340) 775–1510; Fax: (340) 775–2185;
www.renaissancehotels.com/sttsr, www.offshoreresorts.com

Owner: Marriott International
General Manager: David Yamada
Open: Year-round
Credit Cards: All major
U.S. Reservations: Renaissance Hotels and Resorts, (888) 314–3514
Deposit: Two nights in winter; one night in summer
Minimum Stay: Five nights during Christmas
Arrival/Departure: Transfer arranged upon request
Distance from Airport: (Cyril E. King International Airport) 10 miles; taxi one-way, $10
Distance from Charlotte Amalie: 8 miles; taxi one-way, $8.00
Accommodations: 290 rooms including 36 suites; all with terraces (86 rooms in seven poolside buildings; 204 rooms in one-to four-tiered hillside buildings)
Amenities: Air-conditioning; direct-dial telephone; safes; cable television, movies; refrigerator, coffeemaker; bath with tub and shower, bathrobes, hair dryers, toiletries; iron and ironing board; nightly turndown service, room service; shops; beauty salon; shopping shuttle to town center; high-speed Internet access
Electricity: 110 volts
Fitness Facilities/Spa Services: See text
Sports: Two freshwater swimming pools; six tennis courts (four hard surface, two Omni-turf, lighted), clinics, resident USPTA pro, pro shop; volleyball; free nonmotorized water sports including Windrider sailboats, kayaks, windsurfers with instruction; jogging trails; dive facility with daily free instruction; daily sails on on-site trimarans; sport fishing, golf arranged
Dress Code: Smartly casual
Children: All ages; Club Gecko (see text); cribs, high chairs; baby-sitters
Meetings: Up to 650 people; audiovisual facilities
Day Visitors: Yes, with reservations
Handicapped: Entire property wheelchair accessible; specially designated rooms must be requested in advance
Packages: Golf, family, honeymoon, wedding, dive; Inclusive, Semi-Inclusive, Island Explorer, Spa
Rates: Per room, daily, EP. **High Season** (January–April): $259–$339. **Low Season** (May–mid-December): $145–$185. Meal plans available
Service Charge: At discretion of guests
Government Tax: 8 percent

THE RITZ-CARLTON

St. Thomas, U.S.V.I.

Commanding a magnificent setting at the eastern end of St. Thomas with expansive views of the U.S. and British Virgin Islands, The Ritz-Carlton with its Italian Renaissance style and hilltop location could easily have you imagining that you are somewhere on the Italian Riviera.

Terraced in fifteen acres of lavish gardens, the elegant resort was designed by Barbadian architect Ian Morrison, whose signature is the adaptation of various Mediterranean architectural elements to Caribbean settings. The main building and centerpiece of the resort suggests a Venetian Renaissance palace outfitted with a prince's ransom of Italian marble. Its red tile roof and ochre stucco facade are reminders of the Mediterranean style.

From the hotel's impressive entrance reached by a long, flower-lined driveway, you arrive at an imposing valet-attended porte cochere and step into the palazzo and onto beautiful Portuguese marble mosaic floors. These lead you through graceful arched and columned hallways to the reception desk.

This, it turns out, is the upper level of the palazzo, with high-arched Palladian windows that open onto spectacular views of the resort and the islands dotting the turquoise Caribbean waters below. At the center of the building is a small inner courtyard; one of its walls has several lion-head fountains with water cascading gently from one to another.

This imposing structure holds the administrative offices, several fashionable boutiques, a beauty salon, and a concierge desk on the top level; a small fitness center, the Ritz-Kids room and a meeting room on the lower. The Living Room, an all-purpose lounge used for afternoon tea, cocktails, or as a sports bar, opens on to the courtyard. The rest of the resort spans the hillside in both directions and falls to the beach via a flower-festooned stone stairway and a magnificent pool.

Rimming the southern side are multilevel beige stucco buildings with red tile roofs and flower-filled terraces, resembling large villas on the Italian Riviera; each is named for a tropical flower. They house the large guest rooms with fresh new decor reflecting their tropical surroundings. All have large balconies with fabulous views, air-conditioning, ceiling fans, coffeemakers, hair dryers, and enlarging mirrors.

Each carpeted room is furnished with an armoire that hides the television and stocked minibar, a desk and chair, one or two rattan love seats with a coffee table, and either a king-size or two double beds. There are three telephones—by the bed, on the desk, and in the bathroom. In the closet you will find an umbrella along with a digital safe. The marbled bathroom has a long, narrow shelf over two separate sinks along with toiletries, a pair of monogrammed seersucker bathrobes, and iron and ironing board.

On the northern side of the palazzo, the dining pavil-

ion, with pink walls and peaked roofs, houses two air-conditioned restaurants as well as an elegant new ballroom and two meeting rooms. The casual indoor-outdoor cafe serves a light fare of salads, sandwiches, pizzas, and grilled seafood for lunch, and Italian- and Caribbean-inspired selections in the evening. The more elegant and expensive dining room in pink marble under a high ceiling is very romantic and offers a gourmet menu. A lounge by the dining room usually has soft piano music after dinner. In-room dining is available round the clock.

The hills rimming The Ritz-Carlton form something of an amphitheatre cupping the beach. To the south is a mangrove pond with ducks and other birds and at the center is a gorgeous 125-foot-long free-form swimming pool with a vanishing edge on the side toward the sea, allowing the water to spill over like a waterfall—when you look across the pool, the water seems to disappear into the sea. It has sunning space on three sides; the fourth is anchored by a third restaurant, Iguana's, serving breakfast, lunch, and dinner in a pleasant, outdoor setting.

Snorkeling, windsurfing, Sunfish and Hobie Cat sailing, as well as dive instruction, certification, and excursions are all available for an additional charge. The hotel's 53-foot catamaran, Lady Lynsey, offers day sails and cocktail cruises. The tennis complex, with lighted Astroturf courts, has a pro who gives lessons and arranges matches and partners. A horticulturist leads walking tours.

The fitness center has exercise and weight-training equipment and offers aerobics classes and a personal trainer on request. Aromatherapy and other spa treatments can be enjoyed at the Spa Retreat on the beach or in the privacy of your room. The hotel is adding an elaborate spa that is scheduled to open in 2003.

The Ritz-Kids Club, a children's program for ages four to twelve, is available daily, except Sunday, from 9:00 A.M. to 4:00 P.M. On Tuesday it is also available 6:30 to 9:30 P.M., and on Thursday during the evening hours only. The program is supervised by trained counselors and offers a wide range of fun and educational activities. The cost is $10 for a half day; $20 for a full day including lunch; and $30 for the evening. Baby-sitting services are also available.

The Ritz-Carlton will increase in size by one-third by 2003 when a major addition will be completed on the adjacent beach. The Ritz-Carlton should appeal to just about anyone who likes a stylish atmosphere and can afford the tab. Bear in mind that you will need to do quite a lot of walking. There are golf carts to fetch you from your room to the palazzo, but they tend to function on island time—which is to say, slow.

The Ritz-Carlton ✱✱✱✱
6900 Great Bay, St. Thomas, U.S.V.I. 00802
Phone: (340) 775–3333; Fax: (340) 775–4444;
www.ritzcarlton.com/resorts/st_thomas

Owner/Management: THC St. Thomas Corporation
General Manager: Jamie Holmes
Open: Year-round
Credit Cards: All major
U.S. Reservations: (800) 241-3333
Deposit: Three nights; thirty days cancellation
Minimum Stay: None, except during Christmas; inquire
Arrival/Departure: Transfers available
Distance from Airport: (Cyril E. King International Airport) 7 miles (thirty minutes); taxi one-way, $12 per person
Distance from Charlotte Amalie: 6 miles (twenty minutes); taxi one-way, $11.
Accommodations: 148 spacious oceanfront rooms, four one-bedroom suites
Amenities: Air-conditioning, ceiling fans; three international direct-dial telephones; marble bath with tub and shower, two sinks, separate toilet, hair dryer, toiletries, bathrobes; twice-daily maid service with nightly turndown service; stocked minibar; clock, CD players, radio/cable television; safe; beauty salon; laundry and valet service; twenty-four-hour room service
Electricity: 110 volts
Fitness Facilities/Spa Services: See text
Sports: Freshwater swimming pool; snorkeling, windsurfing, Sunfish sailboats, Hobie Cats; scuba instruction, full certification, dive available for additional charge; lighted Astroturf tennis courts, Peter Burwash pro, equipment, lessons; golf at Mahogany Run and deep-sea fishing arranged
Dress Code: Casual by day; casually elegant in evening
Children: All ages; Ritz-Kids Club, age five–twelve; baby-sitters
Meetings: Up to 200 people
Day Visitors: Welcome with reservations
Handicapped: Entire property is wheelchair accessible. Rooms available for physically challenged. However, be aware that property is on hillside and very spread out.
Packages: Honeymoon, wedding, dive, others
Rates: Per room, daily, EP. *High Season* (mid-December–April 30): $545– $2,000. *Shoulder Season* (May–early July and October–mid-December): $350–$1,200. *Low Season:* $250–$750.
Service Charge: At discretion of guests
Government Tax: 8 percent

On the Horizon

This section includes resorts that have opened in the past year or
are due to open soon and hold the promise of being among the best.

ALTAMER

Shoal Bay West, Anguilla, B.W.I.

The story of Altamer reads like a dream. A few years ago an American couple, Michael and Rebecca Eggleton (he, an international banker; she, a CPA) were vacationing on Anguilla when they decided to buy some property and build a beach house. Their seven acres abutted crescent-shaped Shoal Bay West, a secluded beach on the western end of Anguilla with views of St. Martin in the distance across the Caribbean Sea.

They envisioned a reasonably modest home, but by the time they decided to build, the government had enacted laws requiring all beachfront property to be operated as a hotel or villa available for rent to visitors.

Near their property were the futuristic, snow-white villas of Covecastles, designed by well-known architect Myron Goldfinger with interiors by his wife, June. The Eggletons wanted their villa to be consistent with the nearby architecture, but unique in its design. With Goldfinger as the architect, they planned Altamer—a beach house like no other.

Rebecca Eggleton and June Goldfinger set off on several worldwide odysseys to find artists, furniture makers, and artisans to duplicate historic items for use in the decor and to arrange for such extravagances as handmade $10,000 Murano glass light fixtures for the living room.

The resulting collection is stunning. Throughout, the furnishings combine stylish modern pieces with fine antiques and rare art from around the world, with an emphasis on Turkey, Russia, and Italy. Even more exciting, some of the items are available for sale in Altamer's new boutique, and plans are being made to publish a catalogue as well as develop a Web site.

To say that this beach house is over the top might be an understatement. In the ultra modern villa all rooms have floor-to-ceiling windows facing the blue Caribbean waters. Access is via twin towers on its east and west sides, each

with a staircase and one with an elevator for guests' convenience and to accommodate handicapped persons.

The eye is greeted with a fantasylike opulence, with oversize wicker furniture awash in a sea of multihued silk cushions—pink, purple, and periwinkle—arranged in conversation groupings. Vases of floral bouquets are everywhere.

On the first floor are the Great Room with a soaring twenty-one-foot ceiling, sitting areas, a formal dining room with a custom-designed table for twelve, views of the beach from the large sliding glass doors and windows, and a state-of-the-art Viking Professional Gourmet Kitchen where the villa's chef turns out his fabulous creations. Forget calories.

Behind the elongated oval glass dining table is a large three-part painting, *Cloud Triptych,* by Jan Aronson. It is the perfect complement to the ceiling, which seems to touch the sky. There is a second Aronson painting in the room and a priceless antique Russian chest to keep board games of all kinds. Here, too, is a magnificent gilded candelabra—a little something that Rebecca and June picked up in Russia. It's 18-karat gold on bronze and was formerly owned by one of the Czars. Whew!

There are no rugs or carpets, simply a spotlessly clean tile floor. When asked why, Macbeth, the senior butler, is quick to reply, "After all, it's a beach house."

Outside this first floor is the swimming pool, which runs almost the length of the building and is ringed with chaise lounges with canary-yellow cushions. On the far side of the pool is a grove of palm trees with the vibrant blue sea peeking through. It's the Yellow Brick Road, Bali Hai, and Shangri-La in one!

The second floor, with full views of St. Martin and the Caribbean, has a triangle-shaped game room with a wet bar, pool table, and home theater with flat-screen television and a DVD player. Guest rooms One and Two, also with full sea views, are on this level, each with a marble bathroom with a Jacuzzi tub and separate shower. Extending out toward the sea and accessible only from this level is a 50-foot-long Skywalk, allowing guests to lounge, dine, bird-watch, or catch the sunrise at the water's edge.

On the third level is the grand master bedroom, which more than lives up to its name. Measuring 26 feet by 26 feet, it has a 19-foot ceiling, a curved balcony and bar above, and three large skylights for natural lighting. A wicker couch and chairs form a sitting area. A king-size bed swathed in fine Italian linens has a television at its foot. Next to the bed is a bit of whimsy—a pair of slippers said to have belonged to a Turkish sultan's favorite mistress. In the marble bathroom are long twin vanities, a Jacuzzi for two, separate walk-in shower, and wall-mounted television. Directly off the bedroom is a huge private balcony with extensive views. Guest rooms Four and Five with high ceilings and skylights are also on this level.

The fourth-floor balcony over the master bedroom has a sitting area and can be converted into an office with a computer with high-speed Internet access, printer, scanner, and fax. The balcony also has a stainless steel and marble wet bar—handy for guests lounging in privacy on the rooftop patio, some 40 feet above ground level.

A caveat: The other bedrooms, while comfortable, cannot compare to the master bedroom. Those planning to take the villa with friends might want to draw straws to decide who gets the master bedroom first, and then rotate (the butlers will switch the clothing) so all have their turn at the ultimate Altamer luxury.

Near the entrance to the villa in a separate building is a guest room that can accommodate two additional persons. It also houses a fitness center.

But all this is merely the beginning. Before the Eggletons finish, they will have added a restaurant (opened August 2001); a small receptions and executive meetings facility (opened March 2002); two more villas (opening in 2003), each slightly larger than the first villa, with five bedrooms and six baths, six bedrooms and seven baths, and each villa with a fitness room; and a second tennis court.

Most people cannot imagine the experience Altamer offers. Call it contemporary sybaritism—all 12,000 square feet of it, with no detail overlooked, no amenity too small, and no need too great. Service is impeccable. You soon discover that you rarely have to ask for anything. The butlers not only anticipate every need, they seem to read your mind.

Ton de Wit, the former butler at the Royal Palace in The Hague and holder of England's Order of Master in

Royal Household medal, selected and trained the staff that includes three butlers, a gourmet chef, a cook, a manager/concierge, two housekeepers, and two gardeners.

John Macbeth, the senior butler, was at London's Lanesborough Hotel and personal assistant to many celebrities over the years. A man of many talents, Macbeth is also the concierge, wine steward, and host, who creates fun and spontaneous events by fashioning interesting experiences for guests. Typical are his whimsical table settings, whether on the dining terrace, poolside, or on the beach. Assisting Macbeth is Carl Irish, a Montserrat native and natural people-person, who will probably meet you at the airport on arrival; and Sheldon Brookes, an Anguillan, as are the other staff members.

Chef Maurice Leduc, whose forty years of experience ranges from an apprenticeship at Maxim's in Paris to an award-winning French restaurant in Boston and gold medal awards in the International Culinary Exhibition four years in a row, is also in charge of Altamer Restaurant and all catering events at the resort.

From the island's main road, the turn off to Altamer is onto a recently paved road marked by an Altamer sign and leads to the resort's small gatehouse where a security guard welcomes you. Since guests fill out in advance a guest preference form, which includes credit card information as well as menu choices, arrival is like being welcomed into the home of a rich uncle. There are no formalities, save for the entire staff being on hand to greet you.

You are offered iced towels and ushered into the Great Room for drinks. Depending on the time of arrival, you will probably sit down for a "snack" on the terrace, dining at a small table festively decked out with Medici-inspired table settings, brilliant flowers, and contrasting linen. The snack will include fresh-baked bread and perhaps a medley of chilled fresh lobster, shrimp, conch, and scallops on a bed of greens, and a selection of house wines—always three: a red, a white, and a rosé at every lunch and dinner.

By the time you get to your bedroom, your suitcases will have been unpacked and your clothes neatly folded in drawers or placed on hangers in the closet.

Evenings are spent watching movies from the extensive DVD library, lazing in the Great Room listening to CDs from a collection that numbers in the hundreds, or watching the fiber-optic tube around the lip of the pool change color, casting different hues on the water. The remote that controls music throughout the villa can be operated from anywhere in it. The refrigerator in the kitchen is yours to raid at any hour, and Maurice thoughtfully leaves a sweet and some late-night snacks in plain view.

When the time comes to leave, John, Carl, and Sheldon make it easier by packing your gear while you have breakfast or take a last swim.

The sheer elegance and grandeur of Altamer can be overwhelming, but it will appeal to those who crave barefoot elegance in superb surroundings with extreme comfort and excellent service—provided, of course, they can afford it.

Altamer

Box 3001, Shoal Bay West, Anguilla, B.W.I.; or 6800 SW 40th Street, Box 333, Miami, FL 33155

Phone: (264) 498–4000, (888) 652–6888; Fax: (264) 498–1010, e mail: info@altamer.com, www.altamer.com

Owner: Michael and Rebecca Eggleton

General Manager: Rebecca Eggleton

Open: Year-round

Credit Cards: American Express, Visa, MasterCard, Discover

U.S. Reservations: (888) 652–6888, rings to Anguilla office for reservations

Deposit: Three nights to secure reservation, thirty to ninety days balance, depending on time of year; deposit refunded only if cancellation prior to balance due

Minimum Stay: Seven nights

Arrival/Departure: Altamer meets guests at airport and arranges taxi. (Note: Anguilla hotels cannot provide their own transportation for guests due to taxi regulations.)

Distance from Airport: 8 miles; twenty minutes by taxi; one taxi transfer per group included in villa rates

Accommodations: One villa with five bedrooms and six baths with Jacuzzi tubs and separate showers; two bedrooms available in separate quarters; two additional villas (opening in late 2003) with five bedrooms and six baths, six bedrooms and seven baths

Amenities: Air-conditioning, ceiling fans; professional kitchen; high speed Internet connection; flat screen television with DVD player, stereo system; safe; butler and maid service 7:00 A.M. to 10:00 P.M.

Electricity: 110 volts

Fitness Facilities/Spa Services: Fitness center; massage and spa services on request

Sports: Beach, swimming pool; snorkeling, tennis, deep-sea fishing, sailing, diving arranged

Dress Code: Casual

Children: All ages

Packages: Weddings

Rates: Per day, all-inclusive. **High Season** (mid-December–mid-April): $5,429; weekly $38,000. **Low season:** $3,428 and $24,000, respectively. For holidays, Christmas/New Year's, inquire.

Service Charge: 10 percent

Government Tax: 10 percent

THE INN AT OLD BAHAMA BAY

West End, Grand Bahama Island

Perched on the westernmost tip of Grand Bahama Island, Old Bahama Bay is anything but old. On an island where large high-rise resorts dominate the landscape, The Inn at Old Bahama Bay, which opened in May 2001, brings a low-key charm to the island's historic West End community. It has also sparked a renaissance in this corner of the island.

Surrounded by a beautiful turquoise sea on three sides and spread over 150 lush acres, this resort community comprises twenty-four waterfront suites; a seventy-two slip state-of-the-art, full-service marina complete with immigration and customs processing; and fifty-eight building lots—in case you decide you want to stay.

Located only 56 speed-boat miles east of Palm Beach, The Inn at Old Bahama Bay is Grand Bahamas's first luxury boutique hotel. The suites (each measuring 550 to 700 sq. ft.) are housed in two-story, beachfront cottages surrounded by tropical gardens. Each is appointed with custom-designed plantation-style furnishings, a king-size bed or two queens, cable television, DVD player, direct-dial phone with dataport, wet bar with mini-fridge, microwave, and coffeemaker. Each also has a large ocean-view patio or balcony overlooking a beautiful curved strand of white sand fringed with palm trees. Luxury amenities like Frette linens, towels, and robes add the finishing touches to the already fabulous accommodations.

The spacing of the cottages affords a great deal of privacy, making the resort ideal for couples, newlyweds, or small families. Hammocks hang from beachside palms and the 4,000-square-foot freshwater pool and bar almost straddles the beach. Three nature trails wind through the property, offering nature lovers an opportunity to get acquainted with some of the West End's flora and fauna. Besides the walking trails, there are also seven snorkel trails to explore in the area's underwater world.

The Dockside Grille, overlooking the marina, offers inside/outside dining for breakfast, lunch, and dinner, serving international cuisine as well as Bahamian and Caribbean specialties.

Every accommodation comes with trail maps and a laminated underwater field guide complete with pencil to enable snorkelers to document the marine life they see. Three of the snorkel trails are accessible from the resort's beach and the Settlement Point Nature Trail at the opposite side of the peninsula, while the others are located on nearby cays. There is free water-shuttle service to and from these deserted cays and the resort will even arrange a picnic lunch.

For those who still have energy to burn after hiking or snorkeling, the resort has two tennis courts, bicycles, a 1,000-

square-foot fitness center with the latest exercise equipment, a massage pavilion, and a water-sport facility with glass-bottom pedal boats, kayaks, windsurfers, and Hobie Cat sailboats. The water-sport center can also arrange scuba diving and deep-sea fishing.

For those looking for a special place close to Florida shores, Old Bahama Bay should be at the top of the list as an alternative to high rise resorts in Freeport—or Miami, for that matter. And of course, the upscale resort has particular appeal to boaters who can arrive in their private vessels.

The Inn at Old Bahama Bay

Box F-42546, West End, Grand Bahama Island
Phone: (242) 350–6500. Fax: (242) 346–6546;
e-mail: info@oldbahamabay.com; www.oldbahamabay.com

Owners: Holding Capital Group

General Manager: Michel Neutelings

Open: Year-round

Credit Cards: All major

U.S. Reservations: (800) 572–5711

Deposit: 30 percent for confirmation

Arrival/Departure: Complimentary round-trip airport transfers

Distance from Airport: 25 miles

Distance from Freeport: 25 miles

Accommodations: 24 suites (47 suites by end of 2002)

Amenities: Air-conditioning; one king-size bed or two queens; wet bar, mini-fridge, and microwave; direct-dial phone with dataport, DVD player, cable TV, hair dryer, room service; daily housekeeping and turndown service; concierge

Electricity: 110 volts/60Hz

Fitness Facilities/Spa Services: See text

Sports: See text

Dress Code: Casual

Children: Welcome

Meetings: Meeting and banquet space for small groups; business center and heliport

Day Visitors: Must call first to make arrangements

Handicapped: Very limited

Packages: Five-night Romantic Getaway, three-night Endless Weekend, two-night West End Getaway; wedding

Rates: Two people, daily, AP. (January 7–December 21): $290. Extra person in room (maximum of two), $30 daily. Two people, daily MAP, $400. Extra person, $85 daily.

Service Charge: $8.00 per room per day

Government Tax: 12 percent of room rate; included in packages

THE HOUSE

Paynes Bay, St. James, Barbados, W.I.

In autumn 2002, the proprietors of The House at Tamarind Cove, located along "hotel row" on the west coast of Barbados, plan to debut what they say is a new concept in boutique hotel luxury. The idea is simple and sounds almost like a cliché—to make guests feel "at home." Hence, the name, which could come off as brazenly pretentious unless they deliver. And they might.

The House occupies a fully renovated, all-suite private wing of the 162-room Tamarind Cove hotel, owned by the Elegant Hotel Group of London, which operates four other properties in Barbados and one in Antigua. The House is the brainchild of Elegant Hotel's CEO Marcello Pigozzo, who joined the company last year after thirty years with Intercontinental Hotels and Hoteles Sol Melia.

From his understanding, as a seasoned globe-trotter, of the longing for the comforts of home while on the road and his knowledge of the hotel business, Pigozzo saw a conflict and recognized an opportunity. Rather than require a guest to adhere to the policies and procedures of the hotel, hotels should adapt their policies and procedures to the guest. For example: When you make a reservation at almost any hotel in the world, the hotel takes your credit card number and personal information. Yet, upon arrival, it makes you stand in line and give the information all over again. The House plans to eliminate such unnecessary inconveniences.

At The House—a prototype that Pigozzo plans to craft into twenty-five properties worldwide within five years—the concept means, in essence, you can get what you want, as you like it, when you want it. Ask for a Bloody Mary at six o'clock in the morning and it materializes—even though the bar is closed. Got the munchies? There's twenty-four-hour room service from the hotel's signature restaurant, Daphne's, the new Caribbean outpost of the acclaimed celebrity hangout in London. Need any other kind of personal service? Your twenty-four-hour butler is on call.

Of course, there is nothing unique about such niceties—it's the stock-in-trade of boutique hotels and cruise ships. But The House has come up with a challenging innovation—the Service Ambassador, a dedicated staff member who functions as a twenty-four-hour personal concierge or butler and handles everything from taking your breakfast order and bringing you an Evian spritzer on the beach to making your bed and arranging for your wake-up call.

The personalized service begins upon your arrival at

and well appointed, they are elegantly simple in their execution, just as is the rest of the resort, including the open-air lobby, reminiscent of a living room from the pages of *Architectural Digest*, that features white fabrics over dark wood furniture and original modern art on the walls.

Guests at The House can enjoy complimentary water sports including snorkeling, windsurfing, kayaking, sailing, and parasailing. Water skiing is available for a fee. They may use the tennis courts at the hotel's nearby sister properties, Colony Club and Crystal Cove, and they receive preferential tee times at the Barbados Golf Club.

Guests can also use the facilities of Tamarind Cove Hotel next door. These include an air-conditioned fitness center and its restaurants—Sasso, which serves excellent local and continental meat and seafood favorites in a charming covered-patio setting; and Tangerine, the beach-side restaurant. The new Daphne's, sandwiched between The House and Tamarind Cove, features contemporary renditions of Italian fare based on fresh local ingredients. The House serves complimentary high tea daily and your Ambassador leaves freshly made canapés each evening.

The price of this luxury and pampering is not cheap. In high season, a suite with full breakfast, will cost about $1,000 or so per day for two people. But if you place a high value on privacy, personalized service, and the simple luxuries like an exquisite night of sleep or having to ask for something only once, The House might be for you—provided, of course, it meets the challenge it has set for itself.

the Barbados International Airport, where you are greeted by a hotel Ambassador and whisked through customs to a waiting private car. Actually, The House experience begins even before your arrival, when your Ambassador calls you at home to learn your likes, dislikes, and expectations.

Upon your arrival at the hotel, there is no check-in. After entering from a private driveway flanked by tranquil lily ponds and walls of blossoming bougainvillea, you are simply escorted to your suite by your Service Ambassador. While she or he puts away your clothing and personal belongings, you get a complimentary half-hour massage. After that, your Ambassador is always nearby, ready to turn your whims into realities.

Meanwhile, the luxury unfolds. When it's time to sleep, you'll be resting on fine Italian Frette linens. When you go to the private stretch of pristine white-sand beach, you'll be reclining on the plushest and most comfortable cushions money can buy. While you tan, your Ambassador will bring chilled fruit and water along with your Evian.

The House consists of forty-two suites, all with an ocean view, private balcony, and flat-screen plasma satellite television. While the suites are comfortably spacious

The House

Paynes Bay, St. James, Barbados, W.I.
Phone: (800) 326–6898, (246) 432–4424;
e-mail: thehouse@eleganthotels.com;
www.eleganthotels.com

Management: Elegant Hotels Group, London, England
Credit Cards: Most major
U.S. Reservations: Elegant Hotels Reservations, (800) 326–6898
Deposit: Three nights, seven days cancellation
Minimum Stay: Ten nights during Christmas/New Year's, other periods three to seven nights.
Arrival/departure: Complimentary airport meet/assist service to/from hotel
Distance from Airport: Forty minutes; taxi one-way, $45
Children: Twelve and older only
Accommodations: 42 ocean-view suites and rooms
Rates: Per person, double, per day, FAB. To December 18, 2002, $358–$512. *High Season:* To be announced.
Service Charge: 18.25 percent
Government Tax: 18.25 percent

HOTEL KURA HULANDA

Willemstad, Curaçao

Kura hulanda means Dutch courtyard in Papiamentu, the native language of Curaçao. Given that the island is the architectural crown jewel of the Netherlands Antilles, this simple term perfectly denotes the distinctive, charming environment of the Hotel Kura Hulanda.

Opened in late 2001, the hotel is the centerpiece of Project Kura Hulanda, which includes sixty-five historic buildings, mostly former private homes. A sprawling eight-block complex, Project Kura Hulanda showcases meticulously restored eighteenth- and nineteenth-century Dutch colonial architecture and includes an internationally recognized cultural museum, a conference center, and retail shops.

Hotel Kura Hulanda, clustered around several appealing courtyards, is a sixty-seven-room luxury boutique hotel that seems more like a well-executed theme park than a resort hotel. It could also be a movie set, the Dutch colonial equivalent of Dodge City on a studio lot. It is, in fact, an extraordinary fusion of "urban renewal," Caribbean style, and one man's obsessive vision.

Dutch millionaire Jacob Gelt Dekker, along with his longtime partner John R. Padget, made his fortune in rental-car and one-hour-photo businesses in Europe. On a trip to Curaçao after he and Padget had sold off their major business interests at huge profits, Dekker fell in love with the island's extraordinary architecture. Almost overnight, he drew up plans for Project Kura Hulanda.

In a run-down neighborhood of dilapidated houses and broken streets, Dekker and his team carved out, quite literally, an architectural and cultural oasis. For its originality, vision, and commitment to local culture, Kura Hulanda has already been recognized as a UNESCO World Heritage site by the United Nations.

Aimed primarily at well-heeled business travelers and cultural-architectural tourists from Holland, the Caribbean basin, and the United States, Hotel Kura Hulanda is conveniently located in the center of the Otrabanda section of Willemstad, Curaçao's capital, only fifteen minutes from the airport. The brightly colored compound, located above St. Anna Bay near the Queen Emma Bridge, is within easy walking distance of Punda, Willemstad's major downtown district across the retractable pontoon bridge.

The hotel gives the impression of a peaceful village, with tree-lined streets carefully crafted of imported stone and a tour-book façade with some interesting architectural flourishes, such as perfect replicas of historic houses Dekker saw on his travels to Suriname and a charming central courtyard between the lobby and the restaurants and shops. Elsewhere around the property there is a series of intimate courtyards that include an African sculpture garden and an herb and fruit garden. A sophisticated high-tech sound system pipes in music specific to the mood of each courtyard.

Kura Hulanda's spacious, nicely appointed accommodations include double rooms and suites. Because the units are adapted from renovated private homes, no two are the same. As a decorative motif, each room displays a wall hand-painted by a local artisan. Custom-made furniture, including four-poster, mosquito-netted beds from Indonesia, is hand-carved from the finest mahogany and old teak; the handwoven linens are from India; bathrooms are of Indian marble. Rooms also have beautifully hand-carved standing mirrors and bars.

Two signature suites are a 996-square-foot, two-story, one-bedroom Presidential Suite that includes an entertainment center with big-screen television and a fully equipped kitchen; and a sexy yet sophisticated bridal suite with handcrafted furniture made of hammered sterling silver, including a canopied, hand-carved bed worthy of Cleopatra. A pair of luxury, duplex, spa loft suites have huge bathrooms suitable for in-room treatments.

Amenities include air-conditioning, ceiling fans, waffle-weave bathrobes, hair dryers, minibar, remote-controlled satellite TV, portable CD system, and teak butler stands for clothing and comforter. The hotel's interna-

tional appeal is reflected in its telephone system with modem and voice mail available in English, Dutch, French, and Spanish. A wake-up call, for example, can be programmed in one's native tongue.

Kura Hulanda has two swimming pools, including the "eco-pool," a grotto surrounded by natural rock formations and fed by a waterfall, and a more traditional pool near a sculpture garden; there is also a kiddie pool. Hotel guests enjoy access and complimentary transportation to a private beach club eight minutes from the hotel, and preferential golf privileges are available at a nearby golf club. An air-conditioned and fully equipped fitness center has free weights and the latest machines and a sauna and steam room. Guests can view satellite television, watch videos, or listen to CDs on their headsets while doing their cardiovascular workout on stationary bikes or treadmills.

Above the fitness center is the hotel's spa, where guests can enjoy facials, massages, manicures, and pedicures for an additional charge. In-room services are also available. The hotel has a business center, and among its most important facilities in today's post-September 11 world, the complex has an unobtrusive state-of-the-art security system that monitors the grounds around the clock from eighty discreetly placed video cameras.

The tight security and conference facilities make Kura Hulanda an excellent site for corporate meetings. Its facilities include three auditorium-style meeting rooms, closed-circuit television capabilities, and state-of-the-art audiovisual equipment. An executive boardroom accommodates up to twenty people and includes a side bar and private dining room.

For dining, Kura Hulanda offers a number of options, from casual to classy. The hotel's Indian influence is carried through at Jaipur, its signature restaurant serving tandoori oven specialties from traditional chicken and nan breads to shrimp and lamb. The restaurant, set by the rock grotto eco-pool, also has a cozy, alfresco bar. The AstroLab Observatory restaurant, with a courtyard filled with museum-quality maritime navigational instruments, serves breakfast and dinner. For dinner, the specialties are meat and seafood in a pristine, white-tablecloth ambience.

Jacob's Bar offers tapas and cocktails in a Spanish setting with an outdoor dining terrace overlooking the central courtyard. Located just off the lobby, the News Cafe has coffee, tea, and snacks. The hotel has a children's menu with such favorites as chicken nuggets, hamburgers, hot dogs, and peanut butter and jelly sandwiches—all served with French fries—for $3.95.

The Kura Hulanda Museum, which has educational relationships with major universities around the world, including the University of Florida, houses the largest African collection in the Caribbean and a stunning, eye-opening exhibit that chronicles the history of slavery. It also has a small courtyard restaurant serving lunch and dinner.

For travelers more interested in history and culture than beaches and who like being within easy walking distance of Curaçao's main attractions, Kura Hulanda is an attractive new option.

Hotel Kura Hulanda

Langestraat 8, Willemstad, Curaçao
Phone: 011–5999–434–7700; www.kurahulanda.com

Owners/Managers: Dr. Jacob Gelt Dekker and John R. Padget
President/General Manager: Peter Heinen
Open: Year-round
Credit Cards: Most major
U.S. Reservations: Leading Small Hotels of the World at (800) 223–6800; e-mail: reservations@lhw.com
Deposit: Only credit-card guarantee required; cancellation up to twenty-four hours in advance
Minimum Stay: None
Arrival/Departure: Transportation available by taxi only
Distance from Airport: (Hato International Airport) 8 miles
Accommodations: 67 rooms and suites (17 deluxe, 12 superior, 14 standard rooms; 14 junior, three one-bedroom, five deluxe one-bedroom suites; one presidential, one bridal, one executive, and two spa loft suites)
Amenities: Air-conditioning, ceiling fans; marble bathroom, hair dryer, bathrobes; stocked minibar; cable television; teak clothing and comforter butler stand; portable in-room CD player/stereo; 110-outlet by desk, multilingual telephone system with modem and voice mail; safe; room service (7:00 A.M.–11:00 P.M.); nightly turndown service
Electricity: 110/220 volts
Fitness Facilities/Spa Service: Fitness center, spa (see text)
Sports: Two swimming pools; children's pool; transportation to and from private beach club; golf nearby
Dress Code: Casual; shorts and T-shirts not allowed at dinner
Children: All ages
Meetings: Two conference rooms for up to fifty people; auditorium for 160; executive boardroom for twenty with adjacent dining room; closed-circuit television; audiovisual equipment; interpreter/translator system for Dutch, English, French, and Spanish
Packages: Golf, dive, museum, honeymoon
Rates: Per person, double, per day, EP. *High Season* (late December–mid-April): $275–$800. *Low Season* (mid-April–late December): $250–$700. Third adult, children, and MAP rates available.
Service Charge: 12 percent
Government Tax: 7 percent

LA LUNA

St. George's, Grenada, W.I.

The operative word for this new resort is minimalist. In the look of the cottages, in another era, it would have been called bare. But then, it's funky, too. Certainly, La Luna breaks the mold.

Located in the southwestern area of the island between the airport and Grand Anse Beach, La Luna is approached by a rutted dirt stretch until about a quarter-mile before the resort, where a paved road begins. (The government has promised to pave the road, but don't hold your breath.)

Sixteen cottages are set on the hillside in three rows, far enough apart to be private, except for the top row. Each cottage, a cement rectangle, is painted in bright, rather garish, Caribbean colors—blue, purple, yellow—

with a wash effect. (Actually, the color was mixed into the plaster to get the effect.) The porches have bamboo roofs and living room-style furnishings suitable for the outdoors.

But inside, the look is quite different. Each room is furnished with a four-poster, mahogany king-size bed with imported white linens and netting; soft cushions on a concrete slab constitute a sofa, and there is a straight chair and table for reading or writing, a television/VCR and a CD player (tapes and CDs are available at the office at no charge), air-conditioning, and ceiling fan. French doors open onto the porch; white gauze curtains can be pulled over the opening. The rooms have no pictures or adornment of any kind on any of the walls . . . purposely not to distract from the outside view. Only a neutral color area rug covers the concrete floor at the entrance to the bedroom.

The bathroom has a long cement counter painted in

same bright color as the cottage walls. A round basin sits on *top* of the counter—an ultramodern design innovation sometimes found in new, trendy hotels. A better innovation is the three-pronged lamp that allows you to twist one or more prongs to get the lighting you want in the mirror or elsewhere. The bathroom is stocked with top-quality Italian lotions and shampoos.

The shower has several openings in the upper part of its wall, so you can view the sea while showering. There's also a gauze curtain or blind that can be raised, exposing one entire wall to the outdoors. A high bamboo fence outside keeps the neighbors from peeking in. The toilet is separate from the bath in its own closet. One of the best features of the cottage layout is a door opening onto the porch and outside, so you can enter the bathroom upon returning from the beach without tracking sand into the bedroom.

Each cottage has a small, round, sunken whirlpool simulating a mini-plunge pool just outside the bathroom door on the end of the porch not covered by the bamboo roof. It's big enough for two—an ideal perch for watching sunsets as you sip your cocktail or gazing up at starlit skies.

The top row of accommodations is composed of double cottages that connect. They are designed in the same style as the single ones and are sold singly, in which case one guest must cross over the other's porch to get to the second cottage. A drop-down blind acts as a divider between porches.

The lounge area of the main building is attractive. A pavilion in Balinese style, with a roof but no walls, opens directly onto the beach in front. There is a bar on one side with dark furniture and thick white cushions, enhanced by wooden sculpture and objets d'art from Bali, handpicked by the owner, Bernardo Bertucci. The art placed around the lounge and the grounds is unusual, some pieces even quirky, but all interesting. There is also a tiny gift alcove.

A wooden deck at the front of the pavilion and facing the beach has low wooden, cushioned lounges. Below the deck are lounge chairs in the sand along the tree-shaded beach, which is bookended by high cliffs, making it very private.

Beyond the bar is the pool and the main restaurant, a pavilion-style beachside restaurant presided over by an Italian chef who makes good use of Grenadian spices (Grenada is known as the Spice Island of the Caribbean) in his dishes. Be sure to try his great callaloo soup.

The Beach House Restaurant at one end of the beach is an option for guests who want to vary from the hotel dining room. You can also have continental breakfast served on your porch, but there is no regular room service. Rooms have coffee/tea makers and minibars.

La Luna does not have a water-sports facility but does have complimentary kayaks, Hobie Cats, and snorkeling gear available for guests to use and can arrange diving, golf, tennis, and fishing as well as island excursions.

Casual attire is emphasized. Not even shoes are required, but at dinner, guests must wear cover-ups.

For those ready for an away-from-this-world setting where "nothing to do" is touted as the resort's main asset, La Luna awaits discovery.

La Luna

Morne Rouge, P.O. Box 1500, St. George's, Grenada, W.I. Phone: (473) 439–0001; Fax: (473) 439–0600; e-mail: info@laluna.com; www.laluna.com

Owner: Bernardo Bertucci

General Manager: Charles Hossle

Open: Year-round

U.S. Reservations: Direct to the hotel or 880–4LALUNA

Deposit: Three nights; thirty days cancellation

Credit Cards: Amex, Visa, MasterCard

Minimum Stay: Seven nights over Christmas and New Year's

Arrival/Departure: Transfer service not available

Distance from Airport: 2 miles

Accommodations: 16 guest rooms and suites with king beds in 12 cottages, all with private balconies with plunge pools and ocean views

Amenities: Air-conditioning, ceiling fans; safe; direct-dial telephones, CD player, minibar, television/VCR; coffeemaker; hair dryer, bathrobe; twice-daily maid service, including turn-down service; room service for continental breakfast only

Electricity: 220/240 volts

Fitness Facilities/Spa Services: In-room massage

Sports: Swimming pool, beach, kayaks, Hobie Cats, snorkeling gear, mountain bikes—all included in rate.

Dress Code: Casual

Day Visitors: Bar and restaurant only

Handicapped: None, not suitable

Children: Ten years of age and older in high season, on request during remainder of year

Meetings: None

Packages: Romance, diving, escape

Rates: Per cottage, per day, EP. *High Season* (December/January–April): $480–$630. *Low season* (May–mid-December): $270–$370.

Service Charge: 10 percent

Government Tax: 8 percent

TI KAYE VILLAGE

Anse Cochon, St. Lucia

Nestled on a cliffside overlooking the Caribbean Sea, Ti Kaye Village is a small, quiet cottage resort on St. Lucia's west coast by the village of Anse Cochon about halfway between Castries, the capital, and Soufrière, the island's old capital. The resort takes its name from the local patois meaning "small house."

Designed by Wayne Brown, one of the founders of Anse Chastanet Resort and Stonefield Estate in St. Lucia, Ti Kaye Village has thirty-three cottages of traditional West Indian style with gingerbread trim and louvered windows and doors to catch cool Caribbean breezes. All cottages have air-conditioning and are furnished with a king-size, four-poster bed. Each cottage has a large veranda with a hammock for two and a private, spacious garden shower, open to the sky. Some oceanfront cottages have a private plunge pool on the veranda.

Nineteen rooms are in individual cottages; fourteen other rooms are in seven duplex cottages adjoined by a balcony door. These can be rented separately or as a two-bedroom unit and are particularly suited to families or two couples traveling together.

The main pavilion, close to the cottages, has a restaurant, tropical bar, and freshwater swimming pool—all with panoramic views of the Caribbean, a great perch for watching St. Lucia's fabulous sunsets. The restaurant has a European chef.

Ti Kaye Village has a fitness center, massage therapist, and water-sports facilities. A staircase zigzags down 166 steps to a pretty cove with silver sands and calm, crystal-clear waters where guests can get outfitted for snorkeling, diving, and other water sports at The Scuba Center. Ti Kaye has teamed up with Dive Fair Helen Undersea Adventures, a full-fledged PADI Dive Center and an affiliate of Neal Watson Undersea Adventures, to offer some of the best diving in the Caribbean. The Center caters to a wide range of divers from beginners to the most advanced.

The bay Ti Kaye faces is home to the *Lesleen M,* a popular shipwreck dive site and to beautiful coral reefs. Equally significant for divers, the resort is only a ten-minute boat ride to the Soufrière area, which boasts the Anse Chastanet reef and the majestic Pitons with their spectacular walls and reefs. Two-tank boat dives are made each morning, followed by a one-tank afternoon dive. Shore and night dives are also available. Dive Fair Helen has two custom-built dive boats, both with onboard washroom and shower facilities, shade, and ease of entry and exit.

Ti Kaye Village

Anse Cochon, P.O. Box GM 669, Castries, St. Lucia
Phone: (758) 456–8101; Fax: (758) 456–8105;
e-mail: tikaye@candw.lc; www.tikaye.com

Owner: Nicholas Pinnock

General Manager: Jeannine Davies

Open: Year-round

U.S. Reservations: Direct to hotel

Deposit: 30 percent for confirmation; seven days cancellation notice in summer, fourteen days in winter

Credit Cards: Most major

Minimum Stay: Three nights

Arrival/Departure: Upon request, hotel arranges transfers from either airport; see below.

Distance from Airport: *(Hewanorra International Airport)* Eighty minutes, $90 if hotel's shuttle company used, $150 by taxi; or *George F. Charles Airport* (SLU) north of Castries, forty minutes, $60; airport transfers included in honeymoon and dive packages

Accommodations: 33 cottages (19 rooms in individual cottages; 14 rooms in seven duplex cottages; kings only), all with private balconies; three with plunge pools

Amenities: Air-conditioning, ceiling fans; telephone, strong boxes, coffee/tea makers, fridge-minibar, hair dryers; no television (available on request)

Electricity: 110 and 220 volts/50 cycles

Fitness Facilities/Spa Services: Fitness room

Sports: Swimming pool, beach, kayaks, snorkeling, diving

Dress Code: Casual

Day Visitors: Yes

Handicapped: Not appropriate

Children: Twelve years and over

Rates: Per room, per day, single or double, BP. *High Season* (mid-December–mid-April): $195–$300. *Low Season:* $165–$225.

Service Charge: 10 percent

Government Tax: 8 percent

THE CARENAGE BAY BEACH & GOLF CLUB

Canouan, St. Vincent & The Grenadines

NOTE: Carenage Bay Beach will close for one year until May 2003 to add major new facilities. These include a full-fledged spa; four villa buildings, each with beachfront one- and two-bedroom suites; and a complete redesign of the golf course into an eighteen-hole championship course by Jim Fazio, expanding it from 60 acres to 250 acres. It will be ready for play several months prior to the official reopening of the hotel. Surfside, the daytime beachside restaurant and bar, will be upgraded for casual evening dining as well, serving seafood and Caribbean cuisine.

The opening of the multimillion-dollar Carenage Bay Beach and Golf Club in 2000 heralded a new era for the bucolic island of Canouan, known more for beaches and bananas than boutiques and ballrooms.

Until two years earlier, when bulldozers began to shift layers of earth and the resort began to take shape, only the Anglican Church, with a crescent beach at its feet, was on this site. And even the stone church is something of a newcomer, having been brought to the island stone by stone from Britain at the end of the nineteenth century.

Now, the church rises above the sharp roof lines of 172 paint-washed villas, the terra-cotta-hued Town Square, and a free-form freshwater pool that undulates a quarter of a mile parallel to the sea.

The Carenage is a Hollywood blockbuster of a resort, created, financed, owned, and staffed by Italians and tended to by locals from St. Vincent and neighboring islands. Italian financier Antonio Saladino both built the no-expense-spared resort and developed the island's infrastructure, including water system, roads, electricity, and a new, larger, colors-of-carnival airport.

Italian designers have a knack for reinterpreting Caribbean clichés with so much style that they are no longer clichés. In the case of Carenage Bay Beach, Italian architects Luigi Vietti, who designed the Aga Khan's villa in Sardinia, and Antonio Ferrari freely mixed Caribbean colors and designs with exotic motifs from a range of tropical destinations.

Thus, the Indonesian roof lines of the villas contrast with the Mexican furnishings, Indian fabrics, palapas (thatched-roofed shade pavilions), while the walls are enlivened with the colors of mango and papaya and original works of art by Italian artists. The mix works and even the sharp-angled roofs blend into the land-

scape—helped perhaps, because the resort occupies only 100 acres of an 800-acre site. But then, the sea and offshore reef, the green hills, and rugged terrain curving around the beach at either end of the resort are constant reminders that this is the Caribbean, after all. That is, until you visit Big Point.

Big Point is Carenage's answer to Monaco. The White House-like edifice atop a steep hill about a fifteen-minute drive from the resort houses the casino. Yes, a casino. Here, the croupiers are better dressed than the guests, the slot machines discreetly tucked in shadows, and the crystal chandeliers outnumber the hidden cameras in the high ceilings. And yes, it's a big Wow, but you will not be the first to wonder why on a sleepy Grenadine island of only 1,500 inhabitants there would need to be so elaborate a gaming house.

On the other hand, you can easily succumb to the spell of La Bagatelle, the casino's gourmet French restaurant with a selection of thirty-four champagnes and a fabulous view that takes in about the same number of islands and cays. Dinner here is a three-hour event, overseen by a restaurant manager and a maitre d' who know when to hover and when to disappear, when to translate and when to refill.

La Bagatelle is one of Carenage's four restaurants. La Piazza, an octagonal-shaped Italian/Mediterranean restaurant, framed by tall windows, blue-glazed walls, copper pots, and double layers of white tablecloths, has an a la carte dinner-only menu created by Italian television celebrity chef Luigi Bergeretto. It includes unusual dishes such as breadfruit dumpling with octopus, cream of eggplant soup with shrimp, and a dessert of risotto with blueberries and cheese. The finest ingredients—olive oil from Oneglia (Liguria) and rice, pasta, cheeses, and truffles from Peck in Milan—are imported from Italy.

More in the beer-and-barefoot style is the open-air Surfside Bar and Grill, five minutes by golf cart up a hill and around the bend on Godahl Beach. Here you can sip Hairoun, the local beer, munch on a Milanese baguette, and scoop up homemade ice cream served in colorful Italian crockery. When the resort reopens in 2003, Surfside will also be opened for casual evening dining.

The Beach Club Restaurant, comprised of four Balinese-style interconnecting houses, each decorated in its own individual style under a palapa roof and overlooking the pool and beach, rounds out the options. (Incidentally, Amazonas Indians were flown to the island to thatch the palapas in the traditional way.) One area houses the Pink Baron bar. The Beach Club serves a breakfast buffet and for lunch and dinner offers fish and meats from the grill, salads, and authentic Italian pizzas from the wood-burning oven.

Carenage has five categories of accommodations from a deluxe room of 616 square feet to a two-bedroom villa suite with 1,936 square feet. My digs, Villa 76, were big—so big that I lost track of my husband. He settled low in a rattan and cushioned settee on the spacious patio and promptly slid from my view. I mistook the entrance to the second bathroom for a large walk-in closet. The kitchen and dining area with a hand-carved dining room table were better equipped than mine at home. Families do well with the supply of china, utensils, a two-burner range, a half-size stocked refrigerator, an espresso maker, and a selection of coffees and teas.

The living room has a complete entertainment center, two comfortable couches that invite lounging, plenty of lights, an overhead fan, a floor-to-ceiling view of sea and sky, and a sliding door to the patio. Original works of art by Italian artist, Costanzo Rovati, depict objects found on Canouan. Rugs are scattered randomly on the tile floors, air-conditioning is controlled by high-tech wall thermostats (familiarity with Celsius temperatures helps), and phones have Internet connection capabilities.

The bedroom is light and airy with gauze curtains, shutters that open and shut easily, two bureaus, and a vaulted ceiling with a fan. The king-size four-poster bed with Frette linens has slim iron posts rather than the carved mahogany versions more often seen in the Caribbean. (Some guest rooms have handcrafted wood bed frames, custom made in India.) The master bathroom won my heart with its colorful Mexican-tile basins, strong lighting, Bulgari toiletries, large walk-in shower stall, Jacuzzi bathtub, and Frette towels and bathrobes. There is twice-daily maid service and a concierge.

The golf course runs along the seafront on the flat coastal plain and on the hillsides above the resort where Fazio is adding more challenging greens. Golf instruction and rental clubs will be available.

The Health and Fitness Center is being expanded with a full-fledged spa with a wide range of treatments and state-of-the-art exercise equipment.

For other diversions, the resort has three all-weather, lighted tennis courts; Sunfish, snorkel gear, windsurfers, hydro-bikes, and pedalos are available on a complimentary basis. You can walk the pretty white-sand beach and take a day trip on the resort's 51-foot *Canouan Express* catamaran to nearby Tobago Cays. Scuba diving can be arranged. Should you decide to get married, the stone church in the heart of the resort, with beautiful murals and stained glass windows, has been lovingly restored.

But then, you might want to do nothing more ambitious than perch on a stool at the swim-up bar for a chat with the bartender. Should the urge to do something hit you, your golf cart (with a maximum speed of 3 miles per hour flat out) awaits.

The Carenage Bay Beach & Golf Club

Canouan Island, St. Vincent & The Grenadines, West Indies
Phone: (784) 458–8000; Fax: (784) 458–8885;
e-mail: info@canouan.com; www.canouan.com

Owner: Antonio Saladino

General Manager: Bruce Hearn

Open: Closed for expansion; reopening summer 2003

U.S. Reservations: Leading Hotels of The World, (800) 223–6800 or direct to hotel, (784) 482–2148; e-mail: reservations@carenage.com

Deposit: Three nights, within fourteen days of booking; twenty-eight days cancellation

Credit Cards: Most major

Minimum Stay: Ten nights Christmas only

Arrival/Departure: Transfer complimentary

Distance from Airport: Ten minutes

Accommodations: 172 rooms and villa suites with private balconies (king-size beds; twins available)

Amenities: Air-conditioning, ceiling fans; safe; hair dryer; Frette towels, bathrobes, and bed linen; Bulgari toiletries; twice-daily maid service, dual-line telephone with computer fax/Internet; television on request; minibar/refrigerator; fruit basket; concierge; in-room dining.

Electricity: 220 volts/50 cycles

Fitness Facilities/Spa Services: Fitness room, full-service spa (opening 2003), hair salon

Sports: Swimming pool, beach, tennis courts, Sunfish, windsurfing, kayaks, snorkeling, included in rate; eighteen hole golf course

Dress Code: Casually elegant; appropriate dress required on tennis courts and golf course; jackets required at gourmet restaurant and casino; no shorts or jeans after 7:00 P.M.

Day Visitors: Day golf and beach packages available

Handicapped: Limited

Children: All ages; Kids Club for ages four to ten; babysitting service

Meetings: Seven meeting rooms at Town Square; casino ballroom

Rates: Per room, per day, single or double, EP. *High Season* (Christmas/New Year's): $550–$2,150; (January–April): $490–$1,900. *Shoulder Season* (April and November 15–December 15): $375–$1,600. *Low Season* (May–mid-November) $300–$1,375.

Service Charge: 10 percent

Government Tax: 7 percent

BLUE HAVEN HOTEL

Bacolet Bay, Scarborough, Tobago, W.I.

History and nostalgia buffs, listen up. If you are addicted to late-night 1940s and '50s movies set in bewitching tropical isles and have fantasized about romantic nights under star-filled balmy skies, we have just the place for you.

Situated along the southern shores of Tobago at Bacolet Bay, the Blue Haven Hotel, where royalty honeymooned and movie stars frolicked, was once considered one of the leading hotels in the Caribbean and the location for several movies. Rita Hayworth and Robert Mitchum were frequent guests, and Princess Margaret spent part of her honeymoon here. Now, the hotel has been completely and extensively renovated.

Perched on a promontory jutting into the sea and surrounded on three sides by water, Blue Haven's fifteen oceanfront acres were probably part of a fort in colonial days as there are cannons and the remnants of ancient walls dating back to 1770. The new-old hotel is located in a quiet residential neighborhood just outside of Scarborough, Tobago's capital, convenient to the town center, the market, and cultural and historic sites, and a twenty-minute drive from Crown Point International Airport.

From the entrance to Blue Haven, you pass through a hundred-year-old palm alley and tropical gardens to the archways of the old hotel and to the Octagon, an eight-sided lobby with a high, royal-blue ceiling with white beams.

The small hotel has fifty-one rooms including ten junior suites. Twenty-five rooms and two suites are in the renovated old building, and sixteen rooms and eight suites were added in two new wings. Connecting rooms and suites for families are available. The new buildings are covered by a strange-looking floating roof meant to create open space between the ceiling of the guest rooms and the roof for air to pass through and keep the rooms cooler.

Inside, the rooms are comfortably furnished in a somewhat minimalist fashion with white walls, white bed covers, and splashes of color in the works by Johan Jascha on the wall. The rooms have handsome mahogany four-poster or double sleigh beds. All accommodations are air-conditioned and have balconies with sea views. The junior suites have separate sitting and living areas with pull-out sofa.

Telephones with computer jacks, television, hair dryer, and safe are standard in all rooms. The newest rooms have a large window between the bathroom and bedroom that enables guests to see the sea while they are bathing; a shade can be lowered to block the view into the bathroom.

Blue Haven is serious about protecting the environment. In the renovation, it worked to save the historic character of the resort and to use methods to make the

gather for cocktails in the Terrace Bar, just off the lobby. Dinner offers international cuisine with West Indian ingredients and spices.

During the day, guests can choose between the swimming pool or the hotel's secluded beach, said to be the place Robinson Crusoe was stranded in 1659. The hotel has a lighted tennis court, a fitness center, and shuffleboard and can arrange golf, sailing, scuba diving, snorkeling, deep-sea fishing, guided hikes in the rain forest, and bird watching tours. Massages are also available.

Blue Haven Hotel

Robinson Crusoe Beach Resort, Bacolet Bay, Scarborough, Tobago, West Indies
Phone, (868) 660–7400; Fax: (868) 660 7900;
e-mail: bluehaven@bluehavenhotel.com;
www.bluehavenhotel.com

Owners/Managers: Karl and Marilyn Pilstl
Open: Year-round
U.S. Reservations: Direct to the hotel or (800) 232–3237
Deposit: 50 percent on room rate; three room nights if cancellation less than three weeks prior to arrival
Credit Cards: Amex, Visa, MasterCard
Minimum Stay: Seven nights Christmas/New Year's
Arrival/Departure: Transfer service one-way by bus, $12 and limousine, $35
Distance from Airport: Twenty-minute drive
Accommodations: 51 guest rooms and suites with king beds and ocean views (25 rooms and two suites in original building; 16 rooms and ten suites added)
Amenities: Air-conditioning, ceiling fans, safe, direct-dial telephones, television/VCR, coffeemaker; hair dryer
Electricity: 220 volts
Fitness Facilities/Spa Services: Fitness center and massage
Sports: Swimming pool, beach; snorkeling, diving, hiking, deep-sea fishing arranged
Dress Code: Casual
Handicapped: None, not suitable
Children: Three and under are free
Packages: Honeymoon, wedding
Rates: Per room, per day, EP. *High Season* (December/January–mid-April): $260–$390. *Low Season* (mid-April–mid-December): $198–$295.
Service Charge: Included
Government Tax: 10 percent

hotel environmentally sound. it has a solar system to heat the water; rainwater is collected; energy-saving lights and biodegradable detergents are used throughout; the grounds are planted mostly with indigenous plants; local organic farmers are supported—these are only a few of the positive routines the hotel follows.

Breakfast and dinner are served in the colonial-style villa restaurant Shutters on the Bay, while the No Problem Beach Bar is open for lunch. In the evening guests

STONEHAVEN VILLAS

Black Rock, Tobago, W.I.

Stonehaven Villas is a gated complex of fourteen spacious villas climbing a steep hillside on Tobago's west coast from where they enjoy spectacular panoramic views of the Caribbean Sea and tropical sunsets. Behind the villas is the 140-acre Grafton Caledonia Wildlife Sanctuary with forest trails and an afternoon bird-feeding schedule open to visitors.

The villas, French Provincial in style, were designed by the late Swedish architect, Arne Hasselqvist, who created most of the homes on Mustique. Each of the two-story houses, with 3,700 square feet, has three air-conditioned bedrooms, each with a private balcony; three bathrooms, and a large veranda running the length of the house and alongside a private infinity-edge pool.

The villas are comfortably furnished in eighteenth-century French colonial-style mahogany furniture. They have greenheart ceilings from Guyana, oil-rubbed bronze fittings from Chile, marble vanities from Italy, and green granite kitchen counters from Brazil. A bar also has an ice-maker and wine cooler. All villas have cable television. Upon arrival, guests will find fresh flowers in their villa and complimentary breakfast, beach towels, and daily housekeeping service.

The first floor of each villa has an entrance foyer, living room, one bedroom and bathroom, and kitchen with refrigerator, stove, dishwasher, microwave, toaster, coffeemaker, blender, pots, pans, and cooking utensils, as well as fine cutlery, crockery, and glassware for eight. The laundry area has a washer and dryer, iron and ironing board. On the second floor, there are two bedrooms, each with a bathroom and balcony. There is nightly turndown service.

The veranda by the pool is particularly enjoyable in the early morning for breakfast with the sounds of awakening birds all around and in later afternoon to watch the Caribbean sunsets. Each villa has a personal housekeeper who will prepare meals in a fully equipped modern kitchen and provide maid service. Massages, manicures,

and pedicures are available in the privacy of the villa.

Halfway down the hillside, the Clubhouse in pavilion style has an infinity pool, lounge and bar, executive meeting space, and a restaurant presided over by a French chef. The restaurant serves a casual lunch, while dinner has a more elegant ambience.

Stonehaven has facilities for conferences, retreats, weddings, and family reunions. Scuba diving and snorkeling, fishing, sailing, windsurfing, tennis, and golf can be arranged.

Stonehaven has a sister villa group at its feet by the beach. Plantation Beach Villas has six villas designed in colonial West Indies style with gingerbread trim around the windows and doors. The villas have large, teak-floored verandas and they are furnished in island style. There is a swimming pool and beach bar at the water's edge.

Stonehaven Villas

P.O. Box 1079, Grafton Road, Black Rock, Tobago, West Indies
Phone: (868) 639–0102, (868) 639–0361;
e-mail: stonehav@tstt.net.tt; www.stonehavenvillas.com

General Manager: Peter Howard

Open: Year-round

U.S. Reservations: Direct to the hotel or (800) 633–7411

Deposit: 10 percent to confirm reservation; full payment thirty days prior to arrival; ninety days cancellation full refund

Credit Cards: Amex, Visa, MasterCard

Minimum Stay: Four days; six days for Christmas/New Year's

Arrival/Departure: Transfer service for $10 one-way

Distance from Airport: Fifteen-minute drive

Accommodations: 14 three-bedroom villas with king-size beds and ocean views

Amenities: Air-conditioning, ceiling fans; direct-dial telephones, television/VCR; safe; fully equipped kitchen; daily maid service

Electricity: 110 volts

Fitness Facilities/Spa Services: Fitness center and massage

Sports: Swimming pool, beach; snorkeling, diving, hiking, deep-sea fishing arranged

Dress Code: Casual

Handicapped: None, not suitable

Children: Three and under are free

Packages: Honeymoon, wedding

Rates: Per villa, per day for up to four people, EP. **High Season** (December/January–mid-April): $770–$825. **Low Season** (May–mid-December): $395.

Service Charge: 10 percent

Government Tax: 10 percent

TOBAGO HILTON
Lowlands, Tobago, W.I.

Located on the windward side of Tobago's southwestern coast, the Tobago Hilton occupies twenty beachfront acres that are part of Tobago Plantations with a ninety-acre natural lagoon and protected mangrove forest, 3 miles from the capital of Scarborough.

The three-story hotel structure is designed to support the plantation setting of its surroundings. In one direction, the hotel overlooks its new PGA-designed, eighteen-hole championship, par-72 golf course; and in another direction, a huge free-form pool overlooking a white-sand beach and the sea.

The Tobago Hilton has 200 luxurious ocean view rooms and one- or two-bedroom suites with Jacuzzi; all have balconies. They are decorated in colorful island decor and have air-conditioning, ceiling fans, minibar, coffeemaker, direct-dial telephone with dataport, safe, cable television, and bathroom with a magnifying mirror, hair dryer, and separate stall shower and bathtub.

The Tobago Hilton's dining venues include the Coral Reef, which features fresh seafood in an elegant setting; the Plantation Restaurant, offering casual all-day dining; Robinson Crusoe's Pub, which serves cocktails and light fare and has live local entertainment; Friday's, a poolside bar and grill; the Palm Court, a spacious lobby lounge; and Tradewinds, the swim-up pool bar. Room service is also available.

The hotel's facilities include a large teardrop-shaped, freshwater swimming pool with swim-up bar by the beach, two lighted tennis courts, a health club with sauna and massage room, and a variety of water sports.

The new Plantations Golf and Country Club, adjacent to the hotel, is set against the island's windward side in a tropical plantation setting of palm trees, mangroves, and a sugar mill. The 7,000-yard, par-72 course is Tobago's only PGA championship-designed golf course and one of the region's most challenging designs.

Architects Bob Hunt and Marcus Blackburn of PGA Golf Management Ltd. designed the course to reflect Tobago's Caribbean setting and to protect its environment. Characteristic pot bunkers are sunk into the greensides, as on the third hole—a par-4 beauty that stretches onto a peninsula where there are panoramic views of Scarborough and the ocean. Other holes weave their way through palm trees and mangroves and an old sugar mill behind the seventeenth green. Artificial lakes and wetlands developed to regenerate nature are fast becoming a home and breeding ground for migratory ducks and birds.

The Golf Academy, staffed with PGA-qualified pros,

offers lessons for all levels from beginners to advanced, low-handicap players. Video analysis is available. There is a well-stocked pro shop. Rental and trial clubs and packages are also available.

For children age five to seventeen, the hotel offers the Learning Center with daily activities, such as local arts and crafts, nature hikes, glass-bottom boat trips, and games. There are twice-weekly rain forest and marine biology talks.

The Hilton Tobago has more than 6,000 square feet of state-of-the-art meeting space with a large ballroom and two smaller meeting rooms.

Tobago Hilton

Lowlands, Tobago, West Indies,
or P.O. Box 633, Scarborough, Tobago
Phone: (868) 660–8500; Fax: (868) 660–8503;
www.hilton.com

General Manager: Greg Weinlaender
Open: Year-round
U.S. Reservations: 800–HILTONS or direct to hotel
Deposit: One night
Credit Cards: All major
Minimum Stay: None

Arrival/Departure: Transfers can be arranged
Distance from Airport: *(Crown Point International Airport)* fifteen-minute drive
Accommodations: 200 ocean-view rooms (including 22 one- or two-bedroom suites with Jacuzzi; 156 kings and 22 twins, with balcony
Amenities: Air-conditioning, ceiling fans; safe; alarm clock, direct-dial telephone with dataport, cable television; coffeemaker; bathrooms with hair dryer, separate stall shower and bathtub
Electricity: 110 volts
Fitness Facilities/Spa Services: Health club with sauna and massage
Sports: Freshwater swimming pool, beach; two lighted tennis courts; eighteen-hole PGA-designed championship golf course; snorkeling, diving, hiking, deep-sea fishing arranged
Dress Code: Casual
Meetings: Ballroom and two meeting rooms
Packages: Honeymoon, wedding, golf
Rates: Per room, per day, EP. *Year-round:* $225–$490.
Service Charge: 10 percent
Government Tax: 10 percent

The Best of the Best

This chart is meant to help readers locate quickly the resorts that might best meet their particular interests. It is not intended to be a complete inventory of each resort's facilities. Instead, it indicates the especially strong features of each establishment. For example, most beachside resorts in this book offer scuba diving or can arrange it, as we have noted in the text; however, the chart notes only those resorts focused primarily on diving or that have a particularly outstanding dive facility.

	Beachside	Hillside	All-inclusive	Budget	Value	Honeymoon	Romantic	Wedding	Children's Program	Families	Singles	Sports/Active	Dive	Golf	Tennis	Marina	Spa/Fitness Center	Nature Lovers	Hiking	Birding	History	Cuisine	Entertainment	Casino
Anse Chastanet (St. Lucia)	•	•				•	•	•				•	•				•	•	•					
Asa Wright (Trinidad)		•		•	•							•						•	•	•				
Bakoua (Martinique)	•																•							
Biras Creek (British VI)	•		•			•	•	•		•		•					•		•	•				
Bitter End (British VI)	•	•		•	•			•	•	•		•	•				•							
British Colonial Hilton (Bahamas)	•					•						•	•								•			
Buccaneer (USVI)	•					•		•	•	•		•		•	•		•	•			•			
Calabash (Grenada)	•					•											•							
Caneel Bay (USVI)	•					•	•	•				•			•		•	•	•					
Cap Juluca (Anguilla)	•					•	•										•					•		
Capt. Don's Habitat (Bonaire)	•			•									•											
Carl Gustaf (St. Barts)		•				•																•		
Casa de Campo (Dominican Republic)	•	•		•	•			•		•		•		•	•	•	•	•					•	•
Cobblers Cove (Barbados)	•					•	•					•										•		
Coco La Palm (Jamaica)	•			•				•														•		
Compass Point (Bahamas)	•					•					•											•		
Coral Reef Club (Barbados)	•						•	•				•					•				•	•	•	
Cotton House (The Grenadines)	•					•	•															•		
Couples Swept Away (Jamaica)	•	•	•	•	•	•	•					•			•		•						•	
CuisinArt (Anguilla)	•				•		•					•						•				•		
Curtain Bluff (Antigua)	•	•	•		•		•					•			•		•					•		
Dunmore Beach (Bahamas)	•										•											•		
Eden Rock (St. Barts)	•					•	•														•	•		
El Conquistador (Puerto Rico)	•	•		•		•	•	•	•	•				•	•	•	•		•			•	•	•
El Convento (Puerto Rico)				•	•					•											•			
El San Juan (Puerto Rico)	•					•	•		•			•			•		•						•	•

Resort	Beachside	Hillside	All-inclusive	Budget	Value	Honeymoon	Romantic	Wedding	Children's Program	Families	Singles	Sports/Active	Dive	Golf	Tennis	Marina	Spa/Fitness Center	Nature Lovers	Hiking	Birding	History	Cuisine	Entertainment	Casino
Filao Beach (St. Barts)	•									•												•		
Four Seasons Nevis (Nevis)	•	•	•			•			•	•		•		•	•		•	•						
Frangipani (The Grenadines)	•			•																				
Gallery San Juan (Puerto Rico)				•			•				•										•			
Galley Bay (Antigua)	•		•			•						•						•		•				
Glitter Bay (Barbados)	•					•	•	•		•		•					•							
Golden Lemon (St. Kitts)	•					•	•	•													•	•		
Golden Rock (Nevis)		•		•		•	•											•	•			•		
Grace Bay Club (Turks & Caicos Islands)	•					•	•					•			•							•		
Grand Lido Sans Souci (Jamaica)	•	•	•			•	•					•					•							
Green Turtle (Bahamas)	•											•				•		•						
Guanahani (St. Barts)	•	•				•						•					•					•		
Guana Island (British VI)	•	•	•			•				•		•						•	•	•				
Habitation Lagrange (Martinique)		•																•			•	•		
Half Moon Club (Jamaica)	•					•	•	•	•	•		•		•	•		•						•	
Hermitage (Nevis)		•		•		•					•							•				•		
Hibiscus Beach (USVI)	•			•							•													
Hilton Trinidad (Trinidad)		•		•							•						•						•	
Horned Dorset Primavera (Puerto Rico)	•	•				•																•		
Hyatt Dorado Beach (Puerto Rico)	•					•	•		•	•		•		•			•	•					•	•
Hyatt Regency Aruba (Aruba)	•					•	•		•	•		•					•						•	•
Hyatt Regency Grand Cayman (Cayman Islands)	•					•	•		•	•		•				•	•					•		
Isle de France (St. Barts)	•	•				•						•					•					•		
Jamaica Inn (Jamaica)	•					•	•	•									•					•		
Jumby Bay (Antigua)	•					•	•	•	•	•		•			•		•	•	•					
La Samanna (St. Martin)	•	•				•	•	•				•		•	•		•					•		
La Sirena (Anguilla)	•			•						•	•													
LaSource (Grenada)	•	•	•	•		•	•					•	•		•		•	•	•					
LeSport (St. Lucia)	•	•	•	•		•	•					•			•		•	•	•					
Le Toiny (St. Barts)		•					•											•				•		
Little Dix (British VI)	•					•	•	•	•	•				•	•	•	•	•						
Maho Bay (USVI)	•	•		•						•	•							•	•					
Malliouhana (Anguilla)	•	•				•	•		•	•		•			•		•					•		
Marriott Curacao Beach (Curaçao)	•					•			•	•		•					•						•	•
Marriott Frenchman's Reef (USVI)	•					•	•	•		•			•		•									
Meridian Club (Turks & Caicos Islands)	•		•			•												•	•	•				
Montpelier Plantation (Nevis)		•				•		•				•							•	•	•			

	Beachside	Hillside	All-inclusive	Budget	Value	Honeymoon	Romantic	Wedding	Children's Program	Families	Singles	Sports/Active	Dive	Golf	Tennis	Marina	Spa/Fitness Center	Nature Lovers	Hiking	Birding	History	Cuisine	Entertainment	Casino
Necker Island (British VI)		•	•				•			•								•				•		
Nisbet Plantation (Nevis)	•				•	•	•														•			
Ocean Club (Bahamas)	•				•	•	•							•	•		•							
Ottley's Plantation (St. Kitts)		•			•	•	•	•		•				•				•	•			•		
Palm Island (The Grenadines)	•		•		•	•						•						•		•				
Parador Hacienda Gripinas (Puerto Rico)		•		•														•	•					
Parrot Cay (Turks & Caicos)	•					•	•										•	•	•					
Pasanggrahan (St. Maarten)	•			•						•	•													
Peter Island (British VI)	•	•				•	•			•			•			•	•	•	•					
Petit St. Vincent (The Grenadines)	•	•				•	•					•												
Pink Sands (Bahamas)	•					•	•										•							
Pirates Point (Cayman Islands)	•	•			•								•					•		•				
Point Grace (Turks and Caicos Islands)	•											•	•											
Rawlins Plantation (St. Kitts)		•		•														•	•					
Renaissance Grand (USVI)	•	•			•	•	•	•		•					•	•	•						•	
Renaissance Jaragua (Dominican Republic)				•	•					•	•						•					•	•	•
Ritz Carlton Rose Hall (Jamaica)	•					•	•	•	•	•				•	•		•	•				•	•	
Ritz Carlton San Juan (Puerto Rico)	•					•				•		•					•					•	•	•
Ritz Carlton St. Thomas (USVI)	•	•			•					•		•					•					•		
Rockhouse (Jamaica)		•		•	•	•	•											•				•		
Round Hill (Jamaica)	•	•			•	•	•							•	•		•							
Royal Pavilion (Barbados)	•				•	•	•							•			•							
Royal St. Lucian (St. Lucia)	•				•												•							
Runaway Hill (Bahamas)	•			•						•	•							•				•		
Sandals Dunn's River (Jamaica)	•		•	•		•	•	•						•									•	
Sandcastle (British VI)	•				•	•	•											•						
Small Hope Bay (Bahamas)	•				•	•				•	•		•					•	•					
Spice Island Inn (Grenada)	•				•							•	•				•							
Strawberry Hill (Jamaica)		•					•											•	•	•		•		
Sugar Mill (British VI)	•	•			•					•												•		
SuperClubs Breezes Runaway Bay (Jamaica)	•		•	•	•					•				•	•	•	•						•	
Tryall Club (Jamaica)	•	•						•		•				•	•		•				•			
Twelve Degrees North (Grenada)	•	•		•						•														
Village St. Jean (St. Barts)		•		•						•														
Water Club (Puerto Rico)	•			•							•											•		
Westin St. John (USVI)	•	•			•				•	•	•	•				•	•	•	•					
Young Island (St. Vincent)	•	•			•	•						•						•	•					

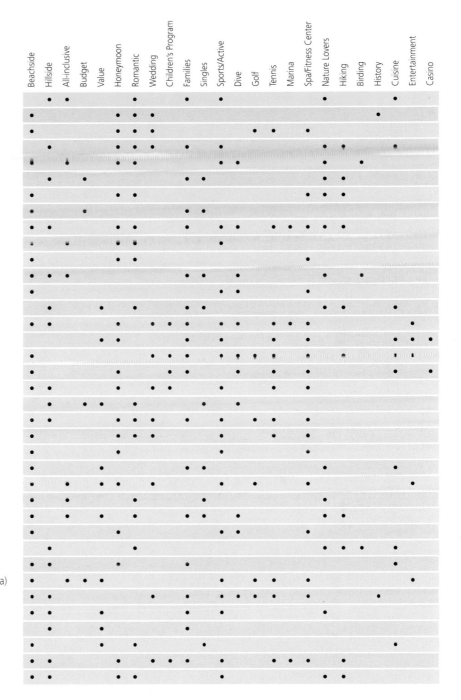

PHOTO CREDITS: Many thanks to the following people and organizations for providing photos: i Parrot Cay; p. iii Parrot Cay; p. iii Martha Morano Public Relations and Marketing; p. iii Photodisc; p. ix Montpelier Plantation Inn; p. v Peter Island Resort Worldwide; p. vi Michael Kleinberg for Kura Hulanda; p. vii Peter Island Resort Worldwide; p. x Ritz-Carlton Resorts of the Caribbean and Mexico; p. xii Michael Kleinberg for Kura Hulanda; p. xiii Couples Resorts; p. xv Tim Imrie; p. 2 Marilyn Marx Public Relations; p. 4 CuisinArt Resort & Spa; p. 5 CuisinArt Resort & Spa; p. 6 La Sirena; p. 7 La Sirena; p. 8 Rolf Gottwald Fotodesign for Malliouhana Hotel; p. 9 Rolf Gottwald Fotodesign for Malliouhana Hotel; p. 11 Curtain Bluff Resort, Antigua; p. 12 Curtain Bluff Resort, Antigua; p. 13 Andrew Innerarity and Willie Alleyne/Galley Bay; p. 14 Andrew Innerarity and Willie Alleyne/Galley Bay; p. 15 Elegant Resorts International; p. 16 Elegant Resorts International; p. 18 KWE Associates, Inc.; p. 19 KWE Associates, Inc.; p. 21 Green Turtle Club and Marina; p. 22 Green Turtle Club and Marina; p. 23 Small Hope Bay Lodge; p. 24 Small Hope Bay Lodge; p. 25 Cookie Kinkead/Dunmore Beach Club; p. 26 Cookie Kinkead/Dunmore Beach Club; p. 27 Cookie Kinkead, Island Outpost, L.L.C.; p. 28 Cookie Kinkead, Island Outpost, L.L.C.; p. 29 Runaway Hill Club; p. 30 Runaway Hill Club; p. 31 Hilton Caribbean; p. 32 Hilton Caribbean; p. 33 Cookie Kinkead, Island Outpost, L.L.C.; p. 34 Cookie Kinkead, Island Outpost, L.L.C.; p. 36 PhotoDisc; p. 39 Cobbler's Cove and LarsenCollinge International; p. 40 Cobbler's Cove and LarsenCollinge International; p. 41 Coral Reef Club; p. 42 Coral Reef Club; p. 44 Fairmont Hotels & Resorts; p. 45 Fairmont Hotels & Resorts; p. 46 Fairmont Hotels & Resorts; p. 47 Fairmont Hotels & Resorts; p. 49 Maduro Dive Fanta-Seas; p. 50 Maduro Dive Fanta-Seas; p. 52 Marco Ricca; p. 53 Marco Ricca; p. 54 Guana Island; p. 55 Guana Island; p. 57 Peter Island Resort Worldwide; p. 58 Dougal Thorton & Associates; p. 59 Dougal Thorton & Associates; p. 60 Max Kim-Bee/Biras Creek Resort; p. 61 Max Kim-Bee/Biras Creek Resort; p. 61 Max Kim-Bee/Biras Creek Resort; p. 62 The Bitter End Yacht Club; p. 62 The Bitter End Yacht Club; p. 64 Rosewood Caribbean Resorts; p. 66 Tim Imrie; p. 66 Tim Imrie; p. 69 KWE Associates, Inc.; p. 70 KWE Associates, Inc.; p. 72 Pirates Point Resort, Ltd.; p. 73 Pirates Point Resort, Ltd.; p. 75 Marriott and Renaissance Offshore Resort Network; p. 76 Marriott and Renaissance Offshore Resort Network; p. 79 Casa de Campo, Dominican Republic; p. 81 Casa de Campo, Dominican Republic; p. 82 Renaissance Jaragua Hotel and Casino; p. 83 Renaissance Jaragua Hotel and Casino; p. 85 The Calabash Hotel; p. 86 The Calabash Hotel; p. 87 Marilyn Marx Public Relations; p. 88 Marilyn Marx Public Relations; p. 89 LarsenCollinge International; p. 90 LarsenCollinge International; p. 91 Twelve Degrees North; p. 94 Cookie Kinkead for Strawberry Hill; p. 95 Cookie Kinkead for Strawberry Hill; p. 96 Elegant Resorts International; p. 97 Elegant Resorts International; p. 98 Ritz-Carlton Resorts of the Caribbean and Mexico; p. 98 Ritz-Carlton Resorts of the Caribbean and Mexico; p. 100 Elegant Resorts International; p. 101 Elegant Resorts International; p. 102 Marcella Martinez Associates Inc.; p. 103 Marcella Martinez Associates Inc.; p. 104 Coco La Palm ; p. 105 Coco La Palm ; p. 106 Couples Resorts; p. 106 Couples Resorts; p. 108 Rockhouse Hotel, Negril Jamaica; p. 109 Rockhouse Hotel, Negril Jamaica; p. 110 photographer Len Kaufman/Spring, O'Brien & Co., Inc.; p. 111 photographer Len Kaufman/Spring, O'Brien & Co., Inc.; p. 112 Marcella Martinez Associates Inc.; p. 112 Marcella Martinez Associates Inc.; p. 114 Sandals Resorts International; p. 114 Sandals Resorts International; p. 116 photographer Len Kaufman/Spring, O'Brien & Co., Inc.; p. 117 photographer Len Kaufman/Spring, O'Brien & Co., Inc.; p. 119 © David Sanger, Martinique Promotion Bureau; p. 120 © David Sanger, Martinique Promotion Bureau; p. 121 © Martinique Tourist Office; p. 122 © Martinique Tourist Office; p. 124 Four Seasons Resort, Nevis; p. 126 Golden Rock Hotel; p. 126 Golden Rock Hotel; p. 127 Golden Rock Hotel; p. 128 The Hermitage; p. 128 The Hermitage; p. 130 Montpelier Plantation Inn; p. 131 Montpelier Plantation Inn; p. 132 Moxley Associates; p. 133 Moxley Associates; p. 135 KWE Associates Inc.; p. 136 KWE Associates Inc.; p. 138 Wyndham El Conquistador Resort & Country Club; p. 141 Wyndham El Conquistador Resort & Country Club; p. 143 Paradores Puertorriqueños; p. 144 Paradores Puertorriqueños; p. 145 Martha Morano Public Relations and Marketing; p. 146 Martha Morano Public Relations and Marketing; p. 147 Wyndham El San Juan Hotel & Casino; p. 147 Wyndham El San Juan Hotel & Casino; p. 147 Wyndham El San Juan Hotel & Casino; p. 149 The Gallery Inn; p. 150 The Gallery Inn; p. 151 Hotel El Convento; p. 151 Hotel El Convento; p. 153 Ritz-Carlton Resorts of the Caribbean and Mexico; p. 154 Ritz-Carlton Resorts of the Caribbean and Mexico; p. 155 The Water Club; p. 156 The Water Club; p. 158 Eden Rock Hotel; p. 159 Eden Rock Hotel; p. 160 P. Verdier/Filao Beach Hotel; p. 161 P. Verdier/Filao Beach Hotel; p. 162 Guanahani; p. 163 Guanahani; p. 164 Hotel Carl Gustaf; p. 165 Hotel Carl Gustaf; p. 166 Michel Hasson/www.phototheque.net; p. 167 Michel Hasson/www.phototheque.net; p. 168 Hotel Le Toiny; p. 169 Hotel Le Toiny; p. 170 Hotel le Village St. Jean; p. 171 Antoine Heckly/Hotel le Village St. Jean; p. 171 Hotel le Village St. Jean; p. 173 Michael Ventura for The Golden Lemon Inn & Villas; p. 174 Michael Ventura for The Golden Lemon Inn & Villas; p. 175 Ottley's Plantation Inn; p. 176 Ottley's Plantation Inn; p. 177 Rawlins Plantation Inn; p. 178 Rawlins Plantation Inn; p. 180 Anse Chastanet Beach Resort; p. 181 Anse Chastanet Beach Resort; p. 182 Marilyn Marx Public Relations; p. 183 Marilyn Marx Public Relations; p. 184 Royal St. Lucian; p. 187 Orient-Express Hotels, Inc.; p. 189 PhotoDisc; p. 190 PhotoDisc; p. 192 Young Island Resorts; p. 193 Young Island Resorts; p. 194 The Frangipani Hotel; p. 195 The Frangipani Hotel; p. 196 Laura Davidson Public Relations; p. 197 G. Gardette/Laura Davidson Public Relations; p. 198 Andrew Innerarity and Willie Alleyne/Palm Island; p. 199 Andrew Innerarity and Willie Alleyne/Palm Island; p. 200 Neil Selkirk for Petit St. Vincent; p. 201 Neil Selkirk for Petit St. Vincent; p. 203 Ian Lambie; p. 204 Raymond A. Mendez; p. 205 Hilton Caribbean; p. 206 Hilton Caribbean; p. 208 Nancy J. Friedman Public Relations; p. 209 Nancy J. Friedman Public Relations; p. 210 Martha Morano Public Relations and Marketing; p. 211 Martha Morano Public Relations and Marketing; p. 212 Parrot Cay; p. 213 Parrot Cay; p. 214 Point Grace; p. 215 Point Grace; p. 217 The Buccaneer Hotel; p. 219 Sandhaus Communications, Inc.; p. 220 Sandhaus Communications, Inc.; p. 220 Sandhaus Communications, Inc.; p. 221 Caneel Bay; p. 223 Maho Bay Camps, Inc.; p. 225 Westin St. John Resort & Villas; p. 225 Westin St. John Resort & Villas; p. 227 Marriott and Renaissance Offshore Resort Network; p. 228 Marriott and Renaissance Offshore Resort Network; p. 229 Marriott and Renaissance Offshore Resort Network; p. 230 Marriott and Renaissance Offshore Resort Network; p. 231 Ritz-Carlton Resorts of the Caribbean and Mexico; p. 234 Altamer Resort; p. 236 Old Bahama Bay; p. 238 The Brandman Agency; p. 239 Michael Kleinberg for Kura Hulanda; p. 241 La Luna; p. 243 Ti Kaye Village; p. 244 Carenage Bay; p. 247 Blue Haven; p. 248 Doug Ashley/Stonehaven Villas; p. 250 Hilton Caribbean. Spot art throughout: PhotoDisc (fountain, sun umbrella, chair with shells, conch); Westin St. John Resort & Villas (fins); Cookie Kinkead/Dunmore Beach Club (flower).

ABOUT THE AUTHOR

Kay Showker is a veteran writer, photographer, and lecturer on travel. Her assignments have taken her to more than one hundred countries in the Caribbean and around the world. She is the author of *Caribbean Ports of Call: A Guide for Today's Cruise Passengers, Western Region* (Globe Pequot, 2001); *Caribbean Ports of Call: North and Northern Region* (Globe Pequot, 2000); *Caribbean Ports of Call: Eastern and Southern Caribbean Region* (Globe Pequot, 2001); *The Outdoor Traveler's Guide to the Caribbean* (Stewart, Tabori & Chang, 1990), which won first runner-up as travel guidebook of the year in the Lowell Thomas Travel Journalism Awards, and the 2003 *Unofficial Guide to Cruises* (John Wiley), which was named Best Travel Guidebook of the Year in 1996. She served as senior editor of *Travel Weekly,* the industry's major trade publication, with which she was associated for eleven years, and writes frequently for such leading travel publications as *National Geographic Traveler, Travel and Leisure,* and *Caribbean Travel* among others. She is a member of America Online's creative team for Cruise Critic, for which she writes the "Ports of Call" segment.

A native of Kingsport, Tennessee, Ms. Showker received a master's degree in international affairs from the School of Advanced International Studies of Johns Hopkins University in Washington, D.C., and a B.A. from Mary Washington College of the University of Virginia; she also studied at the American University at Cairo, Cairo University, and Georgetown University. She was the 1989 recipient of the Marcia Vickery Wallace Award, given annually by the Caribbean Tourism Organization and the government of Jamaica to the leading travel journalist in the Caribbean, and the 1990 Travel Writer of the Year award of the Bahamas Hotel Association. She was the first travel writer to receive the *Sucrier d'Or,* a professional achievement award given by the government of Martinique in 1996, and the Caribbean Tourism Association Award for excellence in journalism. She has served as a consultant to government and private organizations on travel and tourism.